Political Parties

ROBERT MICHELS

POLITICAL PARTIES

A Sociological Study of the Oligarchical Tendencies of Modern Democracy

Translated by EDEN and CEDAR PAUL

Introduction by SEYMOUR MARTIN LIPSET

THE FREE PRESS
A Division of Macmillan Publishing Co., Inc.
NEW YORK

Printed in the United States of America

The Free Press
A Division of Macmillan Publishing Co., Inc.
866 Third Avenue, New York, New York 10022

Library of Congress Catalog Card Number: 61–18564

SECOND FREE PRESS PAPERBACK EDITION 1968

printing number
15 16 17 18 19 20

Author's Preface

MANY OF the most important problems of social life, though their causes have from the first been inherent in human psychology, have originated during the last hundred and fifty years; and even in so far as they have been handed down to us from an earlier epoch, they have of late come to press more urgently, have acquired a more precise formulation, and have gained fresh significance. Many of our leading minds have gladly devoted the best energies of their lives to attempts towards solving these problems. The so-called principle of nationality was discovered for the solution of the racial and linguistic problem which, unsolved, has continually threatened Europe with war and the majority of individual states with revolution. In the economic sphere, the social problem threatens the peace of the world even more seriously than do questions of nationality, and here "the labourer's right to the full produce of his labour" has become the rallying cry. Finally, the principle of self-government, the corner-stone of democracy, has come to be regarded as furnishing a solution of the problem of nationality, for the principle of nationality entails in practical working the acceptance of the idea of popular government. Now, experience has shown that not one of these solutions is as far-reaching in its effects as the respective discoverers imagined in the days of their first enthusiasm. The importance of the principle of nationality is undeniable, and most of the national questions of western Europe can be and ought to be solved in accordance with this principle; but matters are complicated by geographical and strategical considerations, such as the difficulty of determining natural frontiers and the frequent need for the establishment of strategic frontiers; moreover, the principle of nationality cannot help us where nationalities can hardly be said to exist or where they are intertangled in inextricable confusion. As far as the economic problem is concerned, we have numerous solutions offered by the different schools of socialist thought, but the formula of the right to the whole produce of labour is one which can be comprehended more readily in the synthetic than in the analytic field; it is easy to formulate as a general principle and likely as such to command widespread sympathy, but it is exceedingly difficult to apply in actual practice. The present work aims at a critical discussion of the third question, the problem of democracy.

It is the writer's opinion that democracy, at once as an intellectual theory and as a practical movement, has today entered upon a critical phase from which it will be extremely difficult to discover an exit. Democracy has encountered obstacles, not merely imposed from without, but spontaneously surgent from within. Only to a certain degree, perhaps, can these obstacles be surpassed or removed.

The present study makes no attempt to offer a "new system." It is not the principal aim of science to create systems, but rather to promote understanding. It is not the purpose of sociological science to discover, or rediscover, solutions, since numerous problems of the individual life and of the life of social groups are not capable of "solutions" at all, but must ever remain "open." The sociologist should aim rather at the dispassionate exposition of tendencies and counter-operating forces, of reasons and opposing reasons, at the display, in a word, of the warp and the woof of social life. Precise diagnosis is the logical and indispensable preliminary to any possible prognosis.

The unravelment and the detailed formulation of the complex of tendencies which oppose the realization of democracy are matters of exceeding difficulty. A preliminary analysis of these tendencies may, however, be attempted. They will be found to be classifiable at tendencies dependent (1) upon the nature of the human individual; (2) upon the nature of the political struggle; and (3) upon the nature of organization. Democracy leads to oligarchy, and necessarily contains an oligarchical nucleus. In making this assertion it is far from the author's intention to pass a moral judgment upon any political party or any system of government, to level an accusation of hypocrisy. The law that it is an essential characteristic of all human aggregates to constitute cliques and sub-classes is, like every other sociological law, beyond good and evil.

The study and analysis of political parties constitutes a new branch of science. It ocupies an intermediate field between the social, the philosophico-psychological, and the historical disciplines, and may be termed a branch of applied sociology. In view of the present development of political parties, the *historical* aspect of this new branch of science has received considerable attention. Works have been written upon the history of almost every political party in the western world. But when we come to consider *the analysis of the nature of the party*, we find that the field has hardly been touched. To fill this gap in sociological science is the aim of the present work.

The task has been by no means easy. So great was the extent of the material which had to be discussed that the difficulties of concise presentation might well seem almost insuperable. The author has had to renounce the attempt to deal with the problem in all its extension and all its complexity, but rather to confine himself to the consideration of salient features. In the execution of this design he has received the unwearied and invaluable help of his wife, Gisela Michels.

This English translation is from the Italian edition, in the preparation of which I had at my disposal the reviews of the earlier German version. Opportunities for further emendation of the present volume have also been afforded by the criticisms of the recently published French and Japanese translations. But the only event of outstanding importance in the political world since my *Political Parties* was first drafted has been the outbreak of the war which still rages. The author's general conclusions as to the inevitability of oligarchy in party life, and as to the difficulties which the growth of this oligarchy imposes upon the realization of democracy, have been strikingly confirmed in the political life of all the leading belligerent nations immediately before the outbreak of the war and during the progress of the struggle. The penultimate chapter of the present volume, specially written for the English edition, deals with *Party Life in Wartime*. It will be obvious that the writer has been compelled, in this new chapter, to confine himself to the discussion of broad outlines, for we are still too near to the events under consideration for accurate judgment to be possible. Moreover, the flames of war, while throwing their sinister illumination upon the military and economic organization of the states concerned, leave political parties in the shadow. For the time being parties are eclipsed by nations. It need hardly be said, however, that as soon as the war is over party life will be resumed, and that the war will be found to have effected a reinforcement of the tendencies characteristic of party.

ROBERT MICHELS

BASLE, 1915

Contents

Part Two/Autocratic Tendencies of Leaders

Part Three/The Exercise of Power and Its Psychological Reaction upon the Leaders

Part Four/Social Analysis of Leadership

Part Five/Attempts to Restrict the Influence of the Leaders

Introduction

Introduction

> *It is organization which gives birth to the domination of the elected over the electors, of the mandataries over the mandators, of the delegates over the delegators. Who says organization says oligarchy.*

THESE WORDS, first published in 1911, sum up Michels' famous "iron law of oligarchy." In *Political Parties,* Robert Michels, then a young German sociologist, laid down what has come to be the major political argument against Rousseau's concept of direct popular democracy which underlay much of the traditional democratic and socialist theory. For Michels argued that the malfunctioning of existing democracy, in particular the domination by the leadership over the society and popular organizations, was not primarily a phenomenon which resulted from a low level of social and economic development, inadequate education, or capitalist control of the opinion-forming media and other power resources, but rather was characteristic of any complex social system. Oligarchy, the control of a society or an organization by those at the top, is an intrinsic part of bureaucracy or large-scale organization. Modern man, according to him, is faced with an unresolvable dilemma: he cannot have large institutions such as nation states, trade unions, political parties, or churches, without turning over effective power to the few who are at the summit of these institutions.

To demonstrate his thesis that democracy and large-scale social organization are incompatible, Michels examined the behavior of the Socialist parties in Germany and elsewhere which appeared to be, at that time, the most committed to the extension of democracy. Long active personally in the German socialist movement, he presented an intensive analysis of the oligarchic structure of the German Social Democratic Party, then the largest socialist party in the world. An argument that centered on showing the more conservative parties to be internally undemocratic would not have proven his point, since most German and other European conservatives did not believe in democracy, in the right or the ability of the majority to determine social policy. The socialists, however, fought for adult suffrage, free speech, and for popular participation in the operation of governmental and economic institutions at every level. If such parties were themselves undemocratic in their internal structure, presumably the effort to completely democratize society must fail.

What are the causes of this trend to oligarchy? To this question, Michels provided an answer.[1]

Michels' Theory of Organization

Large-scale organizations give their officers a near monopoly of power.

Political parties, trade unions, and all other large organizations tend to develop a bureaucratic structure, that is, a system of rational (predictable) organization, hierarchically organized. The sheer problem of administration necessitates bureaucracy. As Michels stated: "It is the inevitable product of the very principle of organization. . . . Every party organization which has attained to a considerable degree of complication demands that there should be a certain number of persons who devote all their activities to the work of the party." But the price of increased bureaucracy is the concentration of power at the top and the lessening of influence by rank and file members. The leaders possess many resources which give them an almost unsurmountable advantage over members who try to change policies. Among their assets can be counted: *a)* superior knowledge, e.g., they are privy to much information which can be used to secure assent for their programme; *b)* control over the formal means of communication with the membership, e.g., they dominate the organization press; as full-time salaried officials, they may travel from place to place presenting their case at the organization's expense, and their position enables them to command an audience; and *c)* skill in the art of politics, e.g., they are far more adept than nonprofessionals in making speeches, writing articles, and organizing group activities.

The masses are incapable of taking part in the decision-making process and desire strong leadership.

[1] Detailed efforts to summarize and respecify Michels' theory in terms of latter developments may be found in the following: Philip Selznick, "An Approach to a Theory of Bureaucracy," *American Sociological Review* (1943), pp. 47-54; James Burnham, *The Machiavellians* (New York: The John Day Co., 1943), pp. 135-70; C. W. Cassinelli, "The Law of Oligarchy," *American Political Science Review*, 47 (1953), pp. 773-84; and S. M. Lipset, "The Political Process in Trade Unions: A Theoretical Statement," in M. Berger, C. Page, and T. Abel, eds., *Freedom and Control in Modern Society* (New York: D. Van Nostrand Co., 1954), pp. 82-124.

These occupational skills which inhere in the leader's role are power assets which are further strengthened by what Michels' called the "incompetence of the masses." Any effort to sustain membership influence requires, among other things, that the members be involved in the activities of the organization, participating in meetings and being aware of and concerned with the major problems affecting the life of the movement. In actuality, however, relatively few members attend party or union meetings. The pulls of work, family, personal leisure activities, and the like severely limit the amount of actual time and psychic energy which the average person may invest in membership groups or politics. The lower interest and participation are also due to the fact that the membership of any mass organization necessarily has less education and general sophistication than the leadership.

In the mass, and even in the organized mass of the labor parties, there is an immense need for direction and guidance. . . . This . . . is explicable owing to the more extensive division of labor in modern civilized society, which renders it more and more impossible to embrace in a single glance the totality of the political organization of the state and its ever more complicated mechanism. To this misoneism are superadded, and more particularly in the popular parties, profound differences of culture and education among the members. Those differences give to the need for leadership felt by the masses a continually increasing dynamic tendency.[2]

If the facts of organizational life help account for the power of the leaders, they do not explain why there should be conflict between the interests of the officials and the members. Michels specifically rejected the assumption of a representative leadership. He argued that those who become full-time officials of unions, political parties, or who serve as parliamentary representatives, "whilst belonging by social position to the class of the ruled, have in fact come to form part of the ruling oligarchy." That is to say, the leaders of the masses are themselves part of the "power elite," and develop perspectives and

2 Michels' assumptions concerning the "incompetence of the masses" corresponded greatly with those of Lenin who justified his belief in the need for an elitist party of professional revolutionists who would lead the masses into socialism by the description of them as "slumbering, apathetic, hidebound, inert, and dormant." V. I. Lenin, *Left Wing Communism: An Infantile Disorder* (New York: International Publishers, 1940), pp. 74-75. For a summation of more recent evidence concerning the propensity of the underprivileged to rely on strong leadership and to participate less in political activities see S. M. Lipset, *Political Man* (New York: Doubleday and Co., 1960), pp. 97-130, 179-219.

interests derived from their position among the more privileged elements. Hence, many of the policies of mass organizations reflect not the will or interests of the masses, but the will and interests of the leaders. Furthermore Michels stated, in a political party, "it is far from obvious that the interests of the masses which have combined to form the party will coincide with the interests of the bureaucracy in which the party becomes personified. The interests of the body of employees [that is, the party officials] are always conservative, and in a given political situation these interests may dictate a defensive and even a reactionary policy when the interests of the working class demand a bold and aggressive policy; in other cases, although these are very rare, the roles may be reversed. By a universally applicable social law, every organ of the collectivity, brought into existence through the need for the division of labor, creates for itself, as soon as it becomes consolidated, interests peculiar to itself. The existence of these special interests involves a necessary conflict with the interests of the collectivity."

Because the leaders of mass organizations are part of the dominant "political class" this does not necessarily mean that they will not continue to oppose other sections of the political elite. In order to maintain and extend their influence, they must command support from a mass following. Hence they will continue to oppose other elements of the ruling strata such as business and the aristocracy. The objective, however, of the mass-based elite is to replace the power of one minority with that of another, themselves.

When faced with a threat to their authority or office from within the organization, the leaders will become extremely aggressive and will not hesitate to undermine many democratic rights. To lose command of their organization is to lose that which makes them important individuals, and hence they are strongly motivated to preserve their position even if it requires using repressive methods. They legitimize such behavior by pointing out that a mass organization is inevitably an organization maintaining itself by its struggle with powerful and evil opponents. Therefore all efforts to introduce factionalism into the organization, to challenge the appropriateness of party or organization policy, result in aid and comfort to its enemies. Serious criticism of the leadership is thus defined as treachery to the organization itself.

Fifty years ago, Michels sent out a warning to the socialist movement: "The problem of socialism is not merely a problem in economics. . . . Socialism is also an administrative problem, a problem of democracy." He made the prognosis that if socialists adhered to the existing simple relationship between political revolution and social change, a socialist revolution would result in a "dictatorship in the hands of those leaders who have been sufficiently astute and sufficiently powerful to grasp the sceptre of dominion in the name of—socialism. . . . Thus the social revolution would not effect any real modification of the internal structure of the mass. The socialists might conquer, but not socialism, which would perish in the moment of its adherents' triumph."

Michels' predictions that the behavior of the party leaders would reflect bureaucratic conservatism rather than adherence to ideology or defense of their members' interests, were seemingly validated just three years after the book was published. The great German Social Democratic Party, the pride of the Socialist International, the defender of international peace, which opposed the policies of the Kaiser's government and promised to call a general strike in the event of war, supported the war as soon as it was declared in 1914. Even Lenin, critic though he was of the leadership of the German party, could not believe that it was possible for the party to turn so quickly from a violent opponent of German militarism to a jingoistic supporter. He was convinced that the issue of the party newspaper *Vorwarts* calling for support of the war effort was a forgery.

To Michels, this abrupt about face by the Marxist leaders of German socialism was a natural consequence of their social position, for as he put it in the second edition of the book published in 1915, "the life of the party . . . must not be endangered. . . . The party gives way, hastily sells its internationalist soul, and impelled by the instinct of self-preservation, undergoes transformation into a patriotic party. The world war of 1914 has afforded the most effective confirmation of what the author wrote in the first edition of this book concerning the future of socialist parties."

The reaction of most socialist parties to World War I demonstrated that socialist party leaders placed the needs of organizational survival over adherence to doctrine. The Russian Revolution offered an even more dramatic confirmation of his other prediction that a successful socialist revolution would mean not the triumph of democracy for the working class but the replacement of one set of rulers by another.[3] The Revolution led by Nicolai Lenin, a strong advocate of a completely free and democratic society, quickly resulted in one party rule. The Bolsheviks seized power and suppressed all others, even those groups that had supported the Revolution and fought with the Bolsheviks against their military opponents. In 1920, just three years after taking power, the Bolshevik Party began to purge its own ranks. It denied its own members the right to form groups to advocate policies within the party, and within a decade had expelled some of its most important leaders for "the crime" of opposing the will of the party secretary, Joseph Stalin.[4]

The Influence of Political Parties

The seeming accuracy of Michels' predictions concerning the future behavior of political parties and other voluntary democratic organizations, combined with the fact that he specified the processes responsible for such developments, have made *Political Parties* one of the twentieth century's most influential books. It is a classic of Social Science and continues to interest those concerned with political action as well as those interested from a scholarly point of view.

In a recent issue of the socialist magazine *Dissent* (Sumner, 1961), Irving Howe speaks for a whole generation of left-wing intellectuals disturbed by the crimes of Stalinism when he reports that reading *Political Parties* left him "with a permanent feeling of uneasiness."[5] In Poland, the one Iron Curtain country that permitted, if only for a brief period, the analysis of the social roots of Stalinism (after Khrushchev

[3] Thus the editors of *Dissent*, Irving Howe and Lewis Coser find that they can quote *Political Parties* to describe changes in the Communist movement. " 'As the party bureaucracy increases,' wrote Robert Michels in his classic study of early twentieth-century socialism, 'two elements which constitute the essential pillars of every socialist conception undergo an inevitable weakening: an understanding of the wider and more cultural aims of socialism, and an understanding of the international multiplicity of its manifestations. *Mechanism becomes an end in itself.*' In these brilliant sentences Michels anticipated the basic curve of the historical development from the Leninist to the Stalinist movement." *The American Communist Party. A Critical History* (Boston: Beacon Press, 1957), p. 501.

[4] As the Yugoslav formerly second-in-command to Tito, Milovan Djilas, has put it, "the Communist revolution, conducted in the name of doing away with classes, has resulted in the most complete authority of any single new class. Everything else is sham and an illusion." *The New Class. An Analysis of the Communist System* (New York: Frederick A. Praeger, 1957), p. 36.

[5] Some ten years ago, I witnessed the striking effect which a reading of *Political Parties* often has on socialists. A leader of a Latin-American social-democratic party who was introduced to the book as a student in a course on Political Sociology told me that he had bought ten copies and sent them to various leaders of his party. He felt that Michels should be made required reading for all socialists.

acknowledged them), Michels' analysis became a principal source of ideas. After the October revolt of 1956 overthrew the Stalinist regime within the Polish Communist party, an official party magazine published a translation of the final chapter of *Union Democracy* a section which seeks to extend Michels' analysis to problems of democracy in the contemporary labor and socialist movement.[6] Subsequent to this, another more academic Polish journal, *Studies in Political Sociology*, published a detailed summary of *Political Parties*, itself.[7]

The status of *Political Parties* as a classic of social science has been attested to many times. Sigmund Neumann, one of the leading students of comparative political institutions has written: "The study of the sociology of political parties has been completely dominated by Robert Michels' iron law of the oligarchical tendencies of social movements. . . ."[8] The German scholar, Max Weber, who has had perhaps more influence on sociology and the other social sciences than any other single sociologist, was a close personal friend of Michels. According to his political biographer, J. P. Mayer, his writings on political parties were influenced by Michels' work, to a considerable extent. His discussion on the structure of legal political parties is a summary of *Political Parties*.[9] Similarly the British student

[6] See S. M. Lipset, M. Trow, and J. Coleman, "O demokracji zwiqzkowej," *Zeszty teoretyczno-polityczne*, 1-2 (44-45), 1958, pp. 111-124. The original English version of this chapter may be found as Chapter 18 of *Union Democracy* (Glencoe: The Free Press, 1956, reprinted as a Doubleday-Anchor paperback, 1962). The chapter urges that totalitarianism is inevitable in the absence of any institutionalized checks on political power, and legitimate opposition groups.

[7] See Szymon Chodak, "Roberta Michelsa Socjologia Niemieckiej Socjaldemokracji," (Robert Michels' Sociology of German Social Democracy), *Studia Socjologiczno Polityczne*, 1 (1958), pp. 123-62. The English summary of this article ends as follows: "His work became the starting point for a new branch of science—the Sociology of the Party—as well as for the analysis of the development process of the Party, its structural types, the nature of its membership . . ." p. 162. More recently the same Polish sociologist Szyman Chodak has published a book-length study, "Systemy Party Jne Europy Zachodniej" ("Party Systems in Western Europe"), *Studia Socjologiczno Polityczne*, 9 (1961), pp. 7-255. This study contains an interesting and sophisticated critique of Michels which emphasizes that he has defined democracy out of existence, and which attempts to suggest factors which determine variations in types of party structures and practices.

[8] Sigmund Neumann, ed., *Modern Political Parties* (Chicago: University of Chicago Press, 1956), p. 405.

[9] See J. P. Mayer, *Max Weber and German Politics* (London: Faber and Faber, 1956), pp. 81-83; see also Max Weber, *The Theory of Social and Economic Organization* (New York: Oxford University Press, 1947), p. 408. For a discussion of the personal relations between Weber and Michels see H. H. Gerth and C. W. Mills, *From Max Weber: Essays in Sociology* (New York: Oxford University Press, 1946), pp. 19-21. Michels was barred from an academic appointment in Germany because of his membership in the Social Democratic Party, and Weber reacted violently against this.

of comparative politics, James Bryce, summarized the conclusions of his study of governments and parties in sentences which almost paraphrase *Political Parties*. He referred to Michels' work as "well worth reading," and commented that, "The views stated in the text which I had reached by other paths are confirmed by an able writer who has given special study to the subject, R. Michels, in his book entitled *Political Parties*."[10] A prominent French student of contemporary party organizations, Maurice Duverger, acknowledges his intellectual debt to Michels and even takes the title, *Political Parties*, for his own book which analyzes the sources and nature of oligarchy among different types of party organizations.[11] The widely acclaimed recent study of British Political Parties by the Reader in Political Sociology of the London School of Economics, Robert McKenzie, represents an effort "to assess the relevance of certain theories concerning the nature of political parties of which perhaps the most provocative and interesting is that elaborated by Robert Michels. . . ."[12] And though he offers important modifications to Michels' pessimistic conclusions, McKenzie concludes that "this study has shown that there is ample evidence of the working of what Michels calls the 'technical' and 'psychological' factors which tend to ensure the emergence of, and the retention of power by a small group of leaders in each party."[13]

The analysis of political parties is not the only field which has benefitted from Michels' insights. Surveys of the internal life of voluntary organizations, such as medical associations, veterans' groups, pressure groups, and trade unions have yielded evidence to support the "iron law of oligarchy." The labor economist and President of the University of California, Clark Kerr, has summed up the evidence in the following terms:

> The overwhelming majority of all the organizations of man throughout history have been ruled by one-party governments. Most of the time in most parts of the world all organizations have been under one-party rule. In certain parts of the world at certain times in history there have been a few two-party (or multi-party) organi-

[10] James Bryce, *Modern Democracies*, Vol. II (New York: The Macmillan Co., 1921), p. 546.
[11] See Maurice Duverger, *Political Parties* (London: Methuen, 1954), see esp., pp. 134, 169, and 151-82.
[12] Robert McKenzie, *British Political Parties* (London: William Heinemann, 1955), p. 15. Actually Michels' theory is the only one which is subsequently summarized and discussed.
[13] *Ibid.*, p. 587.

zations; but one-party rule is the standard and well-nigh universal case. The trade union is no exception. The International Typographical Union is the single deviant specimen on a national level in the United States.

Even in the democratic United States, the corporation, the political party, the fraternal order, the religious denomination, the farm organization, the welfare group, the student government, are all one-party organizations.[14]

Michels' analysis is of particular pertinence in the study of trade union government.[15] With few exceptions such analyses

[14] *Unions and Union Leaders of Their Own Choosing* (New York: The Fund for the Republic, 1957), p. 12.

The evidence sustaining the oligarchic tendencies of these groups has been summarized in various works. The sociologist, Bernard Barber, reports: "No matter what interest any particular organization represents, we find the existence of an active minority in control." "Participation and Mass Apathy in Associations," in Alvin W. Gouldner, ed., *Studies in Leadership* (New York: Harper and Brothers, 1950), p. 584. Barber goes on to point out the way oligarchy operates in various groups. "The American Legion was founded in 1919 by a small group and is run by a self-perpetuating oligarchy . . . ," and he cites evidence concerning similar patterns in fraternal organizations, Consumers' Cooperatives, and other groups. For discussion of similar points elaborating and citing evidence concerning oligarchy in many groups such as the National Association of Manufacturers and the American Medical Association, see David Truman, *The Governmental Process* (New York: Alfred A. Knopf, 1958), esp. pp. 129-210. In another discussion of the evidence sustaining Michels' thesis that the bureaucracy dominates the organization, Peter Blau points to the various studies analyzing the way in which the directors of corporations control the policies of the corporations regardless of stockholders' wishes. As he indicates, in almost all corporations, the stockholder has "about as much choice in elections as the citizen of a totalitarian nation. He has almost no way of opposing the existing leadership. . . ." *Bureaucracy in Modern Society* (New York: Random House, 1956), p. 108. In the case of business groups we see a major example of the way in which bureaucratization and the entrenchment of oligarchy lead to a situation where the avowed goals of the institution and the clear-cut interests of its "members" (stockholders) are subverted to sustain the "need" of the managers to operate an ever increasing organization. Corporations constantly reinvest capital rather than distribute optimum profits. An excellent study of what is formally one of the least centralized religious denominations in the United States, the American Baptist Convention, reports that Michels' hypotheses are validated in this group as well, that it is a highly bureaucratic organization and that the central leadership has a great deal of authority over activities and policies. And "the effort . . . to stabilize the process of organizational coordination results in the displacement of the original goals by the methods of bureaucratic procedure. 'Thus, from a means, the organization becomes an end.' " See Paul M. Harrison, *Authority and Power in the Free Church Tradition* (Princeton: Princeton University Press, 1959), p. 136. The quote cited by Harrison is from *Political Parties.*

[15] "Investigations of the behavior of British and American unions have confirmed the conclusions which Michels reached fifty years ago about Continental organizations: groups which may espouse the cause of liberal-democracy may in fact themselves be tightly-run oligarchies." Douglas V. Verney, *The Analysis of Political Systems* (London: Routledge and Kegan Paul, 1959), pp. 155-56. In his detailed analysis of the government of American trade unions William Leiserson described them as "one-party" systems. He pointed out that in most unions "Factional divisions among the members in the manner

are concerned with the absence of an active democratic political life. Union after union, in America and in other countries, are revealed as being governed by one-party oligarchies consisting of a political apparatus, able to maintain itself in power indefinitely, and to recruit its own successors through cooptation.

Beyond the concern with the internal politics of voluntary associations, Michels' work has also contributed to the larger study of organization and bureaucracy, and to sociological theory in general. As Philip Selznick has pointed out, "Michels' theory about democratic organization may be seen as a special case of the general recalcitrance of the human tools of action. The tendency for goals to be subverted through the creation of new centers of interest and motivation inheres in all organization. Deviations from rationality are characteristic of military, industrial, and governmental bureaucracies as well as of voluntary associations." Michels has sensitized the student of organization "to pay attention to deviations from professed goals and rational systems. . . ."[16] And Selznick's work, which has been among the most influential in the field of organizational analysis, in large measure began with an effort to systematize and extend Michels' insights into the source of deviations from professed norms.[17] Such deviations may be perceived as adaptations which organizations make to the contradictory demands that are present in the situations in which they operate. In order to fulfill certain objectives necessary to preserve or strengthen the organizations they run, bureaucrats often find that they must violate other objectives to which they are committed. The student of organizations begins, according to Selznick, with the assumption derived from Michels that there will be "deviations from . . . avowed goals," and that such seeming betrayals of institutional committments, like the violations of democratic norms by social-democratic or trade union leaders can be explained by reference to the assumption that bureaucrats are officials who concentrate power in their

---

of political parties are generally looked upon as inimical to unionism. An organized opposition within the unions to the officials chosen to govern them is regarded as not essentially different from attacks by outside opponents. The overwhelming pressure is for unity, unanimity." *American Trade Union Democracy* (New York: Columbia University Press, 1959), p. 75.

[16] Philip Selznick, "The Iron Law of Bureaucracy," *Modern Review* 3 (1950), pp. 162-63.

[17] His article, "An Approach to a Theory of Bureaucracy," "is largely a theoretical restatement of Michels, with an attempt to provide a theoretical statement which eliminates some of his more dubious psychological presuppositions." "The Iron Law of Bureaucracy," *op. cit.*, p. 160.

own hands, and function according to their own interests." His analysis of the T.V.A. reported in his seminal work, *TVA and the Grass Roots,* analyzed the way in which the T.V.A. bureaucracy's "adaptation to conservative interests in the Valley resulted in unanticipated consequences for the role and character of the organization."[18] Here Selznick's description of the conservative adjustments in policy dictated by the needs of an agency to secure backing in order to survive, echoes Michels' warning that the "necessary principle of organization brings other dangers in its train. . . . Organization is, in fact, the source from which the conservative currents flow over the plain of democracy, occasioning disastrous floods and rendering the plain unrecognizable."[19]

Is There an Answer to the Iron Rule of Oligarchy?

From the perspective of a concern with a more democratic and egalitarian society, *Political Parties* is a pessimistic book. Michels, himself, tells us in his last chapter that historical study forces a "stress on the pessimistic aspect of democracy. . . ."[20] Is democracy then a utopian ideal? Must efforts to create free socialist societies inevitably result in a new tyrany?

Marxist and Communist Answers

The socialist and labor movements clearly have had a special obligation to deal with Michels. The traditional Marxist answer has been to deny that bureaucratic organization could result in the emergence of a new ruling class, since such classes require a base not in a technical form of organization, but in the ownership of economic resources. Writing as a Marxist in the early thirties Sidney Hook presented this thesis:

> Michels overlooks . . . the social and economic presuppositions of oligarchic leadership in the past. Political leadership in past societies meant economic power. Education and tradition fostered the tendencies to predatory self-assertion in some classes and at the same time sought to deaden the interest in politics on the part of the masses. In a socialist society in which political leadership is an ad-

[18] *Ibid.*, pp. 163-64.

[19] A general statement of the problem may be found in R. K. Merton, "The Unanticipated Consequences of Purposeful Social Action," *American Sociological Review,* 1 (1936), pp. 894-904.

[20] In a criticism of many sociological analysts of bureaucracy for exaggerating the inherently restrictive aspects of bureaucracy on human freedom and action, Alvin Gouldner refers to the Michelsian approach as being "even more morosely pessimistic than others . . ." See "Metaphysical Pathos and the Theory of Bureaucracy," in S. M. Lipset and N. W. Smelser, eds., *Sociology: The Progress of a Decade* (Englewood-Cliffs: Prentice-Hall, 1961), p. 86.

ministrative function, and, therefore, carries with it no economic power, in which the processes of education strive to direct the psychic tendencies to self-assertion into 'moral and social equivalents' of oligarchical ambition, in which the monopoly of education for one class has been abolished, and the division of labor between manual and mental work is progressively eliminated—the danger that Michels' 'iron law of oligarchy' will express itself in traditional form, becomes quite remote.[21]

In the one important Communist effort to answer Michels, written in the early twenties, Nicolai Bukharin, then second only to Lenin as a Communist theoretician, acknowledged the importance of Michels' critique, and even described *Political Parties,* as a "very interesting book." Bukharin did not strongly challenge Michels' assumption that the power of administrators under socialism would constitute a problem, though, like Hook, he urged the view that in a real socialist society "this power will be the power of society over machines, not over men." However, he did not dwell on this assumption, but rather rested the main burden of his answer on the change in situation of the lower classes:

> [Under socialism] what constitutes an eternal category in Michels' presentation, namely the 'incompetence of the masses' will disappear, for this incompetence is by no means a necessary attribute of every system; it likewise is a product of the economic and technical conditions, expressing themselves in the general cultural being and in the educational conditions. We may say that in the society of the future there will be a colossal overproduction of organizers, which will nullify the *stability* of the ruling groups.

However, Bukharin, writing before the rise of Stalinism, recognized that this was not a sufficient answer, for the period through which Russia was passing, "the *transition period* from capitalism to socialism, *i.e.,* the period of the proletarian dictatorship, is far more difficult." In this situation he stated, "there will inevitably result a *tendency* to 'degeneration,' *i.e.,* the excretion of a leading stratum in the form of a class-germ. This tendency will be retarded by two opposing tendencies; first, by the *growth of the productive forces;* second, by the abolition

[21] *Towards the Understanding of Karl Marx* (New York: John Day Co., 1933), p. 312. It should be noted that Hook though still a socialist and critical of Michels' pessimistic conclusions no longer holds to this more or less orthodox Marxist critique. For his more recent views see his *Reason, Social Myths and Democracy* (New York. John Day Co., 1940), pp. 119 ff., and *The Hero in History* (Boston: Beacon Press, 1955), pp. 240-45.

of the *educational monopoly*. The increasing reproduction of technologists and of organizers in general, out of the working class itself, will undermine this possible new class alignment. The outcome of the struggle will depend on which tendencies turn out to be stronger."[22]

Bukharin clearly did not challenge Michels' description of the structure of socialist and (presumably) Communist parties under capitalism. Actually as has been noted, Michels' emphasis on the "incompetence of the masses" coincides with much of Lenin's analysis in his basic textbook of party organization, *What is to Be Done?* Lenin argued for a small party of professional revolutionists who would lead the masses because they were incompetent to find the correct road without direction.[23] In the very last pages of a book designed to be a basic party guide, Bukharin warned that a socialist society must find a way to undermine "the *stability* of the ruling groups," and he saw the chances of reaching such a solution as problematic. "The outcome of the struggle will depend on which tendencies turn out to be the stronger." Bukharin posited his hope that socialism would not turn out to be another oligarchic society on the belief that a really socialist society will ennoble the lower strata through education and economic development; there would always be a group outside of the governing apparatus who would be both politically self-conscious and competent to take action to prevent the "administrators" from dominating the society.

Over-Deterministic Aspects of the Theory

Michels has been criticized for being over-deterministic, for seeing only the restrictive side of bureaucracy and failing to see it also as a means through which groups may achieve desired objectives. Thus, many of the recent analyses by social scientists have been concerned not only with bureaucratization

22 Nikolai Bukharin, *Historical Materialism. A System of Sociology* (New York: International Publishers, 1925), pp. 309-311. This book deserves much more attention than it now receives. It represents the one sophisticated effort by a major Marxist to come to terms with the emerging body of sociological theory and research. Unfortunately, since Bukharin was murdered by Stalin in 1936 as a "Fascist beast and traitor," the Communist movement lost all interests in his books. Though the American edition of this book was reprinted as late as 1934, socialists and others have been uninterested in a volume which had been a basic text of world Communism.

The emphases in the quotes are all in Bukharin's original text.

23 Lenin's approach to organization has been related to contemporary sociological theory in this area by Philip Selznick, *The Organizational Weapon: A Study of Bolshevik Strategy and Tactics* (New York: McGraw-Hill Book Co., 1952). Reprinted by The Free Press of Glencoe.

as a determinant of organizational behavior which is self-interested, but also with specifying the factors which make certain types of organizations more successful than others. They have been interested to consider factors which make organizations *vary* in their behavior.[24] And among the variables noted are the nature of goals, the ways in which goals and methods are absorbed into the *modus operandi*, the way in which the multi-functions of organizations affect behavior, and the extent to which different kinds of members or clients modify the actions of bureaucrats.[25] Maurice Duverger, Sigmund Neumann, and Robert McKenzie, among others, have shown that Michels has been over-deterministic in his analysis of party behavior. There are clearly significant variations in the organizational structure of different political parties. For example, the two major political parties in the United States differ greatly from the German Social Democratic Party which served Michels as a model, in that they lack central control at the national level and exhibit comparatively little centralization even at the state level. Moreover factionalism is replete in American parties, and turnover in party control is relatively common as compared with most European parties. This variation is partly the result of the two-party pattern in America which, in turn, is largely a consequence of constitutional forms that virtually require the various politically relevant interests throughout the country to unite into two large electoral coalitions. (The primary executive power is determined by the election of a single man, the president or governor, rather than members of parliament.) Diverse groups, which in multiparty nations have independent parties with relatively little internal changes in leadership, form the basis for factions in two-party political systems.[26]

Leaving the problem of oligarchy aside, there still remains the question of representativeness. Some analysts of trade

[24] See Reinhard Bendix, "Bureaucracy: The Problem and its Setting," *American Sociological Review*, 12 (1947), esp. pp. 493-95. In his most recent work, Selznick also has elaborated in detail the effect which variations in leadership behavior have on the ways in which organizations respond to their environment and vary in propensity to attain their goals. See *Leadership in Administration* (Evanston: Row, Peterson and Co., 1957).

[25] For a good sample of the type of work which has been done in this field of inquiry see the articles reprinted in Amitai Etzioni, ed., *Complex Organizations* (New York: Holt, Rinehart and Winston, 1961) and in R. K. Merton, A. P. Gray, B. Hockey, and H. C. Selvin, eds., *Reader in Bureaucracy* (Glencoe: The Free Press, 1952).

[26] Some of the factors which determine the number and type of parties in different countries are discussed in S. M. Lipset, "Party Systems and the Representation of Social Groups," *European Journal of Sociology*, 1 (1960), pp. 50-85.

union activities who acknowledge that almost all unions are controlled by an entrenched administration argue that these unions still fulfill their primary function from the point of view of their members' interests. Thus the English student of unions, V. L. Allen, states in answer to Michels that "the end of trade union activity is to protect and improve the general standards of its members and not to provide workers with an exercise in self-government."[27] He goes on to suggest, however, that this end will be fostered only when "the penalty [to union leaders] for inefficiency, the misuse of resources, or the abuse of power is severe. . . . The voluntary nature of trade unions provides such a penalty. A trade union leader who is in continual fear of losing his members will inevitably take steps to satisfy their wants. . . . A failing membership is a much greater stimulant than a strongly worded resolution."[28]

Some evidence for this thesis may be adduced from the United Mine Workers of America, which for some time in the late 1920s and early 1930s followed conservative trade union policies which jibed with the social doctrines of its dictatorial president, John L. Lewis. Faced with a rapidly declining union membership and the growth of left-wing rivals, Lewis adopted tactics whose militancy has been more marked than those of miners' unions in some other countries under Communist or left-wing socialist leadership. This argument has been made on the most general level of institutional analysis. According to Alvin Gouldner, in all organizations there is "*a need that consent of the governed be given—at least in some measure—to their governors*. . . . And if all organizations must adjust to such a need for consent, is there not built into the very marrow of organization a large element of what we mean by democracy? This would appear to be an organizational constraint that makes oligarchies, and all separation of leaders from those led, no less inherently unstable than democratic organizations."[29]

Furthermore, the problem of representativeness is confused by the absence of genuine alternatives from which members may choose. The absence of any organized opposition group in most unions and other private associations prevents the members from choosing a leader who shares their views. It is difficult to believe, for example, the the differences in the behavior of the two Jewish dominated garment unions in the

27 *Power in Trade Unions* (London: Longmans, Green and Co., 1954), p. 15.
28 *Ibid.*, p. 63.
29 Gouldner, *op. cit.*, p. 88.

1930s and 1940s represented variations in the predominant sentiment of their members. The Amalgamated Clothing Workers' Union under Sidney Hillman was a pillar of the CIO and cooperated with the Communists in New York's American Labor Party. The International Ladies' Garment Workers' Union under David Dubinsky joined the A.F. of L., and formed the vigorously anti-Communist Liberal Party. John L. Lewis endorsed the Republican candidate for U. S. President in 1940, while the large majority of his members were obviously for Franklin Roosevelt.[30] A survey conducted of the membership of the British Medical Association at a time in which the leaders of the association were strongly fighting all proposals for state medicine showed that a majority of the members of the B.M.A. agreed with the government on most issues rather than with their officials.[31] The largest single British union, the Transport and General Workers' Union, shifted from being a stronghold of right-wing Labor politics, under the leadership of Ernest Bevin and Arthur Deakin, to the most important source of strength for the left-wing of the Labor Party, under the General Secretaryship of Frank Cousins. Cousins' succession to this post was not a result of a change in the attitudes of the members, but rather occurred following the death of the two preceding secretaries in one year.[32]

It is difficult to objectively adduce when there is actually a serious cleavage between the interests and conscious objectives of members and those of their leaders. Michels argued that the shift to the "right" prior to World War I of the German trade unions and the Social Democratic Party, demonstrated the way in which the inherent bureaucratic conservatism of leaders deflects organizations from their goals and the beliefs of their members. However, Rose Laub Coser has accumulated evidence which suggests instead that the goals and beliefs of the members changed first.[33] She points out that the rapid im-

30 Irving Bernstein, "John L. Lewis and the Voting Behavior of the C.I.O." *Public Opinion Quarterly* 5 (1941), pp. 233-49.

31 Harry Eckstein, "The Politics of the British Medical Association," *The Political Quarterly*, 26 (1955), pp. 345-59; see also Oliver Garceau, *The Political Life of the American Medical Association* (Cambridge: Harvard University Press, 1941) and Anonymous, "American Medical Association: Power, Purpose and Politics in Organized Medicine," *Yale Law Journal* 63 (1954), pp. 938-1022.

32 For a detailed study of the sources and nature of oligarchy and membership apathy in this union see Joseph Goldstein, *The Government of British Trade Unions* (London: George Allen and Unwin, 1952).

33 *An Analysis of the Early German Socialist Movement* (M.A. Thesis: Department of Sociology, Columbia University, 1951).

provement in the social and economic position of the German working class in the two decades prior to World War I produced a relatively conservative, contented lower stratum, to whom the traditional revolutionary and internationalist ideology advanced by the party leadership up to 1914 had little appeal. Recent public opinion surveys in Britain show that the large majority of the British trade unions and Labor Party membership have supported the policies of the right wing parliamentary leadership of the party, though the left wing was able in 1960 to gain a majority vote on some issues at the Labor Party conference, and continues to retain strength far out of proportion to its actual policy support among the members.[34] In the United States, the International Longshoremen's Association, described by all observers as corrupt, racket-ridden, and dictatorial, expelled from the AFL-CIO and attacked by various public agencies, has been able to win three secret-ballot elections conducted by the government against a well-financed rival backed by the resources and prestige of the AFL-CIO.[35] Similarly, the Teamsters' Union led by Jimmy Hoffa, although also expelled from the AFL-CIO as corrupt, and denounced by government agencies as dictatorial, has been the most rapidly growing union in the United States. This paradox of trade-union membership support for oligarchy, corruption, Communism, Republican politics, or other policies which are clearly at variance with their sentiments and/or interests, may be explained by the way in which unions are perceived by the members. If they are seen primarily as single-purpose organizations, and if the organization fulfills its primary purpose—in the case of unions this is clearly collec-

[34] A public opinion survey conducted in September 1960 about the time that a majority of the delegates to the Trades Union Congress and to the Labor Party Conference endorsed the left program favoring unilateral disarmament by Great Britain found that only 16 per cent of the trade union members supported the proposal that Britain unilaterally give up its nuclear weapons, while 83 per cent favored the policy that Britain should retain such arms until other powers agreed to disarm. See Research Department, Odhem's Press, *Report on a Survey of Opinions Concerning Nuclear Disarmament* (London: 1960). A survey conducted about the same time by the British Gallup Poll on the same issues, also reported relatively little support (24 per cent) among Labor voters for unilateral disarmament. (Gallup did not separate out trade union members in his report.) See *The Gallup Political Index*, Report No. 9, September, 1960. Given these results, it is perhaps not surprising that when the anti-unilateralists within the unions and the Labor Party formed an organization, the Campaign for Democratic Socialism, to reverse party policy, they were able within a year to change the policies which seemingly had had majority support at conventions.

[35] See Daniel Bell, *The End of Ideology* (Glencoe: The Free Press, 1960), pp. 159-60. The election results are presented on pages 186-87.

tive bargaining—its leaders are permitted considerable leeway in other areas, viewed as less salient policy areas.

Though organizations must in some general sense "represent" their members in the struggle for better wages, higher farm prices, greater profits and dividends, the basic assumption of Michels regarding the effect of the division of labor within organizations remains valid. This division, as he said, results in the delegation of effective power to a small group of leaders who are able under most conditions to remain in power. It also appears to be true that such leadership groups develop aims which are often at variance with the original objectives of the organizations and the interests and attitudes of their members.

These generalizations obviously raise important problems concerning the viability of political democracy. Michels, himself, felt that he had proven democracy and socialism to be structurally impossible. When he wrote *Political Parties,* he still strongly favored the struggle for more democracy as a means of reducing oligarchic tendencies. Once having demonstrated that democracy was impossible, that democratic leaders were, in effect, hypocrites, Michels found it difficult to retain any sustained belief in democratic ideologies and movements, even as lesser evils. Theoretically, his analysis posed a problem. *If* in fact all leaders of mass organizations were inherently self-interested conservative oligarchs, from where does the polity secure the leadership to deal with major problems and with the need for social change?

The answer, Michels found years later, was in strong charismatic leaders, "persons endowed with extraordinary congenital qualities, sometimes held to be justly supernatural and in every way always far superior to the general level. By virtue of these qualities such persons are deemed capable (and often they are) of accomplishing great things, and even miraculous things."[36] Only a charismatic leader has the ability to break through the inherent conservatism of organization and to excite the masses to support great things. It is from charisma, rather than democracy or bureaucracy, that greatness can be expected. And it must be related that Michels found his charismatic leader in Benito Mussolini. For him, Il Duce translated "in a naked and brilliant form the aims of the multitude." Not

36 Robert Michels, *First Lectures in Political Sociology* (Minneapolis: University of Minnesota Press, 1949), pp. 122-23. This book contains many of his writings in the 1920's and thirties.

for the charismatic Il Duce and fascism were the vulgar compromises and conservatism dictated by the constraints of bureaucratic and oligarchic democracy. "Rather, its perfect faith in itself, essential basis of this form of charismatic government, furnishes an inherent dynamic tendency. And that for two reasons. The charismatic leader has a past of struggles—victorious struggles. Therefore he is conscious of his qualities which he has demonstrated capable of valuable use. . . . On the other side his future is bound to the proofs that he may furnish of the faithfulness of his star."[37] And Michels, who had been barred from academic appointment in Germany for many years because of his socialism, left his position at the University of Basle to accept a chair at the University of Perugia offered to him personally by Benito Mussolini in 1928.

The "Elitist" Theory of Democracy

If the view of society and organization as divided between elites and followers led Michels to accept the idea that the best government is an avowedly elitist system under the leadership of a charismatic leader, the same view has led other men to strikingly different conclusions, and suggested the need to redefine the concept of democracy, to elaborate the "elitist" theory of democracy. Max Weber and Joseph Schumpeter, among many, have stressed that the distinctive and most valuable element of democracy is the formation of a political elite in the competitive struggle for the votes of a mainly passive electorate.[38] This general view has been elaborated most recently by Talcott Parsons who has argued that the political system provides generalized leadership for the larger social system in setting and attaining collective goals, and that this is acknowledged by interested organizations who supply generalized support to different leadership groups in the expectation of the approval of their special interest measures. Conversely, various social groups form and advocate particular policies which may eventually result in specific decisions by public bodies. The competitive struggle within the political elite, for generalized as well as for specific support, gives those outside the authority-struc-

[37] *Ibid.*, p. 131. Michels' attitude to Il Duce sounds very much like the comments in defense of Fidel Castro offered by some of his supporters.

[38] See J. Schumpeter, *Capitalism, Socialism and Democracy* (New York: Harper and Brothers, 1947), p. 269; *From Max Weber: Essays in Sociology*, *op. cit.*, p. 226. I have discussed and used this approach to democracy in my work. See "Party Systems and the Representation of Social Groups," *op. cit.*, pp. 50-53; *Political Man, op. cit.*, pp. 45-46; and *Union Democracy*, *op. cit.*, 405-12.

ture access to political power.[39] The key term in this approach is *access*. Those who have access to the political elite in the sense that sections of the latter, party leaders, office-holders, officials of mass organizations, must consider how they will react to a given policy, have a share in the effective power, even if their participation is limited to voting every four years or less.[40]

The interchange of leadership for support takes place through what we call the system of representation. The basic structure of this system involves not only the formal mechanisms of government, but the various institutional practices found in democratic society—party systems and interest organizations—that serve to facilitate the interchange between authority and the spontaneous groupings of society which have specific interests. The representation system links authority (legislative, executive, and judicial) with a variety of subgroups such as religions, classes, ethnic groups, occupations, regions, and so forth. Representation is neither simply a means of political adjustment to social pressures nor an instrument of manipulation. It involves both functions, since the purpose of representation is to locate the combinations of relationships between parties and social bases which make possible the operation of efficient government.

The elitist theory of democracy accepts much of Michels' analysis of the internal structure of mass organizations, but it points out that he and others of the so-called Machiavellian school of politics by whom he was influenced, such as Pareto, Mosca, and Sorel, prove the impossibility of democracy within the larger polity by definition, by *seeing any separation* between leaders and followers as *ipso facto* a negation of democracy.[41]

Democracy in the sense of a system of decision-making in which all members or citizens play an active role in the continuous process is inherently impossible. Organizational elites in general do have long-term tenure in office. Michels clearly demonstrated the technical impossibility of terminating the structural division between rulers and ruled within a complex society. Political and organizational elites always have special group interests which are somewhat at variance with those of the people they represent. But even if we accept all of these

[39] See Talcott Parsons, "Voting and the Equilibrium of the American Political System," in E. Burdick and A. Brodbeck, eds., *American Voting Behavior* (Glencoe: The Free Press, 1959), pp. 80-120.

[40] This aproach to democratic power is elaborated in David Truman, *op. cit.*, esp. pp. 264-528.

[41] For a sympathetic presentation of the views of this group see James Burnham, *op. cit.*

points as valid, they do not mean that democracy is impossible; rather they suggest the need for a more realistic understanding of the democratic potential in a complex society.

Michels' view of power rests basically on the assumption that the behavior of all dominant minorities, whether in society at large or in organizations, must primarily be interpreted as following a logic of self-interest, of exploiting the masses to maintain or extend their own privilege and power. In this respect, Michels explicitly accepted the Marxist materialist conception of history. As he himself argued, his theory "completes that conception and reinforces it. There is no essential contradiction between the doctrine that history is the record of a continued series of class struggles and the doctrine that class struggles invariably culminate in the creation of new oligarchies which undergo fusion with the old. The existence of a political class does not conflict with the essential content of Marxism, considered not as an economic dogma, but as a philosophy of history. . . ." This view of political life assumes, as Talcott Parsons has suggested, "that it is only power which 'really' determines what happens in society. Against this, I would place the view that power is only one of several cognate factors in the determination of social events."[42] The power of any organized minority is circumscribed by the internal and external social setting of the polity which it leads. Clearly, mass organizations and political parties have been responsible for many changes which have increased the effective freedom from coercion of the mass of the population (freedom of speech, of movement, guarantees of job security, and so forth) and have equalized opportunity and income. Workers in Scandinavia, Britain, and the United States, are freer and more secure today because political parties which are *dependent on them for support* have been elected to office. The American Medical Association and the unions within the AFL-CIO are dominated by self-perpetuating oligarchies, but the heads of these bodies take sharply conflicting stands on the question of medical care guaranteed by the government. Faced with the need to win the support of a mass electorate, the Republicans in the United States and the Conservatives in Great Britain maintained most of the extensions of the welfare state enacted by their predecessors. To a considerable extent, power may be viewed as the "capacity to mobilize the resources of the society [or an organization] for

[42] *Structure and Process in Modern Societies* (Glencoe: The Free Press, 1960), p. 221.

the attainment of goals for which a general 'public' commitment has been made, or may be made."[43] A primary emphasis on the oligarchic or "power elite" aspects of organizational or political life is clearly inadequate since it leads its exponents to ignore the sources and consequences of controversy. Michels was forced to deny that conflicts among factions, left and right wings, within the socialist movement or other parties, represented anything but struggles for the spoils of office, and, in fact, he hardly alludes to such controversies. Similarly the most recent exponent of elite theory, C. Wright Mills almost completely ignores the existence of political parties in the American power struggle.[44]

In essence, democracy in modern society may be viewed as involving the conflict of organized groups competing for support.[45] Since many organized groups are always actually or potentially out of office or out of favor with those in office in a democratic system, they have an interest in institutionalizing safeguards for democratic rights of speech, press, assembly, etc. This image of democracy as conflict of organized groups and of access by the ruled to their rulers may be far from the ideal of the Greek city state or of small Swiss cantons, but in operation as a system it is far better than any other political system which has been devised to reduce the potential exploitation of man by man. Only by conflict and public commitment to explicit goals can egoistic misuse of power be limited.

While most private governments, unions, professional societies, veterans' organizations, and political parties, will remain one-party systems, since they do not possess the basis for sustained internal conflict, it is important to recognize that many internally oligarchic organizations help to sustain political democracy in the larger society and to protect the interests of their members from the encroachments of other groups. Democracy in large measure rests on the fact that no one group is able to secure a basis of power and command over the majority so that it can effectively suppress or deny the

[43] *Loc. cit.*

[44] C. Wright Mills, *The Power Elite* (New York: Oxford University Press, 1956).

[45] It should be noted that in one of his last articles before his death in Italy in 1936, Michels explicitly attacked this conception of democracy. "The rapid turnover of leaders deceives the inexperienced regarding the true character of authority in democratic countries. It is not the masses that overthrow leaders but rather new leaders who take advantage of the masses who bring this about." "Social Mobility in General with Special Reference to Post-War Mobility," cited in Dino Camavitto, "Roberto Michels—In Memoriam," *American Sociological Review*, 1 (1936), p. 798.

claims of the groups it opposes. The labor movement, with its ideal of equality, has played a major role in fostering institutions of political democracy. In all the political democracies, workers today can speak out and act with much less fear that their acts will affect their ability to earn a livelihood than they could even three decades ago. There are few unions which have as much potential power over their members as employers once had over their workers. (Unfortunately there are some.)

The challenge which Michels threw out that organization meant oligarchy was directed most specifically towards his comrades at the time in the socialist movement. And insofar as socialism has meant *only* a strengthening of state power, of government ownership, it has increased the potential threat to democracy. In large measure, therefore, as the world moves in the direction of a collectivist society, in response to the pressure from the lower strata demanding that the state take responsibility for guaranteeing full employment, a more equitable distribution of goods and services, more equal opportunity, and greater security against the hazards of illness and old age, the problem of the compatibility of socialism and democracy becomes more and more prominent. The emergence of a Communist "new class" more powerful and exploitative than the old ruling class of capitalism offers a constant warning to all democrats, and especially to the socialists among them, of the need to absorb the lessons for democracy spelled out in *Political Parties*. Fortunately modern history records that western socialists have learned these lessons well. Most socialist parties now seek as little government ownership and control as is necessary to further their welfare and egalitarian goals, and they have recognized that multiple forms of ownership, public, cooperative, and private are preferable to any new concentration of power. Further, it is now an accepted principle of all democratic socialist movements that trade unions, even when supporters of socialist objectives, should maintain their independence of the state and of governments controlled by socialist parties. In *The New Class* Milovan Djilas, who is better acquainted than most men with the dangers of concentrating power, points to the differences between the socialist welfare state in the West and the totalitarian system in the East:

> Aside from other differences between [the Communist and Western] systems, there is an essential difference in state ownership and in the role of the state in the economy. Though state ownership is technically present to some extent in both systems, they are two dif-

ferent, even contradictory types of ownership. This applies to the role of the state in the economy as well.

Not a single Western government acts like an owner with relation to the economy. In fact, a Western government is neither the owner of nationalized property nor the owner of funds which it has collected through taxes. *It cannot be an owner because it is subject to change.* It must administer and distribute this property through the control of parliament. In the course of distribution of property, the government is subject to various influences, but it is not the owner. All it does is administer and distribute, well or badly, property which does not belong to it.[46]

To protect the right to change government, to maintain diverse centers of power, to keep open access to authority, this is the task of men who value freedom in the second half of the twentieth century. By an ironic twist of history, one of the principal intellectual weapons in the arsenal of freedom, this brilliant analysis of the endemic threat to freedom inherent in organization, the very tool which industrial man must use to operate his economy and polity, was given to us by a man who died as a supporter of fascist rule in Italy. Let us remember, however, not the admirer of Il Duce, but the man who at the end of his study of the sources of oligarchy wrote:

> Democracy is a treasure which no one will ever discover by deliberate search. But in continuing our search, in laboring indefatigably to discover the undiscoverable, we shall perform a work which will have fertile results in the democratic sense. . . . It is, in fact, a general characteristic of democracy, and hence also of the labor movement, to stimulate and to strengthen in the individual the intellectual aptitudes for criticism and control. . . .
>
> It may be said, therefore, that the more humanity comes to recognize the advantages which democracy, however imperfect, presents over aristocracy, even at its best, the less likely is it that a recognition of the defects of democracy will provoke a return to aristocracy. . . . [N]othing but a serene and frank examination of the oligarchic dangers of democracy will enable us to minimize these dangers, even though they can never be entirely avoided.

This preface represents an effort to acknowledge my great intellectual debt to Robert Michels. In *Union Democracy,* I, together with my colleagues Martin Trow and James Coleman, sought to elaborate on his optimistic side by testing many of the hypotheses which he advanced in the context of the question: what are the conditions which make democracy within

[46] *Op. cit.*, p. 207.

private governments such as trade unions possible? I trust that the wider distribution of his ideas which this new edition makes possible will increase the numbers of those who in politics and in scholarship follow his advice to labor "indefatigably to discover the undiscoverable," for as he perceived, although the ideals of democracy and socialism can never be reached, the continuing struggle for them is the only way they may be approximated.

SEYMOUR MARTIN LIPSET

Berkeley, California
August, 1961

Political Parties

Chapter 1

Democratic Aristocracy and Aristocratic Democracy

THE MOST restricted form of oligarchy, absolute monarchy, is founded upon the will of a single individual. *Sic volo sic jubeo. Tel est mon bon plaisir.* One commands, all others obey. The will of one single person can countervail the will of the nation, and even today we have a relic of this in the constitutional monarch's right of veto. The legal justification of this regime derives its motives from transcendental metaphysics. The logical basis of every monarchy resides in an appeal to God. God is brought down from heaven to serve as a buttress to the monarchical stronghold, furnishing it with its foundation of constitutional law—the grace of God. Hence, inasmuch as it rests upon a supra-terrestrial element, the monarchical system, considered from the outlook of constitutional law, is eternal and immutable, and cannot be affected by human laws or by the human will. It follows that the legal, juridical, legitimate abolition of the monarchy is impossible, a fable of a foolish political dreamer. Lawfully, the monarchy can be abolished by God alone—and God's will is inscrutable.

At the antipodes of the monarchical principle, in theory, stands democracy, denying the right of one over others. *In abstracto,* it makes all citizens equal before the law. It gives to each one of them the possibility of ascending to the top of the social scale, and thus facilitates the way for the rights of the community, annulling before the law all privileges of birth, and desiring that in human society the struggle for pre-eminence should be decided solely in accordance with individual capacity. Whereas the principle of monarchy stakes everything upon the character of a single individual, whence it results that the best possible monarchical government offers to the people as a whole no guarantee for permanently benevolent and technically efficient rule, democracy is, on principle, responsible to the community at large for the prevailing conditions of rule, of which it is the sole arbiter.

We know today that in the life of the nations the two theoretical principles of the ordering of the state are so elastic that they often come into reciprocal contact, "for democracy can either embrace all of the people or be restricted to half of them; aristocracy, on the other hand, can embrace half the people or an indeterminately smaller number."[1] Thus the two forms of government do not exhibit an absolute antithesis, but meet at that point where the participants in power number fifty per cent.

Our Age has destroyed once for all the ancient and rigid forms of aristocracy, has destroyed them, at least, in certain important regions of political constitutional life. Even conservatism assumes at times a democratic form. Before the assaults of the democratic masses it has long since abandoned its primitive aspect, and loves to change its disguise. Today we find it absolutist, tomorrow constitutional, the next day parliamentary. Where its power is still comparatively unrestricted, as in Germany, it appeals exclusively to the grace of God. But when, as in Italy, it feels insecure, it adds to the appeal to the deity an appeal to the popular will. In its outward forms it is capable of the most extensive modifications. In monarchical France the *Franciæ et Navarræ Rex* becomes the *Roy de France,* and the *Roy de France* becomes the *Roi des Français.*

The life of political parties, whether these are concerned chiefly with national or with local politics, must, in theory, necessarily exhibit an even stronger tendency towards democracy than that which is manifested by the state. The political party is founded in most cases on the principle of the majority, and is founded always on the principle of the mass. The result of this is that the parties of the aristocracy have irrevocably lost the aristocratic purity of their principles. While remaining essentially anti-democratic in nature, they find themselves compelled, at any rate in certain periods of political life, to make profession of the democratic faith, or at least to assume the democratic mask. Whereas the democratic principle, from its very nature, by reason of the mutability of the popular will and of the fluctuating character of the majority, tends in theory to transform the Πάντα ῥεῖ of Heraclitus into the reality of national and popular life, the conservative principle erects its edifice upon certain bases or norms which are immutable in their nature, determined by the test of experience to be the best or at any rate the least bad, and consequently claimed as valid *sub specie æternitatis*. Nevertheless, the conservative principle must not be understood in the sense of an unconditional maintenance of the *status quo*. If that principle consisted merely in

[1] Trans. from J. J. Rousseau, *Le Contract social,* Bibliothèque Nationale, 6th ed., Paris, 1871, p. 91.

the recognition of what already exists, above all in the matter of the legal forms prevailing in a given country or period, conservatism would lead to its own destruction. In periods and among nations where the old conservative elements have been expelled from direct participation in power, and have been replaced by innovators fighting under the banner of democracy, the conservative party assumes an aspect hostile to the existing order of the state, and sometimes even a revolutionary character.[2] Thus, however, is effected a metamorphosis of the conservative party, which, from a clique cherishing an aristocratic exclusivism at once by instinct and by conviction, now becomes a popular party. The recognition that only the masses can help to reintroduce the ancient aristocracy in its pristine purity, and to make an end of the democratic regime, transforms the very advocates of the conservative view into democrats. They recognize unreservedly the sufferings of the common people; they endeavor, as did very recently the royalists in the French Republic, to ally themselves with the revolutionary proletariat, promising to defend this against the exploitation of democratic capitalism and to support and even to extend labor organizations—all this is the hope of destroying the Republic and restoring the Monarchy, the ultimate fruit of the aristocratic principle. *Le Roy et les camelots du Roy*—the king and the king's poor—are to destroy the oligarchy of the bloated plutocrats. Democracy must be eliminated by the democratic way of the popular will. The democratic method is the sole one practicable by which an old aristocracy can attain to a renewed dominion. Moreover, the conservatives do not usually wait until they have been actually driven from power before appealing to the masses. In countries where a democratic regime prevails, as in England, they spontaneously turn to the working class wherever this forms the most conspicuous constituent of the masses. In other countries, also, where parlia-

[2] For example, Raumer, writing from Paris in 1830, expressed the matter very well as follows: "All these men [the liberals] regard as revolutionary the abolition of anciently established institutions and evils, whereas by counterrevolution they understand the restoration of these or of other abuses. Their adversaries, on the other hand, understand by revolution the aggregate of all the follies and crimes that have ever been committed, whereas by counterrevolution they mean the re-establishment of order, of authority, of religion, and so on" (Friedrich von Raumer, *Briefe aus Paris und Frankreich im Jahre 1830*, F. A. Brockhaus, Leipzig, 1831, Part II, p. 26).—Cf. also Wilhelm Roscher, *Politik, Geschichtliche Naturlehre der Monarchie, Aristokratie und Demokratie*, Cotta, Stuttgart-Berlin, 1908, 3rd ed., p. 14.—Yet we have to remember that in political matters such judgments of value may be effective means of struggle towards political and sometimes also towards moral ends; but they are apt to lead us astray if we use them to aid us in defining historical tendencies or conceptions.

mentary government is unknown, but where there exists universal and equal suffrage, the parties of the aristocracy owe their political existence to the charity of the masses to whom in theory they deny political rights and political capacity. The very instinct of self-preservation forces the old groups of rulers to descent, during the elections, from their lofty seats, and to avail themselves of the same democratic and demagogic methods as are employed by the youngest, the widest, and the most uncultured of our social classes, the proletariat.

The aristocracy today maintains itself in power by other means than parliamentary; at any rate in most of the monarchies it does not need a parliamentary majority in order to be able to hold the reins by which is guided the political life of the state. But it does need, were it merely for decorative purposes and in order to influence public opinion in its favor, a respectable measure of parliamentary representation. It does not obtain this representation by divulging its true principles, or by making appeal to those who are truly of like mind with itself. A party of the landed gentry which should appeal only to the members of its own class and to those of identical economic interests, would not win a single seat, would not send a single representative to parliament. A conservative candidate who should present himself to his electors by declaring to them that he did not regard them as capable of playing an active part in influencing the destinies of the country, and should tell them that for this reason they ought to be deprived of the suffrage, would be a man of incomparable sincerity, but politically insane. If he is to find his way into parliament he can do so by one method only. With democratic mien he must descend into the electoral arena, must hail the farmers and agricultural laborers as professional colleagues, and must seek to convince them that their economic and social interests are identical with his own. Thus the aristocrat is constrained to secure his election in virtue of a principle which he does not himself accept, and which in his soul he abhors. His whole being demands authority, the maintenance of a restricted suffrage, the suppression of universal suffrage wherever it exists, since it touches his traditional privileges. Nevertheless, since he recognizes that in the democratic epoch by which he has been overwhelmed he stands alone with this political principle, and that by its open advocacy he could never hope to maintain a political party, he dissembles his true thoughts, and howls with the democratic wolves in order to secure the coveted majority.

The influence of popular suffrage upon the outward behavior of conservative candidates is so extensive that when two candidates of the same political views present themselves in a single constituency, each of them is forced to attempt to distinguish himself from his rival by a movement to the left, that is to say, by laying great stress upon his reputedly democratic principles.

Such occurrences serve to confirm the experience that the conservatives also endeavor to regulate their actions in conformity with the fundamental principle of modern politics, a principle destined to replace the religious dictum that many are called but few are chosen, and to replace also the psychological theory that ideals are accessible solely to a minority of choice spirits: this principle may be summed up in the terms of Curtius, who said that the conservative cannot gain his ends with the aid of a small and select body of troops, but must control the masses and rule through the masses.[3] The conservative spirit of the old master-caste, however deeply rooted it may be, is forced to assume, at least during times of election, a specious democratic mask.

Nor does the theory of liberalism primarily base its aspirations upon the masses. It appeals for support to certain definite classes, which in other fields of activity have already ripened for mastery, but which do not yet possess political privileges—appeals, that is to say, to the cultured and possessing classes. For the liberals also, the masses pure and simple are no more than a necessary evil, whose only use is to help others to the attainment of ends to which they themselves are strangers. The first great liberal writer of Germany, Rotteck, reproaches the Queen of France for having, during the Revolution, forced the bourgeoisie to appeal to the common people for aid. He distinguishes between two kinds of democracy, the rule of representatives and the rule of the masses.[4] During the revolution of June, 1830, Raumer, who was in Paris, broke into vigorous lamentation because the masses possessed power, and said that it

[3] Friedrich Curtius, *Ueber Gerechtigkeit und Politik*, "Deutsche Rundschau," xxiii, 1897, fasc. 4, p. 46.

[4] "It was this opposition [of the ultra-monarchical friends of Louis XVI to the well-disposed liberals] which set itself against the idea of bourgeois and political freedom that was spreading, not in France alone, but in all the other civilized countries of Europe, that forced upon the Revolution (which otherwise might have been purely beneficial) its evil and destructive character. It was this which led the representatives of the people to endeavor to avoid the threatened ruin by calling the masses to their aid; it was this which led to the unchaining of the rough and lawless force of the mob, and thus threw open the box of Pandora" (Carl von Rotteck, *Allgemeine Geschichte vom Anfang der historischen Kenntniss bis auf unsere Zeiten*, Herdersche Buchhandlung, Freiburg, 1826, vol. ix, p. 83).

would be extremely difficult "to deprive them of this power without giving them offense and without provoking them to a fresh revolt against their new chiefs";[5] at the same time, in words expressing the dithyrambic spirit of romanticism, he refers to the conditions that obtain in his Prussian fatherland, where king and people "truly live in a higher and purer atmosphere," and where the contented bourgeoisie is not endeavoring to secure additional rights.[6] From the history of the origin of the North German Reichstag we learn that another eminent liberal leader and advocate of liberal views, the historian Heinrich von Sybel, declared himself opposed to universal, equal, and direct suffrage, on the ground (which can be understood solely with reference to the explanations given above regarding the peculiar conceptions the liberals have of the masses) that such a right must signify "the beginning of the end for every kind of parliamentarism"; such a right, he said, was eminently a right of dominion; and he was impelled to utter an urgent warning to the German monarchy not to introduce these dangerous elements of democratic dictatorship into the new federal state. The inward dislike of liberalism for the masses is also apparent in the attitude of the liberal leaders to the principles and institutions of aristocracy. Since the inauguration of universal suffrage and the consequent prospect that there will in the near future be a majority of socialist tendencies among the electorate or in the Lower House, many liberals, so Roscher affirms, have come to take a different view of the powers of the Crown and of the Upper House,[7] as means by which it is possible to prevent decisions of the Lower House being immediately realized in legislative measures. The same author contends that an extension of the suffrage is undesirable "in the absence of a profound statistical inquiry," that is to say, in the absence of a laborious analysis of the numerical relationships that obtain among the various classes of the population[8] Recently, even in that liberal group which in Germany stands nearest to the socialists, the group of "national socialists," there has been evidence of a tendency to consider that it is by no means a bad thing "for obstacles to be imposed upon the influence in political affairs of the mutable and incalculable popular will which finds expression in the Reichstag, for the national socialists consider it desirable that there should exist

[5] Friedrich von Raumer, *Briefe aus Paris*, etc. op. cit., vol. i, p. 176.
[6] Raumer, op. cit., vol. i, p. 264.
[7] Roscher, op. cit., p. 321.
[8] Ibid., p. 336.

also aristocratic elements, independent of the popular will, ever vigilant, armed with the right of veto, to constitute a permanent moderating element."[9]

For an entire century, from the days of Rolteck to those of Naumann, German writers have labored in the sweat of their brow to effect a theoretical conciliation between democracy and military monarchy, and to unite these natural opposites in a higher unity. Hand in hand with their honorable endeavors on behalf of this loftier aim have proceeded their attempts to defeudalize the monarchy to the utmost, with the sole purpose of substituting for the aristocratic guardians of the throne guardians speaking with professorial authority. The task they set themselves was to lay the theoretical foundations, if not of the so-called social monarchy, at least of the popular monarchy. It is evident that such an objective involves a political tendency which has nothing in common with science, but which is not in necessary opposition to or in contradiction with science (it is the *method* which must decide this), being a political tendency which is, qua political, outside the domain of science. It cannot be made a reason for blaming German men of science that there exists in Germany a tendency towards the construction of something resembling the July Monarchy, for this tendency rests within the orbit of politics. But is it plainly a matter for historical censure when we find an attempt to identify the monarchical principle which has for some decades been dominant in Prussianized Germany with the cherished idea of the popular (or social) monarchy. In committing such an error, the majority of German liberal theorists and historians mistake dreams for reality. In this confusion rests the organic defect of all German liberalism, which since 1866 has continually endeavored to disguise its change of front (that is

[9] Martin Rade, in a leading article (*Das Allgemeine Wahlrecht ein Königliches Recht*, "Hessische Landeszeitung," xxiii, No. 25, 1907) favoring the election of the national-socialist Helmuth von Gerlach at Marburg, wrote as follows in order to still the alarms of the adversaries of universal suffrage: "The case would be very different if our Reichstag were the actual director of the government, if it alone could decide the internal and external destinies of our people! But it is merely one among the elements of our constitution! Beside it, or rather above it, stands the Bundesrat (Federal Council), and not the most trifling proposition can become law unless with the assent of the Imperial Chancellor, the Emperor, and the Princes. Certainly the Federal Council will not permanently oppose a strong and reasonable expression of the popular will which it manifested in a constitutional manner in the Reichstag; but such resolutions of the Reichstag as it regards as injudicious it will reject, and often has rejected. By this means, precautions are taken to limit the power of universal suffrage, just as nature takes care that trees do not grow to touch the skies. It is well for our legislation that we have these two Chambers, and not the Reichstag alone."

to say, its partisan struggle against socialism and its simultaneous and voluntary renunciation of all attempts to complete the political emancipation of the German bourgeoisie), by the fallacious assertion that with the unification of Germany and the establishment of the empire of the Hohenzollerns all or almost all the aspirations of its democratic youth have been realized. The fundamental principle of modern monarchy (hereditary monarchy) is absolutely irreconcilable with the principles of democracy, even when these are understood in the most elastic sense. Cæsarism is still democracy, or may at least still claim the name, when it is based upon the popular will; but automatic monarchy, never.

We may sum up the argument by saying that in modern party life aristocracy gladly presents itself in democratic guise, whilst the substance of democracy is permeated with aristocratic elements. On the one side we have aristocracy in a democratic form, and on the other democracy with an aristocratic content.

The democratic external form which characterizes the life of political parties may readily veil from superficial observers the tendency towards aristocracy, or rather towards oligarchy, which is inherent in all party organization. If we wish to obtain light upon this tendency, the best field of observation is offered by the intimate structure of the democratic parties, and, among these, of the socialist and revolutionary labor party. In the conservative parties, except during elections, the tendency to oligarchy manifests itself with that spontaneous vigor and clearness which corresponds with the essentially oligarchical character of these parties. But the parties which are subversive in their aims exhibit the like phenomena no less markedly. The study of the oligarchical manifestations in party life is most valuable and most decisive in its results when undertaken in relation to the revolutionary parties, for the reason that these parties, in respect of origin and of program, represent the negation of any such tendency, and have actually come into existence out of opposition thereto. Thus the appearance of oligarchical phenomena in the very bosom of the revolutionary parties is a conclusive proof of the existence of immanent oligarchical tendencies in every kind of human organization which strives for the attainment of definite ends.

In theory, the principal aim of socialist and democratic parties is the struggle against oligarchy in all its forms. The question therefore arises how we are to explain the development in such parties of the very tendencies against which they have declared war. To furnish an unprejudiced analytical answer to this question constitutes an important part of the task the author has undertaken.

In the society of today, the state of dependence that results from the existing economic and social conditions renders an ideal democracy impossible. This must be admitted without reserve. But the further question ensues, whether, and if so how far, within the contemporary social order, among the elements which are endeavoring to overthrow that order and to replace it by a new one, there may exist in the germ energies tending to approximate towards ideal democracy, to find outlet in that direction, or at least to work towards it as a necessary issue.

Chapter 2

The Ethical Embellishment of Social Struggles

No one seriously engaged in historical studies can have failed to perceive that all classes which have ever attained to dominion have earnestly endeavored to transmit to their descendants such political power as they have been able to acquire. The hereditary transmission of political power has always been the most efficacious means of maintaining class rule. Thus there is displayed in this field the same historical process which in the domain of the sexual life has given rise to the bourgeois family-order and its accessories, the indissolubility of marriage, the severe penalties inflicted upon the adulterous wife, and the right of primogeniture. In so far as we can draw sound conclusions from the scanty prehistoric data that are available, it seems that the bourgeois family owes its genesis to the innate tendency of man, as soon as he has attained a certain degree of economic well-being, to transmit his possessions by inheritance to the legitimate son whom he can with reasonable certainty regard as his own. The same tendency prevails in the field of politics, where it is kept active by all the peculiar and inherent instincts of mankind, and where it is vigorously nourished by an economic order based upon private property in the means of production, and in which therefore, by a natural and psychological analogy, political power comes also to be considered as an object of private hereditary ownership. In the political field, as everywhere else, the paternal instinct to transmit this species of property to the son has been always strongly manifest throughout historic time. This has been one of the principal causes of the replacement of elective monarchy by hereditary monarchy. The desire to maintain a position acquired by the family in society has at all times been so intense that, as Gaetano Mosca has aptly noted, whenever certain members of the dominant class have not been able to have sons of their own (as, for example, was the case with the prelates of the Roman Church), there has arisen with spontaneous and dynamic force the institution of nepotism, as an extreme manifestation of the impulse to self-maintenance and to hereditary transmission.[1]

In a twofold manner aristocracy has introduced itself quite automatically in those states also from which it seemed to be excluded by constitutional principles, by historical considerations, or by reason of the peculiarities of national psychology—alike by way of a revived tradition and by way of the birth of new economic forces. The North Americans, democrats, living under a republican regime and knowing nothing of titles of nobility, by no means delivered themselves from aristocracy when they shook off the power of the English crown. This phenomenon is in part the simple effect of causes that have come into existence quite recently, such as capitalist concentration (with its associated heaping-up of the social power in the hands of the few and consequent formation of privileged minorities), and the progressive reconciliation of the old and rigid republican spirit with the ideas, the prejudices, and the ambitions of ancient Europe. The existence of an aristocracy of millionaires, railway kings, oil kings, cattle kings, etc., is now indisputable. But even at a time when the youthful democracy and the freedom of America had only just been sealed with the blood of its citizens, it was difficult (so we learn from Alexis de Tocqueville) to find a single American who did not plume himself with an idle vanity upon belonging to one of the first families which had colonized American soil.[2] So lively was "aristocratic prejudice" among these primitive republicans! Even at the present day the old families which are Dutch by name and origin constitute in the State of New York a stratum whose aristocratic preeminence is uncontested, a class of patricians lacking the outward attributes of nobility.

When, in the latter half of the seventeenth century, the French bourgeoisie was vigorously pressing upward, it knew no better how to adapt itself to its changed environment than by aping the usages, the mode of life, the tastes, and even the mentality of the feudal nobility. In 1670 Molière wrote his splendid comedy, *Le Bourgeois gentilhomme*. The Abbé de Choisy, who belonged to the *noblesse de robe*, and whose ancestors had filled the distinguished offices of *Maître des Requêtes and Conseiller d'Etat*, relates that his mother had

[1] Gaetano Mosca, *Il Principio aristocratico e il democratico nel passato e nel' avvenire* (inaugural address), Stamperia Paravia, Turin, 1903, p. 22.
[2] Alexis de Tocqueville, *De la démocratie en Amérique*, Gosselin, Paris, 1849, Part II, vol. ii, p. 19.

given him as a maxim of conduct that he should be careful to frequent none but aristocratic salons.[3] With the fervor of the novice, the new arrivals assimilated the spirit and the principles of the class hitherto dominant, and the distinguished members of the bourgeoisie who had entered the service of the state, which was still predominantly feudal, hastened to take new names. The Fouquets, the Le Telliers, the Colberts, the Phélippeaux, and the Desmarets, became the Belle-Isles, the de Louvois, the Seignelays, the de Maurepas, the de Lavrillières, and the de Maillebois.[4] In modern Germany, under our very eyes, there has for the last forty years been proceeding an absorption of the young industrial bourgeoisie into the old aristocracy of birth and the process has of late been enormously accelerated.[5] The German bourgeoisie is becoming feudalized. Here the only result of the emancipation of the *roturier* has been to reinvigorate his old enemy the noble by the provision of new blood and new economic energy. The enriched bourgeois have no higher ambition than to fuse with the nobility, in order to derive from this fusion a kind of legitimate title for their connection with the dominant class, a title which can then be represented, not as acquired, but as existing by hereditary right. Thus we see that the hereditary principle (even when purely fictitious) greatly accelerates the process of social "training," accelerates, that is to say, the adaption of the new social forces to the old aristocratic environment.

In the violent struggle between the new class of those who are rising and the old stratum of those who are undergoing a decadence partly apparent and partly real—a struggle at times waged with dramatic greatness, but often proceeding obscurely, so as hardly to attract attention—moral considerations are drawn into the dance, and pulled this way and that by the various contending parties, who use them in order to mask their true aims. In an era of democracy, ethics constitute a weapon which everyone can employ. In the old regime, the members of the ruling class and those who desired to become rulers continually spoke of their own personal rights. Democracy adopts a more diplomatic, a more prudent course. It has rejected such claims as unethical. Today, all the factors of

[3] Abbé de Choisy, *Mémoires pour servir à l'Histoire de Louis XIV*, Van De Water, Utrecht, 1727, p. 23.

[4] Pierre Edouard Lémontey, *Essai sur l'établissement monarchique de Louis XIV*, Appendix to *Nouveaux Mémoires de Dangeau*, republished by the author, Deterville, Paris, 1818, p. 392.

[5] Cf. the striking examples furnished by Werner Sombart, *Die deutsche Volkswirtschaft im XIX Jahrhundert*, Bondi, Berlin, 1903, pp. 545 et seq.

public life speak and struggle in the name of the people, of the community at large. The government and rebels against the government, kings and the party-leaders, tyrants by the grace of God and usurpers, rabid idealists and calculating self-seekers, all are "the people," and all declare that in their actions they merely fulfil the will of the nation.

Thus, in the modern life of the classes and of the nations, moral considerations have become an accessory, a necessary fiction. Every government endeavors to support its power by a general ethical principle. The political forms in which the various social movements become crystallized also assume a philanthropic mask. There is not a single one among the young class-parties which fails, before starting on its march for the conquest of power, to declare solemnly to the world that its aim is to redeem, not so much itself as the whole of humanity, from the yoke of tyrannical minority, and to substitute for the old and inequitable regime a new reign of justice. Democracies are always glib talkers. Their terminology is often comparable to a tissue of metaphors. The demagogue, that spontaneous fruit of democratic soil, overflows with sentimentality, and is profoundly moved by the sorrows of the people. "The victims nurse their words, the executioners are drunk on their tearful philosophy,"[6] writes Alphonse Daudet in this connection. Every new social class, when it gives the signal for an attack upon the privileges of a class already in possession of economic and political power, inscribes upon its banners the motto: "The Liberation of the entire Human Race!" When the young French bourgeoisie was girding its loins for the great struggle against the nobles and the clergy, it began with the solemn *Déclaration des Droits de l'Homme*, and hurled itself into the fray with the war-cry *Liberté Egalite, Fraternité!* Today we can ourselves hear the spokesmen of another great class-movement, that of the wage-earners, announce that they undertake the class-struggle from no egoistic motives, but on the contrary in order to exclude such motives for ever from the social process. For the refrain of its Hymn of Progress modern socialism ever reiterates the proud words: "Creation of a humane and fraternal society in which class will be unknown!"

The victorious bourgeoisie of the *Droits de l'Homme* did, indeed, realize the republic, but not the democracy. The words *Liberté, Egalité, Fraternité* may be read to this day over the portals of all French prisons. The Commune was the first

[6] Léon A. Daudet, *Alphonse Daudet*, Bibliothèque Charpentier, E. Fasquelle, Paris, 1898, p. 142.

attempt, crowned by a transient success, at a proletarian-socialist government; and despite its communistic principles, and under the pressure of extreme financial stringency, the Commune respected the Bank of France as faithfully as could have done any syndicate of inexorable capitalists. There have been revolutions, but the world has never witnessed the establishment of logical democracy.

Political parties, however much they may be founded upon narrow class interests and however evidently they may work against the interests of the majority, love to identify themselves with the universe, or at least to present themselves as co-operating with all the citizens of the state, and to proclaim that they are fighting in the name of all and for the good of all. It is only the socialist orators who are sometimes found to proclaim that their party is specifically a class party. But they tone down this assertion by adding that in ultimate analysis the interests of their party coincide with those of the entire people. It is, indeed, true that in protesting that it enters the lists in the interests of the whole of humanity the socialist party, representing the most numerous class of the population, is nearer to the truth than are the bourgeois parties when these make the same claim, for they by their very nature are parties of the minority. But the socialist claim is also far from the truth, seeing that the two terms *humanity* and *party* are far from being identical in extension, even if the party under consideration should embrace, or believe itself to embrace, the great majority of humanity. When for opportunist reason the socialist party declares to the electors that socialism proposes to give to all, but to take nothing from any, it suffices to point out that the enormous differences of wealth which exist in society render it impossible to keep any such promise. The giving presupposes a taking away, and if the proletarians wish to bring about an equality of economic status between themselves on the one hand and the Rothschilds, Vanderbilts, and Rockefellers on the other, which could be done only by socializing the means of production and exchange today owned by these various millionaires, it is obvious that the wealth and power of these great bourgeois princes would be considerably diminished. To the same opportunist party tendency we must ascribe the formulation of the socialist theory which, in apparent accordance with the fundamental principle of the Marxist political economy, divides the population into owners of the means of production and non-owners dependent upon these, proceeding to the contention that all the owners must be capitalist in sentiment while all the dependents must be socialists, that is to say, must desire the triumph of socialism. This view is utterly fallacious, for it regards as the unique or most certain criterion for determining the class to which an individual belongs the amount of his income, which is a purely external characteristic, and then proceeds (in a manner which is perhaps effective in political life, but which is eminently contestable on theoretical grounds) to enlarge the concept of the proletariat so that all employees, governmental or private, may be claimed for the party of labor. According to this theory the directors of Krupp or the Minister-Presidents of Prussia, since as such they are nonowners and employees, are dependents upon the means of production, ought to espouse with enthusiasm the cause of Socialism—ought to do so, at least, in so far as they understand their true position in society, in so far as they have become what the socialists term "class-conscious."

The ideal impetuosity of youthful movements aiming at emancipation is depicted by antidemocratic writers as a pious illusion, as the pursuit of a will-o'-wisp, arising from the need to make the particular good assume the aspect of the general good. In the world of hard fact, every class-movement which professes to aim at the good of the entire community is stamped inevitably as selfcontradictory. Humanity cannot dispense with "political classes," but from their very nature these classes are but fractions of society.

PART ONE/LEADERSHIP IN DEMOCRATIC ORGANIZATIONS

A. Technical and Administrative Causes of Leadership

Chapter 1

Introductory—The Need for Organization

DEMOCRACY is inconceivable without organization. A few words will suffice to demonstrate this proposition.

A class which unfurls in the face of society the banner of certain definite claims, and which aspires to the realization of a complex of ideal aims deriving from the economic functions which that class fulfils, needs an organization. Be the claims economic or be they political, organization appears the only means for the creation of a collective will. Organization, based as it is upon the principle of least effort, that is to say, upon the greatest possible economy of energy, is the weapon of the weak in their struggle with the strong.

The chances of success in any struggle will depend upon the degree to which this struggle is carried out upon a basis of solidarity between individuals whose interests are identical. In objecting, therefore, to the theories of the individualist anarchists that nothing could please the employers better than the dispersion and disaggregation of the forces of the workers, the socialists, the most fanatical of all the partisans of the idea of organization, enunciate an argument which harmonizes well with the results of scientific study of the nature of parties.

We live in a time in which the idea of cooperation has become so firmly established that even millionaires perceive the necessity of common action. It is easy to understand, then, that organization has become a vital principle of the working class, for in default of it their success is *a priori* impossible. The refusal of the worker to participate in the collective life of his class cannot fail to entail disastrous consequences. In respect of culture and of economic, physical, and physiological conditions, the proletarian is the weakest element of our society. In fact, the isolated member of the working classes is defenseless in the hands of those who are economically stronger. It is only by combination to form a structural aggregate that the proletarians can acquire the faculty of political resistance and attain to a social dignity. The importance and the influence of the working class are directly proportional to its numerical strength. But for the representation of that numerical strength organization and coordination are indispensable. The principle of organization is an absolutely essential condition for the political struggle of the masses.

Yet this politically necessary principle of organization, while it overcomes that disorganization of forces which would be favorable to the adversary, brings other dangers in its train. We escape Scylla only to dash ourselves on Charybdis. Organization is, in fact, the source from which the conservative currents flow over the plain of democracy, occasioning there disastrous floods and rendering the plain unrecognizable.

Chapter 2

Mechanical and Technical Impossibility of Direct Government by the Masses

IT WAS a Rhenish democrat, Moritz Rittinghausen, who first made a brilliant attempt to give a real basis for direct legislation by the people.[1]

According to this system the entire population was to be divided into sections, each containing a thousand inhabitants, as was done temporarily for some days in Prussia during the elections of the years 1848 and 1849. The members of each section were to assemble in some prearranged place—a school, townhall, or other public building—and to elect a president. Every citizen was to have the right of speech. In this way the intelligence of every individual would be placed at the service of the fatherland. When the discussion was finished, each one would record his vote. The president would transmit the result to the burgomaster, who would notify the higher authorities. The will of the majority would be decisive.

No legislative proposal was to come from above. The government should have no further initiative than to determine that on a given day all the sections should discuss a given argument. Whenever a certain number of the citizens demanded a new law of any kind, or the reform of an existing law, the ministry concerned must invite the people to exercise its sovereignty within a stated time, and to pass for itself the law in question.[2] The law takes organic form from the discussion itself. First of all, the president opens the debate upon the principal question. Subsequently subordinate points are discussed. Then comes the vote. That proposition which has

[1] Moritz Rittinghausen, *Ueber die Organisation der direkten Gesetzgebung durch das Volk,* Social. Demokrat. Schriften, No. 4, Cöln, 1870, p. 10. The merit of having for the first time ventured to put forward practical proposals of this nature for the solution of the social problem unquestionably belongs to Rittinghausen. Victor Considérant, who subsequently resumed the attempt to establish direct popular government upon a wider basis and with a more far-reaching propagandist effect, expressly recognized Rittinghausen as his precursor (Victor Considérant, *La Solution ou Le Gouvernement Direct du Peuple.* Librairie Phalanstérienne, Paris, 1850, p. 61).

[2] In the American constitution those states only are termed *federalist* (the name being here used to imply a democratic character) in which the people assemble for such a legislative purpose, whilst the states with representative popular government are called *republics.*

received the majority of votes is adopted. As soon as all the returns of the voting have been sent to the ministry, a special commission must edit a clear and simple text of the law, formulating it in a manner which is not open to different interpretations, as is the case with most of the laws presented to modern parliaments, for these, as Rittinghausen sarcastically adds, would seem to incorporate a deliberate intention to favor the tendency of lawyers to ambiguity and hair-splitting.

The system here sketched is clear and concise, and it might seem at the first glance that its practical application would involve no serious difficulties. But if put to the test it would fail to fulfil the expectations of its creator.

The practical ideal of democracy consists in the self-government of the masses in conformity with the decisions of popular assemblies. But while this system limits the extension of the principle of delegation, it fails to provide any guarantee against the formation of an oligarchical camerilla. Undoubtedly it deprives the natural leaders of their quality as functionaries, for this quality is transferred to the people themselves. The crowd, however, is always subject to suggestion, being readily influenced by the eloquence of great popular orators; moreover, direct government by the people, admitting of no serious discussions or thoughtful deliberations, greatly facilitates *coups de main* of all kinds by men who are exceptionally bold, energetic, and adroit.

It is easier to dominate a large crowd than a small audience. The adhesion of the crowd is tumultuous, summary, and unconditional. Once the suggestions have taken effect, the crowd does not readily tolerate contradiction from a small minority, and still less from isolated individuals. A great multitude assembled within a small area is unquestionably more accessible to panic alarms, to unreflective enthusiasm, and the like, than is a small meeting, whose members can quietly discuss matters among themselves (Roscher).[3]

It is a fact of everyday experience that enormous public meetings commonly carry resolutions by acclamation or by general assent, whilst these same assemblies, if divided into small sections, say of fifty persons each, would be much more guarded in their assent. Great party congresses, in which are present the *élite* of the membership, usually act in this way. Words and actions are far less deliberately weighed by the crowd than by the individuals or the little groups of which this crowd is composed. The fact is incontestable—a manifesta-

[3] Roscher, op. cit., p. 35 f.

tion of the pathology of the crowd. The individual disappears in the multitude, and therewith disappears also personality and sense of responsibility.

The most formidable argument against the sovereignty of the masses is, however, derived from the mechanical and technical impossibility of its realization.

The sovereign masses are altogether incapable of undertaking the most necessary resolutions. The impotence of direct democracy, like the power of indirect democracy, is a direct outcome of the influence of number. In a polemic against Proudhon (1849), Louis Blanc asks whether it is possible for thirty-four millions of human beings (the population of France at that time) to carry on their affairs without accepting what the pettiest man of business finds necessary, the intermediation of representatives. He answers his own question by saying that one who declares direct action on this scale to be possible is a fool, and that one who denies its possibility need not be an absolute opponent of the idea of the state.[4] The same question and the same answer could be repeated today in respct of party organization. Above all in the great industrial centers, where the labor party sometimes numbers its adherents by tens of thousands, it is impossible to carry on the affairs of this gigantic body without a system of representation. The great socialist organization of Berlin, which embraces the six constituencies of the city, as well as the two outlying areas of Niederbarnim and Teltow-Beeskow-Charlottenburg, has a member-roll of more than ninety thousand.

It is obvious that such a gigantic number of persons belonging to a unitary organization cannot do any practical work upon a system of direct discussion. The regular holding of deliberative assemblies of a thousand members encounters the gravest difficulties in respect of room and distance; while from the topographical point of view such an assembly would become altogether impossible if the members numbered ten thousand. Even if we imagined the means of communication to become much better than those which now exist, how would it be possible to assemble such a multitude in a given place, at a stated time, and with the frequency demanded by the exigencies of party life? In addition must be considered the physiological impossibility even for the most powerful orator of making himself heard by a crowd of ten thousand persons.[5]

[4] Louis Blanc, "L'état dans une démocratie," *Questions d'aujourd'hui et de demain*, Dentu, Paris, 1880, vol. iii, p. 150.
[5] Roscher, op. cit., p. 351.

There are, however, other persons of a technical and administrative character which render impossible the direct self-government of large groups. If Peter wrongs Paul, it is out of the question that all the other citizens should hasten to the spot to undertake a personal examination of the matter in dispute, and to take the part of Paul against Peter.[6] By parity of reasoning, in the modern democratic party, it is impossible for the collectivity to undertake the direct settlement of all the controversies that may arise.

Hence the need for delegation, for the system in which delegates represent the mass and carry out its will. Even in groups sincerely animated with the democratic spirit, current business, the preparation and the carrying out of the most important actions, is necessarily left in the hands of individuals. It is well known that the impossibility for the people to exercise a legislative power directly in popular assemblies led the democratic idealists of Spain to demand, as the least of evils, a system of popular representation and a parliamentary state.[7]

Originally the chief is merely the servant of the mass. The organization is based upon the absolute equality of all its members. Equality is here understood in its most general sense, as an equality of like men. In many countries, as in idealist Italy (and in certain regions in Germany where the socialist movement is still in its infancy), this equality is manifested, among other ways, by the mutual use of the familiar "thou," which is employed by the most poorly paid wage-laborer in addressing the most distinguished intellectual. This generic conception of equality is, however, gradually replaced by the idea of equality among comrades belonging to the same organization, all of whose members enjoy the same rights. The democratic principle aims at guaranteeing to all an equal influence and an equal participation in the regulation of the common interests. All are electors, and all are eligible for office. The fundamental postulate of the *Déclaration des Droits de l'Homme* finds here its theoretical application. All the offices are filled by election. The officials, executive organs of the general will, play a merely subordinate part, are always dependent upon the collectivity, and can be deprived of their office at any moment. The mass of the party is omnipotent.

At the outset, the attempt is made to depart as little as possible from pure democracy by subordinating the delegates al-

[6] Louis Blanc, op. cit., p. 144.

[7] Cf. the letter of Antonio Quiroga to King Ferdinand VII, dated January 7, 1820 (Don Juan van Halen, *Mémoires*, Renouard, Paris, 1827, Part II, p. 382).

together to the will of the mass, by tieing them hand and foot. In the early days of the movement of the Italian agricultural workers, the chief of the league required a majority of four-fifths of the votes to secure election. When disputes arose with the employers about wages, the representative of the organization, before undertaking any negotiations, had to be furnished with a written authority, authorized by the signature of every member of the corporation. All the accounts of the body were open to the examination of the members, at any time. There were two reasons for this. First of all, the desire was to avoid the spread of mistrust through the mass, "this poison which gradually destroys even the strongest organism." In the second place, this usage allowed each one of the members to learn bookkeeping, and to acquire such a general knowledge of the working of the corporation as to enable him at any time to take over its leadership.[8] It is obvious that democracy in this sense is applicable only on a very small scale. In the infancy of the English labor movement, in many of the trade unions, the delegates were either appointed in rotation from among all the members, or were chosen by lot.[9] Gradually, however, the delegates' duties became more complicated; some individual ability becomes essential, a certain oratorical gift, and a considerable amount of objective knowledge. It thus becomes impossible to trust to blind chance, to the fortune of alphabetic succession, or to the order of priority, in the choice of a delegation whose members must possess certain peculiar personal aptitudes if they are to discharge their mission to the general advantage.

Such were the methods which prevailed in the early days of the labor movement to enable the masses to participate in party and trade-union administration. Today they are falling into disuse, and in the development of the modern political aggregate there is a tendency to shorten and stereotype the process which transforms the led into a leader—a process which has hitherto developed by the natural course of events. Here and there voices make themselves heard demanding a sort of official consecration for the leaders, insisting that it is necessary to constitute a class of professional politicians, of approved and registered experts in political life. Ferdinand Tönnies advocates that the party should institute regular examinations for the nomination of socialist parliamentary candidates, and for the

[8] Egidio Bernaroli, *Manuale per la constituzione e il funzionamento delle leghe dei contadini*, Libreria Soc. Ital., Rome, 1902, pp. 20, 26, 27, 52.

[9] Sidney and Beatrice Webb, *Industrial Democracy* (German edition), Stuttgart, 1898, vol. i, p. 6.

appointment of party secretaries.[10] Heinrich Herkner goes even farther. He contends that the great trade unions cannot long maintain their existence if they persist in entrusting the management of their affairs to persons drawn from the rank and file, who have risen to command stage by stage solely in consequence of practical aptitudes acquired in the service of the organization. He refers, in this connection, to the unions that are controlled by the employers, whose officials are for the most part university men. He foresees that in the near future all the labor organizations will be forced to abandon proletarian exclusiveness, and in the choice of their officials to give the preference to persons of an education that is superior alike in economic, legal, technical, and commercial respects.[11]

Even today, the candidates for the secretaryship of a trade union are subject to examination as to their knowledge of legal matters and their capacity as letter-writers. The socialist organizations engaged in political action also directly undertake the training of their own officials. Everywhere there are coming into existence "nurseries" for the rapid supply of officials possessing a certain amount of "scientific culture." Since 1906 there has existed in Berlin a Party-School in which courses of instruction are given for the training of those who wish to take office in the socialist party or in trade unions. The instructors are paid out of the funds of the socialist party, which was directly responsible for the foundation of the school. The other expenses of the undertaking, including the maintenance of the pupils, are furnished from a common fund supplied by the party and the various trade unions interested. In addition, the families of the pupils, in so far as the attendance of these at the school deprives the families of their breadwinners, receive an allowance from the provincial branch of the party or from the local branch of the union to which each pupil belongs. The third course of this school, from October 1, 1908, to April 3, 1909, was attended by twenty-six pupils, while the first year there had been thirty-one and the second year thirty-three. As pupils, preference is given to comrades who already hold office in the party or in one of the labor unions.[12] Those who do not already belong to the labor bureaucracy make it their aim to enter that body, and cherish the secret hope that attendance at the school will smooth their path. Those who fail to attain this

[10] Ferdinant Tönnies, *Politik und Moral,* Neuer Frankf. Verl., Frankfort, 1901, p. 46.
[11] Heinrich Herkner, *Die Arbeiterfrage,* Guttentag, Berlin, 1908, 5th ed., pp. 116, 117.
[12] *Protokoll des Parteitags zu Leipzig,* 1909, "Vorwärts," Berlin, 1909, p. 48.

end are apt to exhibit a certain discontent with the party which, after having encouraged their studies, has sent them back to manual labor. Among the 141 students of the year 1910-11, three classes were to be distinguished: one of these consisted of old and tried employees in the different branches of the labor movement (fifty-two persons); a second consisted of those who obtained employment in the party or the trade unions directly the course was finished (forty-nine persons); the third consisted of those who had to return to manual labor (forty persons).[13]

In Italy, *L'Umanitaria,* a philanthropic organization run by the socialists, founded at Milan in 1905 a "Practical School of Social Legislation," whose aim it is to give to a certain number of workers an education which will fit them for becoming factory inspectors, or for taking official positions in the various labor organizations, in the friendly societies, or in the labor exchanges.[14] The course of instruction lasts for two years, and at its close the pupils receive, after examination, a diploma which entitles them to the title of "Labor Expert." In 1908 there were two hundred and two pupils, thirty-seven of whom were employees of trade unions or of cooperative societies, four were secretaries of labor exchanges, forty-five employees in or members of the liberal professions, and a hundred and twelve working men.[15] At the outset most of the pupils came to the school as a matter of personal taste, or with the aim of obtaining the diploma in order to secure some comparatively lucrative private employment. But quite recently the governing body has determined to suppress the diploma, and to institute a supplementary course open to those only who are already employed by some labor organization or who definitely intend to enter such employment. For those engaged upon this special course of study there will be provided scholarships of £2 a week, the funds for this purpose being supplied in part by *L'Umanitaria* and in part by the labor organizations which wish to send their employees to the school.[16] In the year 1909, under the auspices of the *Bourse du Travail,* there was founded at Turin a similar school (*Scuola Pratica di Cultura e Legislazione Sociale*), which, however, soon succumbed.

In England the trade unions and cooperative societies make

[13] Heinrich Schulz, *Fünf Jahre Parteischule,* "Neue Zeit," anno xxix, vol. ii, fasc. 49, p. 807.

[14] *Scuola Prat. di Legislaz. Sociale* (Programma e Norme), anno iii, Soc. Umanitaria, Milan, 1908.

[15] Ibid., anno iv, Milan, 1909, p. 5.

[16] Rinaldo Rigola, *I funzionari delle organizzazioni,* "Avanti," anno xiv, No. 341.

use of Ruskin College, Oxford, sending thither those of their members who aspire to office in the labor organizations, and who have displayed special aptitudes for this career. In Austria it is proposed to found a party school upon the German model.

It is undeniable that all these educational institutions for the officials of the party and of the labor organizations tend, above all, towards the artificial creation of an *élite* of the working class, of a caste of cadets composed of persons who aspire to the command of the proletarian rank and file. Without wishing it, there is thus effected a continuous enlargement of the gulf which divides the leaders from the masses.

The technical specialization that inevitably results from all extensive organization renders necessary what is called expert leadership. Consequently the power of determination comes to be considered one of the specific attributes of leadership, and is gradually withdrawn from the masses to be concentrated in the hands of the leaders alone. Thus the leaders, who were at first no more than the executive organs of the collective will, soon emancipate themselves from the mass and become independent of its control.

Organization implies the tendency to oligarchy. In every organization, whether it be a political party, a professional union, or any other association of the kind, the aristocratic tendency manifests itself very clearly. The mechanism of the organization, while conferring a solidity of structure, induces serious changes in the organized mass, completely inverting the respective position of the leaders and the led. As a result of organization, every party or professional union becomes divided into a minority of directors and a majority of directed.

It has been remarked that in the lower stages of civilization tyranny is dominant. Democracy cannot come into existence until there is attained a subsequent and more highly developed stage of social life. Freedoms and privileges, and among these latter the privilege of taking part in the direction of public affairs, are at first restricted to the few. Recent times have been characterized by the gradual extension of these privileges to a widening circle. This is what we know as the era of democracy. But if we pass from the sphere of the state to the sphere of party, we may observe that as democracy continues to develop, a backwash sets in. With the advance of organization, democracy tends to decline. Democratic evolution has a parabolic course. At the present time, at any rate as far as party life is concerned, democracy is in the descending phase. It may be enunciated as a general rule that the increase in the power of the leaders is directly proportional with the extension of the organization. In the various parties and labor organizations of different countries the influence of the leaders is mainly determined (apart from racial and individual grounds) by the varying development of organization. Where organization is stronger, we find that there is a lesser degree of applied democracy.

Every solidly constructed organization, whether it be a democratic state, a political party, or a league of proletarians for the resistance of economic oppression, presents a soil eminently favorable for the differentiation of organs and of functions. The more extended and the more ramified the official apparatus of the organization, the greater the number of its members, the fuller its treasury, and the more widely circulated its press, the less efficient becomes the direct control exercised by the rank and file, and the more is this control replaced by the increasing power of committees. Into all parties there insinuates itself that indirect electoral system which in public life the democratic parties fight against with all possible vigor. Yet in party life the influence of this system must be more disastrous than in the far more extensive life of the state. Even in the party congresses, which represent the party-life seven times sifted, we find that it becomes more and more general to refer all important questions to committees which debate *in camera*.

As organization develops, not only do the tasks of the administration become more difficult and more complicated, but, further, its duties become enlarged and specialized to such a degree that it is no longer possible to take them all in at a single glance. In a rapidly progressive movement, it is not only the growth in the number of duties, but also the higher quality of these, which imposes a more extensive differentiation of function. Nominally, and according to the letter of the rules, all the acts of the leaders are subject to the ever vigilant criticism of the rank and file. In theory the leader is merely an employee bound by the instruction he receives. He has to carry out the orders of the mass, of which he is no more than the executive organ. But in actual fact, as the organization increases in size, this control becomes purely fictitious. The members have to give up the idea of themselves conducting or even supervising the whole administration, and are compelled to hand these tasks over to trustworthy persons specially nominated for the purpose, to salaried officials. The rank and file must content themselves with summary reports, and with the appointment of occasional special committees of inquiry. Yet this does not derive from any special change in the rules of the organization. It is by very necessity that a simple employee gradually becomes a "leader," acquiring a freedom of action which he ought not to possess. The chief then becomes accustomed to dispatch important business on his own responsibility, and to decide various questions relating to the life of the party without any attempt to consult the rank and file. It is obvious that democratic control thus undergoes a progressive diminution, and is ultimately reduced to an infinitesimal minimum. In all the socialist parties there is a continual increase in the number of functions withdrawn from the electoral assemblies and transferred to the executive committees. In this way there is constructed a powerful and complicated edifice. The principle of division of labor coming more and more into operation, executive authority undergoes division and subdivision. There is thus constituted a rigorously defined and hierarchical bureaucracy. In the catechism of party duties, the strict observance of hierarchical rules becomes the first article. The hierarchy comes into existence as the outcome of technical conditions, and its constitution is an essential postulate of the regular functioning of the party machine.

It is indisputable that the oligarchical and bureaucratic tendency of party organization is a matter of technical and practical necessity. It is the inevitable product of the very principle of organization. Not even the most radical wing of the various socialist parties raises any objection to this retrogressive evolution, the contention being that democracy is only a form of organization and that where it ceases to be possible to harmonize democracy with organization, it is better to abandon the former than the latter. Organization, since it is the only means of attaining the ends of socialism, is considered to comprise within itself the revolutionary content of the party, and this essential content must never be sacrificed for the sake of form.

In all times, in all phases of development, in all branches of human activity, there have been leaders. It is true that certain socialists, above all the orthodox Marxists of Germany, seek to convince us that socialism knows nothing of "leaders," that the party has "employees" merely, being a democratic party, and the existence of leaders being incompatible with democracy. But a false assertion such as this cannot override a sociological law. Its only result is, in fact, to strengthen the rule of the leaders, for it serves to conceal from the mass a danger which really threatens democracy.

For technical and administrative reasons, no less than for tactical reasons, a strong organization needs an equally strong leadership. As long as an organization is loosely constructed and vague in its outlines, no professional leadership can arise. The anarchists, who have a horror of all fixed organization, have no regular leaders. In the early days of German socialism, the *Vertrauensmann* (homme de confiance) continued to exercise his ordinary occupation. If he received any pay for his work for the party, the remuneration was on an extremely modest scale, and was no more than a temporary grant. His function could never be regarded by him as a regular source of income. The employee of the organization was still a simple workmate, sharing the mode of life and the social condition of his fellows. Today he has been replaced for the most part by the professional politician, *Berzirksleiter* (U.S. ward-boss), etc. The more solid the structure of an organization becomes in the course of the evolution of the modern political party, the more marked becomes the tendency to replace the emergency leader by the professional leader. Every party organization which has attained to a considerable degree of complication demands that there should be a certain number of persons who devote all their activities to the work of the party. The mass provides these by delegations, and the delegates, regularly appointed, become permanent representatives of the mass for the direction of its affairs.

For democracy, however, the first appearance of professional leadership marks the beginning of the end, and this, above all, on account of the logical impossibility of the "representative" system, whether in parliamentary life or in party delegation. Jean Jacques Rousseau may be considered as the founder of this aspect of the criticism of democracy. He defines popular government as "the exercise of the general will" and draws from this the logical inference that "it can never be alienated from itself, and the sovereign—who is nothing but a collective concept—can only be represented by himself. Consequently the instant a people gives itself to representatives, it is no longer free."[17] A mass which delegates its sovereignty, that is to say transfers its sovereignty to the hands of a few individuals, abdicates its sovereign functions. For the will of the people is not transferable. nor even the will of the single

[17] Jean Jacques Rousseau, *Le Contrat social* (lib. cit., pp. 40 et seq.)

individual. However much in practice, during the confused years of the Terror, the doctrine was abandoned by the disciples of the philosopher of Geneva, it was at this time in theory universally admitted as incontrovertible. Robespierre himself accepted it, making a subtle distinction between the "representative of the people" who has no right to exist "because will cannot be represented" and "the agent to whom the people have given primary power."

The experience of attentive observers of the working of the first attempts at a representative system contributed to establish more firmly the theory of the limits of democracy. Towards the middle of the nineteenth century this theory, the outcome of an empirical psychology, was notably enlarged, its claim to general validity was sustained, and it was formulated as the basis of definite rules and precepts. Carlo Pisacane, the theorist, too soon forgotten, of the national and social revolution in Italy, expounds in his *Saggio sulla Rivoluzione* how the men in whose hands supreme political power is placed must, from their very nature as human beings, be subject to passions and to the physical and mental imperfections therefrom resulting. For this reason the tendency and the acts of their rule are in direct contrast with the tendency and the acts of the mass, "for the latter represent the mean of all individual judgments and determinations, and are therefore free from the operation of such influences." To maintain of a government that it represents public opinion and the will of the nation is simply to mistake a part for the whole.[18] He thus considers delegation to be an absurdity. Victor Considérant, a contemporary of Pisacane and the representative of a similar tendency, also followed in the tracks of Rousseau: "If the people delegate their sovereignty, they resign it. The people no longer govern themselves; they are governed. . . . Then, People, delegate your sovereignty! I guarantee you a fate the opposite of Saturn's: your sovereignty will be devoured by your daughter, the Delegation."[19] The theorists of democracy are never tired of asserting that, when voting, the people is at one and the same time exercising its sovereignty and renouncing it. The great democrat Ledru-Rollin, the father of universal and equal suffrage in France, goes so far as to demand the suppression of president and parliament, and the recognition of the general assembly of the people as the sole legislative organ. If people, he continues,

[18] Carlo Pisacane, *Saggio sulla Rivoluzione*, with a preface by Napoleone Colajanni, Lib. Treves di Pietro Virano, Bologna, 1894, pp. 121–5.
[19] Trans. from Victor Considérant, op. cit., pp. 13–15.

find it possible in the course of the year to waste so much time upon public entertainments, holidays, and loafing, they could surely make a better use of their time by devoting it "to strengthening their independence, their greatness and their prosperity."[20]

Victor Considérant fiercely opposed the theory that popular sovereignty is guaranteed by the representative system. Even if we make the theoretical admission that *in abstracto* parliamentary government does indeed embody government by the masses, in practical life it is nothing but a continuous fraud on the part of the dominant class. Under representative government the difference between democracy and monarchy, which are both rooted in the representative system, is altogether insignificant—a difference not in substance but in form. The sovereign people elects, in place of a king, a number of kinglets. Not possessing sufficient freedom and independence to direct the life of the state, it tamely allows itself to be despoiled of its fundamental right. The one right which the people reserves is the "ridiculous privilege" of choosing from time to time a new set of masters.[21] To this criticism of the representative system may be appended the remark of Proudhon, to the effect that the representatives of the people have no sooner been raised to power than they set to work to consolidate and reinforce their influence. They continue unceasingly to surround their positions by new lines of defense, until they have succeeded in emancipating themselves completely from popular control. All power thus proceeds in a natural cycle: issuing from the people, it ends by raising itself above the people.[22] In the forties of the last century these ideas were widely diffused and their truth was almost universally admitted, and in France more particularly by students of social science and by democratic statesmen. Even the clericals mingled their voices with those which condemned the representative system. Louis Veuillot, the Catholic, said: "When I voted, my equality tumbled into the box with my ballot; they disappeared together."[23] Today this theory is the central feature of the political criticism of the various schools of anarchists, who often expound

[20] A. A. Ledru-Rollin, *Plus de Président, plus de Représentants*, ed. de "La Voix du Proscrit," Paris, 1851, 2nd ed., p. 7.

[21] Victor Considérant, op. cit., pp. 11–12.

[22] Cf. P. J. Proudhon, *Les Confessions d'un Révolutionnaire. Pour servir à la Révolution de Février*, Verboeckhoven, Paris, 1868, new ed., p. 286.

[23] Trans. from Louis Veuillot, *Ça et là*, Caume Frères et Duprey, Paris, 1860, 2nd ed., vol. i, p. 368.

it eloquently and acutely.[24] Finally Marx and his followers, who in theory regard parliamentary action as but one weapon among many, but who in practice employ this weapon alone, do not fail to recognize incidentally the perils of the representative system, even when based upon universal suffrage. But the Marxists hasten to add that the socialist party is quite free from these dangers.[25]

Popular sovereignty has recently been subjected to a profound criticism by a group of Italian writers conservative in their tendency. Gaetano Mosca speaks of "the falsity of the parliamentary legend." He says that the idea of popular representation as a free and spontaneous transference of the sovereignty of the electors (collectivity) to a certain number of elected persons (minority) is based upon the absurd premise that the minority can be bound to the collective will by unbreakable bonds.[26] In actual fact, directly the election is finished, the power of the mass of electors over the delegate comes to an end. The deputy regards himself as authorized arbiter of the situation, and really is such. If among the electors any are to be found who possess some influence over the representative of the people, their number is very small; they are the big guns of the constituency or of the local branch of the party. In other words, they are persons who, whilst belonging by social position to the class of the ruled, have in fact come to form part of the ruling oligarchy.[27]

This criticism of the representative system is applicable above all in our own days, in which political life continually assumes more complex forms. As this complexity increases, it becomes more and more absurd to attempt to "represent" a heterogeneous mass in all the innumerable problems which arise out of the increasing differentiation of our political and

[24] Cf., for example, Enrico Malatesta in two pamphlets: *L'anarchia* (Casa ed. Pensiero, Rome, 6th ed., 1907), and *La Politica parlamentare del Partito socialista* (ediz. dell' "Allarme," Turin, 1903). Cf. also Ferdinand Domela Nieuwenhuis, *Het Parlamentarisme in zijn Wezen en Toepassing*, W. Sligting, Amsterdam, 1906, pp. 149 et seq.

[25] Cf. Karl Kautsky, Rosa Luxemburg, and others. In the works of Karl Marx we find traces here and there of a theoretical mistrust of the representative system; see especially this writer's *Revolution u. Kontre-Revolution in Deutschland*, Dietz, Stuttgart, 1896, p. 107.

[26] Cf. Gaetano Mosca, *Questioni pratiche di Diritto constituzionale*, Fratelli Bocca, Turin, 1898, pp. 81 et seq. Also *Sulla Teorica dei Governi e sul Governo parlamentare*, Loescher, Rome, 1884, pp. 120 et seq.

[27] "An electional system simply places power in the hands of the most skillful electioneers" (H. G. Wells, *Anticipations of the Reaction of Mechanical and Scientific Progress upon Human Life and Thought*, Chapman and Hall, London, 1904, p. 58). Of course, this applies only to countries with a republican-democratic constitution.

economic life. To represent, in this sense, comes to mean that the purely individual desire masquerades and is accepted as the will of the mass.[28] In certain isolated cases, where the questions involved are extremely simple, and where the delegated authority is of brief duration, representation is possible. But permanent representation will always be tantamount to the exercise of dominion by the representatives over the represented.

[28] Fouillée writes aptly in this connection: "If I make personal use of my right to go and come from Paris to Marseille, I do not prevent you from going from Paris to Marseille; the exercise of my civil right does not remove yours. But when I send a deputy to the Chamber who will work at your expense for measures you have always protested, this manner of governing myself implies a manner of governing you which distresses you and which could be unjust. Civil right is personal freedom; political right is a right over others as well as oneself." (Trans. from Alfred Fouillée, *Erreurs sociologiques et morales de la Sociologie,* "Revue des deux Mondes," liv. p. 330).

Chapter 3

The Modern Democratic Party as a Fighting Party, Dominated by Militarist Ideas and Methods

LOUIS XIV understood the art of government as have few princes either before or since, and this was the case above all in the first half of his reign, when his spirit was still young and fresh. In his memoirs of the year 1666, he lays down for every branch of the adminstration, and more especially for the conduct of military affairs, the following essential rules: "Resolutions ought to be prompt, discipline exact, commands absolute, obedience punctual."[1] The essentials thus enumerated by the *Roi Soleil* (promptness of decision, unity of command, and strictness of discipline) are equally applicable, *mutatis mutandis,* to the various aggregates of modern political life, for these are in a perpetual condition of latent warfare.

The modern party is a fighting organization in the political sense of the term, and must as such conform to the laws of tactics. Now the first article of these laws is facility of mobilization. Ferdinand Lassalle, the founder of a revolutionary labor party, recognized this long ago, contending that the dictatorship which existed in fact in the society over which he presided was as thoroughly justified in theory as it was indispensable in practice. The rank and file, he said, must follow their chief blindly, and the whole organization must be like a hammer in the hands of its president.

This view of the matter was in correspondence with political necessity, especially in Lassalle's day, when the labor movement was in its infancy, and when it was only by a rigorous discipline that this movement could hope to obtain respect and consideration from the bourgeois parties. Centralization guaranteed, and always guarantees, the rapid formation of resolutions. An extensive organization is *per se* a heavy piece of mechanism, and one difficult to put in operation. When we have to do with a mass distributed over a considerable area, to consult the rank and file upon every question would involve an enormous loss of time, and the opinion thus obtained would

[1] Trans. from *Mémoires de Louis XIV pour l'instruction du Dauphin,* annotées par Charles Deyss, Paris, 1860, vol. ii, p. 123.

moreover be summary and vague. But the problems of the hour need a speedy decision, and this is why democracy can no longer function in its primitive and genuine form, unless the policy pursued is to be temporizing, involving the loss of the most favorable opportunities for action. Under such guidance, the party becomes incapable of acting in alliance with others, and loses its political elasticity. A fighting party needs a hierarchical structure. In the absence of such a structure, the party will be comparable to a savage and shapeless Negro army, which is unable to withstand a single well-disciplined and well-drilled battalion of European soldiers.

In the daily struggle, nothing but a certain degree of cæsarism will ensure the rapid transmission and the precise execution of orders. The Dutch socialist, van Kol, frankly declares that true democracy cannot be installed until the fight is over. Meanwhile, even a socialist leadership must possess authority, and sufficient force to maintain itself in power. A provisional despotism is, he contends, essential, and liberty itself must yield to the need for prompt action. Thus the submission of the masses to the will of a few individuals comes to be considered one of the highest of democratic virtues. "To those who are called to lead us, we promise loyalty and obedience, and we say to them: Men who have been honored as the people's choice, show us the way, we will follow you."[2] It is such utterances as this which reveal to us the true nature of the modern party. In a party, and above all in a fighting political party, democracy is not for home consumption, but is rather an article made for export. Every political organization has need of "a light equipment which will not hamper its movements." Democracy is utterly incompatible with strategic promptness, and the forces of democracy do not lend themselves to the rapid opening of a campaign. This is why political parties, even when democratic, exhibit so much hostility to the referendum and to all other measures for the safeguard of real democracy; and this is why in their constitution these parties exhibit, if not unconditional cæsarism, at least extremely strong centralizing and oligarchical tendencies. Lagardelle puts the finishing touches to the picture in the following words: "And for the use of the proletariat they have reproduced the capitalist tools of domination; they have built a workers' government as harsh as the bourgeois government, a workers' bureaucracy as clumsy as the bourgeois bureaucracy, a central

[2] Trans. from Rienzi [van Kol], *Socialisme et Liberté*, Giard et Brière, Paris, 1898, pp. 243–53.

power which tells the workers what they can and what they cannot do, which shatters all independence and initiative in the union members, and which sometimes must inspire in its victims a regret for capitalistic modes of authority."[3]

The close resemblance between a fighting democratic party and a military organization is reflected in socialist terminology, which is largely borrowed, and especially in Germany, from military science. There is hardly one expression of military tactics and strategy, hardly even a phrase of barrack slang, which does not recur again and again in the leading articles of the socialist press. In the daily practice of the socialist struggle it is true that preference is almost invariably given to the temporizing tactics of Fabius Cunctator, but this depends upon special circumstances, which will be subsequently discussed (Part 6, Chap. 1). The intimate association between party life and military life is manifested also by the passionate interest which some of the most distinguished leaders of German socialism take in military affairs. During his residence in England, the German merchant Frederick Engels, who had once served in the Guards as a volunteer, devoted his leisure to the simultaneous exposition of socialist and of militarist theory.[4] To Bebel, the son of a Prussian non-commissioned officer, the world is indebted for a number of ideas of reform in matters of military technique which have nothing in common with the theoretical socialist antimilitarism.[5] Bebel and Engels, and especially the latter, may even be considered as essentially military writers. This tendency on the part of socialist leaders is not the outcome of mere chance, but depends upon an instinct of elective affinity.

[3] Trans. from Hubert Lagardelle, *Le Parti Socialiste et la Confédération du Travail*, Discussion with J. Guesde, Rivière, Paris, 1907, p. 24.

[4] See in particular Engels' works: *Po und Rhein* (1859); *Savoyen, Nizza und der Rhein* (1860); *Die preussische Militärfrage und die deutsche Arbeiterpartei* (1865); *Der deutsche Bauernkrieg* (1875, Vorwärts-Verlag, Berlin, 1909, 3rd ed. edited by Mehring); *Kann Europa abrüsten?* (Nuremberg, 1893).

[5] Cf., for example, the pamphlet *Nicht stehendes Heer, sondern Volkswehr*, Dietz, Stuttgart, 1908, p. 80; also a large number of speeches in the Reichstag on the military estimates, in which he is never tired of discussing the minutiæ of army reform, and in which in especial he advocates changes in military equipment to render the army more efficient.

B. Psychological Causes of Leadership

Chapter 1

The Establishment of a Customary Right to the Office of Delegate

ONE WHO holds the office of delegate acquires a moral right to that office, and delegates remain in office unless removed by extraordinary circumstances or in obedience to rules observed with exceptional strictness. An election made for a definite purpose becomes a life incumbency. Custom becomes a right. One who has for a certain time held the office of delegate ends by regarding that office as his own property. If refused reinstatement, he threatens reprisals (the threat of resignation being the least serious among these) which will tend to sow confusion among his comrades, and this confusion will continue until he is victorious.

Resignation of office, in so far as it is not a mere expression of discouragement or protest (such as disinclination to accept a candidature in an unpromising constituency), is in most cases a means for the retention and fortification of leadership. Even in political organizations greater than party, the leaders often employ this stratagem, thus disarming their adversaries by a deference which does not lack a specious democratic color. The opponent is forced to exhibit in return an even greater deference, and this above all when the leader who makes use of the method is really indispensable, or is considered indispensable by the mass. The recent history of Germany affords numerous examples showing the infallibility of this machiavellian device for the maintenance of leadership. During the troubled period of transition from absolute to constitutional monarchy, during the ministry of Ludolf Camphausen, King Frederick William IV of Prussia threatened to abdicate whenever liberal ideas were tending in Prussian politics to gain the upper hand over the romanticist conservatism which was dear to his heart. By this threat the liberals were placed in a dilemma. Either they must accept the king's abdication, which would involve the accession to the throne of Prince William of Prussia, a man of ultra-reactionary tendencies, whose reign was likely to be initiated by an uprising among the lower classes; or else they must abandon their liberal schemes, and maintain in power the king now become indispensable. Thus Frederick William always succeeded in getting his own way, and in defeating the schemes of his political opponents. Thirty-five years later Prince Bismarck, establishing his strength with the weapon of his indispensability, consolidated his omnipotence over the German empire which he had recently created, by again and again handing in his resignation to the Emperor William I. His aim was to reduce the old monarch to obedience, whenever the latter showed any signs of exercising an independent will, by suggesting the chaos in internal and external policy which would necessarily result from the retirement of the "founder of the empire," since the aged emperor was not competent to undertake the personal direction of affairs.[1] The present president of the Brazilian republic, Hermes da Fonseca, owes his position chiefly to a timely threat of resignation. Having been appointed Minister of War in 1907, Fonseca undertook the reorganization of the Brazilian army. He brought forward a bill for the introduction of universal compulsory military service, which was fiercely resisted in both houses of parliament. Through his energetic personal advocacy, sustained by a threat of resignation, the measure was ultimately carried, and secured for its promoter such renown, that not only did he remain in office, but in the year 1910 was elected President of the Republic by 102,000 votes against 52,000.

It is the same in all political parties. Whenever an obstacle is encountered, the leaders are apt to offer to resign, professing that they are weary of office, but really aiming to show to the dissentients the indispensability of their own leadership. In 1864, when Vahlteich proposed a change in the rules of the General Association of German Workers, Lassalle, the president, was very angry, and, conscious of his own value to the movement, propounded the following alternative: Either you protect me from the recurrence of such friction as this, or I throw up my office. The immediate result was the expulsion of the importunate critic. In Holland today, Troelstra, the Dutch Lassalle, likewise succeeds in disarming his opponents within the party by pathetically threatening to retire into private life, saying that if they go on subjecting his actions to an inoppor-

1 *Denkwürdigkeiten des Fürsten Chlodwig zu Hohenlohe-Schillingsfürst*, ed. by Friedrich Curtius, Deutsche Verlagsanstalt, Stuttgart and Leipzig, 1907, vol. ii.

tune criticism, his injured idealism will force him to withdraw from the daily struggles of party life. The same thing has occurred more than once in the history of the Italian socialist party. It often happens that the socialist members of parliament find themselves in disagreement with the majority of the party upon some question of importance, such as that of the opportuneness of a general strike; or in the party congresses they may wish to record their votes in opposition to the views of their respective branches. It is easy for them to get their own way and to silence their opponents by threatening to resign. If necessary, they go still further, and actually resign their seats, appealing to the electors as the only authority competent to decide the question in dispute. In such cases they are nearly always re-elected, and thus attain to an incontestable position of power. At the socialist congress held at Bologna in 1904, some of the deputies voted in favor of the reformist resolution, in opposition to the wishes of the majority of the comrades whose views they were supposed to represent. When called to account, they offered to resign their seats, and the party electors, wishing to avoid the expense and trouble of a new election, and afraid of the loss of party seats, hastened to condone the deputies' action. In May, 1906, twenty-four out of the twenty-seven members of the socialist group in the Chamber resigned their seats, in consequence of the difference of views between themselves and the rank and file on the subject of the general strike, which the deputies had repudiated. All but three were re-elected.

Such actions have a fine democratic air, and yet hardly serve to conceal the dictatorial spirit of those who perform them. The leader who asks for a vote of confidence is in appearance submitting to the judgment of his followers, but in reality he throws into the scale the entire weight of his own indispensability, real or supposed, and thus commonly forces submission to his will. The leaders are extremely careful never to admit that the true aim of their threat to resign is the reinforcement of their power over the rank and file. They declare, on the contrary, that their conduct is determined by the purest democratic spirit, that it is a striking proof of their fineness of feeling, of their sense of personal dignity, and of their deference for the mass. Yet if we really look into the matter we cannot fail to see that, whether they desire it or not, their action is an oligarchical demonstration, the manifestation of a tendency to enfranchise themselves from the control of the rank and file.

Such resignations, even if not dictated by a self-seeking policy, but offered solely in order to prevent differences of opinion between the leaders and the mass, and in order to maintain the necessary harmony of views, always have as their practical outcome the subjection of the mass to the authority of the leader.

Chapter 2

The Need for Leadership Felt by the Mass

A DISTINGUISHED French dramatist who devoted his leisure to writing prose studies of serious social questions, Alexandre Dumas fils, once observed that every human advance was, at its outset, opposed by ninety-nine per cent of humanity. "But this is of no importance, seeing that that hundredth to which we belong has, since the beginning of the world, made all the reforms for the ninety-nine others who are well pleased with them but who nevertheless go on protesting against those which still remain to be carried out." In another passage he adds: "Majorities are only the evidence of that which is" whereas "minorities are often the seed of that which will be."[1]

There is no exaggeration in the assertion that among the citizens who enjoy political rights the number of those who have a lively interest in public affairs is insignificant. In the majority of human beings the sense of an intimate relationship between the good of the individual and the good of the collectivity is but little developed. Most people are altogether devoid of understanding of the actions and reactions between that organism we call the state and their private interests, their prosperity, and their life. As de Tocqueville expresses it, they regard it as far more important to consider "whether it is worthwhile to put a road through their land."[2] than to interest themselves in the general work of public administration. The majority is content, with Stirner, to call out to the state, "Get away from between me and the sun!" Stirner makes fun of all those who, in accordance with the views of Kant, preach it to humanity as a "sacred duty" to take an interest in public affairs. "Let those persons who have a personal interest in political changes concern themselves with these. Neither now nor at any future time will 'sacred duty' lead people to trouble themselves about the state, just as little as it is by 'sacred duty' that they become men of science, artists, etc. Egoism alone can spur people to an interest in public affairs, and will spur them —when matters grow a good deal worse."[3]

[1] Trans. from Alexandre Dumas fils, *Les Femmes qui tuent et les Femmes qui votent*, Calman Lévy, Paris, 1880, pp. 54 and 214.
[2] Trans. from Alexis de Tocqueville, op. cit., vol. i, p. 167.
[3] Max Stirner (Kaspar Schmidt), *Der Einzige und sein Eigentum*, Reclam, Leipzig, 1892, p. 272.

In the life of modern democratic parties we may observe signs of similar indifference. It is only a minority which participates in party decisions, and sometimes that minority is ludicrously small. The most important resolutions taken by the most democratic of all parties, the socialist party, always emanate from a handful of the members. It is true that the renouncement of the exercise of democratic rights is voluntary; except in those cases, which are common enough, where the active participation of the organized mass in party life is prevented by geographical or topographical conditions. Speaking generally, it is the urban part of the organization which decides everything; the duties of the members living in country districts and in remote provincial towns are greatly restricted; they are expected to pay their subscriptions and to vote during elections in favor of the candidates selected by the organization of the great town. There is here at work the influence of tactical considerations as well as that of local conditions. The preponderance of the townsmen over the scattered country members corresponds to the necessity of promptness in decision and speed in action to which allusion was made in an earlier chapter.

Within the large towns there goes on a process of spontaneous selection, in virtue of which there is separated from the organized mass a certain number of members who participate more diligently than the others in the work of the organization. This inner group is composed, like that of the pious frequenters of the churches, of two very distinct categories: the category of those who are animated by a fine sense of duty, and the category of those whose attendance is merely a matter of habit. In all countries the number of this inner circle is comparatively small. The majority of the members are as indifferent to the organization as the majority of the electors are to parliament. Even in countries like France, where collective political education is of older date, the majority renounces all active participation in tactical and administrative questions, leaving these to the little group which makes a practice of attending meetings. The great struggles which go on among the leaders on behalf of one tactical method or another, struggles in fact for supremacy in the party, but carried out in the name of Marxism, reformism, or syndicalism, are not merely beyond the understanding of the rank and file, but leave them altogether cold. In almost all countries it is easy to observe that meetings held to discuss questions of the hour, whether political, sensational, or sentimental (such as protection, an attack upon the Government, the Russian revolution, and the like), or those for the discussion of matters of general interest (the discovery of the North Pole, personal hygiene, spiritualism), attract a far larger audience, even when reserved to members of the party, than do meetings for the discussion of tactical or theoretical questions, although these are of vital importance to the doctrine or to the organization. The present writer knows this from personal experience in three typical great cities, Paris, Frankfort-on-the-Main, and Turin. Notwithstanding differences of atmosphere, there was observable in each of these three centers the same indifference to party affairs and the same slackness of attendance at ordinary meetings. The great majority of the members will not attend meetings unless some noted orator is to speak, or unless some extremely striking war-cry is sounded for their attraction, such as, in France, "A bas la vie chère!", or, in Germany, "Down with personal government!" A good meeting can also be held when there is a cinema-show, or a popular scientific lecture illustrated by lantern-slides. In a word, the ordinary members have a weakness for everything which appeals to their eyes and for such spectacles as will always attract a gaping crowd.

It may be added that the regular attendants at public meetings and committees are by no means always proletarians—especially where the smaller centers are concerned. When his work is finished, the proletarian can think only of rest, and of getting to bed in good time. His place at meetings is taken by petty bourgeois, by those who come to sell newspapers and picture-postcards, by clerks, by young intellectuals who have not yet got a position in their own circle, people who are all glad to hear themselves spoken of as authentic proletarians and to be glorified as the class of the future.

The same thing happens in party life as happens in the state. In both, the demand for monetary supplies is upon a coercive foundation, but the electoral system has no established sanction. An electoral right exists, but no electoral duty. Until this duty is superimposed upon the right, it appears probable that a small minority only will continue to avail itself of the right which the majority voluntarily renounces, and that the minority will always dictate laws for the indifferent and apathetic mass. The consequence is that, in the political groupings of democracy, the participation in party life has an echeloned aspect. The extensive base consists of the great mass of electors; upon this is superposed the enormously smaller mass of enrolled members of the local branch of the party, numbering perhaps one-tenth or even as few as one-thirtieth of the electors; above this, again, comes the much smaller number of the members who regularly attend meetings; next comes the group of officials of the party; and highest of all, consisting in part of the same individuals as the last group, come the half-dozen or so members of the executive committee. Effective power is here in inverse ratio to the number of those who exercise it. Thus practical democracy is represented by the following diagram:—

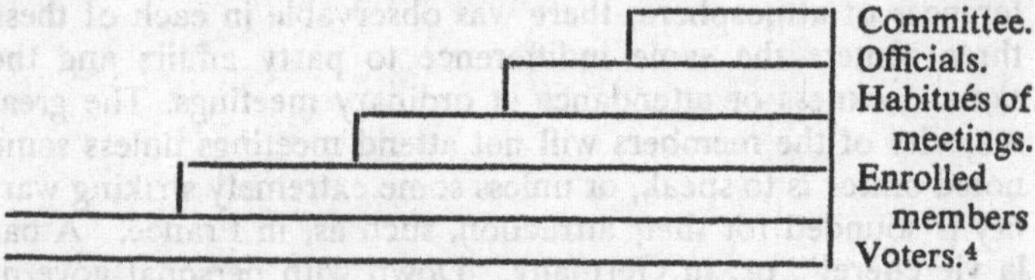

Though it grumbles occasionally, the majority is really delighted to find persons who will take the trouble to look after its affairs. In the mass, and even in the organized mass of the labor parties, there is an immense need for direction and guidance. This need is accompanied by a genuine cult for the leaders, who are regarded as heroes. Misoneism, the rock upon which so many serious reforms have at all times been wrecked, is at present rather increasing than diminishing. This increase is explicable owning to the more extensive division of labor in modern civilized society, which renders it more and more impossible to embrace in a single glance the totality of the political organization of the state and its ever more complicated mechanism. To this misoneism are superadded, and more particularly in the popular parties, profound differences of culture and education among the members. These differences give to the need for leadership felt by the masses a continually increasing dynamic tendency.

This tendency is manifest in the political parties of all countries. It is true that its intensity varies as between one nation and another, in accordance with contingencies of a historical character or with the influences of racial psychology. The German people in especial exhibits to an extreme degree the need for someone to point out the way and to issue orders. This peculiarity, common to all classes not excepting the proletariat, furnishes a psychological soil upon which a powerful directive

[4] This figure must not be regarded as intended to represent such relationships according to scale, for this would require an entire page. It is purely diagrammatic.

hegemony can flourish luxuriantly. There exist among the Germans all the preconditions necessary for such a development: a psychical predisposition to subordination, a profound instinct for discipline, in a word, the whole still-persistent inheritance of the influence of the Prussian drill-sergeant, with all its advantages and all its disadvantages; in addition, a trust in authority which verges on the complete absence of a critical faculty. It is only the Rhinelanders, possessed of a somewhat more conspicuous individuality, who constitute, to a certain extent, an exception to this generalization. The risks to the democratic spirit that are involved by this peculiarity of the German character were well known to Karl Marx. Although himself a party leader in the fullest sense of the term, and although endowed to the highest degree with the qualities necessary for leadership, he thought it necessary to warn the German workers against entertaining too rigid a conception of organization. In a letter from Marx to Schweitzer we are told that in Germany, where the workers are bureaucratically controlled from birth upwards, and for this reason have a blind faith in constituted authority, it is above all necessary to teach them to walk by themselves.[5]

The indifference which in normal times the mass is accustomed to display in ordinary political life becomes in certain cases of particular importance, an obstacle to the extension of the party influence. The crowd may abandon the leaders at the very moment when these are preparing for energetic action. This happens even in connection with the organization of demonstrations of protest. At the Austrian socialist congress held at Salzburg in 1904, Dr. Ellenbogen complained: "I am always anxious when the party leaders undertake any kind of action. It seems simply impossible to arouse the interest of the workers even in matters which one would have expected them to understand. In the agitation against the new military schemes, we found it impossible to organize meetings of a respectable size."[6] In Saxony, in 1895, when it was proposed to restrict the suffrage, that is to say to limit the political rights of thousands of workers, the socialist leaders vainly endeavored to arouse a general agitation, their attempts being rendered nugatory by the general apathy of the masses. The language of the press was inflammatory. Millions of leaflets were dis-

5 Letter from Karl Marx to J. B. von Schweitzer, dated London, October 13, 1868, published, with comments by Ed. Bernstein, "Neue Zeit," xv, 1897, p. 9. Bernstein himself appears to share the views of Marx. (Cf. Ed. Bernstein, *Gewerkschaftsdemokratie*, "Sozial. Monatshefte," 1909, p. 83.)
6 *Protokoll der Verhandlungen, etc.*, J. Brand, Vienna, 1904, p. 90.

tributed. Within the space of a few days a hundred and fifty meetings of protest were held. All was without effect. There was no genuine agitation. The meetings, especially in the outlying districts, were very scantily attended.[7] The leaders, alike the Central Committee and the district organizers, were overwhelmed with disgust at the calm indifference of the mass, which rendered serious agitation altogether impossible.[8] The failure of the movement was due to an error of omission on the part of the leaders. The rank and file did not recognize the importance of the loss they were to suffer because the leaders had neglected to point out all its consequences. Accustomed to being ruled, the rank and file needs a considerable work of preparation before they can be set in motion. In default of this, and when signals which the rank and file do not understand are unexpectedly made by the leaders, they pay no attention.

The most striking proof of the organic weakness of the mass is furnished by the way in which, when deprived of their leaders in time of action, they abandon the field of battle in disordered flight; they seem to have no power of instinctive reorganization, and are useless until new captains arise capable of replacing those that have been lost. The failure of innumerable strikes and political agitations is explained very simply by the opportune action of the authorities, who have placed the leaders under lock and key. It is this experience which has given rise to the view that popular movements are, generally speaking, artificial products, the work of isolated individuals termed agitators (Aufwiegler, Hetzer, Meneurs, Sobillatori), and that it suffices to suppress the agitators to get the upper hand of the agitation. This opinion is especially favored by certain narrow-minded conservatives. But such an idea shows only the incapacity of those who profess to understand the intimate nature of the mass. In collective movements, with rare exceptions, the process is natural and not "artificial." Natural above all is the movement itself, at whose head the leader takes his place, not as a rule of his own initiative, but by force of circumstances. No less natural is the sudden collapse of the agitation as soon as the army is deprived of its chiefs.

The need which the mass feels for guidance, and its incapacity for acting in default of an initiative from without and from above, impose, however, heavy burdens upon the chiefs. The

7 Edmund Fischer, *Der Wilderstand des deutschen Volkes gegen Wahlentrechtungen*, "Sozial. Monatshefte," viii (x), fasc. 10.

8 Edmund Fischer, *Die Sächsische Probe*, "Sozial. Monatshefte," viii, (x), fasc. 12.

leaders of modern democratic parties do not lead an idle life. Their positions are anything but sinecures, and they have acquired their supremacy at the cost of extremely hard work. Their life is one of incessant effort. The tenacious, persistent, and indefatigable agitation characteristic of the socialist party, particularly in Germany, never relaxed in consequence of casual failures, nor ever abandoned because of casual successes, and which no other party has yet succeeded in imitating, has justly aroused the admiration even of critics and of bourgeois opponents. In democratic organizations the activity of the professional leader is extremely fatiguing, often destructive to health, and in general (despite the divison of labor) highly complex. He has continually to sacrifice his own vitality in the struggle, and when for reasons of health he ought to slacken his activities, he is not free to do so. The claims made upon him never wane. The crowd has an incurable passion for distinguished orators, for men of a great name, and if these are not obtainable, they insist at least upon an M.P. At anniversaries and other celebrations of which the democratic masses are so fond, and always during electoral meetings, demands pour in to the central organization, and close always on the same note, "we must have an M.P.!" In addition, the leaders have to undertake all kinds of literary work, and should they happen to be barristers, they must give their time to the numerous legal proceedings which are of importance to the party. As for the leaders of the highest grade, they are simply stifled under the honorary positions which are showered upon them. Accumulation of functions is, in fact, one of the characteristics of modern democratic parties. In the German socialist party we not infrequently find that the same individual is a town-councilor, a member of the diet, and a member of the Reichstag, or that, in addition to two of these functions, he is editor of a newspaper, secretary of a trade union, or secretary of a cooperative society; the same thing is true of Belgium, of Holland, and of Italy. All this brings honor to the leader, gives him power over the mass, makes him more and more indispensable; but it also involves continuous overwork; for those who are not of exceptionally strong constitution it is apt to involve a premature death.

Chapter 3

The Political Gratitude of the Masses

IN ADDITION to the political indifference of the masses and to their need for guidance, there is another factor, and one of a loftier moral quality, which contributes to the supremacy of the leaders, and this is the gratitude felt by the crowd for those who speak and write on their behalf. The leaders acquire fame as defenders and advisers of the people; and while the mass, economically indispensable, goes quietly about its daily work, the leaders, for love of the cause, must often suffer persecution, imprisonment, and exile.

These men, who have often acquired, as it were, an aureole of sanctity and martyrdom, ask one reward only for their services, gratitude. Sometimes this demand for gratitude finds written expression. Among the masses themselves this sentiment of gratitude is extremely strong. If from time to time we encounter exceptions to this rule, if the masses display the blackest ingratitude towards their chosen leaders, we may be certain that there is on such occasions a drama of jealousy being played beneath the surface. There is a demagogic struggle, fierce, masked, and obstinate, between one leader and another, and the mass has to intervene in this struggle, and to decide between the adversaries. But in favoring one competitor, it necessarily displays "ingratitude" towards the other. Putting aside these exceptional cases, the mass is sincerely grateful to its leaders, regarding gratitude as a sacred duty. As a rule, this sentiment of gratitude is displayed in the continual re-election of the leaders who have deserved well of the party, so that leadership commonly becomes perpetual. It is the general feeling of the mass that it would be "ungrateful" if they failed to confirm in his functions every leader of long service.

Chapter 4

The Cult of Veneration Among the Masses

THE SOCIALIST parties often identify themselves with their leaders to the extent of adopting the leaders' names. Thus, in Germany from 1863 to 1875 there were Lassallists and Marxists; whilst in France, until quite recently, there were Broussists, Allemanists, Guesdists, and Jaurèsists. The fact that these personal descriptive terms tend to pass out of use in such countries as Germany may be attributed to two distinct causes: in the first place, there has been an enormous increase in the membership and especially in the voting strength of the party; and secondly, within the party, dictatorship has given place to oligarchy, and the leaders of this oligarchy are inspired by sentiments of mutual jealousy. As a supplementary cause may be mentioned the general lack of leaders of conspicuous ability, capable of securing and maintaining an absolute and indisputable authority.

The English anthropo-sociologist Frazer contends that the maintenance of the order and authority of the state is to a large extent dependent upon the superstitious ideas of the masses, this being, in his view, a bad means used to a good end. Among such superstitious notions, Frazer draws attention to the belief so frequent among the people that their leaders belong to a higher order of humanity than themselves.[1] The phenomenon is, in fact, conspicuous in the history of the socialist parties during the last fifty years. The supremacy of the leaders over the mass depends, not solely upon the factors already discussed, but also upon the widespread superstitious reverence paid to the leaders on account of their superiority in formal culture—for which a much greater respect is commonly felt than for true intellectual worth.

The adoration of the led for the leaders is commonly latent. It reveals itself by signs that are barely perceptible, such as the tone of veneration in which the idol's name is pronounced, the perfect docility with which the least of his signs is obeyed, and the indignation which is aroused by any critical attack upon his personality. But where the individuality of the leader is

[1] J. G. Frazer, *Psyche's Task*, Macmillan, London, 1909, p. 56.

truly exceptional, and also in periods of lively excitement, the latent fervor is conspicuously manifested with the violence of an acute paroxysm. In June 1864, the hot-blooded Rhinelanders received Lassalle like a god. Garlands were hung across the streets. Maids of honor showered flowers over him. Interminable lines of carriages followed the chariot of the "president" with overflowing and irresistible enthusiasm and with frenzied applause were received the words of the hero of the triumph, often extravagant and in the vein of the charlatan, for he spoke rather as if he wished to defy criticism than to provoke applause. It was in truth a triumphal march. Nothing was lacking—triumphal arches, hymns of welcome, solemn receptions of foreign deputations. Lassalle was ambitious in the grand style, and, as Bismarck said of him at a later date, his thoughts did not go far short of asking whether the future German Empire, in which he was greatly interested, ought to be ruled by a dynasty of Hohenzollerns or of Lassalles. We need feel no surprise that all this adulation excited Lassalle's imagination to such a degree that he soon afterwards felt able to promise his fiancée that he would one day enter the capital as president of the German republic, seated in a chariot drawn by six white horses.

In Sicily, in 1892, when the first agricultural laborers' unions, known as *fasci*, were constituted, the members had an almost supernatural faith in their leaders. In an ingenuous confusion of the social question with their religious practices, they often in their processions carried the crucifix side by side with the red flag and with placards inscribed with sentences from the works of Marx. The leaders were escorted on their way to the meetings with music, torches, and Japanese lanterns. Many, drunk with the sentiment of adoration, prostrated themselves before their leaders, as in former days they had prostrated themselves before their bishops.[2] A bourgeois journalist once asked an old peasant, member of a socialist *fascio*, if the proletarians did not think that Giuseppe De Felice Giuffrida, Garibaldi Bosco, and the other young students or lawyers who, though of bourgeois origin, were working on behalf of the *fasci*, were not really doing this with the sole aim of securing their own election as county councilors and deputies. "De Felice and Bosco are angels come down from heaven!" was the peasant's brief and eloquent reply.[3]

It may be admitted that not all the workers would have

[2] Adolfo Rossi, *Die Bewegung in Sicilien*, Dietz, Stuttgart, 1894, pp. 8 and 35.
[3] Rossi, op. cit., p. 34.

replied to such a question in this way, for the Sicilian populace has always had a peculiar tendency to hero-worship. But throughout southern Italy, and to some extent in central Italy, the leaders are even today revered by the masses with rites of a semi-religious character. In Calabria, Enrico Ferri was for some time adored as a tutelary saint against governmental corruption. In Rome also, where the tradition of the classic forms of paganism still survives, Ferri was hailed in a public hall, in the name of all the "proletarian quirites," as "the greatest among the great." The occasion for this demonstration was that Ferri had broken a window as a sign of protest against a censure uttered by the President of the Chamber (1901).[4] In Holland, in the year 1886, when Domela Nieuwenhuis was liberated from prison, he received from the people, as he himself records, greater honors than had ever been paid to any sovereign, and the halls in which he addressed meetings were profusely adorned with flowers. Such an attitude on the part of the mass is not peculiar to backward countries or remote periods; it is an atavistic survival of primitive psychology. A proof of this is afforded by the idolatrous worship paid today in the department of the Nord (the most advanced industrial region in France) to the Marxist prophet, Jules Guesde. Moreover, in certain parts of England, we find that the working classes give their leaders a reception which recalls the days of Lassalle.

The adoration of the chiefs survives their death. The greatest among them are canonized. After the death of Lassalle, the Allgemeiner Deutscher Arbeiterverein, of which he had been absolute monarch, broke up into two sections, the "fraction of the Countess Hatzfeld" or "female line," as the Marxist adversaries sarcastically styled it, and the "male line" led by J. B. von Schweitzer. While quarreling fiercely with one another, these two groups were at one, not only in respect of the honor they paid to Lassalle's memory, but also in their faithful observance of every letter of his program. Nor has Karl Marx escaped this sort of socialist canonization, and the fanatical zeal with which some of his followers defend him to this day strongly recalls the hero-worship paid to Lassalle. Just as Christians used to give and still give to their infants the names of the founders of their religion, St. Peter and St. Paul, so socialist parents in certain parts of central Italy call their boys Lassallo and their girls Marxina, as an emblem of the new faith. Moreover, the zealots often have to pay heavily for their

[4] Enrico Ferri, *La Questione meridionale,* "Asino," Rome, 1902, p. 4.

devotion, in quarrels with angry relatives and with recalcitrant registration officials, and sometimes even in the form of serious material injury, such as loss of employment. Whilst this practice is at times no more than a manifestation of that intellectual snobbery from which even the working-class environment is not wholly free, it is often the outward sign of a profound and sincere idealism. Whatever its cause, it proves the adoration felt by the masses for the leaders, an adoration transcending the limits of a simple sense of obligation for services rendered. Sometimes this sentiment of hero-worship is turned to practical account by speculative tradesmen, so that we see in the newspapers (especially in America, Italy, and the southern Slav lands) advertisements of "Karl Marx liqueurs" and "Karl Marx buttons"; and such articles are offered for sale at public meetings. A clear light is thrown upon the childish character of proletarian psychology by the fact that these speculative activities often prove extremely lucrative.

The masses experience a profound need to prostrate themselves, not simply before great ideals, but also before the individuals who in their eyes incorporate such ideals. Their adoration for these temporal divinities is the more blind in proportion as their lives are rude. There is considerable truth in the paradoxical phrases of Bernard Shaw, who defines democracy as a collection of idolators, in contradistinction to aristocracy, which is a collection of idols.[5] This need to pay adoring worship is often the sole permanent element which survives all the changes in the ideas of the masses. The industrial workers of Saxony have during recent years passed from fervent Protestantism to socialism. It is possible that in the case of some of them this evolution has been accompanied by a complete reversal of all their former intellectual and moral valuations; but it is certain that if from their domestic shrines they have expelled the traditional image of Luther, it has only been in order to replace it by one of Bebel. In Emilia, where the peasantry has undergone a similar evolution, the oleograph of the Blessed Virgin has simply given place to one of Prampolini; and in southern Italy, faith in the annual miracle of the liquefaction of the blood of St. Januarius has yielded before a faith in the miracle of the superhuman power of Enrico Ferri, "the Scourge of the Camorra." Amid the ruins of the old moral world of the masses, there remains intact the triumphal column of religious need. They often behave towards their leaders after the manner of the sculptor of ancient Greece who, having

[5] Bernard Shaw, *The Revolutionist's Handbook.*

modelled a Jupiter Tonans, prostrated himself in adoration before the work of his own hands.

In the object of such adoration, megalomania is apt to ensue.[6] The immeasurable presumption, which is not without its comic side, sometimes found in modern popular leaders, is not dependent solely on their being self-made men, but also upon the atmosphere of adulation in which they live and breathe. This overweening self-esteem on the part of the leaders diffuses a powerful suggestive influence, whereby the masses are confirmed in their admiration for their leaders, and it thus proves a source of enhanced power.

[6] George Sand writes: "I've worked all my life to be modest. I declare that I would not want to live fifteen days in the company of fifteen persons who were convinced that I cannot make a mistake. Perhaps I might finally be convinced myself." (Trans. from George Sand, *Journal d'un voyageur pendant la guerre*, M. Lévy Frères, Paris, 1871, pp. 216-217.)

Chapter 5

Accessory Qualities Requisite to Leadership

IN THE opening days of the labor movement, the foundation of leadership consisted mainly, if not exclusively, in oratorical skill. It is impossible for the crowd to escape the æsthetic and emotional influence of words. The fineness of the oratory exercises a suggestive influence whereby the crowd is completely subordinated to the will of the orator. Now the essential characteristic of democracy is found in the readiness with which it succumbs to the magic of words, written as well as spoken. In a democratic regime, the born leaders are orators and journalists. It suffices to mention Gambetta and Clemenceau in France; Gladstone and Lloyd George in England; Crispi and Luzzatti in Italy. In states under democratic rule it is a general belief that oratorical power is the only thing which renders a man competent for the direction of public affairs. The same maxim applies even more definitely to the control of the great democratic parties. The influence of the spoken word has been obvious above all in the country in which a democratic regime first came into existence. This was pointed out in 1826 by an acute Italian observer: "The English people, so prudent in the use of its time, experiences, in listening to a public speaker, the same pleasure which it enjoys at the theater when the works of the most celebrated dramatists are being played."[1] A quarter of a century later, Carlyle wrote: "No British man can attain to be a statesman or chief of workers till he has first proved himself a chief of talkers."[2] In France, Ernest-Charles, making a statistical study of the professions of the deputies, showed that, as far as the young, impetuous, lively, and progressive parties are concerned, almost all the parliamentary representatives are journalists and able speakers.[3] This applies not only to the socialists, but also to the national-

[1] Giuseppe Pecchio, *Un' Elezione di Membri del Parlamento in Inghilterra*, Lugano, 1826, p. 109.

[2] Thomas Carlyle, *Latter Day Pamphlets*, No. V, "Stump-Orator," Thomas Carlyle's Works, "The Standard Edition," Chapman and Hall, London, 1906, vol. iii, p. 167.

[3] J. Ernest-Charles, *Les Lettrés du Parlement*, "La Revue," 1901, vol. xxxix, p. 361.

ists and to the anti-semites. The whole modern history of the political labor movement confirms the observation. Jaurès, Guesde, Lagardelle, Hervé, Bebel, Ferri, Turati, Labriola, Ramsay Macdonald, Troelstra, Henriette Roland-Holst, Adler, Daszynski—all, each in his own fashion, are powerful orators.

On the other hand, it is the lack of oratorical talent which largely explains why, in Germany, such a personality as that of Eduard Bernstein has remained in comparative obscurity, notwithstanding the vigor of his doctrinal views and his great intellectual influence; why, in Holland, Domela Nieuwenhuis has in the end lost his leading position; why, in France, a man possessed of so much talent and cultivation as Paul Lafargue, closely connected by family ties with Karl Marx, failed to attain such a position in the councils of the party as Guesde, who is far from being a man of science, or even a man of very powerful intelligence, but who is a notable orator.

Those who aspire to leadership in the labor organizations fully recognize the importance of the oratorical art. In March 1909 the socialist students of Ruskin College, Oxford, expressed discontent with their professors because these gave to sociology and to pure logic a more important place in the curriculum than to oratorical exercises. Embryo politicians, the students fully recognized the profit they would derive from oratory in their chosen career. Resolving to back up their complaint by energetic action, they went on strike until they had got their own way.

The prestige acquired by the orator in the minds of the crowd is almost unlimited. What the masses appreciate above all are oratorical gifts as such, beauty and strength of voice, suppleness of mind, badinage; whilst the content of the speech is of quite secondary importance. A spouter who, as if bitten by a tarantula, rushes hither and thither to speak to the people, is apt to be regarded as a zealous and active comrade, whereas one who, speaking little but working much, does valuable service for the party, is regarded with disdain, and considered but an incomplete socialist.

Unquestionably, the fascination exercised by the beauty of a sonorous eloquence is often, for the masses, no more than the prelude to a long series of disillusionments, either because the speaker's practical activities bear no proportion to his oratorical abilities, or simply because he is a person of altogether common character. In most cases however, the masses, intoxicated by the speaker's powers, are hypnotized to such a degree that for long periods to come they see in him a magnified image of their own ego. Their admiration and enthusiasm for the orator are, in ultimate analysis, no more than admiration and enthusiasm for their own personalities, and these sentiments are fostered by the orator in that he undertakes to speak and to act in the name of the mass, in the name, that is, of every individual. In responding to the appeal of the great orator, the mass is unconsciously influenced by its own egoism.

Numerous and varied are the personal qualities thanks to which certain individuals succeed in ruling the masses. These qualities, which may be considered as specific qualities of leadership, are not necessarily all assembled in every leader. Among them, the chief is the force of will which reduces to obedience less powerful wills. Next in importance come the following: a wider extent of knowledge which impresses the members of the leader's environment; a catonian strength of conviction, a force of ideas often verging on fanaticism, and which arouses the respect of the masses by its very intensity; self-sufficiency, even if accompanied by arrogant pride, so long as the leader knows how to make the crowd share his own pride in himself; in exceptional cases, finally, goodness of heart and disinterestedness, qualities which recall in the minds of the crowd the figure of Christ, and reawaken religious sentiments which are decayed but not extinct.

The quality, however, which most of all impresses the crowd is the prestige of celebrity. As we learn from modern psychology, a notable factor in the suggestive influence exercised by a man is found in the elevation to which he has climbed on the path leading to the Parnassus of celebrity. Tarde writes: "Actually, when a mind acts upon our own thought, it is with the collaboration of many other minds through whom we see it, and whose opinion, without our knowledge, is reflected in our own. We muse vaguely on the esteem shown him . . . on the admiration he inspires. . . . If he is a famous man, the number of his admirers impresses us, confusedly, *en masse*, and this influence takes on an air of objective solidarity, of impersonal reality, creating the prestige proper for great figures."[4] It suffices for the celebrated man to raise a finger to make for himself a political position. It is a point of honor with the masses to put the conduct of their affairs in the hands of a celebrity. The crowd always submits willingly to the control of distinguished individuals. The man who appears before them crowned with laurels is

[4] Trans. from G. Tarde, *L'Action internationale*, p. 334.

considered a priori to be a demigod. If he consents to place himself at their head it matters little where he has gained his laurels, for he can count upon their applause and enthusiasm. It was because Lassalle was celebrated at once as poet, philosopher, and barrister that he was able to awaken the toiling masses, ordinarily slumbering or drawn in the wake of the bourgeois democracy, to group them round his own person. Lassalle was himself well aware of the effect which great names produce upon the crowd, and for this reason he always endeavored to secure for his party the adhesion of men of note. In Italy, Enrico Ferri, who while still a young man was already a university professor, and had at the same time acquired wide distinction as the founder of the new Italian school of criminology, had merely to present himself at the Socialist Congress of Reggio Emilia in the year 1893 to secure the leadership of the Italian Socialist Party, a leadership which he retained for fifteen years. In like manner, Cesare Lombroso, the anthropologist, and Edmondo De Amicis, the author, had no sooner given in their adhesion to the socialist party than they were immediately raised to positions of honor, one becoming the confidential adviser and the other the official Homer of the militant Italian proletariat. Yet not one of these distinguished men had become a regular subscribing member; they had merely sent certain congratulatory telegrams and letters. In France, Jean Jaurès, already distinguished as an academic philosopher and as a radical politician, and Anatole France, the celebrated novelist, attained to leading positions in the labor movement as soon as they decided to join it, without having to undergo any period of probation. In England, when the poet William Morris, at the age of forty-eight, became a socialist, he immediately acquired great popularity in the socialist movement. Similar was the case in Holland of Herman Gorter, author of the fine lyric poem *Mei*, and the poetess Henriette Roland-Holst. In contemporary Germany there are certain great men, at the zenith of their fame, who are intimate sympathizers with the party, but have not decided to join it. It may, however, be regarded as certain that if Gerhard Hauptmann, after the success of his *Weavers*, and Werner Sombart, when his first published writings had attracted such wide attention, had given in their official adhesion to the German socialist party, they would now be amongst the most honored leaders of the famous three million socialists of Germany. In the popular view, to bear a name which is already familiar in certain respects constitutes the best title to leadership. Among the party leaders will be found men who have acquired fame solely within the ranks of the party, at the price of long and arduous struggles, but the masses have always instinctively preferred to these those leaders who have joined them when already full of honor and glory and possessing independent claims to immortality. Such fame won in other fields seems to them of greater value than that which is won under their own eyes.

Certain accessory facts are worth mentioning in this connection. History teaches that between the chiefs who have acquired high rank solely in consequence of work for the party and those who have entered the party with a prestige acquired in other fields, a conflict speedily arises, and there often ensues a prolonged struggle for dominion between two factions. As motives for this struggle, we have, on the one side, envy and jealousy, and, on the other, presumption and ambition. In addition to these subjective factors, objective and tactical factors are also in operation. The great man who has attained distinction solely within the party commonly possesses, when compared with the "outsider," the advantage of a keener sense for the immediately practical, a better understanding of mass-psychology, a fuller knowledge of the history of the labor movement, and in many cases clearer ideas concerning the doctrinal content of the party program.

In this struggle between the two groups of leaders, two phases may almost always be distinguished. The new arrivals begin by detaching the masses from the power of the old leaders, and by preaching a new evangel which the crowd accepts with delirious enthusiasm. This evangel, however, is no longer illuminated by the treasury of ideas which as a whole constitute socialism properly so-called, but by ideas drawn from the science or from the art in which these great men have previously acquired fame, and it is given a suggestive weight owing to the admiration of the great amorphous public. Meanwhile, the old leaders, filled with rancor, having first organized for defense, end by openly assuming the offensive. They have the natural advantage of numbers. It often happens that the new leaders lose their heads because, as great men, they have cherished the illusion that they are quite safe from such surprises. Are not the old leaders persons of mediocre ability, who have acquired their present position only at the price of a long and arduous apprenticeship? In the view of the newcomers, this apprenticeship does not demand any distinguished intellectual qualities, and from their superior platform they look down with mingled disdain and compassion. There are, however, additional reasons why the men of independent distinction almost invariably succumb in such a struggle. Poets, æsthetes, or men of science, they refuse to submit to the general discipline of the party, and attack the external forms of democracy. But this weakens their position, for the mass cherishes such forms, even when it is ruled by an oligarchy. Consequently their adversaries, though no more truly democratic, since they are much cleverer in preserving the appearance of democracy, gain credit with the crowd. It may be added that the great men are not accustomed to confront systematic opposition. They become enervated when prolonged resistance is forced upon them. It is thus easy to understand why, in disgust and disillusion, they so often abandon the struggle, or create a little private clique for separate political action. The few among them who remain in the party are inevitably overthrown and thrust into the background by the old leaders. The great Lassalle had already found a dangerous competitor in the person of the simple ex-workman, Julius Vahlteich. It is true that Lassalle succeeded in disembarrassing himself of this opponent, but had he lived longer, he would have had to sustain a merciless struggle against Liebknecht and Bebel. William Morris, after he had broken with the old professional leaders of the English labor movement, was reduced to the leadership of his little guard of intellectuals at Hammersmith. Enrico Ferri, who at his first entrance into the party had to encounter the tenacious mistrust of the old leaders, subsequently committed theoretical and practical errors which ended by depriving him once for all of his position as official chief of the Italian socialists. Gorter and Henriette Roland-Holst, after having for some years aroused intense enthusiasm, were finally overthrown and reduced to complete impotence by the old notables of the party.

Thus the dominion dependent upon distinction acquired outside the party is comparatively ephemeral. But age in itself is no barrier whatever to the power of the leaders. The ancient Greeks said that white hairs were the first crown which must decorate the leaders' foreheads. Today, however, we live in an epoch in which there is less need for accumulated personal experience of life, for science puts at every one's disposal efficient means of instruction that even the youngest may speedily become thoroughly well instructed. Today everything is quickly acquired, even that experience in which formerly consisted the sole and genuine superiority of the old over the young. Thus, not in consequence of democracy, but simply owing to the technical type of modern civilization, age has lost much of its value, and therefore has lost, in addition, the respect which it inspired and the influence which it exercised. It might rather be said that age is a hindrance to progress within the party, just as in any other career which it is better to enter in youth because there are so many steps to mount. This is true at least in the case of well organized parties, and where there is a great influx of new members. It is certainly different as far as concerns leaders who have grown old in the service of the party. Age here constitutes an element of superiority. Apart from the gratitude which the masses feel towards the old fighter on account of the services he has rendered to the cause, he also possesses this great advantage over the novice that he has a better knowledge of his trade. David Hume tells us that in practical agriculture the superiority of the old farmer over the young arises in consequence of a certain uniformity in the effects of the sun, the rain, and, the soil upon the growth of plants, and because practical experience teaches the rules that determine and guide these influences.[1] In party life, the old hand has a similar advantage. He possesses a profounder understanding of the relationships between cause and effect which form the framework of popular political life and the substance of popular psychology. The result is that his conduct is guided by a fineness of perception to which the young have not yet attained.

1 David Hume, *Inquiries Concerning the Human Understanding:* "Why is the aged husbandman more skilful in his calling than the young beginner but because there is a certain uniformity in the operation of the sun, rain, and earth towards the production of vegetables; and experience teaches the old practitioner the rules by which this operation is governed and directed?" (Clarendon Press edition, edited by Selby-Bigge, Oxford, 1902, p. 85.)

Chapter 6

Accessory Peculiarities of the Masses

To ENABLE us to understand and properly to appreciate the superiority of the leaders over the mass it is necessary to turn our attention to the characteristics of the rank and file. The question arises, what are these masses?

It has already been shown that a general sentiment of indifference towards the management of its own affairs is natural to the crowd, even when organized to form political parties.

The very composition of the mass is such as to render it unable to resist the power of an order of leaders aware of its own strength. An analysis of the German trade unions in respect of the age of their members gives a sufficiently faithful picture of the composition also of the various socialist parties. The great majority of the membership ranges in age from 25 to 39 years.[1] Quite young men find other ways of employing their leisure; they are heedless, their thoughts run in erotic channels, they are always hoping that some miracle will deliver them from the need of passing their whole lives as simple wage-earners, and for these reasons they are slow to join a trade union. The men over forty, weary and disillusioned, commonly resign their membership (unless retained in the union by purely personal interest, to secure out-of-work pay, insurance against illness, and the like). Consequently there is lacking in the organization the force of control of ardent and irreverent youth and also that of experienced maturity. In other words, the leaders have to do with a mass of members to whom they are superior in respect of age and experience of life, whilst they have nothing to fear from the relentless criticism which is so peculiarly characteristic of men who have just attained to virility.

Another important consideration as to the composition of the rank and file who have to be led is its fluctuating character. It seems, at any rate, that this may be deduced from a report of the socialist section of Munich for the year 1906. It contains statistics, showing analytically the individual duration of membership. The figures in parenthesis indicate the total number

1 Adolf Braun, *Organisierbarkeit der Arbeiter*, "Annalen für soziale Politik und Gesetzebung," i, No. 1, p. 47.

of members, including those members who had previously belonged to other sections.

MEMBERSHIP CLASSIFIED ACCORDING TO DURATION

			%	
Less than 6 months	1,502	about	23	(1,582)
From 6 months to 2 years	1,620	"	24	(1,816)
" 2 to 3 years	684	"	10	(995)
" 3 to 4 "	1,020	"	15	(1,965)
" 4 to 5 "	507	"	7½	(891)
" 5 to 6 "	270	"	4	(844)
" 6 to 7 "	127	"	2	(604)
" 7 to 8 "	131	"	2	(1,289)
More than 8 "	833	"	12½	(1,666)[2]

The fluctuating character of the membership is manifest in even greater degree in the German trade unions. This has given rise to the saying that a trade union is like a pigeon-house where the pigeons enter and leave at their caprice. The German Metalworkers' Federation (Deutscher Metallarbeiterverband) had, during the years 1906 to 1908, 210,561 new members. But the percentage of withdrawals increased in 1906 to 60, in 1907 to 83, and in 1908 to 100.[3] This shows us that the bonds connecting the bulk of the masses to their organization are extremely slender, and that it is only a small proportion of the organized workers who feel themselves really at one with their unions. Hence the leaders, when compared with the masses, whose composition varies from moment to moment, constitute a more stable and more constant element of the organized membership.

[2] Robert Michels, *Die deutsche Sozialdemokratie, I, Sozial Zusammensetzung,* Arch. für Sozialwissenschaft, xxiii, fasc. 2.

[3] A. von Elm, *Führer und Massen,* "Korrespondenzblatt der Generalkommission," xxi, No. 9.

C. Intellectual Factors

Chapter 1

Superiority of the Professional Leaders in Respect to Culture, and Their Indispensability; the Formal and Real Incompetence of the Mass

IN THE infancy of the socialist party, when the organization is still weak, when its membership is scanty, and when its principal aim is to diffuse a knowledge of the elementary principles of socialism, professional leaders are less numerous than are leaders whose work in this department is no more than an accessory occupation. But with the further progress of the organization, new needs continually arise, at once within the party and in respect of its relationships with the outer world. Thus the moment inevitably comes when neither the idealism and enthusiasm of the intellectuals, nor yet the goodwill with which the proletarians devote their free time on Sundays to the work of the party, suffice any longer to meet the requirements of the case. The provisional must then give place to the permanent, and dilettantism must yield to professionalism.

With the appearance of professional leadership, there ensues a great accentuation of the cultural differences between the leaders and the led. Long experience has shown that among the factors which secure the dominion of minorities over majorities—money and its equivalents (economic superiority), tradition and hereditary transmission (historical superiority)—the first place must be given to the formal instruction of the leaders (so-called intellectual superiority). Now the most superficial observation shows that in the parties of the proletariat the leaders are, in matters of education, greatly superior to the led.

Essentially, this superiority is purely formal. Its existence is plainly manifest in those countries in which, as in Italy, the course of political evolution and a widespread psychological predisposition have caused an afflux into the labor party of a great number of barristers, doctors, and, university professors. The deserters from the bourgeoisie become leaders of the proletariat, not in spite of, but because of, that superiority of formal instruction which they have acquired in the camp of the enemy and have brought with them thence.

It is obvious that the dynamic influence of these newcomers over the mass of workers will diminish in proportion as their own number increases, that a small nucleus of doctors and barristers in a great popular party will be more influential than a considerable quantity of intellectuals who are fiercely contending for supremacy. In other countries, however, such as Germany, whilst we find a few intellectuals among the leaders, by far the greater number of these are ex-manual workers. In these lands the bourgeois classes present so firm a front against the revolutionary workers that the deserters from the bourgeoisie who pass over to the socialist camp are exposed to a thoroughgoing social and political boycott, and, on the other hand, the proletarians, thanks to the wonderful organization of the state, and because highly developed capitalist manufacturing industry demands from its servitors high intelligence, have attained to the possession of a considerable, if elementary, degree of scholastic instruction, which they earnestly endeavor to amplify by private study. But the level of instruction among the leaders of working-class origin is no longer the same as that of their former workmates. The party mechanism, which, through the abundance of paid and honorary posts at its disposal, offers a career to the workers, and which consequently exercises a powerful attractive force, determines the transformation of a number of proletarians with considerable intellectual gifts into employees whose mode of life becomes that of the petty bourgeois. This change of condition at once creates the need and provides the opportunity for the acquisition, at the expense of the mass, of more elaborate instruction and a clearer view of existing social relationships. Whilst their occupation and the needs of daily life render it impossible for the masses to attain to a profound knowledge of the social machinery, and above all of the working of the political machine, the leader of working-class origin is enabled, thanks to his new situation, to make himself intimately familiar with all the technical details of public life, and thus to increase his superiority over the rank and file. In proportion as the profession of politician becomes a more complicated one, and in proportion as the rules of social legislation become more numerous, it is necessary for one who would understand politics to possess wider experience and more extensive knowledge. Thus the gulf between the leaders and the rest of the party becomes ever wider, until the moment arrives in which the leaders lose all true sense of solidarity with the class from which they have sprung, and there ensues a new class-division between ex-proletarian captains and proletarian common soldiers. When the workers choose leaders for themselves, they are with their own hands creating new masters whose principal means of dominion is found in their better instructed minds.

It is not only in the trade-union organization, in the party administration, and in the party press, that these new masters make their influence felt. Whether of working-class or of bourgeois origin, they also monopolize the party representation in parliament.

All parties today have a parliamentary aim. (There is only one exception, that of the anarchists, who are almost without political influence, and who, moreover, since they are the declared enemies of all organization, and who, when they form organizations, do so in defiance of their own principles, cannot be considered to constitute a political party in the proper sense of the term.) They pursue legal methods, appealing to the electors, making it their first aim to acquire parliamentary influence, and having for their ultimate goal "the conquest of political power." It is for this reason that even the representatives of the revolutionary parties enter the legislature. Their parliamentary labors, undertaken at first with reluctance, but subsequently with increasing satisfaction and increasing professional zeal, remove them further and further from their electors. The questions which they have to decide, and whose effective decision demand on their part a serious work of preparation, involve an increase in their own technical competence, and a consequent increase in the distance between themselves and their comrades of the rank and file. Thus the leaders, if they were not "cultured" already, soon become so. But culture exercises a suggestive influence over the masses.

In proportion as they become initiated into the details of political life, as they become familiarized with the different aspects of the fiscal problem and with questions of foreign policy, the leaders gain an importance which renders them indispensable so long as their party continues to practice a parliamentary tactic, and which will perhaps render them important even should this tactic be abandoned. This is perfectly natural, for the leaders cannot be replaced at a moment's notice, since all the other members of the party are absorbed in their everyday occupations and are strangers to the bureaucratic mechanism. This special competence, this expert knowledge, which the leader acquires in matters inaccessible, or almost inaccessible, to the mass, gives him a security of tenure which conflicts with the essential principles of democracy.

The technical competence which definitely elevates the leaders above the mass and subjects the mass to the leaders, has its influence reinforced by certain other factors, such as routine, the social education which the deputies gain in the chamber, and their special training in the work of parliamentary committees. The leaders naturally endeavor to apply in the normal life of the parties the maneuvers they have learned in the parliamentary environment, and in this way they often succeed in diverting currents of opposition to their own dominance. The parliamentarians are past masters in the art of controlling meetings, of applying and interpreting rules, of proposing motions at opportune moments; in a word, they are skilled in the use of artifices of all kinds in order to avoid the discussion of controversial points, in order to extract from a hostile majority a vote favorable to themselves, or at least, if the worst comes to the worst, to reduce the hostile majority to silence. There is no lack of means, varying from an ingenious and often ambiguous manner of putting the question when the vote is to be taken, to the exercise on the crowd of a suggestive influence by insinuations which, while they have no real bearing on the question at issue, none the less produce a strong impression. As referendaries (*rapporteurs*) and experts, intimately acquainted with all the hidden aspects of the subject under discussion, many of the deputies are adepts in the art of employing digressions, periphrases, and terminological subtleties, by means of which they surround the simplest matter with a maze of obscurity to which they alone have the clue. In this way, whether acting in good faith or in bad, they render it impossible for the masses, whose "theoretical interpreters" they should be, to follow them, and to understand them, and they thus elude all possibility of technical control. They are masters of the situation.[1]

The intangibility of the deputies is increased and their privileged position is further consolidated by the renown which they acquire, at once among their political adversaries and among their own partisans, by their oratorical talent, by their

1 It is interesting to note that the developing bourgeoisie of the seventeenth century found itself in relation to the monarchy in the same state of intellectual inferiority as that in which today are the democratic masses in relation to their leaders, and for very similar reasons. The ingenious Louis XIV expressed the point in the following words: In Franche Comté, "all authority is found, then, in the hands of Parliament which, like an assembly of simple bourgeois, would be easy either to fool or to frighten." (Trans. from Dreyss, op. cit., vol. ii, p. 328).

specialized aptitudes, or by the charm of their intellectual or even their physical personalities. The dismissal by the organized masses of a universally esteemed leader would discredit the party throughout the country. Not only would the party suffer from being deprived of its leaders, if matters were thus pushed to an extreme, but the political reaction upon the status of the party would be immeasurably disastrous. Not only would it be necessary to find substitutes without delay for the dismissed leaders, who have only become familiar with political affairs after many years of arduous and unremitting toil (and where is the party which between one day and the next would be able to provide efficient substitutes?); but also it has to be remembered that it is largely to the personal influence of their old parliamentary chiefs that the masses owe their success in social legislation and in the struggle for the conquest of general political freedom.

The democratic masses are thus compelled to submit to a restriction of their own wills when they are forced to give their leaders an authority which is in the long run destructive to the very principle of democracy. The leader's principal source of power is found in his indispensability. One who is indispensable has in his power all the lords and masters of the earth. The history of the working-class parties continually furnishes instances in which the leader has been in flagrant contradiction with the fundamental principles of the movement, but in which the rank and file have not been able to make up their minds to draw the logical consequences of this conflict, because they feel that they cannot get along without the leader, and cannot dispense with the qualities he has acquired in virtue of the very position to which they have themselves elevated him, and because they do not see their way to find an adequate substitute. Numerous are the parliamentary orators and the trade-union leaders who are in opposition to the rank and file at once theoretically and practically, and who, none the less, continue to think and to act tranquilly on behalf of the rank and file. These latter, disconcerted and uneasy, look on at the behavior of the "great men," but seldom dare to throw off their authority and to give them their dismissal.

The incompetence of the masses is almost universal throughout the domains of political life, and this constitutes the most solid foundation of the power of the leaders. The incompetence furnishes the leaders with a practical and to some extent with a moral justification. Since the rank and file are incapable of looking after their own interests, it is necessary that they should have experts to attend to their affairs. From this point of view it cannot be always considered a bad thing that the leaders should really lead. The free election of leaders by the rank and file presupposes that the latter possess the competence requisite for the recognition and appreciation of the competence of the leaders. To express it in French, *la désignation des capacités suppose elle-même la capacité de la désignation.*

The recognition of the political immaturity of the mass and of the impossibility of a complete practical application of the principle of mass-sovereignty, has led certain distinguished thinkers to propose that democracy should be limited by democracy itself. Condorcet wished that the mass should itself decide in what matters it was to renounce its right of direct control.[2] This would be the voluntary renunciation of sovereignty on the part of the sovereign mass. The French Revolution, which claimed to translate into practice the principle of free popular government and of human equality, and according to which the mutable will of the masses was in the abstract the supreme law, established through its National Assembly that the mere proposal to restore a monarchical form of government should be punishable by death.[3] In a point of such essential importance the deliberative power of the masses must yield to the threat of martial law. Even so fanatical an advocate of popular sovereignty as Victor Considérant was forced to acknowledge that at the first glance the machinery of government seemed too ponderous for it to appear possible for the people as such to make the machine work, and he therefore proposed the election of a group of specialists whose duty it should be to elaborate the text of the laws which the sovereign people had voted in principle. Bernstein also denies that the average man has sufficient political competence to render unrestricted popular sovereignty legitimate. He considers that a great part of the questions that have to be decided consist of peculiar problems concerning which, until all men become living encyclopedias, a few only will have interest and knowledge. To attain to an adequate degree of information regarding such questions, so that a carefully considered judgment can be given, requires a rare sense of responsibility such as cannot at

2 Condorcet, *Progrès de l'Esprit humain*, ed. de la Bib. Nat., p. 186.

3 Adolphe Thiers, *Histoire de la Révolution Française*, Brockhaus, Leipzig, 1846, vol. ii, p. 141. The same spirit of illogical amalgamation of unlimited popular sovereignty with the most rigid and despotic tutelage exercised over this alleged sovereign by its leaders, dominates most of the speeches of the Jacobins. (Cf., for example, *Œuvres de Danton*, recueilliés et annotées par A. Vermorel, Cournol, Paris, pp. 119 et seq.)

present be attributed to the majority of the citizens. Even Kautsky could not but recognize the difficulty of the problem thus presented to the labor movement; he has pointed out that it is not every province of social life which is suitable for democratic administration, and that democracy must be introduced gradually, and will not be completely realized until those interested shall have become capable of forming an independent judgment upon all decisive questions; and he shows that the possibility of realizing democratic administration will be greater in proportion as the cooperation of all the persons concerned in the decision of the issues becomes possible.

The incompetence of the masses, which is in last analysis always recognized by the leaders, serves to provide a theoretical justification for the dominion of these. In England, which owes to Thomas Carlyle the theory of the supreme importance of great men, or "heroes," and where that theory has not, as in Germany, been utterly expelled from the official doctrine of socialism by the theory of historical materialism, even socialist thought has been profoundly influenced by the great men theory. The English socialists, in fact, including those of the most various tendencies, have openly declared that if democracy is to be effective it must assume the aspect of a benevolent despotism. "He [the leader] has a scheme to which he works, and he has the power to make his will effective."[4] In all the affairs of management for whose decision there is requisite specialized knowledge, and for whose performance a certain degree of authority is essential, a measure of despotism must be allowed, and thereby a deviation from the principles of pure democracy. From the democratic point of view this is perhaps an evil, but it is a necessary evil. Socialism does not signify everything *by* the people, but everything *for* the people.[5] Consequently the English socialists entrust the salvation of democracy solely to the good will and to the insight of the leaders. The majority determined by the counting of heads can do no more than lay down the general lines; all the rest, which is tactically of greater importance, devolves upon the leaders. The result is that quite a small number of individuals—three, suggests Bax—effectively controls the policy of the whole party. Social democracy is not democracy, but a party fighting to attain to democracy. In other words, democracy is the end,

[4] James Ramsay Macdonald, *Socialism and Society*, Independent Labour Party, London, 1905, pp. xvi, xvii.

[5] Ernest Belfort Bax, *Essays in Socialism New and Old*, Grant Richards, London, 1906, pp. 174, 182.

but not the means.[6] The impossibility of the means being really democratic is conspicuously shown by the character of the socialist party as an undertaking endowed with certain financial characteristics, and one which, though created for ideological aims, depends for its success, not only upon the play of economic forces, but also upon the quality of the persons who have assumed leadership and responsibility. Here, as elsewhere, the saying is true that no undertaking can succeed without leaders, without managers. In parallelism with the corresponding phenomena in industrial and commercial life, it is evident that with the growth of working-class organization there must be an accompanying growth in the value, the importance, and the authority of the leaders. The principle of the division of labor creates specialism, and it is with good reason that the necessity for expert leadership has been compared with that which gives rise to specialism in the medical profession and in technical chemistry. Specialism, however, implies authority. Just as the patient obeys the doctor, because the doctor knows better than the patient, having made a special study of the human body in health and disease, so must the political patient submit to the guidance of his party leaders, who possess a political competence impossible of attainment by the rank and file.

Thus democracy ends by undergoing transformation into a form of government by the best, into an aristocracy. At once materially and morally, the leaders are those who must be regarded as the most capable and the most mature. Is it not, therefore, their duty as well as their right to put themselves at the head, and to lead not merely as representatives of the party, but as individuals proudly conscious of their own personal value?

[6] Bax, ibid.

PART TWO/AUTOCRATIC TENDENCIES OF LEADERS

Chapter 1

The Stability of Leadership

NO ONE who studies the history of the socialist movement in Germany can fail to be greatly struck by the stability of the group of persons leading the party.

In 1870-71, in the year of the foundation of the German Empire, we see two great personalities, those of Wilhelm Liebknecht and August Bebel, emerge from the little group of the faithful to the new socialist religion to acquire leadership of the infant movement by their energy and their intelligence. Thirty years later, at the dawn of the new century, we find them still occupying the position of the most prominent leaders of the German workers. This stability in the party leadership in Germany is very striking to the historian when he compares it with what has happened in the working-class parties elsewhere in Europe. The Italian socialist party, indeed, for the same reasons as in Germany, has exhibited a similar stability. Elsewhere, however, among the members of the Old International, a few individuals only of minor importance have retained their faith in socialism intact into the new century. In Germany, it may be said that the socialist leaders live in the party, grow old and die in its service.

We shall subsequently have occasion to refer to the smallness, in Germany, of the number of deserters from the socialist camp to join the other parties. In addition to these few who have completely abandoned socialism, there are some, who, after working on behalf of the party for a time, have left politics to devote their energies to other fields. There are certain men of letters, who rose in the party like rockets, to disappear with corresponding rapidity. After a brief and sometimes stormy activity, they have quitted the rude political stage to return to the peaceful atmosphere of the study; and often their retirement from active political life has been accompanied by a mental estrangement from the world of socialist thought, whose scientific content they had perhaps never assimilated. Among such may be mentioned: Dr. Paul Ernst, at one time editor of the "Volkstribüne"; Dr. Bruno Wille, who led the section of *Die Jungen* (the Young Men) to the assault upon the veterans of the party who were captained by Bebel and Liebknecht

(1890); Dr. Otto Erich Hartleben, once dramatic critic of "Vorwärts," but never a conspicuous member of the party; Dr. Ludwig Woltmann, delegate of the Rhenish manufacturing town of Barmen to the Congress of Hanover in 1899, where he was engaged in the defense of Bernstein, and who, after writing some socialist books which constitute notable contributions to sociology, subsequently devoted himself entirely to "political anthropology" with a strong nationalist flavor; Ernst Gystrow (Dr. Willy Hellpach); and several others, for the most part talented and highly cultured men who have made names for themselves in German belletristic literature or in German science, but who were not suited for enduring political activities. It has also happened more than once in the history of the social democracy that men dominated by a fixed idea, and inspired by the hope of concentrating upon the realization of this idea the whole activity of socialist propaganda, or of simply annexing socialism to the service of this obsession, have rushed into the party, only to leave it as suddenly with a chilled enthusiasm as soon as they perceived that they were attempting the impossible. At the Munich Congress of 1902, the pastor, Georg Welker of Wiesbaden, a member of the sect of *Freireligiosen* (Broad Church), inspired by all the ardor of a neophyte, wished to substitute for the accepted socialist principle that religion is to be considered as a private matter the tactically dangerous device *Ecrasez l'infâme*. Again, at the first Congress of Socialist Women, which was held contemporaneously with the Munich Socialist Congress, Dr. Karl von Oppel, who had recently returned from Cape Colony and was a new member of the socialist party, emphasized the need for the study by socialists of foreign languages, and even foreign dialects, to enable them to come into more intimate contact with their brethren in other lands, and in his peroration insisted that the use of the familiar "thou" should be made universal and compulsory in the intercourse of socialist comrades. Such phenomena are characteristic of the life of all parties, but are especially common among socialists, since socialism exercises a natural force of attraction for cranks of all kinds. Every vigorous political party which is subversive in its aims is predestined to become for a time an exercise ground for all sorts of innovators and quacksalvers, for persons who wish to cure the ills of travailing humanity by the use of their chosen specifics, employed exclusively in smaller or larger doses—the substitution of friction with oil for washing with soap and water, the wearing of all-wool underclothing, vegetarianism, Christian science, neomalthusianism, and other fantasies.

More serious than the loss of such casual socialists were the losses which the party sustained during the period of the early and fierce application of the antisocialist laws. At this time, in the period of reaction from 1840 to 1850, a large proportion of the leaders were forced to emigrate to America.[1] Still more serious were the losses sustained by the party during the Bismarckian regime. Bebel declares that at this time the number of those who were deprived of their means of livelihood and were forced to seek work and asylum on foreign soil ran into several hundreds. Of the nucleus of those who before the passing of the anti-socialist laws which unchained the tempest against the socialists, had worked actively in the party as propagandists, editors, and deputies, more than eighty left Germany, which most of them never revisited. "This involved a great draining of our energies."[2] In the worst years the exodus was particularly strong. Thus in the year 1881, just before the elections had demonstrated the indomitable vitality of the German Socialist Party, Friedrich Wilhelm Fritzsche (ob. 1905) and Julius Vahlteich, the critic of Lassalle, both of them at one time leaders in the party of Lassalle and socialist deputies to the Reichstag, crossed the Atlantic never to return.[3] Notwithstanding the storm which raged for more than ten years against the socialist party, the number of those whose socialist activity survived this period of terror was very large. Obviously, then, in times of comparative calm the stability of the leaders must be considerably greater. The author has examined the lists of those present at the congresses held in 1893 by three of the international socialist parties, namely, the German social democrats, the Parti Ouvrier (Guesdistes) in France, and the Italian socialist party, in order to ascertain the names of those who in the year 1910 were still in the first rank of the fighters on behalf of socialism in their respective countries. The results of this inquiry, which cannot claim

[1] Among these refugees, in the early fifties, was F. A. Sorge, one of the founders of the "Neue Zeit." When by the influence of Marx the General Council of the International had in 1872 been transferred from London to New York, Sorge assumed the largely imaginary function of secretary of the Council, and subsequently, after the extinction of the Old International, devoted himself entirely to music. Another refugee was the poet Robert Schweichel, who returned to Germany after fifty years in America.

[2] *Protokoll der Verhandlungen des Parteitags zu Halle a/S.*, 1890, p. 29.

[3] Vahlteich, however, though lost to the German labor movement, was not lost to socialism, for as editor of the German socialist daily published in New York he continued to play an active part in the life of the party until his death in 1915.

that the reelection of these leaders is taken as a matter of course, but even that a certain pressure is exercised in order to secure their reelection. It is true that in theory every elector is free to erase the printed names and to write in others, and that this is all the easier since the vote is secret. None the less, the printed ballot paper remains an effective expedient. There is a French phrase, *corriger la fortune*; this method enables the leaders to *corriger la democratie*.[5] A change in the list of names, although this is simply the exercise of an electoral right established by the rules, is even regarded as a nuisance by most of the delegates, and is censured by them should it occur. This was characteristically shown at the Dresden congress in 1903. When the report spread through the congress that the revolutionary socialists of Berlin intended to remove from among the names on the ballot paper the name of Ignaz Auer, of whom they disapproved on account of his revisionist tendencies (an accusation which they subsequently repelled with indignation), the widespread anger aroused by the proposed sacrilege sufficed to overthrow the scheme.

It is in this manner that the leaders of an eminently democratic party, nominated by indirect suffrage, prolong throughout their lives the powers with which they have once been invested. The reelection demanded by the rules becomes a pure formality. The temporary commission becomes a permanent one, and the tenure of office an established right. The democratic leaders are more firmly established in their seats than were ever the leaders of an aristocratic body. Their term of office comes greatly to exceed the mean duration of ministerial life in monarchical states. It has been calculated that in the German Empire the average official life of a minister of state is four years and three months. In the leadership, that is to say in the ministry, of the socialist party we see the same persons occupying the same posts for forty years in succession. Naumann writes of the democratic parties: "Here changes in the leading offices occur less rapidly than in those of the secretaries of state of the ministers. The democratic method of election has its own peculiar loyalty. As far as individual details are concerned it is incalculable, and yet on general lines we can count upon its activity with more certainty than upon the policy of princes. Through all democracy there runs a current of slow-moving tradition, for the ideas of the masses

[5] Regarding identical practices employed by the "party machine" in America, cf. Ostrogorsky, *La Democratie et l'Organisation des Parties politiques*, Calman Lévy, Paris, 1903, vol. ii, p. 200.

these parties were indeed secured. A persevering and logical application of democratic principles should in fact get rid of all personal considerations and of all attachment to tradition. Just as in the political life of constitutional states the ministry must consist of members of that party which possesses a parliamentary majority, so also in the socialist party the principal offices ought always to be filled by the partisans of those tendencies which have prevailed at the congresses. Thus the old party dignitaries ought always to yield before youthful forces, before those who have acquired that numerical preponderance which is represented by at least half of the membership plus one. It must, moreover, be a natural endeavor not to leave the same comrades too long in occupation of important offices, lest the holders of these should stick in their grooves, and should come to regard themselves as God-given leaders. But in those parties which are solidly organized, the actual state of affairs is far from corresponding to this theory. The sentiment of tradition, in cooperation with an instinctive need for stability, has as its result that the leadership represents always the past rather than the present. Leadership is indefinitely retained, not because it is the tangible expression of the relationships between the forces existing in the party at any given moment, but simply because it is already constituted. It is through gregarious idleness, or, if we may employ the euphemism, it is in virtue of the law of inertia, that the leaders are so often confirmed in their office as long as they like. These tendencies are particularly evident in the German social democracy, where the leaders are practically irremovable. The practice of choosing an entirely new set of leaders every two years ought long ago to have become general in the socialist party, as prototype of all democratic parties. Yet, as far as the German socialists are concerned, not merely does no such practice exist, but any attempt to introduce it provokes great discontent among the rank and file. It is true that one of the fundamental rules of the party, voted at the Mainz congress in 1900, lays down that at every annual congress the party must "renew," by ballot and by absolute majority, the whole of the executive committee, consisting of seven persons (two presidents, two vice-presidents, two secretaries, and a treasurer). This would be the true application of the democratic principle, but so little is it commonly observed in practice, that at every congress there are distributed to the delegates who are about to elect their new leaders printed ballot papers bearing the names of all the members of the retiring committee. This proves, not merely that the reelection of these leaders is taken as a matter of course, but even that a certain pressure is exercised in order to secure their reelection. It is true that in theory every elector is free to erase the printed names and to write in others, and that this is all the easier since the vote is secret. None the less, the printed ballot paper remains an effective expedient. There is a French phrase, *corriger la fortune*; this method enables the leaders to *corriger la democratie.*[5] A change in the list of names, although this is simply the exercise of an electoral right established by the rules, is even regarded as a nuisance by most of the delegates, and is censured by them should it occur. This was characteristically shown at the Dresden congress in 1903. When the report spread through the congress that the revolutionary socialists of Berlin intended to remove from among the names on the ballot paper the name of Ignaz Auer, of whom they disapproved on account of his revisionist tendencies (an accusation which they subsequently repelled with indignation), the widespread anger aroused by the proposed sacrilege sufficed to overthrow the scheme.

It is in this manner that the leaders of an eminently democratic party, nominated by indirect suffrage, prolong throughout their lives the powers with which they have once been invested. The reelection demanded by the rules becomes a pure formality. The temporary commission becomes a permanent one, and the tenure of office an established right. The democratic leaders are more firmly established in their seats than were ever the leaders of an aristocratic body. Their term of office comes greatly to exceed the mean duration of ministerial life in monarchical states. It has been calculated that in the German Empire the average official life of a minister of state is four years and three months. In the leadership, that is to say in the ministry, of the socialist party we see the same persons occupying the same posts for forty years in succession. Naumann writes of the democratic parties: "Here changes in the leading offices occur less rapidly than in those of the secretaries of state of the ministers. The democratic method of election has its own peculiar loyalty. As far as individual details are concerned it is incalculable, and yet on general lines we can count upon its activity with more certainty than upon the policy of princes. Through all democracy there runs a current of slow-moving tradition, for the ideas of the masses

[5] Regarding identical practices employed by the "party machine" in America, cf. Ostrogorsky, *La Democratie et l'Organisation des Parties politiques*, Calman Lévy, Paris, 1903, vol. ii, p. 200.

change only step by step and by gentle gradations. While in the monarchical organism there is an abundance of ancient forms, we find no less in the democratic organism that the longer it exists the more does it become dominated by tenaciously established phrases, programs and customs. It is not until new ideas have been in progress up and down the country for a considerable time that these ideas can penetrate the constituted parties through the activity of particular groups that have adopted them, or as an outcome of a spontaneous change of opinion among the rank and file. This natural tenacity of parliaments which are the outcome of popular election is indisputable, be it advantageous or disadvantageous to the community."[6] In democratically constituted bodies elsewhere than in Germany a simliar phenomenon is manifest. In proof of this, reference may be made to a paragraph in the rules drawn up on February 3, 1910, by the Italian General Confederation of Labor as to the proclamation of the general strike. The rule begins by declaring, in perfect conformity with democratic principles, that the declaration of a general strike must always be preceded by a referendum to the branches. To the terms of this referendum were to be appended the minutes of the session at which the Confederation of Labor had decided to submit the question. But the rule adds that if there should be disagreement between the executive council of the Federation and the results of the reference to the branches, if, for instance, the council had rejected the general strike while the referendum showed that the rank and file favored it, this difference must not be taken to imply a vote of censure on the leaders.[7] This shows that in the working-class organizations of Italy ministerial responsibility is not so strongly established as in the Italian state, where the ministry feels that it must resign if, when it has brought forward a bill, this bill is rejected by the majority of the Chamber. As far as concerns England, we learn from the Webbs that the stability of the officials in the labor organizations is superior to that of the employees in the civil service. In the Amalgamated Association of Operative Cotton-Spinners we actually find that there is a rule to the effect that the officials shall remain in office indefinitely, as long as the members are satisfied with them.[8]

An explanation of this phenomenon is doubtless to be found in the force of tradition, whose influence assimilates, in this

[6] Friedrich Naumann, *Demokratie und Kaisertum*, ed. cit., p. 53.
[7] "Stampa," February 3, 1910.
[8] Sidney and Beatrice Webb, op. cit., vol. i, p. 16.

respect, the revolutionary masses to the conservatives. A contributory cause is one to which we have already referred, the noble human sentiment of gratitude. The failure to reelect a comrade who has assisted in the birth of the party, who has suffered with it many adversities, and has rendered it a thousand services, would be regarded as a cruelty and as an action to be condemned. Yet it is not so much the deserving comrade as one who is tried and expert whom the collectivity approves above all others, and whose collaboration must on no account be renounced. Certain individuals, simply for the reason that they have been invested with determinate functions, become irremovable, or at least difficult to replace. Every democratic organization rests, by its very nature, upon a division of labor. But wherever division of labor prevails, there is necessarily specialization, and the specialists become indispensable. This is especially true of such states as Germany, where the Prussian spirit rules, where, in order that the party may be safely steered through all the shoals and breakers that result from police and other official interference and from the threats of the penal laws, the party can be assured of a certain continuity only when a high degree of stability characterizes the leadership.

There is an additional motive in operation. In the working-class organization, whether founded for political or for economic ends, just as much as in the life of the state, it is indispensable that the official should remain in office for a considerable time, so that he may familiarize himself with the work he has to do, may gain practical experience, for he cannot become a useful official until he has been given time to work himself into his new office. Moreover, he will not devote himself zealously to his task, he will not feel himself thoroughly at one with the aim he is intended to pursue, if he is likely to be dismissed at any moment; he needs the sense of security provided by the thought that nothing but circumstances of an unforeseen and altogether extraordinary character will deprive him of his position. Appointment to office for short terms is democratic, but is quite unpractical alike on technical and psychological grounds. Since it fails to arouse in the employee a proper sense of responsibility, it throws the door open to administrative anarchy. In the ministries of lands under a parliamentary regime, where the whole official apparatus has to suffer from its subordination to the continuous changes in majorities, it is well known that neglect and disorder reign supreme. Where the ministers are changed every few months, every one who attains to power thinks chiefly of making a profitable use of that power while it lasts. Moreover, the confusion of orders and regulations which results from the rapid succession of different persons to command renders control extraordinarily difficult, and when abuses are committed it is easy for those who are guilty to shift the responsibility on to other shoulders. "Rotation in office," as the Americans call it, no doubt corresponds to the pure principle of democracy. Up to a certain point it is adapted to check the formation of a bureaucratic spirit of caste. But this advantage is more than compensated by the exploitive methods of ephemeral leaders, with all their disastrous consequences. On the other hand, one of the great advantages of monarchy is that the hereditary prince, having an eye to the interests of his children and his successors, possesses an objective and permanent interest in his position, and almost always abstains from a policy which would hopelessly impair the vital energies of his country, just as the landed proprietor usually rejects methods of cultivation which, while providing large immediate returns, would sterilize the soil to the detriment of his heirs.

Thus, no less in time of peace than in time of war, the relationships between different organizations demand a certain degree of personal and tactical continuity, for without such continuity the political authority of the organization would be impaired. This is just as true of political parties as it is true of states. In international European politics, England has always been regarded as an untrustworthy ally, for her history shows that no other country has ever been able to confide in agreements concluded with England. The reason is to be found in this, that the foreign policy of the United Kingdom is largely dependent upon the party in power, and party changes occur with considerable rapidity. Similarly, the party that changes its leaders too often runs the risk of finding itself unable to contract useful alliances at an opportune moment. The two gravest defects of genuine democracy, its lack of stability (*perpetuum mobile democraticum*) and its difficulty of mobilization, are dependent on the recognized right of the sovereign masses to take part in the management of their own affairs.

In order to bind the leader to the will of the mass and to reduce him to the level of a simple executive organ of the mass, certain primitive democracies have at all times sought to apply, in addition to the means previously enumerated, measures of moral coercion. In Spain, the patriotic revolutionary Junta of 1808 insisted that thirty proletarians should accompany the general who was to negotiate with the French, and these compelled him, in opposition to his own convictions, to reject all Napoleon's proposals. In modern democratic parties, there still prevails the practice, more or less general according to the degree of development these parties have attained, that the rank and file send to the congresses delegates who are fettered by definite instructions, the aim of this being to prevent the delegate from giving upon any decisive question a vote adverse to the opinion of the majority of those whom he represents. This precaution may be efficacious in certain cases, where the questions concerned are simple and clear. But the delegate, since he has no freedom of choice, is reduced to the part of puppet, and cannot allow himself to be influenced by the arguments he hears at the congress or by new matters of fact which are brought to light in the course of the debate. But the result is, that not only is all discussion rendered superfluous in advance, but also that the vote itself is often falsified, since it does not correspond to the real opinions of the delegates. Of late fixed instructions have less often been given to the delegate, for it has become manifest that this practice impairs the cohesion so urgently necessary to every party, and provokes perturbations and uncertainties in its leadership.

In proportion as the chiefs become detached from the mass they show themselves more and more inclined, when gaps in their own ranks have to be filled, to effect this, not by way of popular election, but by cooptation, and also to increase their own effectives wherever possible, by creating new posts upon their own initiative. There arises in the leaders a tendency to isolate themselves, to form a sort of cartel, and to surround themselves, as it were, with a wall, within which they will admit those only who are of their own way of thinking. Instead of allowing their successors to be appointed by the choice of the rank and file, the leaders do all in their power to choose these successors for themselves, and to fill up gaps in their own ranks directly or indirectly by the exercise of their own volition.

This is what we see going on today in all the working-class organizations which are upon a solid foundation. In a report presented to the seventh congress of Italian labor organizations, held at Modena in 1908, we find it stated that the leaders must recognize capable men, must choose them, and must in general exercise the functions of a government.[9] In England these desiderata have already received a practical application,

[9] Fausta Pagliari, *Le Organizzazioni e i loro Impiegati*, Tip. Coop., Turin, 1908, p. 8.

for in certain cases the new employees of the organization are directly chosen by the old officials.[10] The same thing happens in Germany, where about one-fifth of the trade-union employees are appointed by the central power. Moreover, since the trade-union congresses are composed almost exclusively of employees, the only means of which the individual organized workers can avail themselves for the expression of their personal opinions is to be found in contributions to the labor press.[11] In the French labor movement, which claims to be the most revolutionary of all, the secretary of the Confédération Generale du Travail possesses the right of nomination when there is a question of electing new representatives to the executive committee of the federation. He exercises this right by sending to those Bourses du Travail which are not represented on the executive, a list of the comrades whom he considers suitable for this position, recommending the election of these.[12]

In the German Socialist Party, the individual *Landesvorstände*, or provincial committees, and the central executive claim the right of veto over the selection of candidates. But this right of veto gives them a privilege of an essentially oligarchical character, elevating the committees to the rank of a true government, and depriving the individual branches of one of the fundamental rights of all democracy, the right of individual liberty of action. In Holland, again, the socialist candidatures for parliament must be approved by the party executive, and this executive is as irremovable as that of the German party. It rarely happens that an old member of the executive whose term of office has expired fails to obtain reelection should he desire it. It is in Holland also that we see such conspicuous pluralism among the party officials.

In the nomination of candidates for election we find, in addition, another grave oligarchical phenomenon, nepotism. The choice of the candidates almost always depends upon a little clique, consisting of the local leaders and their assistants, which suggests suitable names to the rank and file. In many cases the constituency comes to be regarded as a family property. In Italy, although democratic principles are greatly honored, we not infrequently find that when a representatives dies, or can no longer continue in office, the suffrages of the constituency

10 Sidney and Beatrice Webb, *The History of Trade Unionism*, new edition, Longmans, London, 1907, vol. i, p. 87.

11 Cf. Paul Kampffmeyer, *Die Entwicklung der deutschen Gewerkschaften*, p. 114.

12 Fernand Pelloutier, *Histoire des Bourses du Travail*, Schleicher Frères, Paris, 1902, p. 150.

are transferred without question to his son or to his younger brother, so that the position is kept in the family.

Those who love paradox may be inclined to regard this process as the first symptom marking the passage of democracy from a system of plebiscitary Bonapartism to one of hereditary monarchy.

Chapter 2

The Financial Power of the Leaders and of the Party

IN THE German Socialist Party desertion and treason on the part of the leaders have been rare. This is conspicuous in contrast with what has happened in the French Socialist Party, especially as regards the parliamentary group of the latter. The elections of August 20, 1893, sent to the Palais Bourbon six socialist deputies: Paulin Méry, Alphonse Humbert, A. Abel Hovelacque, Alexandre Millerand, Pierre Richard, and Ernest Roche. Of these, one only, the distinguished linguist and anthropologist, Hovelacque, remained faithful to the party to his death; the other five are now declared enemies of the Socialist Party. The part played by Millerand in socialism, a great one as is well known, came to an end in 1904. In his electoral address of May, 1906, the term "socialist" had passed into the background; he was running in opposition to the official socialist candidate, the sociologist Paul Lafargue, the son-in-law of Marx; his rôle was now that of an anticollectivist and patriotic bourgeois reformer. The other socialist ex-deputies in the above list had deserted their colors at an even earlier date. The trifling political shock which is associated with the name of General Boulanger sufficed to overthrow the house of cards which represented the socialist convictions of these warriors on behalf of the revolutionary proletariat of France. Today they are all vowed to the service of the clerico-nationalist reaction. Paulin Méry became one of the Boulangist leaders; in May, 1906, when, in the second ballot, he was opposed to the bourgeois radical, Ferdinand Buisson, the socialists of his constituency unhesitatingly cast their votes in favor of his opponent. At the time of the Dreyfus affair, Alphonse Humbert was one of the most ardent defenders of the general staff of the army. Ernest Roche, at one time a disciple of Auguste Blanqui, and then, in conjunction with Edouard Vaillant, one of the most noted leaders of the Blanquists, is now the lieutenant of Henri Rochefort; in a recent parliamentary election in the seventeenth arrondissement of Paris he was defeated by the reformist socialist Paul Brousse, although Brousse, the sometime anarchist and theoretical father of the propaganda by deed in western Europe, had recently forfeited the goodwill of the more revolutionary section of the workers (Brousse, as President of the Paris municipal council, had received Alfonso XIII as guest at the Hôtel de Ville, and this conduct was hardly in conformity with socialist principles). It is true that even today Roche still belongs to a *Parti Blanquiste ni Dieu ni Maître* which announces week by week in the "Intransigeant" meetings of a more or less private character, but this party is really fictitious, for though it has a few branches it does not count in political life; in all practical political questions this petty group works hand in hand with the antisemites and the nationalists, and in matters of theory, whenever Roche has occasion to allude to them, he proclaims himself *le champion incorruptible de la République, du Socialisme et de la Patrie,* his anticapitalism being extremely tame, but his jingoism fanatical.[1]

In contrast with this, the German Socialist Party shares with the Italian and the Belgian parties the good fortune of possessing faithful and devoted leaders. The leadership of the German party has been again and again reinforced by valuable accessions from the other parties of the left, such as Auguste Bebel, the bourgeois democrat, Max Quarck and Paul Bader, of the "Frankfurter Zeitung," Paul Göhre and Max Maurenbrecher, who had previously founded the National Socialist Party in opposition to the socialists. On the other hand, it has suffered no extensive losses of significant personalties by desertion to the bourgeois camp. The only exceptions to this generalization relate to leaders of minor importance, such as Max Lorenz,[2] ex-editor of the "Leipzige Volkszeitung," who subsequently passed through the gate of National Socialism to gain a secure position as editor of the "Antisozialdemokratische Korrespondenz"; the young Count Ludwig Reventlow, who in 1906 became a deputy in the antisemite interest; and a few other academic personalities of minor importance, besides one or two exceptional converted proletarians, such as the basketmaker Fischer. It would not be right to regard as treason in the strict sense of the term a simple passage from the Socialist Party properly so-called to some other form of militant socialism, such as happened in the case of socialists as fervent and convinced as the deputy Johann Most, the noted binder of Augsburg, and Wilhelm Hasselmann, the chemist, another dep-

[1] Cf. Michels, *Die deutsche Sozialdemocratie im internationalen Verbande,* "Arch. f. Sozialw.," vol xxv, pp. 213 et seq.

[2] Max Lorenz has written a number of small socialist works, and is author of the reformist book *Die marxistische Sozialdemokratie,* Wiegand, Leipzig, 1896.

uty, who after 1890 broke openly with the party, to adhere first to antiparliamentary socialism and subsequently to anarchism. To speak of these men as "deserters" would be to identify the notion of desertion of the organized party with desertion of the idea of working-class emancipation. But even if we count as deserters from socialism those who have gone over to the ranks of the anarchists, we are compelled to admit that among the apostates from the German Socialist Party there has not been one of those who have occupied a leading position in the party.

The fighting proletariat in Germany has hitherto been spared the spectacle of its former representatives seated on the government benches surrounded by the enemies of the socialists. There has in Germany been no such figure as Aristide Briand, yesterday advocate of the general strike and counsel for the defense of men prosecuted for antimilitarism, who had expressly declared himself in full sympathy with the anti-militarist theory *plutôt l'insurrection que la guerre*, and today, as Minister of Public Instruction, approving no less vigorously and explicitly the measures of repression enforced by his colleagues in the Cabinet against antimilitarists. Germany has not known a John Burns, who as a labor leader in 1886 played a prominent part in the organization of huge demonstrations of the unemployed, at which open reference was made to the possible need for destroying the palaces and sacking the shops, and whose activities had led to a panic in the bourgeois world of the English capital, but who a few years later as President of the Local Government Board, when a motion was brought forward in Parliament at the instance of the Labor Representation Committee demanding the intervention of Parliament on behalf of the unemployed, replied that he was neither a public-house politician nor a soft-hearted philanthropist prepared to squander the money of hard-working citizens upon the so-called unemployed, and who advised the workers to save their money in good times and not to spend it upon unworthy objects. Such disillusionments, experienced at the hands of men in whose sincerity and firmness of character the organized workers had an ingenuous confidence, have a politically discouraging and morally enervating effect. They tend to lead the workers to indifferentism, or to one-sided specializations, such as the new unionism, or an exclusive belief in the cooperative movement, or, again, to certain forms of libertarian aspiration, and to alienate them from the thought of political organization, and from a considered and measured parliamentary activity.

We see this, above all, in France, where the case of Briand was merely a sequel to that of Millerand, and the case of Millerand a sequel, if you will, to the case of Louis Blanc, and where the great mass of the manual workers are split up into the two sections of those who advocate the most defiant abstentionism and of those whose minds are dominated by the spirit which the French aptly term *jemenfichisme*.[3] The fact that the socialist parties of Germany, Italy, and Belgium have hitherto been free from the disturbing and demoralizing effects of such episodes furnishes the chief if not the only reason for the unlimited and often blind confidence which is displayed, as no unprejudiced observer of the members of these parties can fail to notice, in the "tried and trusted" leaders. In Germany, indeed, the authority which this spirit gives to the party leaders, and which continually accentuates the tendency towards centralization, is enormously reinforced by the spirit of organization, by the intense need for guidance, which characterizes the German proletariat, and also by the comparative poverty of the party in individuals of intellectual pre-eminence and of those possessing economic independence. Owing to these exceptional conditions, the leaders are preserved from the disintegrating influence of personal and tactical dissensions, which would otherwise have led them into conflicts with the masses of the party similar to those that have raged with such violence in Italy and in Holland, notwithstanding the stability and the authoritative position of the socialist leaders in these latter countries.

It may be said of the German socialist leaders that they have not yet lost contact with the masses; that there still pre-

[3] Quite recently a number of the most eminent socialist leaders in France have passed over into the governmental camp and are thus in violent conflict with their former comrades. Among these may be mentioned René Viviani, now Minister of State; the university professor V. Augagneur, at one time socialist mayor of Lyons and subsequently governor of the Island of Madagascar; Gabriel Deville, disciple of Marx, and one of the founders of the Parti Ouvrier; Alexandre Zévaès, formerly one of the ablest of the Guesdists leaders and at that time a strict Marxist; Joseph Sarraute; and many others. De Pressensé writes very truly, "How many men has the [French working class] seen who, after being prodigal with words of revolt and often arousing high excitement—ceaselessly working at their revolutionary propaganda—have scarcely risen to power when they cynically turn against their own past and against their dupes? They have made it a crime to keep faith with their own predictions. Mercilessly, unscrupulously they become apostles of social reaction. . . . Nevertheless, it seems to me that nothing could be more senseless or fatal than to abandon ourselves to social apathy because of such actions, to give way to an idiotic delegation of authority which would make us as much the toy of these vile politicians as we were formerly of a naive credulity, an uncritical enthusiasm." (Trans. from Francis de Pressensé, *L'Affaire Durant, ou la nouvelle Affaire Dreyfus*, "Le mouvement socialiste," xiii, No. 227).

vails complete harmony between the form and the content of their tactics even when there should be a conflict between these; that the community of ideas between leaders and led has not yet been broken; and, to sum up, that the executive committee of the party, and also (though perhaps less perfectly) the parliamentary socialist group, still represent the average opinion of the comrades throughout the country. The confidence which the organized German workers give to those that represent them in the complex game of politics is based upon the security which the leaders offer at once from the moral and the political point of view. This security incontrovertibly exists. The manner in which the masses entrust their interests to the leaders is, historically at least, legitimate and explicable. But the causes of the stability of the leaders are naturally, like all causes, complex. Among various explanations, it has been suggested that all the virtue of the German labor leaders lies in the fact that they have never been exposed to serious temptations, so that it resembles that of a young woman who has never been courted. There is a certain element of truth in this explanation, in so far as we have to do with that special political virtue which consists in the faithful defense of the party flag. In a state where parliamentary government does not exist, where the ministers of state are chosen by the sovereign from among the leading officials of the administration without any regard to the parliamentary majority, and where consequently no direct path to office is open to popular representatives, the possibility of intellectual corruption, that is to say of a more or less complete change of front on the part of the socialist leaders under the influence of a desire for ministerial office, is *ipso facto* excluded, just as is excluded an adhesion to the party of bourgeois social reform of the revolutionary socialists who aim at changing the very base of the existing economic order. On the other hand, Arturo Labriola, who has followed the German movement with keen interest and lively sympathy, is undoubtedly right in his caustic prediction that as soon as the day comes when the German Government is willing to afford itself the luxury of a lukewarm liberal ministry, since the socialists are really not difficult to satisfy, the "reformist infection" will spread far even in Germany. He adds that the germs of this infection are already widely diffused.[4]

Yet although it is true that the feudal structure of the German Empire, which is still reflected in the laws and in the col-

[4] Arturo Labriola, *Riforme e Rivoluzione Sociale,* Soc. Edit. Milan, Milan, 1904, p. 17.

lective mentality of the country, imposes necessary limits upon the ambition of the labor leaders, it must be admitted that the fact we are now considering does not find an adequate explanation in the mere lack of temptation. Moreover, temptation, in the vulgar and material sense of the term, is no more lacking in Germany than elsewhere. No government, however autocratic, has ever neglected a chance of corrupting the austere virtue of the leaders of any movement dangerous to authority, by the distribution of a portion of those secret service funds which every state has at its disposal, and which have been voted by the popular representatives themselves. Nevertheless, it may be affirmed that the leaders of the German labor movement, even if they do not possess that evangelical morality of which we find so many examples in the early days of the Italian labor movement, have yet always resisted any attempts to corrupt their integrity by bribes. We need hardly reckon as an exception, the case which has not yet been fully cleared up of the president of the Allgemeiner Deutsche Arbeiterverein, Johann Baptist von Schweitzer, in the year 1872, for it seems probable that the fiery Bebel, who secured Schweitzer's condemnation and expulsion from the party, was in reality altogether in the wrong.[5] Even the subordinates in the leadership of the party, those whom we may speak of as the non-commissioned officers, have usually proved altogether inaccessible to the blandishments of the police. They have sometimes accepted bribes, but always to hand them over at once to "Vorwärts" or some other socialist paper, in which there has then appeared an invitation to the owner of the money to come and claim it personally within a certain number of days, since if unclaimed it would be handed over to the party funds.

The unshaken fidelity of the German socialist leaders rests upon powerful reasons, and some of these are ideal in nature. The characteristic love of the German for his chosen vocation, devotion to duty, years of proscription and of persecution shared with other comrades, the isolation from the bourgeois

[5] Although, so far as is known, Bebel continued to the end of his life to maintain the justice of the accusation he brought in 1872 (cf. August Bebel, *Aus meinem Leben*, Dietz Nachf., Stuttgart, 1911, Part II, p. 130), the official historian of the party, Franz Mehring (*Geschichte der deutschen Sozialdemokratie*, ed. cit., vol. iv, pp. 66 et seq.), takes the opposite view. Commenting on Schweitzer's declaration after his exclusion from the Verein, Mehring remarks: "We cannot read without emotion the wise and dignified leave-taking of the man who in difficult times had so firmly steered the ship of the social democracy, who had rendered so many invaluable services to the class-conscious proletariat, and who, enmeshed in the consequences of his own best actions, committed more than one unjust action, but suffered far greater injustice in return."

world of the workers and their representatives, the invincible conviction that only a party of a compact and solid structure will be able to translate into action the lofty aims of socialism, and the consequent aversion for any socialist struggle conducted by free-lances outside the ranks of the organized party—such are some of the numerous reasons which have combined to produce in the minds of the German socialists a love for their organization enabling it to resist the most violent storms. This attachment to the party, often manifested by fine and moving actions, certainly represents one of the most solid elements in the foundation upon which has been erected the edifice of German socialism. It enables us to understand the conduct of the socialist leaders during and after numerous crises which, in the view of the profane, would necessarily terminate in the open abandonment of the party by a number of its leaders. It is their love for the party, with which the great majority of the comrades feel themself to be identified, which has led such men as Eduard Bernstein and Kurt Elsner to retain their membership after violent conflicts which had almost led to their expulsion. It is proper to add that in the course of this struggle these men have always preserved the personal dignity without which a self-respecting man cannot possibly remain among his companions-at-arms.

These ideal motives are reinforced by motives, no less important, of a material order. The practice of paying for the services rendered to the party by its employees creates a bond which many of the comrades hesitate to break, and this for a thousand reasons. The pecuniary remuneration for services to the party which is given by the German social democracy immunizes the party employees against the grosser forms of temptation. Whereas in France, England, Holland, Italy, and elsewhere, socialist propaganda, spoken and written, is effected chiefly by volunteers, in the German Socialist Party gratuitous propaganda is practically unknown. Elsewhere than in Germany, socialist activity is based upon individual enthusiasm, individual initiative, and individual devotion; but in Germany it reposes upon loyalty, discipline, and the sentiment of duty, encouraged by pecuniary remuneration. In the history of the non-German socialist parties, for example, we find important periodicals, such as the "Avanguardia Socialista" of Milan and the "Nieuwe Tijd" of Amsterdam, which have been founded by individual initiative, and which are maintained by the political idealism of a few individuals. These continue to carry on their work although the expenses of the venture often exceed the income, and although those who write for the papers in question are unpaid or almost wholly unpaid. In Germany, on the other hand, the "Vorwärts" of Berlin, the "Leipziger Volkszeitung" and the "Neue Zeit" were founded and sustained by the party as a whole, and have a paid editorial staff and paid contributors. It would nevertheless be quite wrong to suppose that socialist propagandists and socialist officials are paid on a scale which enables them with the hard-earned pence of the workers to lead that luxurious existence which, with an ignorance bordering on impudence, is often ascribed to them by the "respectable" press and the loungers of the clubs. The life of a socialist journalist is far from resembling that of a spendthrift or a libertine; his day's work is by no means an easy one, his labors demand an abundance of self-denial and sacrifice and are nervously exhausting; whilst the remuneration he receives is a modest one when compared with the gravity and the difficulty of his task. No one will deny this who has even an elementary acquaintance with the conditions of work and pay in the socialist press and with the life led by the employees of the party. Men of the ability and education of Karl Kautsky, Max Quarck, Adolf Müller, and a hundred others, would have been able, had they chosen to devote themselves to some other service than that of the workers, to obtain a material reward much greater than that which they secure in their present positions.

This reference to the practice of the German Socialist Party of remunerating all services rendered was necessary to enable the reader to understand rightly certain peculiarities of German socialist life. But it must not be supposed that there is no unpaid socialist work in Germany. In country districts where the organization is still poor, and in the case of small weekly papers whose financial resources are inconsiderable, much gratuitous work is done by the socialists. In not a few places, moreover, the local comrades do not receive pay for any of the speeches they make. A witness to the idealism which, despite all difficulties, continues to flourish in the working class is the way in which during elections and at other times many working-class socialists sacrifice their Sunday rest in order to do propagandist work in the country, vigorously distributing leaflets, electoral addresses, socialist calendars, etc. This gratuitous work is often carried out, not only under conditions involving the patient endurance of exposure and privation, but also in face of all kinds of abuse and of the danger of arrest on the most trivial pretexts, and of attacks made by excited antisemitic or clerical peasants.

In general, however, the German practice is to pay for all services to the party, from the most trifling notice contributed to a newspaper to the lengthiest public discourse. Whilst this deprives the party to a large extent of the spirit of heroism and enthusiasm, and of work done by voluntary and spontaneous collaboration, it gives to the organization a remarkable cohesion, and an authority over the personnel which, though doubtless detracting from its elasticity and its spirit of initiative, and, in essence, tending to impair the very socialist mentality, constitutes none the less one of the most important and indispensable bases of the party life.

Able critics of socialist affairs, such as Ernst Günther, have endeavored to explain the fact that persons of recognized ability and worth have preferred as a rule to subject themselves to the party-will rather than to break completely with the organization, by the suggestion that had they decided otherwise they would have imperilled their political existence, and would have renounced "the possibility of continuing to represent efficiently the interests of the workers."[6] It is unquestionable that the socialist platform is now the best one from which to advocate the interests of the workers, and is historically the most appropriate, so that the renunciation of this platform almost always involves the loss of the opportunity for defending working-class interests. But it is no less indisputable that "to the average man the close association of his own economic existence with his dependence upon the Socialist Party seems a sufficient excuse" for the sacrifice of his own convictions in order to remain in a party with which he is in truth no longer in full sympathy.[7]

It has been written:

> Staatserhaltend sind nur jene,
> Die vom Staate viel erhalten.[8]

For all their exaggeration, there is a nucleus of truth in these words, and the criticism applies with equal justice to the party

[6] Ernst Günther, *Die Revisionistische Bewegung in der deutschen Sozialdemokratie*, Jahrbuch für Gesetzgebung (Schmoller, anno xxx (1906), fasc. 1, p. 253).

[7] Günther, op. cit.

[8] There is a word-play here which renders a literal translation impossible. The general significance is that those only can be counted upon to support the state who receive much at the hands of the state.—Much in the same way as in England the reactionaries are accustomed to say (though here without any intention to gibe) that those only who have a "stake in the country" can be trusted to care for its interests!

as to the state. The practice of paying for all services rendered, tends in no small degree to reinforce the party bureaucracy, and favors centralized power. Financial dependence upon the party, that is to say upon the leaders who represent the majority, enshackles the organization as with iron chains. The most tenaciously conservative members of the organization are, in fact, those who are most definitely dependent upon it. When this dependence attains to a certain degree of intensity, it exercises a decisive influence upon the mentality. It has been noted that in those countries in which members of parliament are not salaried, but where the party organizations themselves provide for the support of their parliamentary representatives, the deputies have a very strong sense of dependence upon the members of their organizations. Where, on the contrary, members of parliament are remunerated by the state, they feel themselves before all to be parliamentarians, even though they may owe their election exclusively to the Socialist Party.

It is well known that the numerical strength of the trade unions depends to a very considerable extent upon the economic advantages which the unions offer to their members. The success of the trade-union movement from this point of view has suggested to the German socialists that the Socialist Party should extend to the rank and file of the membership some of the advantages which have hitherto been the exclusive privilege of the party bureaucracy. Otto Gerisch, treasurer of the party and member of the executive committee, referred to this possibility in a speech on the problem of organization, made at the Bremen Congress of 1904.[9] After quoting facts proving the superiority of the trade-union organization over that of the party, he stated that in his view the real reason of this superiority was to be found in the "accumulation of benefits" which the unions provided for their members. He added that the workers did not prove faithful to their unions until these organizations undertook the practice of mutual aid on the large scale, but that thereafter the membership increased enormously and became far more stable. Continuing this train of thought, he said: "It is characteristic that the Königsberg comrades, who, in view of the advanced position they occupy in the German socialist movement, must certainly be held to possess extensive experience in matters of organization and propaganda, provide subsidies to members of the party to meet

[9] *Protokoll über die Verhandlungen des Parteitages der sozialdemokratischen Partei Deutschlands, abgehalten zu Bremen, Sept. 10-24, 1904,* Verlag "Vorwärts," Berlin, p. 272.

funeral expenses. This practice has been introduced for a very good reason. We are at a disadvantage in the Socialist Party as compared with the trade unions, in that we cannot offer any direct advantages to our members. But this will not always be the case." It seems doubtful if these words are to be interpreted as a direct announcement of the intention to introduce a system of mutual life-insurance, or whether Gerisch merely intended a warm recommendation of such a measure. Oda Olberg, who was present at the congress on behalf of the Italian socialist paper "Avanti," interpreted the words in the former sense, and described the speech as a "menace of degeneration."[10] It is certain that in the German Socialist Party tendencies exist towards laying greater stress upon such material advantages, tendencies which might lead to the transformation of the party organization into a socialistically tinged proletarian assurance society. It is evident that an evolution in this direction would attract to the party hundreds of thousands of new members, so that there would be a considerable accession of strength. At the same time the apparatus of the socialist bureaucracy would be greatly developed. The effects which such an evolution would have upon the real strength of the party vis-à-vis the state, upon its moral impetus, its internal unity, and its tactical cohesion, are questions which cannot be discussed here. For our purpose it has been enough to draw attention to the influence which the practice of paying for services rendered has upon the maintenance and the reinforcement of the organization.

In aristocratic regimes, so long, at least, as the aristocracy retains its essentially plutocratic character, the elected officials are usually unpaid. Their functions are purely honorary, even when they require the whole time of those who undertake them. They are members of the dominant class, are assumed to be rich, to make it a point of honor to spend money for the public good, and to occupy, even at considerable pecuniary

[10] Cf. leading article, *Il Congresso di Brema*, "Avanti," anno viii, No. 2,608. Oda Olberg writes: "Frankly, we cannot conceive a socialist party which attracts and retains its members by offering them economic advantages. We consider that it would be far better to have a handful of devoted comrades who have joined our ranks, not for lucre, but impelled by the socialist faith, ready for every sacrifice, willing to give themselves, rather than a whole army of members who have entered the party regarding it as a mutual aid society." This view is estimable from the moral and socialist outlook, but its utterance shows that Oda Olberg has an inadequate understanding of the most conspicuous quality of the masses; unless it be that she has abandoned her Marxism, that after the Blanquist manner she is willing to renounce the democratic criterion of majority rule, and that she looks to find salvation solely from the action of a small but intelligent minority.

sacrifice, eminent positions in the service of the state. A similar practice prevails even in modern democracies. The Lord Mayor of London and his colleagues in the other great cities of England are unpaid. The same is true of the Italian Syndics. Inasmuch as the entertainment allowances, etc., are usually altogether inadequate, the holders of such offices must be men of considerable private means to enable them to support the necessary charges, and they must therefore be either wealthy parvenus or men born to wealth. Similar considerations apply to Italian parliamentary representation. In Italy the government opposes the idea of paying salaries to members of parliament, on the ground that it would be improper for the elected of the nation to receive base money for their activities. The consequence is that in Italy, since the Italian socialist party is a poor one, the manual workers are *a priori* excluded from parliament. Among the thirty-six socialist deputies in the Italian chamber during 1909, two only had been manual workers (trade-union leaders). In such conditions it is likely that the party representation in the legislature will be restricted to persons with private means, to those, that is to say, who have time and money which they are able to devote to an unremunerative occupation, and one which demands frequent changes of residence. In France, moveover, where the salaries of the deputies are on a liberal scale, it has been noted that the poorest constituencies are represented in parliament by the richest members.

Even in certain democratic parties the assumption of official positions in the party may be regarded as an honorary office, especially where the organization is not well supplied with means. Thus there not infrequently arises within the party a peculiar form of financial authority, since the comrades who are better endowed with means, gain and retain influence through the pecuniary services which they render. A plutocratic supremacy of this nature exists in the press of those parties which, lacking means for the independent maintenance of their own organs, are forced to depend upon the pecuniary assistance given by well-to-do comrades. The result, of course, is that these latter, as principal shareholders in the newspaper, possess a natural right of controlling its policy. A typical example of this is found in France, where for a time "l'Humanité" was supported by a syndicate of wealthy Jews. Again, in choosing delegates to the party congresses, the preference is often given to those who are able and willing to pay their own traveling expenses. In this way it results that the congresses, which constitute the supreme authority of the party, often come to be chiefly composed, like the parliamentary group in certain countries, of persons who are comparatively well-to-do. This is what happens in Italy, France, Holland, etc. As far as Germany is concerned, this is less likely to occur, partly because very few members of the Socialist Party are well off, and partly because of the flourishing condition of the party finances. In Germany, therefore, the financial superiority of the rich comrade over the poor one is often replaced by the superiority of the rich branch. It is naturally very difficult for the organizations that are short of money to send delegates to the party congress, especially if this is held in a distant city. Consequently these poor branches, when they are unable to appoint as delegate some one who has the time, the means, and the will to undertake the journey at his own expense, are compelled to abandon the idea of being represented at the congress. It should be added that public opinion within the party has often shown itself strongly adverse to the practice, stigmatizing the delegates who are appointed on these terms as "mandataries by accommodation," and regarding the conferring and the acceptance of such a mandate as a treason to the party and as a form of corruption. At the Bremen congress of 1904, in the case of Fehndrich, it was loudly denounced as a veritable crime. Such accusations are often unjust, for more spirit of sacrifice and love of duty are commonly needed to induce a comrade to attend a congress at his own cost than would be the case if he had a week's holiday at the expense of his local branch.

Nevertheless it remains true that as regards representation at party congresses, the smaller sections are in a position of serious inferiority. Numerous proposals have been made for the remedy of this state of affairs. For instance, in order to realize the democratic postulate of the equal representation of all districts, in the years 1903 and 1904 the section of Marburg proposed that all the costs of delegation should be defrayed by the central treasury. This proposal was not accepted, and consequently another attempt was made to find a remedy, and this has taken the form of uniting numerous local branches into provincial federations. Thus the rules of the provincial federation of Hesse-Nassau contain a clause to the following effect: "Those local branches of the federation which are unable to pay the costs of delegation to the congress will draw lots every year to select one among their number, and the branch thus chosen will have the right to send a delegate to the congress at the expense of the federation." It may be noted in passing that five of the branches out of the ten of which the federation consists have to avail themselves of this privilege.

A party which has a well-filled treasury is in a position, not only to dispense with the material aid of its comparatively affluent members, and thus to prevent the acquirement by these of a preponderant influence in the party, but also to provide itself with a body of officials who are loyal and devoted because they are entirely dependent on the party for their means of subsistence. Before the year 1906, when the payment of members was conceded by the German state, the German Socialist Party had provided the salaries of its deputies. In this way the party leaders, poor men for the most part, were enabled to enter parliament without being in a position to emancipate themselves from the party, or to detach themselves from the majority of the parliamentary group of socialists—as has happened in France with the formation of the group of "independent socialists." The French Socialist Party has been forced to recognize the danger involved in the existence of leaders who are not economically dependent on the party. In those countries in which the representatives of the people are not paid by the government nor salaried by the party, the danger of plutocracy arises from the fact that the members of parliament must necessarily be men of means; but in France such a danger arises in the opposite way, for here not only are the deputies paid, but they are paid at the high rate of £600 a year. Consequently it has occurred to the French socialists to adopt a measure which shall at once reduce the financial supremacy of its representatives at the Palais Bourbon and provide a steady accession to the party funds, and they have decreed that every deputy elected under the ægis of the party must pay over one-fifth of his salary, £120 per annum, to the party treasury. Many of the French socialist deputies, in order to elude this obligation, have simply resigned their membership of the party. Among the causes which in the year 1905 led to the formation of the new parliamentary socialist group, the so-called independent socialists, the chief was certainly the desire to escape this heavy tax, and to preserve intact for themselves the fine round sum paid as salary by the state. Even in the case of the deputies who, in order to preserve their seats, have found it expedient to accept as a matter of principle their liability to the party treasury, the majority have shown little alacrity in the discharge of this liability. Year after year, in fact, at the party congresses, there have been interminable discussions as to the means to be adopted to compel the recalcitrant socialist deputies to discharge their financial obligations. And yet (and here is one of the ironies of history) it has not taken long to discover that to despoil the deputies of a portion of their salary does not after all constitute the most efficacious means of preventing the formation within the party of an oligarchy of plutocrats. From the report made to the congress of Nîmes (1910) by the executive committee it appears that of the 128,000 francs which constitute the party revenue, more than half, 67,250 francs to be precise, was made up by the contributions of the socialist members of parliament. Such a state of affairs is eminently calculated to favor the predominance of the deputies, who become the financial props of the party administration, and thus are persons of importance whom the rank and file must treat with all possible respect.

Speaking generally, when the manual workers become employers it is not found that they are easy masters. They are prone to mistrust, and are extremely exacting. Were it not that these employees have as a rule abundant means of escaping from the influence of their many-headed masters, they would be worse treated—so runs the complaint—than by any private employer. In relation to the salaried officials, every member of the organization considers himself a capitalist and behaves accordingly. Moreover, the manual workers often lack any criterion for the appreciation of intellectual labor.

In Rome, many societies for cooperative production make it a principle to pay their commercial and technical managers on the same scale as their manual workers. In Germany, too, for a long time the same tendency prevailed. At the assembly of the Christian miners held at Gelsenkirchen in 1898, the demand found expression that Brust, one of the leaders, should continue manual work as a miner, since otherwise he would forfeit the esteem of his comrades. At the socialist congress held at Berlin in 1892 a motion was discussed for many hours in accordance with which no employee of the party was to be paid a salary exceeding £125 per annum; whilst at the congress of Frankfort in 1894 the proposal to increase the salary of the two party secretaries by £25 had to be withdrawn, since the voting was indecisive, although the ballot was taken several times. For a long time in the German Socialist Party there continued to prevail the erroneous view that the salaries paid to the party employees, and even the disbursements made to propagandists on account of expenses and time lost, were a sort of gratuity, a "pourboire." In the case of the socialist newspapers, the editor was often worse paid than the business manager and even than the compositors. Matters have changed since then, but there always exists a tendency on the part of the manual workers which induces them to endeavor to keep down the salaries of the party officials to the level of what is paid to a factory hand. A few years ago a trade union passed a motion to the effect that the employees of the union should be paid by the hour, and on the same scale as that which prevailed in the branch of industry to which they belonged as trade unionists. Even now, in fixing the salaries of their own employees, many of the comrades adopt as a principle that the remuneration ought to be less than that which is paid for the same work by capitalist employers. Speaking generally, however, it may be said that the German working class is now accustomed to pay its employees liberally. This improvement is explicable, in part, from the improved financial position of the trade unions and of the Socialist Party. But there is another reason. The employees have succeeded in withdrawing the question of their salaries from the publicity of the congresses and of reserving the discussion of this question for private committees.

In France, on the other hand, the tendency among the workers to stint their employees has gained ground, especially of late, since the deputies to the Chamber have been allotted salaries of £600 a year. The indignation against the "Quinze Mille" (15,000 francs) has been so great that in many cases the manual workers have been unwilling to pay their employees in the trade unions more than the tenth part of this sum, the modest annual salary of £60. During 1900-1901, the three employees of the Confédération Générale du Travail (the secretary, the treasurer, and the organizer) received in all only 3,173 francs (i.e., a little over £40 a year each). The two chief employees of the Printers' Federation receive an annual salary of £144 each, whilst the treasurer receives £48 a year. The Metal-workers' Federation regards itself as extraordinary in engaging three employees at a salary of £112 per annum and (in 1905) seven district secretaries at salaries of £95 each.

In Italy there has not yet come into existence a numerous general staff of employees salaried by the Socialist Party and the trade-union organizations. This is chiefly explicable by lack of funds. For many years it has been necessary to improvise secretaries, administrators, and treasurers of trade unions and local branches, to find them from day to day by appealing to the goodwill and devotion of the comrades. Before 1905, the Printers' Federation was the only one which had special employees for bookkeeping and for the administration of the funds. Even today the life of the labor organizations is extremely rudimentary and is exposed to great vicissitudes. Of late years, indeed, the number of permanent employees of the federations and the Bourses du Travail has undergone a continuous increase, but these employees are still very badly paid. We are told by Rigola that the salary has been raised from 100 lire to 200 lire a month, and that "no self-respecting organization will now offer less." But this increase does not suffice to provide a remedy, for 200 lire will not induce a skilled workman to abandon his trade to become a trade-union leader. Nothwithstanding this, if we are to believe the trade unionists, even in Italy some of the trade-union leaders are already manifesting that tendency to grow fat and idle for which the leaders of the rich English labor organizations have sometimes been reproached.

The meagerness of the salaries paid to their employees by the Socialist Party and the trade unions is not due solely to that employers' arrogance and arbitrariness from which the working class is by no means exempt when it becomes an employer. Where the younger organizations are concerned, the trouble may arise simply from lack of means. Moreover, in paying at a low rate there is a practical end in view, the desire being that the employees should serve for love of the cause, and not with an eye to the material advantages attaching to their office. It was hoped that in this way the idealism of the leaders would be artificially fostered, and that it would be possible to prevent them from raising themselves above the social level of their proletarian comrades. During the early and revolutionary period of the labor movement, whether economic or political, such attempts were made in every country of the world. The labor organizations have not always been satisfied with paying their employees on a stingy scale, but members of the party or the union have even been forbidden to accept the money which the state paid to those who became members of parliament. Among the reasons which in the year 1885 induced the socialists of Berlin to abstain from participation in the elections to the Prussian Landtag, the chief was the consideration that the fifteen marks a day which the members of this body receive would tend to lift the socialist members out of their class.

In practice, however, the grudging payment of the leaders which at least in the early days of the trade-union movement was a deliberate policy, has proved to be a very untrustworthy safeguard against possible breaches of duty.

For the great majority of men, idealism alone is an inadequate incentive for the fulfillment of duty. Enthusiasm is not an article which can be kept long in store. Men who will stake their bodies and their lives for a moment, or even for some months in succession, on behalf of a great idea often prove incapable of permanent work in the service of the same idea even when the sacrifices demanded are comparatively trifling. The joy of self-sacrifice is comparable to a fine gold coin which can be spent grandly all at once, whereas if we change it into small coin it dribbles imperceptibly away. Consequently, even in the labor movement, it is necessary that the leaders should receive a prosaic reward in addition to the devotion of their comrades and the satisfaction of a good conscience. Quite early in the history of the organizations formed by the Italian agricultural workers we find in a manual written for the guidance of these that if the *capolega* or chief of the union is to do his duty it would be well to pay him for his work.[11]

For two additional reasons it is necessary that the employees should be adequately paid. The first of these is a moral one, belonging to the department of socialist ethics. The laborer is worthy of his hire. In Marxist terminology, the worker who does not receive pay correspondent to the social value of his work is being exploited. The other reason belongs to the sphere of practical politics. To pay the leaders poorly as a matter of principle is dangerous precisely because it stakes everything upon the single card of idealism. Eduard Bernstein is right in contending that underpayment leads to corruption and demoralization.[12] The leader who is poorly paid is more likely to succumb to temptation, more likely to betray the party for gain, than one who, being well paid, finds in his occupation a safe and sufficient income. Moreover, the payment of the leaders at a low rate renders difficult the application of another preventive means against the establishment of an oligarchy, for it hinders frequent changes in the personnel of the leading employees, and thus indirectly favors the formation of an oligarchy. In France, where it is still the rule to pay the trade-union leaders very small salaries, there is lacking a new generation of leaders ready to take the place of the old, and for this

11 Egidio Bernaroli, op. cit., p. 27.

12 Eduard Bernstein, *Die Demokratie in der Sozialdemokratie*, "Sozial. Monatsh.," September 3, 1908, p. 1108.

reason at the trade-union congresses the same members continually appear as delegates.

If, however, the non-payment of the party leaders or their remuneration on a very moderate scale does not afford any safeguard for the observance of democratic principles on the part of the officials, we have on the other hand to remember that an increase in the financial strength of the party, which first renders liberal payment of the officials possible, contributes greatly to nourish the dictatorial appetites of the members of the party bureaucracy, who control the economic forces of the party in virtue of their position as administrators. In the history of Christianity we learn that as the wealth of the Church increased, there increased also the independence of the clergy, of the ecclesiastical employees, vis-à-vis the community. As representatives of the community they were in charge of the goods. Consequently all those who had need of these goods, or wished in any way to speculate upon them, were dependent upon the clergy. This applied not only to mendicants and to all kinds of receivers of alms, but also to those whose aim it was to swell the ranks of the clergy, or to succeed to the positions of these, all aspirants to sacerdotal honors. For the administration of the funds and for the conduct of affairs, Christianity needed a graded corps of employees. This was the origin of the hierarchy which changed the inner meaning of Christianity and perverted its aims. A similar danger is encountered by all democratic parties which possess an elaborate financial administration. This danger is especially marked in the case of the German Socialist Party, whose central organization in the year 1908 employed merely in its printing office 298 persons, and all of these, having no share whatever in the net profits, nor any rights in the management of the social property, depend upon the party just as they might depend upon any ordinary private employer. In the hands of the party bureaucracy are the periodical press, the publication and sale of the party literature, and the enrollment of orators in the list of paid propagandists. All these sources of income can at any time be closed to undesirable competitors or to dissatisfied members of the rank and file, and this power is utilized in actual practice. The concentration of power in those parties which preach the Marxist doctrine is more conspicuous than the concentration of capital predicted by Marx in economic life. For some years past the leaders of the German Socialist Party have employed numerous methods of oppression, such as the threat to give no aid either in men or money on behalf of the electoral propaganda of a candidate from whose views they dissent, although the local comrades give this candidate their full confidence. It is hardly necessary to say that such a practice as this accords ill with the principles of liberty and fraternity. In this way have come into existence strict relationships of dependence, of hierarchical superiority and inferiority, engendered by the invisible force of the great god Money, and this within the bosom of the working-class party which has taken as its motto Blanqui's phrase, *ni Dieu ni Maître.*

Brief allusion may be made in conclusion to another kind of economic pressure which labor organizations are able to exercise. Publicans whose houses are frequented chiefly or exclusively by members of the working class, or small shopkeepers whose customers consist mainly of working women, are indirectly if not directly dependent, in the economic sense, upon the party and upon the trade union. They are dependent, that is to say, upon the leading personalities in these organizations, who, by declaring a boycott, can involve them in absolute ruin.

Chapter 3

The Leaders and the Press

THE PRESS constitutes a potent instrument for the conquest, the preservation, and the consolidation of power on the part of the leaders. The press is the most suitable means of diffusing the fame of the individual leaders among the masses, for popularizing their names. The labor press, and this applies equally to the trade-union journals and to those which devote themselves predominantly to political ends, is full of panegyrics concerning the personalities of the leaders, of references to their "disinterestedness and self-sacrificingness," to their "ardent idealism, conjoined with a vigorous force of conviction and with invincible tenacity," qualities which, we are told, have alone made it possible for them to create the great working-class organizations. Such flattering phrases as are from time to time used of the socialist leaders by the capitalist press (mostly dictated by motives of electoral opportunism) are complacently reproduced by socialist journals, and whether taken at par value or not they serve, by their diffusion among the socialist rank and file, to increase the prestige of the leaders.

It is true that the press cannot exert the immediate influence which the popular propagandist exercises over his audience in public meetings, debates, and party congresses. In compensation for this defect, however, the circle of influence of the written word is far more extensive. The press can be used with effect to influence public opinion by cultivating a "sensation" —a point in which modern party democracy exhibits a fundamental trait which it shares with Bonapartism. This means is frequently employed by the leaders in order to gain or to retain the sympathy of the masses, and to enable them to keep the guidance of the movement in their own hands. The democratic press is also utilized by the leaders in order to make attacks (more or less masked) upon their adversaries; or to launch grave accusations against persons of note in the world of politics or finance. These attacks may or may not be established upon a sufficient foundation of proof, but at any rate they serve to raise a duststorm. Sometimes, again, the leaders endeavor to ingratiate themselves with the masses by employing in respect of their capitalist opponents, coarse and insulting language which recalls the proverbial "Billingsgate." All means are good to the popularity hunter, and he varies them to suit his environment.

The manner in which the leaders make use of the press to secure their domination naturally varies from one country to another in accordance with variation in national customs. Where the party organization and the force at its disposal are still weak, the influence of the leaders is direct and personal. The consequence is that in France, in England, and in Italy, where the popular character still presents a strongly individual stamp, the democratic leader presents himself as personally responsible for what he writes, and signs his articles in full. An article which appears in "Le Socialiste" in Paris will attract attention, not so much on account of its own merits, but because at the foot it displays in large type the signature of a Jules Guesde. The leader imposes his influence upon the masses directly, manifesting his opinion openly, often giving it the form of a decree, published in the most conspicuous part of the paper. From the æsthetic and ethical points of view, this is, moreover, the best form of journalism, for the reader has a right to know the source of the wares which are offered him, and this altogether apart from the consideration that to all public activity there should be applied the fundamental moral principle that each one is responsible to all for his conduct. For the aspirants to leadership, again, the practice of signing newspaper articles has the incontestable advantage that it makes their names known to the masses, and this facilitates their gradual rise in the scale of representative honors until they attain to the highest.

In other countries, as for instance in Germany, the faith of the masses in authority is so robust that it does not require to be sustained by the prestige of a few conspicuous individualities. Hence journalism is here almost always anonymous. The individual contributor disappears behind the editorial staff. The journal does not serve to diffuse the writers' names far and wide, and regular readers are often totally ignorant of the individualities of the staff. This explains the comparative unimportance of the personal rôle played by German publicists when compared with those of most other countries; it explains their small part in public life, and the trifling social consideration they enjoy. But this must not be taken to mean that the anonymous press fails to serve the leaders as an instrument of domination. Since the German journalist is identified with the whole editorial staff, and even with the entire party, the result is that his voice appeals to the public with the entire force of this collective authority. His personal ideas thus acquire a prominence and attain an influence which would otherwise be lacking. What the individual member of the staff loses through his anonymity, in respect of direct influence upon the masses, is gained by the journalist leaders as a group. The editorial "we," uttered in the name of a huge party, has a much greater effect than even the most distinguished name. The "party," that is to say the totality of the leaders, is thus endowed with a special sanctity, since the crowd forgets that behind an article which thus presents itself under a collection aspect there is concealed in the great majority of cases but one single individual. In Germany it is not difficult to observe that the anonymous polemical and other articles of "Vorwärts," the central organ of the party, are regarded by the rank and file, and especially in Prussia, as a sort of periodical gospel, as a Bible in halfpenny numbers. It is more especially for the publication of violent personal attacks that anonymous journalism furnishes convenient and almost tempting opportunities, guaranteeing moral and legal impunity. Behind the shelter thus afforded by anonymity those of base and cowardly nature are apt to lurk in order that they may launch thence in safety their poisoned arrows against their personal or political adversaries. The victim of aggression is thus for four separate reasons placed in a position of inferiority. The rank and file consider the censure which has been expressed against him as having been uttered in the name of a principle or a class, as emanating from a superior and impersonal region, and as consequently of an extremely serious character and practically indelible. On the other hand, the whole editorial staff feels itself responsible for what has been published, for the anonymous article is regarded as published with the unanimous consent of the collectivity; the result is that the whole staff makes common cause with the aggressor, and this renders it almost impossible to secure any reparation for the wrong which hs been committed. Further, the person attacked does not know who is the aggressor, whereas if he knew the latter's name he might be able to understand the motives for the attack instead of being forced to fight a shadow. Finally, if he is by chance able to unveil the personality of the aggressor, journalistic etiquette forbids him to undertake his defense on lines directed against the aggressor individually, and he is thus deprived of one of the most efficient methods of defense. It recently happened that a writer in the German socialist press, who had attacked another member of the party, when this latter made a reply which unquestionably demanded a rejoinder, refused to continue the discussion because the person attacked had addressed his reply, not to the editorial staff generally, but "to one single member of that staff," who was in fact the aggressor. The reason given for this refusal was that in thus replying to an individual instead of to the staff the second writer had "infringed the most elementary decencies of party life."[1]

The obliteration of personality in German journalism has favored the institution, in connection with the socialist press of that country, of what are known as "correspondence bureaux." These organizations, which are managed by some of the writers of the party, transmit every day to the socialist press information relating to special branches, such as foreign politics, cooperative questions, and legislative problems. The bureaux owe their origin in great part to the spirt of intense economy which dominates the party press. They confer upon this press a stamp of great uniformity, since dozens of newspapers receive their inspiration from the same source. Further, they insure the supremacy of a small closed group of official journalists over the independent writers—a supremacy which is manifested chiefly in the economic sphere, since those who write for the correspondence bureaux seldom play any notable part in the political life of the party.

In all cases the press remains in the hands of the leaders and is never controlled by the rank and file. There is often intercalated between the leaders and the mass an intermediate stratum of press commissaries who are delegated by the rank and file to exercise a certain supervision over the editorial staff. In the most favorable circumstances, however, these functionaries cannot aspire to more than a very small share of power, and constitute merely a sort of inopportune and untechnical supplementary government. Speaking broadly it may be said that it is the paid leaders who decide all the political questions which have to do with the press.

[1] "Frankfurter Volksstimme," 1909, No. 175.

Chapter 4

The Position of the Leaders in Relation to the Masses in Actual Practice

IN THE political organizations of the international proletariat, the highest order of the leaders consists chiefly of members of parliament. In proof of this it suffices to mention the names of a few men who were or are the most distinguished socialist leaders of their day, at the same time men of note as parliamentarians: Bebel, Jaurés, Guesde, Adler, Vandervelde, Troelstra, Turati, Keir Hardie, Macdonald, Pablo Iglesias. Hyndman is an exception only because he has never succeeded in winning an election. The section of the English party to which he belongs is unrepresented in parliament.

The fact here noted indicates the essentially parliamentary character of the modern socialist parties. The socialist members of parliament are those who have especially distinguished themselves in the party by their competence and by their capacity. But in addition to this superiority, recognized and consecrated by the party itself, there are two reasons for the great authority exercised by the socialist parliamentarian. In the first place, in virtue of his position, he largely escapes the supervision of the rank and file of the party, and even the control of its executive committee. He owes his comparative independence to the fact that the parliamentary representative is elected for a considerable term of years, and can be dispossessed by no one so long as he retains the confidence of the electors. In the second place, and even at the moment of his election, his dependence on the party is but indirect, for his power is derived from the electoral masses, that is to say, in ultimate analysis from an unorganized body. It is true that in certain countries the independence of the party organization thus enjoyed by the parliamentary deputies is subject to limits more or less strict according to the degree of organization and cohesion of the party. But even then the respect and the power enjoyed by the parliamentarians remains unquestioned, since it is they who within the party fill the principal offices, and whose power predominates to a notable degree in the party executive. This is true, above all, of Germany. Where the rules forbid the deputy to function also as a member of the executive committee (in Italy, for example, only one deputy, chosen by the parliamentary group, can sit on the party executive), much friction is apt to arise between the two groups of leaders, impairing the authority of both. But, for the reasons expounded above, the influence of the parliamentary group commonly predominates.

The influence of parliamentarism is particularly great in the German social democracy. This is clearly shown by the attitude towards the party commonly assumed by the socialists in parliament. There is no other socialist party in the world in which the conduct of its representatives in parliament is subject to so little criticism. The socialist members of the Reichstag frequently make speeches in that body which might be expected to give rise to the liveliest recriminations, and yet neither in the party press nor at the congresses is to be heard a word of criticism or of disapproval. During the discussions in the Reichstag concerning the miners' strike in the basin of the Ruhr (1905), the deputy Hué spoke at the maximum program of the party as "utopian," and in the socialist press there was manifested no single symptom of revolt. On the first occasion on which the party departed from its principle of unconditional opposition to all military expenditure, contenting itself with simple absention when the first credit of 1,500,000 marks was voted for the war against the Hereros, this remarkable innovation, which in every other socialist party would have unquestionably evoked a storm from one section of the members, even if there might have been manifested cheerful approval by another, aroused among the German socialists no more than a few dispersed and timid protests. Subsequently, at the Bremen congress of 1904, when the deputies had to give an account of their conduct, very few delegates were found to express disapproval. It is, further, remarkable to what a degree the power of the parliamentary group becomes consolidated as the party increases throughout the country. In earlier days, far less important questions aroused much more acute struggles between the party and the parliamentary group. Today, the socialist masses in Germany have accustomed themselves to the idea that the decisive struggle on behalf of the aims they have at heart will be carried out in parliament, and for this reason they scrupulously avoid doing anything which might make difficulties for their parliamentary representatives. This conviction constantly determines the conduct of the masses in relation to their leaders. Hence in many questions the conduct of the parliamentary group is really decisive, *suprema lex*. All vigorous criticism, though made in accordance with the basic principles of socialism, is at once repudiated by the rank and file if it tend to weaken the position of the parliamentary group.

Those who, notwithstanding this, venture to voice such criticism are immediately put to silence and are severely stigmatized by the leaders. Two examples may be given in illustration, The "Leipziger Volkszeitung," in the year 1904, in a leading article entitled *The Usury of Bread*, vented its anger in somewhat violent terms upon the political leaders of the capitalist parties. Thereupon in the Reichstag certain orators of the right and of the center, when Prince Bülow had himself read this article to the house, adducing it as an evil example of journalistic methods, made a great display of indignation against the socialists. When this happened, Bebel, who had hitherto been a declared friend of the "Leipziger Volkszeitung," did not hesitate to repudiate the article in open parliament, though his conduct was here in flagrant contradiction with the best established traditions of democracy, and with the essential principle of party solidarity. At the congress of Bremen in 1904, Georg von Vollmar openly condemned the first attempts at anti-militarism made in Germany by certain members of the party. He did this with the express approval of most of the delegates and without arousing any disapproval from the others. Yet antimilitarism is a logical consequence of socialism, and for such a party as the socialist, anti-militarist propaganda must surely be a matter of primary importance. Vollmar, however, justified his attitude by remarking that if a systematic anti-militarist propaganda were to be undertaken, the Minister of War would have a pretext ready to his hand for disregarding all the protests and complaints which might be made by the socialist deputies on account of the differential treatment of soldiers known to hold socialist views. If, for example, the party representatives in parliament were to take action against the secret inquiries which the authorities are accustomed to make and to transmit to the district commanders, sending the names of recruits who before enlistment have been in the habit of frequenting socialist meetings and have even been known as local leaders, the minister could readily reply, and with effect, that socialists, being antimilitarists, are enemies of their country and as such deserve to be handled with all possible rigor. Vollmar concluded by saying: "Antimilitarist propaganda will make it impossible for the socialist in parliament to continue to assert that socialists fulfil their military duties no less patriotically than nonsocialists, and that for this reason it is unjust to subject them to exceptional treatment."[1]

It is well known that great efforts have been made by the parliamentary socialist groups in every country to secure for their members *ex-officio* the right to vote at the party congresses. In Germany this right was recognized in 1890 by the congress of Berlin, with the unimportant restriction that in questions concerning their parliamentary activities the rights of the members of the group in congress should be purely deliberative. Despite some opposition, this right was confirmed in the new rules of the party which were passed at the Jena congress in 1905. It is obvious that the deputy, even if he does not as such possess the right to vote, will not find much difficulty in securing delegation to the congress. Auer once said that those deputies who are not thus delegated must be poor fellows indeed.[2] Nevertheless they have been saved this trifling trouble. Thus the members of the parliamentary group are admitted to an active participation in the most intimate deliberations of the party, not as delegates approved by a vote of the branch to which they belong, but as representatives of the entire electorate of their constituency for the whole period for which they are elected to the legislature. This involves an express recognition of their position as leaders (and a further admission that this leadership owes its origin in part to non-party sources), and obviously raises them to the position of super-comrades independent of the rank and file of the party, or makes them irremovable delegates for so long as they may remain members of the Reichstag. This institution is certainly peculiar to Germany. In other countries identical rules apply for the appointment of all delegates to the congress, whether these may happen to be parliamentary representatives or not.[3] In France and Holland, for instance, the deputies can take part in the congresses, and are able to vote in these only if they are specially delegated for the purpose. In Italy, the members of the executive committee and the members of the parliamentary group cannot speak in the congress unless they are charged by the executive committee to present a report of some

1 *Protokoll des Parteitags zu Bremen*, 1904, p. 186.

2 "In any case, since, in view of their responsibilities to the party, their presence at the congress may be indispensable, it should not be made necessary for them to go about begging for a mandate" (*Protokoll des Parteitags zu Berlin*, 1890, p. 122).

3 "Avanti," No. 3433. Nevertheless, in these other countries the leading rôles in the socialist congresses are played by the parliamentary representatives.

kind. In Italy, as in France and Holland, they can vote only when regularly delegated.

Yet in view of their greater competence in various questions, the socialist parliamentary groups consider themselves superior even to the congresses, which are in theory the supreme courts of the party, and they claim an effective autonomy. The members of the parliamentary group obey a natural tendency to restrict more and more the circle of questions which must be submitted to the congress for decision, and to make themselves the sole arbiters of the party destinies. In Germany, many of the socialist deputies put forward a claim in 1903 to decide for themselves, independently of the party congresses, whether the parliamentary group should or should not accept the vice-presidency of the Reichstag for one of its members, and whether, if this post were accepted, the socialist vice-president should conform to the usage attaching to his office, and put in appearances at court. In Italy, the socialist and the republican parliamentary groups have secured complete independence of the executives of their respective parties. The socialist group has even been accused at times of accepting deputies who are not even regular members of the party, men who contend that their electors would look askance should they adhere officially to the local socialist organization.

The parliamentary leaders of the socialist as well as those of the capitalist parties assume the right to constitute a closed corporation, cut off from the rest of their party. The parliamentary group of the German socialists has on more than one occasion, and of its own initiative, disavowed the actions of considerable sections of the party. The most notable of such disavowals have been those of the article *The Usury of Bread*, in the "Leipziger Volkszeitung" (1904),[4] and that of the anti-militarist agitation of Karl Liebknecht (1907). In the former instance, the "Leipziger Volkszeitung" could very well console itself for the disapproval of the "fifty-seven comrades" (i.e. the members of the parliamentary group) as that of an infinitesimal minority of the party—in accordance with the historic and typically democratic utterance of the Abbé Sieyès on the eve of the French Revolution, when he said that the

[4] The declaration made by the party executive in the affair of the "Leipziger Volkszeitung" begins as follows: "On Saturday, the 10th inst., when, after the speech of comrade von Vollmar, the Imperial Chancellor brought up for discussion the subject of the article in the 'Leipziger Volkszeitung' of December 2nd, those members of the parliamentary group who were present agreed to instruct comrade Bebel to state in his speech that the group regretted the publication of this article and repudiated responsibility for it."

rights of the king bore to those of his subjects the ratio of 1:30,000,000. As a matter of pure theory, and considering the democratic principles of the party, the paper here hit the right nail on the head; but in practice its contention had no significance, for to the ineffective right of principle there was opposed the right of the stronger, immanent in the leadership.

The local branches of the party follow their deputies. In the congresses the great majority of the delegates accept as a matter of habit the guidance of the men of note. At the Bremen congress in 1904 the German socialists rejected the idea of the general strike as a general absurdity; at Jena, in 1905, they acclaimed it as an official weapon of the party; at Mannheim, in 1906, they declared it to be utopian. All the individual phases of this zigzag progress were hailed with the conscientious applause of the mass of the delegates in the congress and of the comrades throughout the country, who exhibited on each occasion the same lack of critical faculty and the same unthinking enthusiasm. In France, the little handful of men who constituted the general staff of the French Marxists when these still formed a separate party under the leadership of Jules Guesde was so permeated with the authoritarian spirit that at the party congresses the executive committee (Comité National) was not elected in due form, but was appointed *en bloc* by acclamation; it was impossible for the chiefs to conceive that the rank and file of the party could dream of refusing to follow their leaders. Moreover, the congresses were conducted *in camera*. Reports were published in an extremely condensed form so that no one could check the speakers. In the German Socialist Congresses, and in the reports of these assemblies, it is easy to distinguish between a higher and a lower circle of delegates. The report of what is said by the "ordinary" delegates is greatly abbreviated, whilst the speeches of the big guns are reproduced verbatim. In the party press, too, different measures are applied to the comrades. In the year 1904, when "Vorwärts," then edited by Eisner, did not publish a letter sent by Bebel, the latter moved heaven and earth with his complaints, saying that freedom of opinion was being suppressed in the party and that it was "the most elementary right" for all the comrades to have their letters printed in the party organs. Yet it is hardly possible to ignore that the "right" which Bebel thus invoked is in practice proportional to a comrade's degree of elevation in the party. The excitement over the non-appearance of Bebel's letter shows that his case was an exceptional one.

In the trade-union movement, the authoritative character of the leaders and their tendency to rule democratic organizations on oligarchic lines, are even more pronounced than in the political organizations.[5]

Innumerable facts recorded in the history of trade-union organizations show to what an extent centralized bureaucracy can divert from democracy a primarily democratic working-class movement. In the trade union, it is even easier than in the political labor organization, for the officials to initiate and to pursue a course of action disapproved of by the majority of the workers they are supposed to represent. It suffices here to refer to the two famous decisions of the trade-union congress at Cologne in 1905. In one of these the leaders declared themselves to be opposed (in opposition to the views of the majority) to the continued observance of the 1st of May as a general labor demonstration of protest. In the second, the discussion of the general strike was absolutely forbidden. By these and similar occurrences the oligarchical practices of the leaders are sufficiently proved, although some of writers continue to dispute the fact.[6]

For a good many years now, the executive committees of the trade-union federations have endeavored to usurp the exclusive right to decide on behalf of the rank and file the rhythm of the movement for better wages, and consequently the right to decide whether a strike is or is not "legitimate." Since the leaders of the federation are in charge of the funds, which often amount to a considerable sum, the dispute reduces itself in practice to a question as to who is to decide whether a strike shall or shall not be subsidized. This question is one which involves the very life of the democratic right of the organized masses in the trade unions to regulate their own affairs. When the leaders claim that they alone have a right to decide in a matter of such importance, and still more when they already largely possess this right, it is obvious that the

[5] "In the socialist party, owing to the nature of the matters with which it has to deal and owing to the characteristics of the political struggle, narrower limits are imposed upon bureaucracy than in the case of the trade-union movement" (Rosa Luxemburg, *Massenstreik, Partei, und Gewerkschaften*, ed, cit., p. 61). This cautious expression of the differences may be accepted.

[6] Heinrich Ströbel, for instance, a writer on the staff of "Vorwärts." "We at least do not believe that the majority of trade-union members favour tactics differing from those pursued by the trade-union officials. Unfortunately the majority of the trade unions, owing to the 'neutrality' which they have observed for some years, have become politically indifferent, and judge the trade-union movement in practice only from the outlook of the petty and immediate interests of their respective trades" (H. Ströbel, *Gewerkschaften und sozialistische Geist*, "Neue Zeit," xxiii, vol. ii, No. 44).

most essential democratic principles are gravely infringed. The leaders have openly converted themselves into an oligarchy, leaving to the masses who provide the funds no more than the duty of accepting the decisions of that oligarchy. This abuse of power may perhaps find justification on tactical grounds, the leaders alleging in defense of their procedure the supreme need that a strike should be declared cautiously and in unison. They claim the right to decide the merits of the question on the sole ground that they know better than the workers themselves the conditions of the labor market throughout the country and are consequently more competent to judge the chances of success in the struggle. The trade-union leaders add that since the stoppage of work in a town necessarily impairs the financial strength of the union in that town, and sometimes disturbs the conditions of work of a whole series of organized workers, it is for the leaders to decide when and where a strike should be declared. Thus they consider that their action is justified by the democratic aim of safeguarding the interests of the majority against the impulsive actions of the minority.

We are not here concerned, however, with the causation of the oligarchy which prevails in the trade unions. It suffices to point out how little difference exists between the tendencies of proletarian oligarchies and those of such oligarchies as prevail in the life of the state—governments, courts, etc. It is interesting to note that in Germany, as elsewhere, the socialist leaders do not hesitate to admit the existence of a well-developed oligarchy in the trade-union movement; while the leaders of the trade unions, in their turn, draw attention to the existence of an oligarchy in the socialist party; both groups of leaders unite however in declaring that as far as their own organizations are concerned these are quite immune to oligarchical infection.

Nevertheless, the trade-union leaders and the leaders of the Socialist Party sometimes combine upon a course of action which, were it undertaken by either group of leaders alone, those of the other group would not fail to stigmatize as grossly undemocratic. For example, in the serious question of the 1st of May demonstration, one of primary democratic importance in the year 1908, the executive committee of the Socialist Party and the general committee of the trade unions issued by common accord an announcement definitely decreeing from above the conduct of the separate political and trade-union organizations. In a question thus profoundly affecting the individual trade unions and local socialist committees, the executives regarded it as quite unnecessary to ask these for their opinion. Such conduct shows how much justification there is for the criticism which each of the two branches of the working-class movement directs against the other. Moreover, the question which has been debated whether the local trades councils might not be directly represented at the trade-union congresses is after all merely one of the enlargement of the oligarchical circle.

Let us next briefly consider the third form of the working-class movement, cooperative organizations, and in particular the organizations for cooperative production, as those which in their very nature should incorporate most perfectly the democratic principle.

As far as concerns distributive cooperative societies, it is easy to understand that these cannot be directly governed by the mass of the members. As Kautsky has shown, we are here concerned with an enterprise whose functions are essentially commercial, and therefore outside the competence of the rank and file. For this reason, the principal business activities of these societies must be entrusted to the employees and to a few experts. "Unless we consider buying as cooperation, in which case the customers of an ordinary shopman are also cooperators with the shopman, the members of a cooperative society have nothing more to do with the management than have the shareholders of a limited company; they choose their managing committee, and then leave the machine to run itself, waiting till the end of the year to express their approval or disapproval of the management, and to pocket their dividends.[7] In actual fact, the distributive cooperative societies present in general a monarchical aspect. Read, for example, what was written by a well-disposed critic concerning the cooperative society "Vooruit" of Ghent, which is led by Edouard Anseele, the socialist, and which is definitely socialist in its tendency: "Prosperity and good administration do not come about without some sacrifice of the workmen's sacred liberty. The 'Vooruit' bears the imprint of the strong personality which created it. . . . A powerful will in laying claim to responsibilities (while others retreat from them) almost always becomes intoxicated with itself. M. Anseele, has deliberately assumed the impetuous, imperious, brusque manners of the most bourgeois captains of industry, and 'Vooruit' functions mainly on the principle of authority."[8]

[7] Karl Kautsky, *Konsumvereine und Arbeiterbewegung*, ed. cit., p. 17.
[8] Trans. from "Pourquoi pas?" Brussels, anno ii, No. 97.

Societies for cooperative production, on the other hand, and especially the smaller of these, offer in theory the best imaginable field for democratic collaboration. They consist of homogeneous elements belonging to the same stratum of the working class, of persons following the same trade, and accustomed to the same manner of life. In so far as the society needs a management, this management can readily be effected by all the members in common, since all possess the same professional competence, and all can lend a hand as advisers and coadjutors. In a political party it is impossible that every member should be engaged in important political work, and it is for this reason that in the political party there necessarily exists a great gulf between the leaders and the rank and file. But in a society for cooperative production, for bootmaking for example, all the members are equally competent in the making of boots, the use of tools, and knowledge of the quality of leather. There do not exist among them any essential differences in matters of technical knowledge. Yet despite the fact that the circumstances are thus exceptionally favorable for the constitution of a democratic organism, we cannot as a general rule regard productive cooperatives as models of democratic auto-administration. Rodbertus said on one occasion that when he imagined productive associations to have extended their activities to include all manufacture, commerce, and agriculture, when he conceived all social work to be effected by small cooperative societies in whose management every member had an equal voice, he was unable to avoid the conviction that the economic system would succumb to the cumbrousness of its own machinery.[9] The history of productive cooperation shows that all the societies have been faced with the following dilemma: either they succumb rapidly owing to discord and powerlessness resulting from the fact that too many individuals have the right to interfere in their administration; or else they end by submitting to the will of one or of a few persons, and thus lose their truly cooperative character. In almost all cases such enterprises owe their origin to the personal initiative of one or a few members. They are sometimes miniature monarchies, being under the dictatorship of the manager, who represents them in all internal and external relations, and upon whose will they depend so absolutely that

[9] Karl Rodbertus, *Offener Brief an das Komitee des deutschen Arbeitervereins zu Leipzig*, in F. Lassalle's *Politische Reden und Schriften*, ed. cit., vol. ii, p. 9.

if he dies or resigns his post they run the risk of perishing. This tendency on the part of the productive cooperative societies is further accentuated by their character as aggregates of individuals whose personal advantages decrease in proportion as the number of the members increases. Thus from their very nature they are subject to the same immutable psychological laws which governed the evolution of the medieval guilds. As they become more prosperous, they become also more exclusive, and tend always to monopolize for the benefit of the existing members the advantages they have been able to secure. For example, by imposing a high entrance fee they put indirect obstacles in the way of the entry of new members. In some cases they simply refuse to accept new members, or pass a rule establishing a maximum membership. When they have need of more labor-power they supply this need by engaging ordinary wage-laborers. Thus we not infrequently find that a society for cooperative production becomes gradually transformed into a joint-stock company. It even happens occasionally that the cooperative society becomes the private enterprise of the manager. In both these cases Kautsky is right in saying that the social value of the working-class cooperative is then limited to the provision of means for certain proletarians which will enable them to climb out of their own class into a higher. Rodbertus described labor associations as a school for the education of the working class, in which the manual workers could learn administration, discussion, and within limits the art of government.[10] We have seen to how small an extent this statement is applicable.

In the democratic movement the personal factor thus plays a very considerable part. In the smaller associations it is often predominant. In the larger organizations, larger questions commonly lose the personal and petty characteristics which they originally possessed, but all the same the individuals who bring these questions forward, and who in a sense come to personify them, retain their influence and importance. In England, three or four men, Macdonald, Keir Hardie, Henderson, and Clynes, for instance, enjoy the confidence of the socialist masses so unrestrictedly that, as an able observer declares, it is impossible to exercise an influence upon the rank and file except by influencing these leaders.[11] In Italy, the first among the leaders of the trade-union organizations has affirmed that those only

10 Rodbertus, op. cit., p. 9.

11 M. Beer's report on the 9th annual congress of the British Labour Party, "Fränkische Tagespost," anno xli, No. 28 (1909).

which are headed by a good organizer can continue in existence. "Categories of the most various trades, found in the most diverse environments, have been unable to secure organization and to live through crises, except in so far as they have been able to find first-class men to manage their affairs. Those which have had bad leaders have not succeeded in establishing organizations; or the organizations if formed have proved defective."[12] In Germany, the supreme authority of Bebel was manifested by a thousand signs,[13] from the joy with which he was hailed wherever he went, to the efforts always made in the various congresses by the representatives of different tendencies to win him over to their side. Moreover, the working-class leaders are well aware of their ascendancy over the masses. Sometimes political opportunism leads them to deny it, but more commonly they are extremely proud of it and boast of it. In Italy, and in other countries as well, the socialist leaders have always claimed that the bourgeoisie and the government are greatly indebted to them for having held the masses in check, and as having acted as moderators to the impulsive crowd. This amounts to saying that the socialist leaders claim the merit, and consequently the power, of preventing the social revolution, which, according to them, would, in default of their intervention, have long ago taken place. Disunion in parties, although often evoked by objective necessities, is almost always the work of the leaders. The masses never oppose the reconciliation of their chiefs, partly, no doubt, because the differences between the leaders, in so far as they are of an objective character, are for the most part outside the narrow circle of interests and the limited understanding of the rank and file.

The esteem of the leaders for the masses is not as a rule very profound, even though there are some among them who profess great enthusiasm for the masses and repay with interest the honor which these render. In the majority of cases the veneration is a one-sided affair, if only for the reason that the leaders have had an opportunity of learning the miseries of the crowd by first-hand experience. Fournière said that the socialist leaders regarded the crowd, which had entrusted them with the fulfilment of its own aspirations and which consisted of devoted followers, as a passive instrument in their own hands, as a series of ciphers whose only purpose was to increase the value

12 Rinaldo Rigola, *I Funzionari delle Organizzazioni*, "Avanti," anno xiv, No. 341.

13 Cf. the excellent description given by Albert Weidner, *Bebel*, "Der Arme Teufel," anno ii, No. 21 (1903).

of the little figure standing to the left. "If he has only one in his power, he counts for only ten: if he has six, he counts for a million."[14]

The differences in education and competence which actually exist among the members of the party are reflected in the differences in their functions. It is on the ground of the incompetence of the masses that the leaders justify the exclusion of these from the conduct of affairs. They contend that it would be contrary to the interests of the party if the minority of the comrades who have closely followed and attentively studied the questions under consideration should be overruled by the majority which does not really possess any reasoned opinion of its own upon the matters at issue. This is why the chiefs are opposed to the referendum, at any rate as far as concerns its introduction into party life. "The choice of the right moment for action demands a comprehensive view which only a few individuals in the mass can ever possess, whilst the majority are guided by momentary impressions and currents of feeling. A limited body of officials and confidential advisers, in closed session, where they are removed from the influence of colored press reports, and where every one can speak without fearing that his words will be bruited in the enemy's camp, is especially likely to attain to an objective judgment."[15]

To justify the substitution of the indirect vote for the direct vote, the leaders invoke, in addition to political motives, the complicated structure of the party organization. Yet for the state organization, which is infinitely more complicated, direct legislation by means of the initiative and the referendum is an integral part of the socialist program. The antinomy which underlies these different ways of looking at the same thing according as it presents itself in the politics of the state or in those of the party pervades the whole life of the latter.

The working-class leaders sometimes openly avow, with a sincerity verging on cynicism, their own superiority over the troops they command, and may go so far as to declare their firm intention to refuse to these latter any facility for dictating the leaders' conduct. The leaders even reserve to themselves the right of rebelling against the orders they receive. A typical example, among many, is the opinion expressed on this subject by Filippo Turati, an exceptionally intelligent and well-informed man and one of the most influential members of the Italian Socialist Party, in a labor congress held at Rome in

[14] E. Fournière, *La sociocratie*, ed. cit., p. 117.

[15] Eduard Bernstein, *Gewerkschaftsdemokratie*, "Sozial. Monatsh.," 1909, p. 86.

1908. Referring to the position of the socialist deputy in relation to the socialist masses, he said: "The socialist parliamentary group is always at the disposal of the proletariat, as long as the group is not asked to undertake absurdities."[16] It need hardly be said that in each particular case it is the deputies who have to decide whether the things they are asked to do are or are not "absurd."

The accumulation of power in the hands of a restricted number of persons, such as ensues in the labor movement today, necessarily gives rise to numerous abuses. The "representative," proud of his indispensability, readily becomes transformed from a servitor of the people into their master. The leaders, who have begun by being under obligations to their subordinates, become in the long run the lords of these: such is the ancient truth which was recognized by Goethe when he made Mephistopheles say that man always allows himself to be ruled by his own creatures. The very party which fights against the usurpations of the constituted authority of the state submits as by natural necessity to the usurpations effected by its own constituted authorities. The masses are far more subject to their leaders than to their governments and they bear from the former abuses of power which they would never tolerate from the latter. The lower classes sometimes react forcibly against oppression from above, and take bloody reprisals, as happened in the French Jacqueries, in the German Peasants' Wars, in the English revolts under Wat Tyler and Jack Cade, and more recently in the revolts of the Sicilian Fasci in 1893; whereas they do not perceive the tyranny of the leaders they have themselves chosen. If at length the eyes of the masses are opened to the crimes against the democratic ideal which are committed by their party leaders, their astonishment and their stupor are unbounded. If, however, they then rise in rebellion, the nature of their criticisms shows how little they have understood the true character of the problem. Far from recognizing the real fount of the oligarchical evil in the centralization of power within the party, they often consider that the best means of counteracting oligarchy is to intensify this very centralization.

[16] This speech was made in a Convegno pro Amnistia on March 31, 1908, reported in the Turin "Stampa," xvii, No. 92.

Chapter 5

The Struggle Between the Leaders and the Masses

THOSE WHO defend the arbitrary acts committed by the democracy, point out that the masses have at their disposal means whereby they can react against the violation of their rights. These means consist in the right of controlling and dismissing their leaders. Unquestionably this defense possesses a certain theoretical value, and the authoritarian inclinations of the leaders are in some degree attenuated by these possibilities. In states with a democratic tendency and under a parliamentary regime, to obtain the fall of a detested minister it suffices, in theory, that the people should be weary of him. In the same way, once more in theory, the ill-humor and the opposition of a socialist group or of an election committee is enough to effect the recall of a deputy's mandate, and in the same way the hostility of the majority at the annual congress of trade unions should be enough to secure the dismissal of a secretary. In practice, however, the exercise of this theoretical right is interfered with by the working of the whole series of conservative tendencies to which allusion has previously been made, so that the supremacy of the autonomous and sovereign masses is rendered purely illusory. The dread by which Nietzsche was at one time so greatly disturbed, that every individual might become a functionary of the mass, must be completely dissipated in face of the truth that while all have the right to become functionaries, few only possess the possibility.

With the institution of leadership there simultaneously begins, owing to the long tenure of office, the transformation of the leaders into a closed caste.

Unless, as in France, extreme individualism and fanatical political dogmatism stand in the way, the old leaders present themselves to the masses as a compact phalanx—at any rate whenever the masses are so much aroused as to endanger the position of the leaders.

The election of the delegates to congresses, etc., is sometimes regulated by the leaders by means of special agreements, whereby the masses are in fact excluded from all decisive influence in the management of their affairs. These agreements often assume the aspect of a mutual insurance contract. In the German Socialist Party, a few years ago, there came into existence in not a few localities a regular system in accordance with which the leaders nominated one another in rotation as delegates to the various party congresses. In the meetings at which the delegates were appointed, one of the big guns would always propose to the comrades the choice as delegate of the leader whose "turn" it was. The comrades rarely revolt against such artifices, and often fail even to perceive them. Thus competition among the leaders is prevented, in this domain at least; and at the same time there is rendered impossible anything more than passive participation of the rank and file in the higher functions of the life of that party which they alone sustain with their subscriptions.[1] Notwithstanding the violence of the intestine struggles which divide the leaders, in all the democracies they manifest vis-á-vis the masses a vigorous solidarity. "They perceive quickly enough the necessity for agreeing among themselves so that the party cannot escape them by becoming divided."[2] This is true above all of the German social democracy, in which, in consequence of the exceptional solidity of structure which it possesses as compared with all the other socialist parties of the world, conservative tendencies have attained an extreme development.

When there is a struggle between the leaders and the masses, the former are always victorious if only they remain united. At least it rarely happens that the masses succeed in disembarrassing themselves of one of their leaders. At Mannheim, a few years ago, the organized workers did actually dismiss one of their chiefs, but not without arousing intense indignation among the leaders, who described this act of legitimate rebellion as a crime on the part of the rank and file, and were careful to obtain another post for the poor victim of popular anger. In the course of great political agitations and in extensive economic struggles undertaken by the masses against the will of their leaders these soon reacquire the supremacy which they may for a moment have lost. Then it often happens that the leaders, over the heads of the crowd and in opposition to its expressed will, contravening the fundamental principles of democracy and ignoring all the legal, logical, and economic bonds which unite the paid leaders to the paying masses, make peace

1 Similar phenomena have been observed in party life in America (Astrogorsky, *La Démocratie, etc.*, ed, cit., vol. ii, p. 196).

2 Trans. from Antoine Elisée Cherbuliez, *Théorie des Garantis constitutionelles*, Ab. Cherbuliez, Paris, 1838, vol. ii, p. 253.

with the enemy, and order the close of the agitation or the resumption of work. This is what happened in the last Italian general strike, and also in the great strikes at Crimmitschau, Stetten, Mannheim, etc. The masses in such cases are often sulky, but they never rebel, for they lack power to punish the treachery of the chiefs. After holding tumultuous meetings in which they declare their legitimate and statutory displeasure, they never fail to provide their leaders with the democratic fig-leaf of a bill of indemnity. In 1905 the miners of the Ruhr basin were enraged against their leaders when these had taken it upon themselves to declare the great miners' strike at an end. It seemed as if on this occasion the oligarchy was at length to be called to account by the masses. A few weeks later, tranquility was completely restored, as if it had never been disturbed. The leaders had defied the anger of their followers, and had nevertheless remained in power. In Turin, in October, 1907, on the third day of the general strike, the workers had decided by a large majority that the strike should be continued, but the leaders (the executive committee of the local branch of the party and the committees of the local trade unions) went counter to this decision, which ought to have been valid for them, by issuing a manifesto in which they counselled the strikers to return to work. In the meetings of the party and of the trades council which followed upon these events the breach of discipline was condoned. The rank and file dreaded the resignation of the leaders and the bad appearance which their organizations would have displayed in face of the bourgeoisie when deprived of their best known and most highly esteemed men. Thus the governing bodies of democratic and socialist parties can in case of need act entirely at their own discretion, maintaining a virtual independence of the collectivity they represent, and in practice making themselves omnipotent.

Such a condition of affairs is essentially oligarchical, and manifold are its consequences in the movements that have been initiated under the banner of democracy. One of the chief of these consists in the daily infringement on the part of the executive of the tactical resolutions whose fulfilment is entrusted to the executive as a sacred charge by the numerous leaders of the second rank who make up the congresses and assemblies of the party; hence arises the practice which becomes continually more general of discussing *en petit comité* questions of the greatest importance, and of confronting the party subsequently with accomplished facts (for example, electoral congresses are not summoned until *after* the elections, so that the leaders decide on their sole responsibility what is to be the electoral platform). Again, there are secret negotiations among different groups of leaders (as happened in Germany in the case of the 1st of May demonstration and in that of the general strike), and secret understandings with the government. Once more, silence is often maintained by the members of the parliamentary group upon matters which have been discussed by the group and upon decisions at which they have arrived, and this practice is censured by members of the executive only when they themselves are kept in the dark, but is approved by them when it is merely the masses who are hoodwinked.

There is no indication whatever that the power possessed by the oligarchy in party life is likely to be overthrown within an appreciable time. The independence of the leaders increases concurrently with their indispensability. Nay more, the influence which they exercise and the financial security of their position become more and more fascinating to the masses, stimulating the ambition of all the more talented elements to enter the privileged bureaucracy of the labor movement. Thus the rank and file becomes continually more impotent to provide new and intelligent forces capable of leading the opposition which may be latent among the masses.[3] Even today the masses rarely move except at the command of their leaders. When the rank and file does take action in conflict wtih the wishes of the chiefs, this is almost always the outcome of a misunderstanding. The miners' strike in the Ruhr basin in 1905 broke out against the desire of the trade-union leaders, and was generally regarded as a spontaneous explosion of the popular will. But it was subsequently proved beyond dispute that for many months the leaders had been stimulating the rank and file, mobilizing them against the coal barons with repeated threats of a strike, so that the mass of the workers, when they entered on the struggle, could not possibly fail to believe that they did so with the full approval of their chiefs.

It cannot be denied that the masses revolt from time to time, but their revolts are always suppressed. It is only when the dominant classes, struck by sudden blindness, pursue a policy which strains social relationships to the breaking-point, that the party masses appear actively on the stage of history and overthrow the power of the oligarchies. Every autonomous move-

[3] Thus Pareto writes: "If B [the new élite] took the place of A [the old élite] by slow infiltration, and if the social circulation is not interrupted, C [the masses] are deprived of the leaders who could incite them to revolt." (Trans. from Vilfredo Pareto, *Les Systèmes socialistes*, Giard and Brière, Paris, 1892, vol. i, p. 35).

ment of the masses signifies a profound discordance with the will of the leaders. Apart from such transient interruptions, the natural and normal development of the organization will impress upon the most revolutionary of parties an indelible stamp of conservatism.

Chapter 6

The Struggle Among the Leaders Themselves

THE THESIS of the unlimited power of the leaders in democratic parties, requires, however, a certain limitation. Theoretically the leader is bound by the will of the mass, which has only to give a sign and the leader is forced to withdraw. He can be discharged and replaced at any moment. But in practice, as we have learned, for various reasons the leaders enjoy a high degree of independence. It is none the less true that if the Democratic Party cannot dispense with autocratic leaders, it is at least able to change these. Consequently the most dangerous defect in a leader is that he should possess too blind a confidence in the masses. The aristocratic leader is more secure than the democratic against surprises at the hands of the rank and file. It is an essential characteristic of democracy that every private carries a marshal's baton in his knapsack. It is true that the mass is always incapable of governing; but it is no less true that each individual in the mass, in so far as he possesses, for good or for ill, the qualities which are requisite to enable him to rise above the crowd, can attain to the grade of leader and become a ruler. Now this ascent of new leaders always involves the danger, for those who are already in possession of power, that they will be forced to surrender their places to the newcomers. The old leader must therefore keep himself in permanent touch with the opinions and feelings of the masses to which he owes his position. Formally, at least, he must act in unison with the crowd, must admit himself to be the instrument of the crowd, must be guided, in appearance at least, by its goodwill and pleasure. Thus it often seems as if the mass really controlled the leaders. But whenever the power of the leaders is seriously threatened, it is in most cases because a new leader or a new group of leaders is on the point of becoming dominant, and is inculcating views opposed to those of the old rulers of the party. It then seems as if the old leaders, unless they are willing to yield to the opinion of the rank and file and to withdraw, must consent to share their power with the new arrivals. If, however, we look more closely into the matter, it is not difficult to see that their submission is in most cases no more than an act of foresight intended to obviate the influence of their younger rivals. The submission of the old leaders is ostensibly an act of homage to the crowd, but in intention it is a means of prophylaxis against the peril by which they are threatened—the formation of a new élite.

The semblance of obedience to the mass which is exhibited by the leaders assumes, in the case of the feebler and the more cunning among them, the form of demagogy. Demagogues are the courtesans of the popular will. Instead of raising the masses to their own level, they debase themselves to the level of the masses. Even for the most honest among them, the secret of success consists in "knowing how to turn the blind impulsiveness of the crowd to the service of their own ripely pondered plans."[1] The stronger leaders brave the tempest, well-knowing that their power may be attacked, but cannot be broken. The weak or the base, on the other hand, give ground when the masses make a vigorous onslaught; their dominion is temporarily impaired or interrupted. But their submission is feigned; they are well aware that if they simply remain glued to their posts, their quality as executants of the will of the masses will before long lead to a restoration of their former dominance. One of the most noted leaders of German socialism said in a critical period of tension between the leaders and the masses, that he must follow the will of the masses in order to guide them.[2] A profound psychological truth is hidden in this sarcasm. He who wishes to command must know how to obey.

It has been affirmed that popular revolutions usually end by destroying their leaders. In proof there have been quoted the names of Rienzi, Masaniello, and Michele di Lando, for Italy, and of Danton and Robespierre, for France. For these and many similar instances the observation is a true one. It would, however, be an error to accuse the crowd of rising against its leaders, and to make the masses responsible for their fall. It is not the masses which have devoured the leaders: the chiefs have devoured one another with the aid of the masses. Typical examples are that of Danton, who was overthrown by Robespierre, and that of Robespierre, who was destroyed by the surviving Dantonists.

The struggle which arises between the leaders, and their mutual jealousies, induce them to employ active measures and

1 Kochanowski, *Urzeitklänge, und Wetterleuchten Geschichtlicher Gesetze in den Ereignissen der Gegenwart*, Wagner, Innsbruck, 1910, p. 10.

2 "Ich bin ihr Führer, also muss ich ihnen folgen." (Cf. Adolf Weber, *Der Kampf zwischen Kapital u. Arbeit*, ed. cit., p. 369.)

often to have recourse to artifices. Democratic deputies endeavor to disarm their adversaries within the party, and at the same time to acquire a new prestige in the eyes of the masses, by displaying in parliament "a formidable activity on behalf of the common cause." This is regarded at once as a democratic duty and as a measure of personal precaution. Since the great majority of the deputies, electors, and comrades have no precise ideas concerning the functions he exercises, and are continually inclined to accuse him of slackness, the deputy is from time to time forced to recall himself to their memories. It is this need which has given rise to not a few of those speeches to which the Germans give the name of *Dauerreden* (interminable speeches), and it has also been the cause of more than one "scene" in the various parliaments of Austria, France, England, and Italy. It is, in fact, held that the most efficacious means for retaining the attention of the masses and of rendering them proud of their leaders is to be found in the provocation of those personal incidents which are far more interesting to the great public and far more within the scope of its intelligence than a report upon the utilization of water power or upon a commercial treaty with the republic of Argentina. Moreover, it has to be remembered that in many countries, and above all in Italy, such scenes are recorded in the capitalist press with the greatest abundance of detail, whilst serious speeches are summed up in a few lines, and with especial brevity when the speaker is a socialist. Thus even in normal times the oratorical activity of the parliamentary representatives of the democratic parties is considerable. In Italy, the socialist deputies have boasted that between March 25 and July 10, 1909, they spoke in the Chamber 212 times. The figure represents 20.4 per cent of all the speeches made in parliament during the period, whilst the socialist deputies at this time constituted only 8 per cent of the members.[3] Such loquacity serves not merely to maintain the prestige of the party in the eyes of its opponents, but it is also a matter of personal interest to each deputy, being a means to secure his reelection in competition, not only with enemies in other parties, but also with jealous rivals belonging to his own organization.

The differences which lead to struggles between the leaders arise in various ways. Reference has previously been made to the inevitable antagonism between the "great men" who have acquired a reputation in other fields, and who now make adhesion to the party, offering it their services as generals, and the old-established leaders, who have been socialists from the

[3] Cf. the account given by Oddino Morgari, "Avanti," August 12, 1909.

first. Often conflict arises simply between age and youth. Sometimes the struggle depends upon diversity of social origin, as when there is a contest between proletarian leaders and those of bourgeois birth. Sometimes the difference arises from the objective needs of the various branches of activity into which a single movement is subdivided, as when there is a struggle between the political Socialist Party and the trade-union element, or within the political party between the parliamentary group and the executive. In some cases there is a horizontal stratification, causing a struggle between one stratum of the bureaucracy and another: at other times the stratification is vertical, as when there occurs a conflict between two local or national groups of leaders; between the Bavarian socialists and the Prussian; between those of Frankfort and those of Hanau; between the French followers of Vaillant, Jaurès, and Hervé, and the German adherents of Bebel and von Vollmar (in the antimilitarist discussion at the international congress of Stuttgart). Often enough struggles among the socialists are the outcome of racial differences. The unceasing contests in the international congresses between the German socialists and the French afford in more than one respect a parallel with the Franco-German War of 1870. In these same congresses there participates a third group, misunderstood and heterogeneous, the representatives of English socialism, hostile to all the others and encountered with the enmity of all. In most cases, however, the differences between the various groups of leaders depend upon two other categories of motives. Above all there are objective differences and differences of principle in general philosophical views, or at least in the mode in which the proximate social evolution is conceived, and consequent divergences of opinion as to the most desirable tactics: this leads to the manifestation of the various tendencies known as reformist and Marxist, syndicalist and political socialist, and so on. In the second place, we have the struggles that depend on personal reasons: antipathy, envy, jealousy, a reckless attempt to grasp the first positions, demagogy. Enrico Ferri said of his opponent Filippo Turati: "He hates me because he thinks there is not room for two cocks in the same foul-house."[4] In most cases the two series of motives are somewhat confounded in practice; and in the long run we find that those of the former series tend to be replaced by those of the latter, inasmuch as differences of principle and of the intellectual order soon become personal and

[4] Speech made by Ferri at Suzzara, reported in "Stampa," anno xlvii, No. 358 (December 27, 1909).

lead to a profound hostility between the representatives of the various theories. Conversely it is clear that motives of the second series, since those who are influenced by them are ashamed to display them in their true colors, always endeavor to assume the mantle of theory; personal dislike and personal hostility pompously masquerade as differences of views and tactics.

The oligarchy which issues from democracy is menaced by two grave dangers: the revolt of the masses, and (in intimate relationship with this revolt, of which it is often the result) the transition to a dictatorship when one among the oligarchs succeeds in obtaining supreme power. Of these two dangers, one comes from below, whilst the other arises within the very bosom of the oligarchy: we have rebellion on one side, and usurpation on the other. The consequence is that in all modern popular parties a spirit of genuine fraternity is conspicuously lacking; we do not see sincere and cordial mutual trust; there is a continual latent struggle, a spirit of irritation determined by the reciprocal mistrust of the leaders, and this spirit has become one of the most essential characteristics of every democracy. The mistrust of the leaders is directed above all against those who aspire to command their own organizations. Every oligarchy is full of suspicion towards those who aspire to enter its ranks, regarding them not simply as eventual heirs but as successors who are ready to supplant them without waiting for a natural death. Those who have long been in possession (and this applies just as much to spiritual and psychical possession as to material) are proud of their past, and are therefore inclined to look down upon those whose ownership is of more recent date. In certain Sicilian towns, struggles go on between two parties who in popular phrase are ironically termed *i ricchi* and *gli arricchiti* (the wealthy and those who have attained to wealth). The former consist of the old landed gentry; whilst the latter, the parvenus, are merchants, contractors for public works, manufacturers, and the like. A similar struggle makes its appearance in modern democratic parties, although it is not in this case characterized by any flavor of economic distinction. Here also we have a struggle between the *détenteurs d'emploi et les chercheurs d'emploi*, or as the Americans put it, between the "ins" and the "outs." The latter declare war on the former, ostensibly on the ground of eternal principle, but in reality, in most cases, because in such opposition they find the most effective means of forcing their way into the circle of the chiefs. Consequently in meetings they display themselves as implacable theoretical adversaries, "talking big" solely in order to intimidate the accepted leaders, and in order to induce them to surrender a share of the spoil to these turbulent comrades. Often enough, the old leaders resist, and maintain their ground firmly; in such cases their opponents, changing front, abandon the attitude of struggle, and attach themselves to the triumphal care of the men in power, hoping thus to attract favor, and, by a different route, to realize their own ambitions.

The struggle between the old leaders and the aspirants to power constitutes a perpetual menace to freedom of speech and thought. We encounter this menace in every democratic organization in so far as it is well ordered and solidly grounded, and in so far as it is operating in the field of party politics (for in the wider life of the state, in which the various parties are in continual reciprocal concussion, it is necessary to leave intact a certain liberty of movement). The leaders, those who already hold the power of the party in their hands, make no concealment of their natural inclination to control as strictly as possible the freedom of speech of those of their colleagues from whom they differ. The consequence is that those in office are great zealots for discipline and subordination, declaring that these qualities are indispensable to the very existence of the party. They go so far as to exercise a censorship over any of their colleagues whom they suspect of rebellious inclinations, forcing them to abandon independent journals, and to publish all their articles in the official organs controlled by the leaders of the majority in the party. The prohibition, in the German Socialist Party, of collaboration on the part of its members with the capitalist press, is in part due to the same tendency; whilst the demand that the comrades should have nothing to do with periodicals which, though socialist, are founded with private capital and are not subject to the official control of the party executive, arises solely from this suspicion on the part of the leaders.

In the struggle against the young aspirants, the old leader can as a rule count securely upon the support of the masses. The rank and file of the working-class parties have a certain natural distrust of all newcomers who have not been openly protected or introduced into the party by old comrades; and this is above all the case when the newcomer is derived from another social class. Thus the new recruit, before he can come into the open with his new ideas, must submit, if he is not to be exposed to the most violent attacks, to a long period of quarantine. In the German Socialist Party, this period of quarantine is especially protracted, for the reason that the German party has been longer established than any of the others, and because its leaders therefore enjoy an exceptional prestige. Many of them were among the actual founders of the party, and their personalities have been consecrated by the baptism of fire which they suffered during the enforcement of the anti-socialist laws. A socialist who has had his party card in his pocket for eight or ten years is often regarded in his branch as a "young" member. This tendency is reinforced by the respect for age which is so strong among the Germans, and by the tendency towards hierarchy of which even the democracy has not been able to divest itself. Finally, it may be added that the bureaucracy of the German labor movement, like every strongly developed bureaucracy, tends instinctively towards exclusivism. Consequently in the German social democracy, in contradistinction to other socialist parties which are less solidly organized, we find that not merely the recently enrolled member of the party (the so-called *Fuchs*), but also the ordinary member who does not live in the service and by the service of the party but has preserved his outward independence as a private author or in some other capacity, and has therefore not been incorporated among the cogwheels of the party machine, very rarely succeeds in making his influence felt. There can be no doubt that this fact plays a large part in the causation of that lack of a number of capable young men, displaying fresh energies, and not greatly inferior to the old leaders, a lack which has often been deplored. The annual congresses of the Socialist Party have even been spoken of as "congresses of the party officials." The criticism is not unjust, for among the delegates to the socialist congresses the percentage of party and trade-union officials is enormous. It is above all in the superior grades of the organization that the tendencies we are here analyzing are especially conspicuous. In Germany, the management of the Socialist Party is not entrusted to young men, as often happens in Italy, or to free publicists, as in France, but to old members, *des anciens,* elderly officials of the party. Moreover, the conservative psychology of the masses supports the aspirations of the old leaders, for it would never occur to the rank and file to entrust the care of their interests to persons belonging to their own proper sphere, that is to say, to those who have no official position in the party and who have not pursued a regular bureaucratic career.

Often the struggle between the old leaders in possession of power and the new aspirants assumes the aspects of a struggle between responsible and irresponsible persons. Many criticisms leveled by the latter against the former are beside the mark, because the leaders have grave responsibilities from which the aspirants are free. This freedom gives the aspirants a tactical advantage in their conflict with the old leaders. Moreover, precisely because they are irresponsible, because they do not occupy any official position in the party, the opponents are not subject to that simulacrum of democratic control which must influence the conduct of those in office.

In order to combat the new chiefs, who are still in a minority, the old leaders of the majority instinctively avail themselves of a series of underhand methods through which they often secure victory, or at least notably retard defeat. Among these means, there is one which will have to be more fully discussed in another connection. The leaders of what we may term the "government" arouse in the minds of the masses distrust of the leaders of the "opposition" by labeling them incompetent and profane, terming them spouters, corrupters of the party, demagogues, and humbugs, whilst in the name of the mass and of democracy they describe themselves as exponents of the collective will, and demand the submission of the insubordinate and even of the merely discontented comrades.

In the struggle among the leaders an appeal is often made to loftier motives. When the members of the executive claim the right to intervene in the democratic functions of the individual sections of the organization, they base this claim upon their more comprehensive grasp of all the circumstances of the case, their profounder insight, their superior socialist culture and keener socialist sentiment. They often claim the right of refusing to accept the new elements which the inexpert and ignorant masses desire to associate with them in the leadership, basing their refusal on the ground that it is necessary to sustain the moral and theoretical level of the party. The revolutionary socialists of Germany demand the maintenance of the centralized power of the executive committee as a means of defense against the dangers, which would otherwise become inevitable as the party grows, of the predominant influence of new and theoretically untrustworthy elements. The old leaders, it is said, must control the masses, lest these should force undesirable colleagues upon them. Hence they claim that the constituencies must not nominate parliamentary candidates without the previous approval of the party executive.

The old leaders always endeavor to harness to their own chariot the forces of those new movements which have not yet found powerful leaders, so as to obviate from the first all competition and all possibility of the formation of new and vigorous intellectual currents. In Germany, the leaders of the Socialist Party and the trade-union leaders at first looked askance at the Young Socialist movement. When, however, they perceived that this movement could not be suppressed, they hastened to place themselves at its head. There was founded for the guidance of the socialist youth a "Central Committee of Young German Workers," comprising four representatives from each of the three parties, that is to say, four from the executive of the Socialist Party, four from the general committee of trade unions, and four from the Young Socialist (the representatives of the latter being thus outnumbered by two to one).[5] The old leaders endeavor to justify the tutelage thus imposed on the Young Socialists by alleging (with more opportunist zeal than logical acuteness) the incapacity of the youthful masses, if left to their own guidance, of wisely choosing their own leaders and of exercising over these an efficient control.

We have by no means come to an end of our enumeration of the weapons at the disposal of the old leaders in their conflict with the new aspirants to power. Charlemagne effected the final subjugation of the Saxon tribal chiefs by making them counts. In this way he not only increased the brilliancy of their position, but also gave them a restricted share in his own power. This means has been practiced again and again in history, where an old ruler has wished to render harmless, insubordinate but influential chiefs, and thus to prevent a rebellion against his own authority. Oligarchies employ this stratagem with just as much success as monarchies. The feudal state of Prussia appointed to the privy council the most defiant among the leaders of its bourgeoisie. At a time when the youthful German bourgeoisie was still filled with a rebellious spirit towards the nobility and towards the traditional authority of the state, this tendency aroused much bitterness. Thus Ludwig Börne wrote in 1830: "Wherever a talented force of opposition has made itself apparent and has secured respect from those in authority, it is chained to the professorial chair, or is controlled by being harnessed to the government. If the governmental ranks are full, so that no place can be found for the new energies, a state livery is at least provided for the authors by giving them titles and orders. In other cases the dangerous elements are isolated from the people by immuring them in some noble's castle or princely court. It is for this reason that nowhere else do we find so many privy councillors

[5] "Fränkische Tagespost," anno xxxix, No. 191, Supplement 2.

as in Germany, where the courts are least inclined to take any one's advice."[6] In the Spanish elections of 1875, we learn that so great was the popular indifference that the government had matters altogether in its own hands, but in order to be secure in any event it thoughtfully selected a certain number of opposition candidates.[7] It seems that things are much the same in Spain even today.[8] These tactics are not confined to states that are still permeated by feudal conceptions. Where plutocratic rule is supreme, corruption persists unchanged, and it is only the corruptor who is different. This is plainly shown by Austin Lewis when he writes: "The public ownership contingent in politics being composed of the middle and subjugated class have neither the political ability nor the vital energy necessary for the accomplishment of the task which they have undertaken. The brains of the smaller middle class have already been bought by the greater capitalists. Talent employed in the service of the chiefs of industry and finance can command better prices than can be obtained in the uncertain struggle for economic standing which members of the middle class have to wage. The road to professional and political preferment lies through the preserves of the ruling oligarchy, whose wardens allow no one to pass, save servants in livery. Every material ambition of youth is to be gratified in the service of the oligarchy, which shows, generally, an astuteness in the selection of talent that would do credit to a bureaucrat or a Jesuit."[9]

Of late years the ruling classes in the countries under a democratic regime have hoped to impose obstacles in the way of the revolutionary labor movement by conceding posts in the ministry to its most conspicuous leaders, thus gaining control over the revolutionary impulse of the proletariat by allowing its leaders to participate in power, though cautiously and in an extremely restricted measure. The oligarchy which controls the modern democratic party has often employed the same means to tame the opposition. If the leaders of the opposition within the party are dangerous because they have a large following among the masses, and if they are at the same time few in number, the old party-leaders endeavor to hold them in check and to neutralize their influence by the

[6] Ludwig Börne, *Aus meinem Tagebuche*, Reclam, Leipzig, p. 57.
[7] *Denkwürdigkeiten des Fürsten Hohenlohe*, ed. cit., p. 376.
[8] Nicolas Salmerton y Garçia, *L'état espagnol et la Solidarité catalone*, "Le Courier Européen," iv, No. 23.
[9] Austin Lewis, *The Rise of the American Proletarian*, Charles H. Kerr & Co., Chicago, 1907, pp. 189-90.

conciliatory methods just described. The leaders of the opposition receive high offices and honors in the party, and are thus rendered innocuous—all the more so seeing that they are not admitted to the supreme offices, but are relegated to posts of the second rank which give them no notable influence, and they are without hope of one day becoming a majority. On the other hand, they divide with their ancient adversaries the serious weight of responsibility which is generated by common deliberations and manifestations, so that their activities become confounded with those of the old leaders.

In order to avoid having to divide their power with new elements, especially such as are uncongenial by tendency or mental characteristics, the old leaders tend everywhere with greater or less success to acquire the right of choosing their own colleagues, thus depriving the masses of the privilege of appointing the leaders they themselves prefer.

The path of the new aspirants to power is always beset with difficulties, bestrewn with obstacles of all kinds, which can be overcome only by the favor of the mass. Very rarely does the struggle between the old leaders and the new end in the complete defeat of the former. The result of the process is not so much a *circulation des élites* as a *réunion des élites*, an amalgam, that is to say, of the two elements. Those representing the new tendency, as long as their footing is still insecure, seek all sorts of side paths in order to avoid being overthrown by the powers-that-be. They protest that their divergence from the views of the majority is trifling, contending that they are merely the logical advocates of the ancient and tried principles of the party, and express their regret that the old leaders display a lack of true democratic feeling. Not infrequently it happens that they avert the blows directed against them by craftily creeping behind the backs of their established and powerful opponents who are about to annihilate them, solemnly declaring, when wrathful blows are directed against them, that they are in complete accord with the old leaders and approve of all their actions, so that the leaders seem to beating the air. On many occasions in the recent history of the socialist parties, the reformist minorities, in order to avoid destruction, have bowed themselves beneath the yoke of the so-called revolutionary majorities by voting (with a fine practical and tactical sense, but with an entire lack of personal pride and political loyalty) resolutions which were drafted precisely in order to condemn the political views dear to the minority. In two cases only does it sometimes happen that the relationships between the two tendencies become strained to the breaking-point. In the first place this may happen when the leaders of one of the two factions possess a profound faith in their own ideas, and are characterized at once by tactical fanaticism and theoretical irreconcilability—or, in other words, when the objective reasons which divide them from their opponents are felt with an unaccustomed force and are professed with an unwonted sincerity. In the second place it may happen when one of the parties, in consequence of offended dignity or reasonable susceptibility, finds it psychologically impossible to continue to live with the other, and to carry on within the confines of the same association a continued struggle for dominion over the masses. The party will then break up into two distinct organisms, and in each of these there will be renewed the oligarchical phenomena we have been describing.

One of the most interesting chapters in the history of the struggles between leaders deals with the measures which these leaders adopt within their own closed corporations in order to maintain discipline—that is to say, in order to preserve the cementing force of the will of the majority. In the struggle which the various groups of leaders carry on for the hegemony of the party, the concept of democracy becomes a lure which all alike employ. All means are good for the conquest and preservation of power. It is easy to see this when we read the discussions concerning the system to be employed for the appointment of the party executive. The various tendencies manifested in this connection all aim at the same end, namely, at safeguarding the dominance of some particular group. Thus in France the Guesdists, whose adherents are numerous but who control a small number only of the groups, advocate a system of proportional representation; the Jauressists, on the other hand, who are more influential in respect of groups than of members, and also the Hervéists, oppose proportional representation within the party, for they fear that this would give the Guesdists group too great a facility for the enforcement of its own special methods of action, and they propose to maintain the system of local representation or of representation by delegation.

In the American Congress, each party possesses a special committee which exercises a control over the attendance of its members at the sessions, and which on the occasion of decisive votes issues special summonses or "whips." When an interesting bill is before the house, the party committee also summons a *caucus,* that is to say, a private meeting of the parliamentary group, and this decides how the congressmen are to vote. All members of the party are bound by the decision of such a caucus. Naturally no immediate punishment is possible of those who rebel against the authority of the caucus; but at the next election the independent congressman is sure to lose his seat, for the party-managers at Washington will not fail to report to their colleagues, the bosses of the local constituency, the act of insubordination committed by the congressman concerned. The most vital of all the caucuses is that which precedes the election of the president of the congress. The ideas and sympathies of the speaker have a decisive influence upon the composition of the committees and therefore upon the whole course of legislation. For this reason his election is of fundamental importance, and is preceded for several weeks by intrigues and vote-hunting campaigns. Doubtless it is not in every case that the votes are decided in advance at a meeting of the group. Where laws of minor importance are concerned, every member of congress is free to vote as he pleases. But in times of excitement obedience is exacted, not only to the decisions of the caucus, but also to the authority of the party leaders. This last applies especially to Congress, for in the Senate the members are extremely jealous of their absolute equality. On the other hand, the caucus has an even greater importance in the case of the Senate, for here the groups are smaller and the caucus can therefore function more efficiently. The groups in Congress may number more than two hundred members, whereas those of the Senate rarely exceed fifty.[10]

The parliamentary group of the German social democracy is likewise dominated, as far as its internal structure is concerned, by a most rigorous application of the principle of subordination. The majority of the parliamentary group decides the action of all its members on the various questions submitted to the Reichstag or to the diets, exercising what is known as the *Fraktionszwang* (group coercion). No individual member has the right to independent action. Thus the parliamentary group votes as a single entity, and this not merely in questions of a distinctively socialist bearing, but also in those which are independent of socialist ideas, which each might decide according to his own personal conceptions. It was very different in the French parliament during the fratricidal struggle between the Jauressists and the Guesdists before the attainment of socialist unity in France, for at that time each

[10] Bryce, *The American Commonwealth*, abridged ed., Macmillan, New York, 1907, pp. 152-3.

deputy used to vote as he pleased. But the German example shows that liberty of opinion no longer exists where the organization demands common action and where it has some force of penetration in political life.

In certain cases, however, all these preventive measures fail of their effect. This happens when the conflict is not simply between a minority and a majority within the group, but between the group and one single member who possesses outside parliament, in certain sections of the party, the full support of the subordinate leaders. When a conflict occurs in such conditions, the deputy, though isolated, is sure of victory. The electors, in fact, usually follow with great docility the oscillations and evolutions of their parliamentary representatives, and they do this even in constituencies where socialist voters predominate. The ministers Briand, Viviani, and Millerand have been expelled from the French Socialist Party, but the former members of the socialist organizations in their constituencies have remained faithful to these leaders, resigning from the Socialist Party, and continuing as electors to give the ex-socialists their support. Analogous were the cases of John Burns in England (Battersea) and of Enrico Ferri in Italy (Mantua). It was enough in Ferri's case that at an appropriate moment he should reveal a new truth to produce immediately a collective change in the political opinions of an entire region. Having first been, with Ferri, revolutionary and irreconcilable, this region became converted in a single night, always following Ferri, to the principle of class cooperation and of participation in ministerial activity. In Germany, the party executive had to make use of all its authority in order, at the last minute, to induce the comrades of Chemnitz to withdraw their support from their deputy Max Schippel, and those of Mittweida from Otto Göhre, when these two deputies had displayed heterodox leanings.

The tendency of the deputy to set himself above his party is most plainly manifest precisely where the party is strongly organized; especially, therefore, in the modern labor parties; and within these, again, more particularly in the reformist sections. The reformist deputies, as long as they have not upon their side a majority within the party, carry on an unceasing struggle to withdraw themselves from the influence of the party, that is to say, from the mass of the workers who are organized as a party. In this period of their evolution they transfer their dependence upon the organized mass of the local socialist section of the electors of the constituency, who constitute a gray, unorganized, and more or less indifferent mass. Thus from the organized masses, who may be under the influence of their opponents within the party, they appeal to the mass of the electors, with the contention that it is to these latter alone, or at least chiefly, that they have to give an account of their political conduct. It is right to recognize that this appeal to the electorate as the body which has conferred a political mandate is frequently based upon genuinely democratic sentiments and principles. Thus, at the International Socialist Congress of London (1893), the four French socialist deputies refused to make use of the mandates which had been conferred upon them by political or corporative groups, thus defying the rules of admission to the congress. After extremely violent discussions they were ultimately admitted simply as deputies, having raised the question of principle whether an important constituency capable of returning a socialist deputy to the Chamber should not have the same rights which are granted to a local socialist or trade-union branch, especially when it is remembered that such a branch may consist of a mere handful of members. It is true that in certain circumstances a constituency inspired by socialist sentiment, even if it be not socialistically organized, constitutes a better basis, in the democratic sense, for political action than a small socialist branch whose members are mostly petty bourgeois or lawyers;[11] and even if a large local organization exists, the constituency as a whole is a better basis than a badly attended party meeting for the selection of a candidate.

From our study of the intricate struggles which proceed between the leaders of the majority and those of the minority, between the executive organs and the masses, we may draw the following essential conclusions.

Notwithstanding the youth of the international labor movement, the figures of the leaders of that movement are more imposing and more imperious than those displayed in the history of any other social class of modern times. Doubtless the labor movement furnishes certain examples of leaders who have been deposed, who have been abandoned by their adherents. Such cases are, however, rare, and only in exceptional instances do they signify that the masses have been stronger than the leaders. As a rule, they mean merely that a

[11] It is well to remind English readers that on the Continent, and especially in France and Italy, barristers play a conspicuous part in the oligarchy of socialism, corresponding with that which in England they play in the old political parties.—Translators' Note.

new leader has entered into conflict with the old, and, thanks to the support of the mass, has prevailed in the struggle, and has been able to dispossess and replace the old leader. The profit for democracy of such a substitution is practically nil.

Whenever the Catholics are in a minority, they become fervent partisans of liberty. In proof of this we need merely refer to the literature issued by the Catholics during the *Kulturkampf* under the Bismarckian regime and during the struggle between Church and State which went on a few years ago in France. In just the same way the leaders of the minority within the Socialist Party are enthusiastic advocates of liberty. They declaim against the narrowness and the authoritative methods of the dominant group, displaying in their own actions genuine democratic inclinations.

As soon as the new leaders have attained their ends, as soon as they have succeeded (in the name of the injured rights of the anonymous masses) in overthrowing the odious tyranny of their predecessors and in attaining to power in their turn, we see them undergo a transformation which renders them in every respect similar to the dethroned tyrants. Such metamorphoses as these are plainly recorded throughout history. In the life of monarchical states, an opposition which is headed by hereditary princes is rarely dangerous to the crown as an institution. In like manner, the opposition of the aspirants to leadership in a political party, directed against the persons or against the system of the old leaders, is seldom dangerous. The revolutionaries of today become the reactionaries of tomorrow.

Chapter 7

Bureaucracy. Centralizing and Decentralizing Tendencies

THE ORGANIZATION of the state needs a numerous and complicated bureaucracy. This is an important factor in the complex of forces of which the politically dominant classes avail themselves to secure their domination and to enable themselves to keep their hands upon the rudder.

The instinct of self-preservation leads the modern state to assemble and to attach to itself the greatest possible number of interests. This need of the organism of the state increases *pari passu* with an increase among the multitude, of the conviction that the contemporary social order is defective and even irrational—in a word with the increase of what the authorities are accustomed to term discontent. The state best fulfils the need for securing a large number of defenders by constituting a numerous caste of officials, of persons directly dependent upon the state. This tendency is powerfully reinforced by the tendencies of modern political economy. On the one hand, from the side of the state, there is an enormous supply of official positions. On the other hand, among the citizens, there is an even more extensive demand. This demand is stimulated by the ever-increasing precariousness in the position of the middle classes (the smaller manufacturers and traders, independent artisans, farmers, etc.) since there have come into existence expropriative capitalism on the grand scale, on the one hand, and the organized working classes on the other—for both these movements, whether they wish it or not, combine to injure the middle classes. All those whose material existence is thus threatened by modern economic developments endeavor to find safe situations for their sons, to secure for these a social position which shall shelter them from the play of economic forces. Employment under the state, with the important right to a pension which attaches to such employment, seems created expressly for their needs. The immeasurable demand for situations which results from these conditions, a demand which is always greater than the supply, creates the so-called "intellectual proletariat." The numbers of this body are subject to great fluctuations. From time to time the state, embarrassed by the increasing demand for positions in its service, is forced to open the sluices of its bureaucratic canals in order to admit thousands of new postulants and thus to transform these from dangerous adversaries into zealous defenders and partisans. There are two classes of intellectuals. One consists of those who have succeeded in securing a post at the manger of the state, whilst the other consists of those who, as Scipio Sighele puts it, have assaulted the fortress without being able to force their way in.[1] The former may be compared to an army of slaves who are always ready, in part from class egoism, in part for personal motives (the fear of losing their own situations), to undertake the defense of the state which provides them with bread. They do this whatever may be the question concerning which the state has been attacked and must therefore be regarded as the most faithful of its supporters. The latter, on the other hand, are sworn enemies of the state. They are those eternally restless spirits who lead the bourgeois opposition and in part also assume the leadership of the revolutionary parties of the proletariat. It is true that the state bureaucracy does not in general expand as rapidly as do the discontented elements of the middle class. None the less, the bureaucracy continually increases. It comes to assume the form of an endless screw. It grows ever less and less compatible with the general welfare. And yet this bureaucratic machinery remains essential. Through it alone can be satisfied the claim of the educated members of the population for secure positions. It is further a means of self-defense for the state. As the late Amilcare Puviani of the University of Perugia, the political economist to whom we are indebted for an important work upon the legend of the state, expresses it, the mechanism of bureaucracy is the outcome of a protective reaction of a right of property whose legal basis is weak, and is an antidote to the awakening of the public conscience.[2]

The political party possesses many of these traits in common with the state. Thus the party in which the circle of the *élite* is unduly restricted, or in which, in other words, the oligarchy is composed of too small a number of individuals, runs the risk of being swept away by the masses in a moment of democratic effervescence. Hence the modern party, like the modern state, endeavors to give to its own organization the widest possible base, and to attach to itself in financial bonds the largest pos-

[1] Scipio Sighele, *L'Intelligenza della Folla*, Bocca, Turin, 1903, p. 160.
[2] Amilcare Puviani, *Teoria della Illusione finanziaria*, R. Sandron, Milan-Naples-Palermo, 1903, pp. 258 et seq.

sible number of individuals. Thus arises the need for a strong bureaucracy, and these tendencies are reinforced by the increase in the tasks imposed by modern organization.

As the party bureaucracy increases, two elements which constitute the essential pillars of every socialist conception undergo an inevitable weakening: an understanding of the wider and more ideal cultural aims of socialism, and an understanding of the international multiplicity of its manifestations. Mechanism becomes an end in itself. The capacity for an accurate grasp of the peculiarities and the conditions of existence of the labor movement in other countries diminishes in proportion as the individual national organizations are fully developed. This is plain from a study of the mutual international criticisms of the socialist press. In the days of the so-called "socialism of the émigrés," the socialists devoted themselves to an elevated policy of principles, inspired by the classical criteria of internationalism. Almost every one of them was, if the term may be used, a specialist in this more general and comprehensive domain. The whole course of their lives, the brisk exchange of ideas on unoccupied evenings, the continued rubbing of shoulders between men of the most different tongues, the enforced isolation from the bourgeois world of their respective countries, and the utter impossibility of any "practical" action, all contributed to this result. But in proportion as, in their own country, paths of activity were opened for the socialists, at first for agitation and soon afterwards for positive and constructive work, the more did a recognition of the demands of the everyday life of the party divert their attention from immortal principles. Their vision gained in precision but lost in extent. The more cotton-spinners, boot and shoe operatives, or brushmakers the labor leader could gain each month for his union, the better versed he was in the tedious subtleties of insurance against accident and illness, the greater the industry he could display in the specialized question of factory inspection and of arbitration in trade disputes, the better acquainted he might be with the system of checking the amount of individual purchases in cooperative stores and with the methods for the control of the consumption of municipal gas, the more difficult was it for him to retain a general interest in the labor movement, even in the narrowest sense of this term. As the outcome of inevitable psycho-physiological laws, he could find little time and was likely to have little inclination for the study of the great problems of the philosophy of history, and all the more falsified consequently would become his judgment of international questions. At the same time he would incline more and more to regard every one as an "incompetent," an "outsider," an "unprofessional," who might wish to judge questions from some higher outlook than the purely technical; he would incline to deny the good sense and even the socialism of all who might desire to fight upon another ground and by other means than those familiar to him within his narrow sphere as a specialist. This tendency towards an exclusive and all-absorbing specialization, towards the renunciation of all far-reaching outlooks, is a general characteristic of modern evolution. With the continuous increase in the acquirements of scientific research, the polyhistor is becoming extinct. His place is taken by the writer of monographs. The universal zoologist no longer exists, and we have instead ornithologists and entomologists; and indeed the last become further subdivided into lepidopterists, coleopterists, myrmecologists.

To the same of the "non-commissioned officers" who occupy the inferior grades of the party bureaucracy may be aptly applied what Alfred Weber said of bureaucracy in general at the congress of the *Verein für Sozialpolitik* held in Vienna in 1909. Bureaucracy is the sworn enemy of individual liberty, and of all bold initiative in matters of internal policy. The dependence upon superior authorities characteristic of the average employee suppresses individuality and gives to the society in which employees predominate a narrow petty-bourgeois and philistine stamp. The bureaucratic spirit corrupts character and engenders moral poverty. In every bureaucracy we may observe place-hunting, a mania for promotion, and obsequiousness towards those upon whom promotion depends; there is arrogance towards inferiors and servility towards superiors. Wolfgang Heine, who in the German Socialist Party is one of the boldest defenders of the personal and intellectual liberty of the members, who is always in the breach to denounce "the tendency to bureaucracy and the suppression of individuality," goes so far, in his struggle against the socialist bureaucracy, as to refer to the awful example of the Prussian state. It is true, he says, that Prussia is governed in accordance with homogeneous principles and by a bureaucracy which must be considered as a model of its kind; but it is no less true that the Prussian state, precisely because of its bureaucratic characteristics, and notwithstanding its external successes, is essentially retrogressive. If Prussia does produce any distinguished personalities, it is unable to tolerate their existence, so that

Prussian politics tends more and more to degenerate into a spiritless and mechanical regime, displaying a lively hostility to all true progress.[3] We may even say that the more conspicuously a bureaucracy is distinguished by its zeal, by its sense of duty, and by its devotion, the more also will it show itself to be petty, narrow, rigid, and illiberal.

Like every centralizing system, bureaucracy finds its justification in the fact of experience that a certain administrative unity is essential to the rapid and efficient conduct of affairs. A great many functions, such as the carrying out of important statistical inquiries, can never be satisfactorily effected in a federal system.

The outward form of the dominion exercised by the leaders over the rank and file of the socialist party has undergone numerous changes *pari passu* with changes in the historical evolution of the labor movement.

In Germany, the authority of the leaders, in conformity with the characteristics of the nation and with the insufficient education of the masses, was at first displayed in a monarchical form; there was a dictatorship. The first labor organization on German soil was the *Allgemeiner Deutscher Arbeiterverein* of Ferdinand Lassalle. This organization was founded in 1873 and lasted until 1875, when it became fused with the internationalist and Marxist section of German socialism, the "Eisenachers." The personal creation of a man of extraordinary force of character, it received even in its smallest details the stamp of his personality. It has been contended that Lassalle's association was founded upon the model of the *Nationalverein*, a German national league which was extremely influential at that epoch. This may be true in respect of the base of the Arbeiterverein, but is certainly not true of its summit. The Arbeiterverein, like the Nationalverein, was a unitary society whose members were dispersed throughout Germany and did not form any properly organized local branches. The membership was not local but national, each member being directly dependent upon the central organization. But whereas in the Nationalverein the central executive was a committee of several members, the Arbeiterverein was autocratically ruled by a single individual, Ferdinand Lassalle, who exercised, as did his successor Johann Baptist von Schweitzer, as president of the party of German workers, a power comparable with that of the doge of the Venetian Republic, and indeed a power

[3] Wolfgang Heine, *Demokratische Randbemerkungen zum Fall Göhre*, "Soz. Monatsh.," viii (x), fasc. 4.

even more unrestricted, since the president's power was not, as was that of the doge, subject to any kind of control through oligarchical institutions. The president was an absolute monarch, and at his own discretion nominated his subordinate officials, his plenipotentiaries, and even his successor. He commanded, and it was for the others to obey. This structure of the organization was not the outcome merely of the personal qualities of Lassalle, of his insatiable greed for power, and of that egocentric character which made him, despite his genius, so poor a judge of men; it corresponded also to his theoretical view of the aim of all party organization. In his famous speech at Ronsdorf he said: "Wherever I have been I have heard from the workers expressions of opinion which may be summarized as follows: 'We must forge our wills into a single hammer, and place this hammer in the hands of a man in whose intelligence, characters, and, good-will we have the necessary confidence, so that he can use this hammer to strike with!' . . . The two contrasts which our statesmen have hitherto believed incapable of being united, freedom and authority, whose union they have regarded as the philosopher's stone—these contrasts are most intimately united in our Verein, which thus represents in miniature the coming social order!" Thus in the eyes of the president his dictatorship was not simply a sad necessity temporarily forced upon a fighting organization, but dictatorship was the ultimate aim of the labor movement. In the days of Lassalle, the labor movement in Germany was still weak, and, like a little boy, was still urgently in need of paternal guidance. When the father came to die he made testamentary arrangements for the provision of a guardian (for the German labor movement could still be an object of testamentary depositions). After Lassalle's death, the decisive executive power, the quintessence (if the term be permitted) of the structure of the young labor movement, continued to rest at the most absolute disposal of a single individual, Schweitzer. This authoritative tendency was an outcome, not so much of the historical necessity of the moment, as of the traditions and of the racial peculiarities of the German stock. With the lapse of time this characteristic has been notably attentuated by theoretical and practical democracy, and by the varying necessities of the case; above all by the appearance of a typically southern socialism, less rigid than that of Prussia and of Saxony, and jealous of its own autonomy. But the tendency has not disappeared, nor can it disappear.

Whilst there was thus forming in Germany the massive

organization of the followers of Lassalle, the leaders of the International Association adopted a different form of organization. The International Working-men's Association was characterized by mutual jealousy on the part of the various national sections, and this was a potent obstacle in the way of any tendency towards dictatorship. Thus there came into existence in London the General Council, the supreme authority of the International, consisting of a handful of members belonging to the different countries represented in the organization. But the powers of this executive were in many respects hardly less restricted than those of the president of the Allgemeiner Deutscher Arbeiterverein. The General Council forbade the associations which were affiliated to it to elect presidents, regarding this as contrary to democratic principles. Yet as far as concerned itself, it proudly asserted, through the mouth of the most conspicuous among its members, that the working class had now discovered a "common leadership."[4] It nominated from among its own members the officers necessary for the general conduct of its business, such as the treasurer, the general secretary, and the corresponding secretaries for the different countries, nor did it hesitate on occasions, to allot several offices to the same individual. Engels, though a German, was for some time secretary for four different countries —Spain, Italy, Portugal, and Denmark.[5] It may be added that the secretariat carried with it important prerogatives, such as the right of recognizing newly constituted sections, the right to grant or refuse pecuniary subsidies, and the adjustment of disputes among the comrades. It is unquestionable that for several years the General Council was subject, in respect of all its most significant practical and theoretical manifestations, to the iron will of one single man, Karl Marx. The conflict in the General Council between the oligarchy *de jure* and the monarchy *de facto* was the inner cause of the rapid decline of the Old International. The General Council and especially Marx were accused of being the negation of socialism because, it was said, in their disastrous greed for power, they had introduced the principle of authority into the politics of the workers.[6] At first these accusations were directed from without, coming

[4] (Marx), *L'Alliance de la Démocratie Socialiste et l'Association Int. des Travailleurs,* Rapports et Documents, London-Hamburg, 1873, p. 25.

[5] Letter from F. Engels to Sorge, March 17, 1872 (*Briefe u. Auszüge aus Briefen von Joh. Phil. Becker, Jos. Dietzgen, Fried. Engels, Karl Marx, u. A. an F. A. Sorge u. A.,* Dietz Nachf., Stuttgart, 1906, p. 54).

[6] James Guillaume, *L'Internationale, Documents et Souvenirs,* Cornély, Paris, 1907, vol. ii.

from the groups that were not represented on the General Council: the accusers were Bakunin, the Italians, and the Jurassians. The General Council, however, easily got the upper hand. At The Hague congress in 1872, the "authoritarians," making use of means characteristic of their own tendencies (the hunting of votes, the calling of the congress in a town which was little accessible to some of the opponents and quite inaccessible to others),[7] obtained a complete victory over the anti-authoritarians. Before long, however, voices were raised within the Council itself to censure the spirit of the autocracy. Marx was abandoned by most of his old friends. The French Blanquists ostentatiously separated themselves from him when he had arbitrarily transferred the General Council to New York. The two influential leaders of the English trade unions who were members of the General Council, Odger and Lucraft, quarreled with Marx because they had not been consulted about the manifesto in favor of the Paris Commune to which their signatures were attached. The German refugees in England, Jung and Eccarius, declared that it was impossible to work with persons as dictatorial as Marx and Engels. Thus the oligarchs destroyed the larval monarchy.

In 1889 the so-called New International was founded. The socialists parties of the various countries agreed to undertake common deliberations, and to meet from time to time in congresses for this purpose. Therewith the "idea of internationalism" (to quote a phrase employed by Jaeckh) underwent a transformation. The Old International had worked along the lines of the greatest possible centralization of the international proletariat, "so that it might be possible, at any place at which the economic class-struggle became especially active, to throw there immediately into the scale the organized power of the working class."[8] The New International, on the other hand, took the form of an extremely lax system, a union of elements which were strangers one to another; these elements were national organizations of a very rigid form, each confined

[7] *Idem*, p. 327; cf. also a letter from Marx to Sorge, dated London, June 21, 1872, in which Marx begs Sorge to send him a number of blank voting cards for certain friends in America whom he mentions by name (*Briefe u. Auszüge aus Briefen*, ed. cit., p. 33).—The locale of the congress was a convenient one for the English, the French, and the Germans, who were on the whole favorable to the General Council, but extremely inconvenient for the Swiss, the Spaniards, and the Italians, who were on the side of Bakunin. Bakunin himself, who was living in Switzerland, was unable to attend the congress, for to reach The Hague he must have crossed Germany or France, and in both these countries he was liable to immediate arrest.

[8] Cf. Gustav Jaeckh, *Die Internationale*, Leipz. Buchdr. Akt. Ges., Leipzig, 1904, p. 218.

within the limits of its own state. In other words, the New International is a confederation of autonomous states, and lacks any unitary and homogeneous organization. The Old International was an individual dictatorship, masquerading as an oligarchy. The New International may be compared to the old States General of the Netherlands; it is a federal republic, consisting of several independent oligarchies. The General Council of London was all-powerful. The modern Secrétariat Socialiste International, whose seat is in Brussels, is nothing but an office for the exchange of letters, devoid of all authority. It is true that the international socialist congresses have sometimes furnished an opportunity for thoroughly self-conscious and vigorous national oligarchies to attempt usurpations in the international field. Thus, in particular, the German social democracy, when forced upon the defensive at the Stuttgart congress of 1907, endeavored, and not without success, to impose upon other socialist parties its own particular tactics, the verbal revolutionarism which had originated in the peculiar conditions of Germany.[9] The international unification of tactics has always been limited by the varying needs of the different national oligarchies. In other words, whilst national supremacies are still possible in the contemporary socialist International, it is no longer possible for the socialist party of one country to exercise a true hegemony over the other national parties. The dread of being dominated increases in each national party in proportion as it becomes firmly established, consolidating its own existence and rendering itself independent of other socialist parties. International concentration is checked by the competition of the various national concentrations. Each national party stands on guard to prevent the others from extending their sphere of influence.[10] The result is that the international efficiency of the resolutions voted at the international congresses is almost insignificant. At the International Socialist Congress of Amsterdam, in 1904, the Belgian Anseele made it clear that he would not regard himself as bound by an international vote forbidding socialists to participate in bourgeois governments.[11] Thus, again, Vollmar, with the approval

[9] Cf. R. Michels, *Die deutsche Sozialdemokratie im Internationalen Verbande*, "Arch. für Sozialwiss.," anno 1907). This is a detailed study of the conditions of fact and the complex of causes which rendered it possible for the German party to exercise such a pressure upon the other parties in the International; it deals also with the subsequent decline of its hegemony.

[10] Eduard Bernstein expressed himself similarly as long ago as 1893. Cf. *Zur Geschichte u. Theorie des Sozialismus*, Edelheim, Berlin-Berne, 1901, p. 143.

[11] Cf. speech by Eduard Anseele, *Protokoll des internat. Soz. Congress, 1904*, "Vorwärts," Berlin, 1904, pp. 47–9.

of the Germans, speaking at the International Socialist Congress at Stuttgart in 1907, repudiated any interference on the part of the French in the military policy of the German socialists, protesting in advance against any international resolution regulating the conduct of the socialists of all countries in case of war.[12] Considered from close at hand the international socialist congresses present an aspect similar to that of the minor German principalities of the eighteenth century, consisting of nobles, ecclesiastics, and a few burgomasters, assemblies whose chief preoccupation was to avoid yielding to the prince a jot of their "freedoms," that is to say of their peculiar privileges. In just the same way, the various national socialist parties, in their international congresses, defend with the most jealous care all their prerogatives and their national particularism, being all determined to yield not an inch of ground in favor of His Majesty the International.

The national oligarchies are willing to recognize the authority of international resolutions only when by an appeal to the authority of the International they can quell a troublesome faction in their own party. Sometimes the leaders of the minority secure an international bull to authenticate the purity of their socialist sentiments as contrasted with the majority, whom they accuse of heresy. Sometimes, on the other hand, it is the leaders of the majority who endeavor, on the international field, to gain a victory over the leaders of the minority, whom they have been unable to subdue within the limits of their national organization. A typical example of the former case is furnished by the action of the Guesdist minority, at the congress of Amsterdam in 1904, which endeavored to discredit in the opinion of the International the ideas of their great cousin Jaurès in matters of internal policy. The maneuver proved effective, for the Guesdists succeeded in attaching Jaurès to their chariot, and in holding him prisoner within the serried ranks of the unified French party. An example of the second mode of action is afforded by the conduct of the Italian and German Socialist Parties in appealing to the decisions of the international congresses (Paris, 1889; Zurich, 1893; London, 1895) in order to get rid of their anti-parliamentary and anarchist factions.

Side by side with this international decentralization, we see today a vigorous national centralization. Certain limitations, however, must be imposed on this generalization.

12 Cf. speech by George von Vollmar, *Protokoll des internat. Soz. Congress, 1907*, "Vorwärts," Berlin, 1907, p. 93.

In the modern labor movement, within the limits of the national organizations, we see decentralizing as well as centralizing tendencies at work. The idea of decentralization makes continuous progress, together with a revolt against the supreme authority of the central executive. But it would be a serious error to imagine that such centrifugal movements are the outcome of the democratic tendencies of the masses, or that these are ripe for independence. Their causation is really of an opposite character. The decentralization is the work of a compact minority of leaders who, when forced to subordinate themselves in the central executive of the party as a whole, prefer to withdraw to their own local spheres of action (minor state, province, or commune). A group of leaders which finds itself in a minority has no love for strong national centralization. Being unable to rule the whole country, it prefers to rule at home, considering it better to reign in hell than serve in heaven. Vollmar, for example, who in his own land possesses so great an influence that he has been called the uncrowned king of Bavaria, cannot consent to play second fiddle in the German national organization. He would rather be first in Munich than second in Berlin!

The rallying cry of the majority is centralization, while that of the minority is autonomy. Those of the minority, in order to gain their ends, are forced to carry on a struggle which often assumes the aspect of a genuine fight for liberty, and this is reflected in the terminology of the leaders, who declare themselves to be waging war against the new tyranny. When the leaders of the minority feel themselves exceptionally strong, they push their audacity to the point of attempting to deny the right to existence of the majority, as impersonated in the central executive. At the Italian Socialist Congress held at Imola in 1902, the leader of the Italian reformists, Filippo Turati, joined with his friends in putting forward a formal proposal to suppress the central executive. It was necessary, he said, to substitute for this obsolete, dictatorial, and decrepit institution the complete autonomy of the local organizations, or at least to replace it by a purely administrative and executive organism consisting of three specialist employees. He added that it was a form of jacobinism to wish to govern the whole party from above. The opponents of this democratic conception rejoined with an effective argument when they pointed out that if the central executive were abolished, the parliamentary deputies would remain the sole and uncontrolled masters of the party. Consequently, whenever it became necessary to take action upon some urgent question, when time was lacking to make a direct reference to the party as a whole, it would be the parliamentary group, deriving its authority not from the party but from the electorate, which would decide upon the line of conduct to be pursued. If we accept the hypothesis that a true democracy may exist within the party, the tendency to the subdivision of powers is unquestionably anti-democratic, while centralization is, on the other hand, the best way of giving incontestable validity to the will of the masses. From this point of view, Enrico Ferri was perfectly right when he told the reformists that the proposed abolition of the central executive would be equivalent to the suppression of the sovereignty of the members in general, since the executive is the legitimate expression of the mass-will, and derives its rights from the party congresses.

This decentralizing movement which manifests itself within the various national socialist parties does not conflict with the essential principle of oligarchy. The minority in opposition, which has been thus careful to withdraw itself from the control of the central executive, proceeds within its own sphere of dominion to constitute itself into a centralized power no less unrestricted than the one against which it has been fighting. Thus such movements as we have been considering represent no more than an attempt to effect a partition of authority, and to split up the great oligarchies into a number of smaller oligarchies. In France and in Italy every socialist deputy endeavors to become as independent as possible of the central executive of his party, making himself supreme in his local organization. A similar process may be observed in Germany, where the persistence of numerous petty states, mutually independent, and each governed by its own parliament, has hitherto prevented the constitutional and administrative unification of the party throughout the country, and has greatly favored decentralizing tendencies. In consequence of this state of affairs we find in Germany that all the parties in the separate states, from Bavaria to Hesse, desire autonomy, independence of the central executive in Berlin. But this does not prevent each one of them from exercising a centralized authority within its own domain.

The decentralizing currents in German Socialism, and more particularly those of the German south, are adverse to centralization only as far as concerns the central executive of Berlin, whilst within their own spheres they resist federalism with the utmost emphasis. Their opposition to the centralization in Berlin takes the form of a desire in the local parties to retain financial independence of the central treasury. At the Schweinfurt congress in 1906, Ehrhart, socialist deputy to the Bavarian diet, said: "It comes to this, the central executive has the management of the money which goes to Berlin, but it is for us to decide how we shall spend the money which is kept here."[13] Hugo Lindenmann of Würtemberg, one of the most ardent adversaries of the Prussianization of the party and an advocate of federalism has declared that it is undesirable to deplete the local finances of the South German states in favor of the central treasury in Berlin, where the executive is always inclined to a policy of hoarding money for its own sake.

The struggles within the modern democratic parties over this problem of centralization versus decentralization are of great scientific importance from several points of view. It would be wrong to deny that the advocates of both tendencies bring forward a notable array of theoretical considerations, and occasionally make valid appeals to moral conceptions. We have, however, to disabuse our minds of the idea that the struggle is really one for or against oligarchy, for or against popular sovereignty or the sovereignty of the party masses. The tendency to decentralization of the party rule, the opposition to international centralization (to the far-reaching authority of the international bureaux, committees, congresses), or to national centralization (to the authority of the party executives), has nothing to do with the desire for more individual liberty.

The democratic tendency may be justified by practical reasons, and in particular by differences in the economic or social situation of the working classes in the various districts, or by other local peculiarities. The tendencies to local, provincial, or regional autonomy are in fact the outcome of effective and ineradicable differences of environment. In Germany, the socialists of the south feel themselves to be divided as by an ocean from their comrades of the north. They claim the rights of self-government and participation in government because they live in countries where parliamentarism already possesses a glorious history dating from more than a century back, whereas Prussia is still thoroughly imbued with the authoritarian and feudal spirit. They claim it also because in the south agriculture is carried on mainly under a system of petty proprietorship, whereas in the central and eastern provinces of Germany large landed estates predominate. The result is that class differences, with their consequent differences of mental out-

[13] "Volksstimme" of Frankfort, March 6, 1906.

look, are less conspicuous in the south than in the north, so that the opposition to the socialists is of a different character in the two regions. In the struggles between the northern and the southern leaders within the Socialist Party, struggles which are often lively and at times extremely violent, each section levels the same accusation against the other, declaring it to belong to a country in which civilization is comparatively backward and where theoretical conceptions are obsolete. The socialists of the north contend that those of the south are still living in a petty bourgeois, pacific, countrified environment, whereas they themselves, in the land of large-scale manufacture, represent the future. The men of the south proudly reply that it is they who live in conditions to which their comrades of the north have yet to attain, by abolishing the large landed estates and by suppressing the class of junkers.

Similar environmental differences divide the Italian socialists. Here also the socialists of the south demand complete autonomy, contending that the theoretical basis of socialism in the south is different from that in the north. They say that in the former kingdom of Naples the actual conditions of production and distribution are not such as to establish a sharp distinction between the two classes which according to classical socialism exist everywhere in strife. Consequently the introduction into this region of the Marxist revolutionary propaganda would marshal against socialism, not the great and medium landowners alone, but also the petty proprietors. Whilst the socialists of the plain of the Po fiercely oppose a duty upon grain because this would increase the cost of living for the laboring masses agglomerated in great cities, the socialists of the south have on several occasions declared in favor of the existing protectionist system, because its suppression would bring about a crisis in production in a region where proletarians and employers all alike live by agriculture. Again, in the north, where manufacturing industry is dominant, the socialists disapproved of the Tripolitan campaign, whereas in the south, where they are for the most part agriculturists, an enthusiastic sentiment in favor of territorial expansion prevailed. In addition to these reasons, which may be termed intrinsic because they derive from the objective differences between the north and the south, we find that an opposition between the socialists of the two areas arises from the attitude of the government in the respective regions. The Italian government is double-faced, being liberal in the north, but often very much the reverse in the south, for here it is largely in the hands of the local coteries which, in a region where the voters are scattered, become the sole arbiters in times of election. In the year 1902, when Giolitti was in power, this duplex attitude of the government gave rise to a serious difference within the Socialist Party, for the socialists of the north did not disguise their ardent desire to participate in government, while those of the south (although their tendencies were rather reformist than revolutionary) attacked the government fiercely.

Thus, as has been shown at length, the various tendencies towards decentralization which manifest themselves in almost all the national parties, while they suffice to prevent the formation of a single gigantic oligarchy, result merely in the creation of a number of smaller oligarchies, each of which is no less powerful within its own sphere. The dominance of oligarchy in party life remains unchallenged.

PART THREE/THE EXERCISE OF POWER AND ITS PSYCHOLOGICAL REACTION UPON THE LEADERS

Chapter 1

Psychological Metamorphosis of the Leaders

THE APATHY of the masses and their need for guidance has as its counterpart in the leaders a natural greed for power. Thus the development of the democratic oligarchy is accelerated by the general characteristics of human nature. What was initiated by the need for organization, administration, and strategy is completed by psychological determinism.

The average leader of the working-class parties is morally not lower, but on the whole higher, in quality than the average leaders of the other parties. This has sometimes been unreservedly admitted by the declared adversaries of socialism. Yet it cannot be denied that the permanent exercise of leadership exerts upon the moral character of the leaders an influence which is essentially pernicious. Yet this also, from a certain point of view, is perhaps good. The bitter words which Labruyère applied to the great men of the court of Louis XIV, that the imitative mania and veneration exhibited towards them by the masses would have grown into an absolute idolatry, if it had occurred to any of them to be simply good men as well as great ones—these words, *mutatis mutandis*, could be applied with equal truth to the leaders of the vast democratic movements of our own days.[1]

In the majority of instances, and above all at the opening of his career, the leader is sincerely convinced of the excellence of the principles he advocates. Le Bon writes with good reason: "The leader has usually been at one time the led. He himself has been hynotized by the idea of which he afterwards becomes the apostate."[2] In many cases the leader, at first no more than a single molecule of the mass, has become detached from this involuntarily, without asking whither his instinctive action was leading him, without any personal motive whatever. He has been pushed forward by a clearer vision, by a profounder sentiment, and by a more ardent desire for the general good; he has been inspired by the elasticity and seri-

[1] Labruyère, *Caractères*, Penaud, Paris, p. 156.

[2] Trans. from Gustave le Bon, *Psychologie des Foules*, ed. cit., p. 106. Cf. also S. G. Hobson, *Boodle and Cant*, "International Socialist Review," Chicago, 1902, ii, No. 8, p. 585.

ousness of his character and by his warm sympathy for his fellows. It is obvious that this will be true above all where the leader does not find already established a solid organization capable of offering remunerative employment, but where his first step must be to found his own party. But this must not be taken to mean that wherever a well-organized party already exists the leader seeks at the outset to gratify his personal interests.

It is by no means always by deliberate desire that people become officers of the masses. Using familiar French terms we may express this more clearly by saying that not every *arrivé* was at first an *arriviste*. But he who has once attained to power will not readily be induced to return to the comparatively obscure position which he formerly occupied. The abandonment of a public position obtained at the cost of great efforts and after many years of struggle is a luxury which only a "grand seigneur" or a man exceptionally endowed with the spirit of self-sacrifice can afford. Such self-denial is too hard for the average man.

The consciousness of power always produces vanity, an undue belief in personal greatness. The desire to dominate, for good or for evil, is universal.[3] These are elementary psychological facts. In the leader, the consciousness of his personal worth, and of the need which the mass feels for guidance, combine to induce in his mind a recognition of his own superiority (real or supposed), and awake, in addition, that spirit of command which exists in the germ in every man born of woman. We see from this that every human power seeks to enlarge its prerogatives. He who has acquired power will almost always endeavor to consolidate it and to extend it, to multiply the ramparts which defend his position, and to withdraw himself from the control of the masses. Bakunin, the founder of anarchizing socialism, contended that the possession of power transformed into a tyrant even the most devoted friend of liberty.[4] It is certain that the exercise of power produces a profound and ineffaceable change in the character. This is admirably described by Alphonse Daudet when he writes: "Quickly enough, if it involves politics, our natures turn their worst side: enthusiasm becomes hypocrisy; eloquence, verbosity and humbug; slight scepticism, fraud; love

[3] "Love of power, as well as of independence and freedom, are the inherent human passions." (Holbach, *Systèmes sociales, ou Principes naturelles de la Morale et de la Politique*, Niogret, Paris, 1822, vol. i, p. 196).

[4] Bakunin, *Il Socialismo e Mazzini*, F. Serantoni, Rome-Florence, 1905, p. 22.

of light, lust for gain and luxury at any price; sociability and the need to please turn into laxity, weakness, and cant."[5] To retain their influence over the masses the leaders study men, note their weaknesses and their passions, and endeavor to turn these to their own advantage.

When the leaders are not persons of means and when they have no other source of income, they hold firmly to their positions for economic reasons, coming to regard the functions they exercise as theirs by inalienable right. Especially is this true of manual workers who, since becoming leaders, have lost their aptitude for their former occupation. For them, the loss of their positions would be a financial disaster, and in most cases it would be altogether impossible for them to return to their old way of life. They have been spoiled for any other work than that of propaganda. Their hands have lost the callosities of the manual toiler, and are likely to suffer only from writer's cramp.

Those leaders, again, who are refugees from the bourgeoisie are used up after having devoted a few years to the service of the Socialist Party. It was as youthful enthusiasts that they joined the organized workers and soon attained to dominant positions. The life they then had to lead, however great may have been its advantages in certain respects, was one full of fatigue and hardship, and, like all careers in which fame can be acquired, was extremely exhausting to the nervous system. Such men grow old before their time. What are they to do? They have become estranged from their original profession, which is altogether out of relation with their chosen vocation of professional politician. A barrister, indeed, can continue to practice his profession, and may even devote almost all his time to it, without being forced to abandon the party. The political struggle and the life of the lawyer have more than one point of contact, for is not the political struggle a continuous act of advocacy? The barrister who plays a leading part in public life will find many opportunities for the gratification of his love of oratory and argument, and will have no lack of chances for the display of the power of his lungs and the expressiveness of his gestures. It is very different with men of science. These, if they plan an active part in the life of the party, be it as journalists, as propagandists, or as parliamentary deputies, find that their scientific faculties undergo a slow but progressive atrophy. Having become absorbed in the daily political round, they are dead for their discipline, for they no longer have time for the

[5] Trans. from Léon Daudet, *Alphonse Daudet*, ed. cit., p. 179.

serious study of scientific problems and for the continuous development of their intellectual faculties.

There are, however, additional reasons for the mental transformation which the leaders undergo as the years pass.

As far as concerns the leaders of bourgeois origin in the working-class parties, it may be said that they have adhered to the cause of the proletariat either on moral grounds, or from enthusiasm, or from scientific conviction. They crossed the Rubicon when they were still young students, still full of optimism and juvenile ardor. Having gone over to the other side of the barricade to lead the enemies of the class from which they sprang, they have fought and worked, now suffering defeats and now gaining victories. Youth has fled; their best years have been passed in the service of the party or of the ideal. They are ageing, and with the passing of youth, their ideals have also passed, dispersed by the contrarieties of daily struggles, often, too, expelled by newly acquired experiences which conflict with the old beliefs. Thus it has come to pass that many of the leaders are inwardly estranged from the essential content of socialism. Some of them carry on a difficult internal struggle against their own scepticism; others have returned, consciously or unconsciously, to the ideals of their presocialist youth.

Yet for those who have been thus disillusioned, no backward path is open. They are enchained by their own past. They have a family, and this family must be fed. Moreover, regard for their political good name makes them feel it essential to persevere in the old round. They thus remain outwardly faithful to the cause to which they have sacrificed the best years of their life. But, renouncing idealism, they have become opportunists. These former believers, these sometime altruists, whose fervent hearts aspired only to give themselves freely, have been transformed into sceptics and egoists whose actions are guided solely by cold calculation.

As we have previously seen, these new elements do not join the party with the declared or even the subconscious aim of attaining one day to leadership; their only motives have been the spirit of sacrifice and the love of battle. Visionaries, they see a brother in every comrade and a step towards the ideal in every party meeting. Since, however, in virtue of their superiority (in part congenital and in part acquired), they have become leaders, they are in the course of years enslaved by all the appetites which arise from the possession of power, and in the end are not to be distinguished from those among their colleagues who became socialists from ambition, from those who have from the first deliberately regarded the masses as no more than an instrument which they might utilize towards the attainment of their own personal ambitions.

It cannot be denied that the factor of individuality plays its part in all this, for different individualities react differently to the same environment. Just as women and girls in similar erotic situations act differently in accordance with their varying degrees of congenital sexual irritability and with the differences that have been induced in them by moral education, remaining immaculate, becoming demi-vierges, or yielding to advances, so also the specific qualities of the leaders, in so far as these are acquired and not immanent, manifest themselves differently in different individuals in face of the numerous temptations to which they are exposed in party life. The sense of satiety which arises in those who have attained their end varies greatly in intensity from person to person. There are similar variations in adaptability to a new and anti-democratic environment, or to an environment hostile to the ideas which the individual has at heart. Some socialists, for instance, are so greatly intimidated by the parliamentary milieu that they are ashamed in that milieu to make use of the expressions "class struggle" and "collectivism," although it is to the unwearying insistence upon these ideas that they owe their present position. Others among their comrades find amid all the circumstances of their new life that right feeling and that old courage of conviction which cannot be prescribed by any formal rules. It is absurd to maintain, as does Giuseppe Prezzolini, that in the parliamentary atmosphere it is as impossible for a deputy to preserve his socialist purity as it would be for a Joseph to remain chaste while frequently visiting brothels.[6] Such a view is false, if only for the reason that here, as in all social phenomena, we have to consider the personal as well as the environmental factor. It is nevertheless true that in the course of party evolution, as the led becomes a subordinate leader, and from that a leader of the first rank, he himself undergoes a mental evolution, which often effects a complete transformation in his personality. When this happens, the leader often sees in his own transformation nothing more than a reflex of a transformation in the surrounding world. The times have changed, he tells us, and consequently a new tactic and a new theory are necessary. A greater maturity of judgment corresponds to the greater maturity of the new age. The reformist and revisionist theory in

[6] G. Prezzolini, *La Teoria sindacalista*, Perrella, Naples, 1909, p. 65.

the International Socialist Party is largely the outcome of the psychological need to furnish an explanation and an excuse for the metamorphosis which has taken place in the leaders. A few years ago, one of the leaders of the Italian clericals, after declaring that triumphant reformism, having an evolutionary and legalist character, was in these respects preferable to strict syndicalism, went on to say that in his view the basis of reformist socialism was still the materialist conception of man, of life, and of history, but further corrupted by contact with the utilitarian and Epicurean spirit of the free-thinking bourgeoisie, and that it was consequently even more profoundly anti-Christian than the ideas of the ultra-revolutionists.[7] There is a kernel of truth in this idea. However much we are forced to recognize that reformism sometimes manifests itself as a sane rebellion against the *apriorism* of orthodox Marxist dogma, and as a scientific reaction against the phraseology of pseudo-revolutionary stump-orators, it is nevertheless incontestable that reformism has a logical and causal connection with the insipid and blasé sociolism and with the decadent tendencies which are so plainly manifest in a large section of the modern bourgeois literary world. In many instances, in fact, reformism is no more than the theoretical expression of the scepticism of the disillusioned, of the outwearied, of those who have lost their faith; it is the socialism of nonsocialists with a socialist past.

It is above all the sudden passage from opposition to participation in power which exercises a powerful influence on the mentality of the leaders. It is evident that in a period of proscriptions and persecutions of the new doctrine and its advocates on the part of society and of the state, the morality of the party leaders will maintain itself at a much higher level than in a period of triumph and of peace, if only for the reason that in the former conditions those of egoistic temperament and those inspired by narrow personal ambition will hold aloof from the party since they have no desire for the martyr's crown. These considerations apply, not merely to the old leaders who have been members of the party during its days of tribulation, and whose qualities, if not completely corrupted by the sun of governmental favor (so as to lead them to abandon the cause of the proletariat), are yet so greatly changed as to render them almost unrecognizable by the masses; but it is equally true of the new leaders who do not put in an appear-

[7] Filippo Media, *Il Partito socialista in Italia dall' Internazionale al Riformismo*, Lib. ed. Florentina, Florence, 1909, p. 46.

ance until the sun has begun to shine upon the party. As long as the struggle on behalf of the oppressed brings to those engaged in it nothing more than a crown of thorns, those members of the bourgeoisie who adhere to socialism must fulfil functions in the party exacting great personal disinterestedness. Bourgeois adherents do not become a danger to socialism until the labor movement, abandoning its principles, enters the slippery paths of a policy of compromise. At the international congress of Amsterdam, Bebel exclaimed with perfect truth, in answer to Jaurès: "When a socialist party forms an alliance with a section of the bourgeoisie, and institutes a policy of cooperation with the government, not only does it repel its own best militants, driving them into the ranks of the anarchists, or into isolated action, but it also attracts to itself a swarm of bourgeois of very dubious value."[8] In Italy, during the period of persecutions, all scientific investigators bore striking witness to the high moral qualities of the socialist leaders. No sooner, however, had the Socialist Party (towards 1900) begun to display friendship for the government than voices were heard on all hands deploring a deterioration in the composition of the party, and denouncing the numerous elements entering the party simply because they regarded it as the best means by which they could secure a share in the loaves and fishes of public administration.[9] Wherever the socialists have gained control of the municipalities, wherever they run peoples' banks and distributive cooperative societies, wherever they have remunerative posts at their disposal, we cannot fail to observe a notable decline in their moral level, and to see that the ignorant and the self-seeking now constitute the majority among them.

[8] From the report in "Het Volk," v, No. 1341. In the German *Protokoll* (which, be it remarked in passing, is extremely inadequate) this passage is not reported. Bebel's observation is in flat contradiction with what he has frequently said in the Reichstag, that in his view the carrying of socialism into effect after the victory would be greatly facilitated by the inevitable adhesion to the various branches of the new administration of numerous competent elements from the official bureaucracy. (Cf. August Bebel, *Zukunftstaat und Sozialdemokratie*, p. 13; speech in Reichstag, February 3, 1893.)

[9] Cf. R. Michels, *Il Proletariato e la Borghesia, etc.*, ed. cit., p. 348; Romeo Soldi, *Die politische Lage in Italien*, "Neue Zeit," xxi, No. 30, p. 116; Giovanni Lerda, *Sull' Organizzazione politica del Partito socialista italiano,* a report to the Italian socialist congress of 1902, Coop. Tip.-Ed., Imola, 1902, p. 10; Filippo Turati, *Il Partito socialista e l'attuale Momento politico,* "Critica Sociale," Milan, 3rd ed., 1901.

Chapter 2

Bonapartist Ideology

NAPOLEON I, as head of the state, desired to be regarded as the chosen of the people. In his public activities, the emperor boasted that he owed his power to the French people alone. After the battle of the Pyramids, when his glory began to attain its acme, the general imperiously demanded that there should be conferred on him the title of *premier représentant du peuple*, although hitherto the style of "popular representative" had been exclusively reserved for members of the legislative bodies.[1] Later, when by a plebiscite he had been raised to the throne of France, he declared that he considered his power to repose exclusively upon the masses.[2] The Bonapartist interpretation of popular sovereignty was a personal dictatorship conferred by the people in accordance with constitutional rules.

The Cæsarism of Napoleon III was founded in still greater measure upon the principle of popular sovereignty. In his letter to the National Assembly written from London on May 24, 1848, the pretender to the crown recognized the French Republic which was the issue of the February revolution and was founded upon universal suffrage. At the same time he claimed for himself, and at the expense of the exiled king Louis Philippe, a hereditary right to insurrection and to the throne. This recognition and this claim were derived by him from the same principle. With simultaneous pride and humility he wrote: "In the presence of a king elected by two hundred deputies, I could remember that I am the inheritor of an empire founded on the consent of four million Frenchmen; in the presence of the national sovereignty (the result of universal suffrage) I can't and don't wish to claim any rights but those of a French citizen."[3] But Napolean III did not merely recognize in popular sovereignty the source of his power, he further made that sovereignty the theoretical basis of all his practical activities. He made himself popular in France by declaring that he regarded himself as merely the executive organ of the collective

[1] Louis Napoléon Bonaparte, *Idées napoléoniennes*, 1839, Italian ed., Pelazza, Turin, 1852, p. 74.
[2] Ibid. p. 119.
[3] Eugène Tenot, *Paris en Décembre 1851. Etudes historiques sur le Coup d'Etat*, Le Chevalier, Paris, 1868, p. 10.

will manifested in the elections, and that he was entirely at the disposition of that will, prepared in all things to accept its decisions. With great shrewdness, he continually repeated that he was no more than an instrument, a creature of the masses. While still president he declared in a speech that he was prepared as circumstances might dictate either for *abnégation* or for *persévérance*, or, in other words, that he was as ready to go or to remain. It was the pure Bonapartist spirit which was expressed by Ollivier, the keeper of the seals, when in the Chamber, in one of the stormy sittings of the summer of 1870, he declared: "We belong to you; you will reject us when you wish, we will always be there to submit to your reproaches and your imprecations."[4]

Bonapartism recognized the validity of the popular will to such an extreme degree as to concede to that will the right of self-destruction: popular sovereignty could suppress itself. Yet if we look at the matter from a purely human point of view, popular sovereignty is inalienable. Moreover, if we think of succeeding generations, it seems illogical and unjust that those of this generation should claim the moral right of renouncing on behalf of their descendants. Consequently the democrats of the Napoleonic epoch insisted most energetically that the power of popular sovereignty was limited to this extent, that it did not carry with it any right of abdication. Bonapartism is the theory of individual dominion originating in the collective will, but tending to emancipate itself of that will and to become sovereign in its turn. In its democratic past it finds a shield against the dangers which may threaten its anti-democratic present. In Bonapartism, the rule of Cæsar (as was said by a wit of the last years of the second empire) becomes a regular organ of the popular sovereignty. "He will be democracy personified, the nation made man."[5] It is the synthesis of two antagonistic concepts, democracy and autocracy.

Once elected, the chosen of the people can no longer be opposed in any way. He personifies the majority, and all resistance to his will is antidemocratic. The leader of such a democracy is irremovable, for the nation, having once spoken, cannot contradict itself. He is, moreover, infallible, for "he who is elected by six million votes carries out the will of the people; he does not betray them." It is reasonable and necessary that the adversaries of the government should be exterminated in

[4] Garnier Pagès, *L'Opposition et l'Empire. Dernière Séance du Corps Législatif, 1870*. Bibl. Démocratique, Paris, 1872, p. 157.

[5] Edouard Laboulaye, *Paris en Amérique*, Charpentier, Paris, 1869, 24th ed., p. 381.

the name of popular sovereignty, for the chosen of the people acts within his rights as representative of the collective will, established in his position by a spontaneous decision.[6] It is the electors themselves, we are assured, who demand from the chosen of the people that he should use severe repressive measures, should employ force, should concentrate all authority in his own hands.[7] One of the consequences of the theory of the popular will being subsumed in the supreme executive is that the elements which intervene between the latter and the former, the public officials, that is to say, must be kept in a state of the strictest possible dependence upon the central authority, which, in its turn, depends upon the people.[8] The least manifestation of liberty on the part of the bureaucracy would be tantamount to a rebellion against the sovereignty of the citizens. The most characteristic feature of this view is the idea that the power of the chief of the state rests exclusively upon the direct will of the nation. Bonapartism does not recognize any intermediate links. The *coup d'état* of December 2, 1851, was represented as an emancipation of the people from the yoke of parliament, and as having for its necessary corollary a plebiscite. Victor Hugo compared the relationship between the parliament and the ministry under Napoleon III to the relationship between master and servants, the master (the ministry) being appointed by the emperor, and the servants (the parliament) being elected by the people.[9] This affirmation, though incontestable in fact, is theoretically inexact. In theory, every act of Bonapartism was perfectly legitimate, even if it led to the shedding of the blood of the citizens. The plebiscite was a purifying bath which gave legitimate sanction to every illegality. Napoleon III, when he received the formal announcement of his triumph in the plebiscite, declared that if in the *coup d'état* he had infringed the laws it was only in order to reenter the paths of legality: "Je ne suis sorti de la légalité que pour rentrer dans le droit." He was granted absolu-

[6] Such were the expressions used by Louis Napoleon in a speech at Lyons, immediately after he had been elected Life-President of the Republic (E. Tnot, *Paris en Décembre 1851*, ed. cit., p. 26).—When he first assumed the presidency in December 1848, Louis Napoleon, speaking to the Chamber, solemnly enunciated the principle: "I shall see as enemies of the country all those who wish by illegal means to change what the whole of France has established." Trans. from (V. Hugo, *Napoléon le Petit*, ed. cit., p. 16).

[7] Napoleon III maintained that it was only on account of the democratic instincts of the first Napoleon that the emperor had not abolished the legislative bodies. The people would have had no objection to their abolition (*Idées Napoléoniennes*, ed. cit., p. 71).

[8] *Ibid.* p. 38.

[9] V. Hugo, *Napoléon le Petit*, Jeffs., London, 1852, pp. 79, 80.

tion by seven million votes.[10] This sanction by plebiscite, three times repeated by the French people, and given to the illegal government of the third Napoleon—confirmed as it was by innumerable and noisy demonstrations of popular sympathy—gave to accommodating republicans a ready pretext for passing from the side of the opposition to that of the monarchy. Was not this plebiscitary Cæsarism established upon the same foundation as the republic of their dreams? Emilie Ollivier divided the forms of government into the two great categories of personal and national government. The ruler in the case of a national government is no more than "a delegate of the nation to exercise social rights."[11] In this manner his republican conscience was tranquilized and his conversion to Bonapartism could present itself as logical and in conformity with his principles.

The history of modern democratic and revolutionary parties and trade unions exhibits phenomena similar to those we have been analyzing. The reasons are not far to seek. In democratic crowds, Bonapartism finds an eminently favorable soil, for it gives the masses the illusion of being masters of their masters; moreover, by introducing the practice of delegation it gives this illusion a legal color which is pleasing to those who are struggling for their "rights." Delegation and the abdication by the people of the direct exercise of power, are accomplished in strict accordance with all the rules by a deliberate act of the popular will and without that metaphysical divine intervention vaunted on its own behalf by the detested hereditary and legitimate monarchy. The chosen of the people thus seems to be invested in his functions by a spontaneous act of the popular will; he appears to be the creature of the people. This way of looking at the relations between the masses and the leaders is agreeable to the *amour propre* of every citizen, who says to himself: "Without me he would not be what he is; I have elected him; he belongs to me."

There is another reason, at once psychological and historical, why the masses accept without protest a certain degree of tyranny on the part of their elected leaders: it is because the crowd submits to domination more readily when each one of its units shares the possibility of approximating to power, and even of acquiring some power for himself. The bourgeois and the French peasants in the middle of the nineteenth century,

10 Emile Ollivier, *Le 19 janvier. Compte Rendu aux Electeurs de la III Circonscription de la Seine*, Paris, 1869, 7th ed., p. 119.
11 E. Tenot, *Paris en Décembre 1851*, ed. cit., pp. 206, 207.

imbued with democratic ideas, detested legitimate monarchy, but they gladly gave their votes to the third Napoleon, remembering how readily many of their fathers had become great dignitaries under his glorious uncle.[12]

Similarly in the case of political parties, the weight of an oligarchy is rarely felt when the rights of the masses are codified, and when each member may in the abstract participate in power.

In virtue of the democratic nature of his election, the leader of a democratic organization has more right than the born leader of the aristocracy to regard himself as the emanation of the collective will, and therefore to demand obedience and submission to his personal will. As a socialist newspaper puts it: "The party executive is the authority imposed by the party as a whole and thus incorporating the party authority. The first demand of democratic discipline is respect for the executive."[13] The absolute obedience which the organized mass owes to its leaders is the outcome of the democratic relationships existing between the leaders and the mass, and is merely the collective submission to the collective will.

The leaders themselves, whenever they are reproached for an anti-democratic attitude, appeal to the mass will from which their power is derived by election, saying: "Since the masses have elected us and re-elected us as leaders, we are the legitimate expression of their will and act only as their representatives."[14] It was a tenet of the old aristocracy that to disobey the orders of the monarch was to sin against God. In modern democracy it is held that no one may disobey the orders of the oligarchs, for in so doing the people sin against themselves, defying their own will spontaneously transferred by them to their representatives, and thus infringing democratic principle. In democracies, the leaders base their right to command upon the democratic omnipotence of the masses. Every employee of

[12] Alexandre Herzen, *De l'autre Rive,* Geneva, 1871, 3rd ed., p. 119.—In the light comedy *Le Gramin de Paris* by Bayard and Vanderburgh the words of the general typify the rôle of Napoleonism among the French common people: "We were children of Paris . . . printers . . . sons of wheelwrights . . . we had courage . . . we wanted to make our own way . . . perhaps we would have stopped en route . . . without the Emperor! . . . who appeared there . . . who caught us up in his whirlwind. . . . Chance was everything!" (Trans. by Velhagen, Bielefeld, 1861, 4th ed., p. 77).

[13] Düsseldorfer "Volkszeitung," November 13, 1905.

[14] This argument is repeatedly employed by socialist speakers. Their reasoning is that the very fact that the leaders are still leaders proves that they have the support of the masses—otherwise they would not be where they are. (Cf. Karl Legien's speech at the socialist congress of Jena (*Protokoll,* "Vorwärts," Berlin, 1905, p. 265); also P. J. Troelstra, *Inzake Partijleiding. Toelichtingen en Gegevens,* ed. cit., p. 97.)

the party owes his post to his comrades, and is entirely dependent upon their good will. We may thus say that in a democracy each individual himself issues, though indirectly, the orders which come to him from above.[15] Thus the reasoning by which the leaders' claim to obedience is defended and explained is, in theory, clear and unanswerable. In practice, however, the election of the leaders, and above all their re-election, is effected by such methods and under the influence of suggestions and other methods of coercion so powerful that the freedom of choice of the masses is considerably impaired. In the history of party life it is undeniable that the democratic system is reduced, in ultimate analysis, to the right of the masses, at stated intervals, to choose masters to whom in the interim they owe unconditional obedience.

Under these conditions, there develops everywhere in the leaders, alike in the democratic political parties and in the trade unions, the same habit of thought. They demand that the masses should not merely render obedience, but that they should blindly and without murmuring carry out the orders which they, the leaders, issue deliberately and with full understanding of the circumstances. To the leaders it is altogether inconceivable that the actions of the supreme authority can be subjected to criticism, for they are intimately convinced that they stand above criticism, that is to say above the party. Engels, who was endowed with an extremely keen sense of the essence of democracy, regarded it as deplorable that the leaders of the German Socialist Party could not accustom themselves to the idea that the mere fact of being installed in office did not give them the right to be treated with more respect than any other comrade.[16]

It is especially exasperating to the leaders when the comrades are not content with mere criticism, but act in opposition to the leaders' advice. When they speak of their differences with those whom they regard as inferiors in education and intelligence, they are unable to restrain their moral indignation at such a profound lack of discipline. When the masses "kick against the advice of the leaders they have themselves chosen," they are accused of a great lack of tact and of intelligence. In the conference of trade union executives held from February

[15] We owe to Georges Sorel the rediscovery of the relationships between democracy in general and absolutism, and their point of intersection in centralization. Cf., for instance, his *Les Illusions du Progrès*, Rivière, Paris, 1908, pp. 9 et seq.

[16] F. Engels, in a letter dated March 21, 1891; also Karl Marx, in a letter dated September 19, 1879 (*Briefe u. Auszüge aus Briefen, etc.*, ed. cit., pp. 361 and 166).

19 to 23, 1906—a conference which marks an important stage in the history of the German labor movement—Paul Müller, employee of a trade union, complained bitterly that his revolutionary comrades of the Socialist Party were endeavoring "to estrange the members of the unions from the leaders they had chosen for themselves. They have been directly incited to rebellion against their leaders. They have been openly urged to breaches of discipline. What other expressions can be used when in meetings we are told that the members ought to fight against their leaders?"[17]

Whenever a new current of opposition manifests itself within the party, the leaders immediately endeavor to discredit it with the charge of demagogy. If those of the comrades who are discontented with the leaders make a direct appeal to the masses, this appeal—however lofty may be its motives, however sincere the convictions of those who make it, however much they may be justified by a reference to fundamental democratic rights—is repudiated as inexpedient, and is even censured as a wicked attempt to break up the party, and as the work of vulgar intriguers. We have to remember, in this connection, that the leaders, who hold in their hands all the mechanism of power, have the advantage of being able to assume an aureole of legality, whereas the masses, or the subordinate leaders who are in rebellion, can always be placed in an unfavorable light of illegality. The magic phrase with which the leaders invariably succeed in stifling embarrassing opposition in the germ is "the general interest." In such circumstances they exhibit a notable fondness for arguments drawn from the military sphere. They maintain, for instance, that, if only for tactical reasons, and in order to maintain a necessary cohesion in face of the enemy, the members of the party must never refuse to repose perfect confidence in the leaders they have freely chosen for themselves. It is in Germany, above all, that in the trade union organizations the authoritarian spirit is developed with especial force, and that the leaders are prone to attribute to their adversaries the "criminal intention" of attempting "to dissolve trade union discipline." Even the socialist leaders make similar charges against their opponents. If we translate such an accusation from the language of the trade union leaders into that of government officials, the charge becomes one of "inciting to revolt against constituted authority." If the critics are not officials of the party, if they are mere sympathizers or

[17] *Partei u. Gewerkschaften*, textual reprint from the § § P. and G. of the *Protokoll*, p. 4.

friends, they are then in the eyes of the attacked leaders intrusive and incompetent persons, without any right whatever to form an opinion on the matter. "On no account must the faith of the people be disturbed! Such is the principle in accordance with which all lively criticism of the objective errors of the movement are stigmatized as an attack on the movement itself, whilst the elements of opposition within the party are habitually execrated as enemies who wish to destroy the party."[18]

The general conduct of the leaders of democratic parties and the phraseology typically employed by them (of which our examples might be multiplied a hundredfold) suffice to illustrate how fatal is the transition from an authority derived from "the favor of the people" to a right based upon "the grace of God"—in a word, to the system which in French history we know by the name of Bonapartism. A right of sovereignty born of the plebiscite soon becomes a permanent and inviolable dominion.

[18] Rosa Luxemburg, writing of the trade-union leaders in *Massenstreik, Partei u. Gewerkschaften*, p. 61.

Chapter 3

Identification of the Party with the Leader ("Le Parti c'est Moi")

WE HAVE shown that in their struggle against their enemies within the party the leaders of the labor movement pursue a tactic and adopt an attitude differing very little from those of the "bourgeois" government in its struggle with "subversive" elements. The terminology which the powers-that-be employ is, *mutatis mutandis,* identical in the two cases. The same accusations are launched against the rebels, and the same arguments are utilized in defense of the established order: in one case an appeal is made for the preservation of the state; in the other, for that of the party. In both cases, also, there is the same confusion of ideas when the attempt is made to define the relationships between thing and person, individual and collectivity. The authoritarian spirit of the official representatives of the German Socialist Party (a spirit which necessarily characterizes every strong organization) exhibits several striking analogies with the authoritarian spirit of the official representatives of the German empire. On the one side we have William II, who advises the "malcontents," that is to say those of his subjects who do not consider that all is for the best in the best of all possible empires, to shake the dust off their feet and go elsewhere. On the other side we have Bebel, exclaiming that it is time to have done once for all with the eternal discontents and sowings of discord within the party, and expressing the opinion that the opposition, if it is unable to express itself as satisfied with the conduct of affairs by the executive, had better "clear out."[1] Between these two attitudes, can we find any difference other than that which separates a voluntary organization (the party), to which one is free to adhere or not as one pleases, from a coercive organization (the state), to which all must belong by the fact of birth?[2]

[1] August Bebel, speech to the Dresden congress, *Protokoll,* p. 308.

[2] In the text, the writer has repeatedly mentioned the name of Bebel when he has wished to illustrate by typical examples the conduct of the leaders towards the masses. Yet it would be erroneous to regard Bebel as a typical leader. He was raised above the average of leaders, not only by his great intellectual gifts, but also by his profound sincerity, the outcome of a strong and healthy temperament, which often led him to say things openly which others would have left unsaid and to do things openly which others would have left con-

It may perhaps be said that there is not a single party leader who fails to think and to act, and who, if he has a lively temperament and a frank character, fails to speak, after the example of Le Roi Soleil, and to say *Le Parti c'est moi.*

The bureaucrat identifies himself completely with the organization, confounding his own interests with its interests. All objective criticism of the party is taken by him as a personal affront. This is the cause of the obvious incapacity of all party leaders to take a serene and just view of hostile criticism. The leader declares himself personally offended, doing this partly in good faith, but in part deliberately, in order to shift the battleground, so that he can present himself as the harmless object of an unwarrantable attack, and arouse in the minds of the masses towards his opponents in matters of theory that antipathy which is always felt for those whose actions are dictated by personal rancor. If, on the other hand, the leader is attacked personally, his first care is to make it appear that the attack is directed against the party as a whole. He does this not only on diplomatic grounds, in order to secure for himself the support of the party and to overwhelm the aggressor with the weight of numbers, but also because he quite ingenuously takes the part for the whole. This is frequently the outcome, not merely of a blind fanaticism, but of firm conviction. According to Netchajeff, the revolutionary has the right of exploiting, deceiving, robbing, and in case of need utterly ruining, all those who do not agree unconditionally with his methods and his aims, for he need consider them as nothing more than *chair à conspiration.* His sole objective must be to ensure the triumph of his essentially individual ideas, without any respect for persons—*La Révolution c'est moi!* Bakunin uttered a sound criticism of this mode of reasoning when he said that its hidden source was to be found in Netchajeff's unconscious but detestable ambition.

---

cealed. It was for this reason that "Kaiser Bebel" was frequently exposed to the suspicion of being exceptionally autocratic in his conduct and undemocratic in his sentiments. Nevertheless, a thorough analysis of Bebel's character and of his conduct on various memorable occasions would establish that, side by side with a marked tendency to self-assertion and a taste for the intrinsic forms of rule, he exhibited strong democratic leanings, which distinguished him from the average of his colleagues, just as much as he was distinguished from them by the frankness with which he always displayed his dictatorial temperament. This is not the place for such an analysis, but the writer felt it was necessary to guard against a false interpretation of his references to Bebel by a brief allusion to the complexity of character of this remarkable man. In ultimate analysis, Bebel was no more than a representative of his party, but he was one in whom the individual note was never suppressed by the exigencies of leadership or of demagogy.

The despotism of the leaders does not arise solely from a vulgar lust of power or from uncontrolled egoism, but is often the outcome of a profound and sincere conviction of their own value and of the services which they have rendered to the common cause. The bureaucracy which is most faithful and most efficient in the discharge of its duties is also the most dictatorial. To quote Wolfgang Heine: "The objection is invalid that the incorruptibility and efficiency of our party officials, and their love for the great cause, would suffice to raise a barrier against the development of autocracy within the party. The very opposite is true. Officials of high technical efficiency who unselfishly aim at the general good, like those whom we are fortunate enough to possess in the party, are more than all others inclined, being well aware of the importance of their own services, to regard as inalterable laws whatever seems to them right and proper, to suppress conflicting tendencies on the ground of the general interest, and thus to impose restraints upon the healthy progress of the party."[3] Similarly, where we have to do with excellent and incorruptible state officials like those of the German empire, the megalomaniac substitution of thing for person is partly due to the upright consciences of the officials and to their great devotion to duty. Among the members of such a bureaucracy, there is hardly one who does not feel that a pin-prick directed against his own person is a crime committed against the whole state. It is for the same reason that they all hold together *comme les doigts de la main*. Each one of them regards himself as an impersonation of a portion of the whole state, and feels that this portion will suffer if the authority of any other portion is impaired. Further, the bureaucrat is apt to imagine that he knows the needs of the masses better than these do themselves, an opinion which may be sound enough in individual instances, but which for the most part is no more than a form of megalomania. Undoubtedly the party official is less exposed than the state official to the danger of becoming fossilized, for in most cases he has work as a public speaker, and in this way he maintains a certain degree of contact with the masses. On the other hand, the applause which he seeks and receives on these occasions cannot fail to stimulate his personal vanity.

When in any organization the oligarchy has attained an advanced stage of development, the leaders begin to identify with themselves, not merely the party institutions, but even the

[3] W. Heine, *Demokratisch Randbemerkungen zum Fall Göhre*, "Soz. Monatsh.," viii (x), fasc. iv, p. 284.

party property, this phenomenon being common both to the party and to the state. In the conflict between the leaders and the rank and file of the German trade unions regarding the right to strike, the leaders have more than once maintained that the decision in this matter is morally and legally reserved for themselves, because it is they who provide the financial resources which enable the workers to remain on strike. This view is no more than the ultimate consequence of that oligarchical mode of thought which inevitably leads to a complete forgetfulness of true democratic principles. In Genoa, one of the labor leaders, whose influence had increased *pari passu* with the growing strength of the organized proletariat of the city, and who, enjoying the unrestricted confidence of his comrades, had acquired the most various powers and had filled numerous positions in the party, regarded himself as justified, when as a representative of the workers he made contracts with capitalists and concluded similar affairs, in feathering his own nest in addition to looking after the workers' interests.[4]

[4] This was the barrister, Gino Murialdi, who in youth had made many sacrifices for the movement. He was in receipt of a regular salary from the trade unions and cooperative societies, but this did not prevent him from accepting money from the employers when he was negotiating with them as the workers' representative. When taken to task on this account, he said that by his exertions he had obtained such brilliant advantages for the workers, that he saw no reason why he should not secure for himself a little extra profit at the cost of the employers. Murialdi's actions led to a violent quarrel between him and the other leaders in Genoa, and ultimately caused his expulsion from the Socialist Party. Cf. "Avanti," anno xiii (1909), Nos. 1 and 42.

PART FOUR/SOCIAL ANALYSIS OF LEADERSHIP

Chapter 1

Introductory. The Class Struggle and Its Disintegrating Influence upon the Bourgeoisie

THE MASSES are not easily stirred. Great events pass before their eyes and revolutions are accomplished in economic life without their minds undergoing profound modifications. Very slowly do they react to the influence of new conditions.

For decades, and even for centuries, the masses continue to endure pasively outworn political conditions which greatly impede legal and moral progress.[1] Countries which from the economic point of view are fairly well advanced, often continue to endure for lengthy periods a political and constitutional regime which derives from an earlier economic phase. This is especially noteworthy in Germany, where an aristocratic and feudal form for government, the outcome of economic conditions which the country has outlived, has not yet been able to adapt itself to an economic development of the most advanced capitalist character.

These historical phenomena, which at first sight appear paradoxical, arise from causes of two different orders. In the first place it may happen that classes or sub-classes representing an extinct economic form may survive from a time in which they were the authentic exponents of the then dominant economic relationships; they have been able to save from the wreck a sufficiency of moral prestige and effective political force to maintain their dominion in the new phase of economic and civil development, and to do this even in opposition to the expressed will of the majority of the people. These classes succeed in maintaining themselves in power by the strength of their own political energy and with the assistance of numerous elements essentially foreign to themselves, but which they can turn to their own advantage by suggestive influences. Most

1 "Unreflectingly, sometimes with a sigh, but often without a thought of the possibility of better things, the nations have borne for centuries, and continue to bear, all the burdens and all the shames imposed upon them by tyranny, like the lower animals, who with satisfaction and even gratitude accept a bare subsistence from the hand of the master to whom they belong, and who makes use of them and chastises them at his will" (Carl von Rotteck, *Allgemeine Geschichte, etc.*, ed. cit., p. 81).

commonly, however, we find that the classes representing a past economic order continue to maintain their social predominance only because the classes representing the present or future economy have as yet failed to become aware of their strength, of their political and economic importance, and of the wrongs which they suffer at the hands of society. Moreover, a sense of fatalism and a sad conviction of impotence exercise a paralyzing influence in social life. As long as an oppressed class is influenced by this fatalistic spirit, as long as it has failed to develop an adequate sense of social injustice, it is incapable of aspiring towards emancipation. It is not the simple *existence* of oppressive conditions, but it is the *recognition of these conditions by the oppressed,* which in the course of history has constituted the prime factor of class struggles.

The mere existence of the modern proletariat does not suffice *per se* to produce a "social problem." The class struggle, if it is not to remain a nebulous theory, in which the energy is for ever latent, requires to be animated by class consciousness.

It is the involuntary work of the bourgeoisie to arouse in the proletariat that class consciousness which is necessarily directed against the bourgeoisie itself. History is full of such ironies. It is the tragical destiny of the bourgeoisie to be instructor of the class which from the economic and social point of view is its own deadly enemy. As Karl Marx showed in his *Communist Manifesto,* the principal reason for this is found in the unceasing struggle which the bourgeoisie is forced to carry on "at once with the aristocracy, with those sections of its own class whose interests are opposed to industrial progress, and with the bourgeoisie of all foreign countries." Unable to carry on this struggle effectively by its own unaided powers, the bourgeoisie is continually forced "to appeal to the proletariat, to demand its aid, and thus to launch the proletariat into the political mêlée, thus putting into the hands of the proletariat a weapon which the latter will turn against the bourgeoisie itself.[2] Under yet another aspect the bourgeoisie appears as the instructor, as the fencing-master of the working class. Through its daily contact with the proletariat there results the detachment from its own body of a small number of persons who devote their energies to the service of the working classes, in order to inflame these for the struggle against the existing order, to make them feel and understand the deficien-

[2] Karl Marx, *The Communist Manifesto,* "Vorwärts," Berlin, 1901, 6th ed., p. 16.

cies of the prevailing economic and social regime. It is true that the number of those who are detached from the bourgeoisie to adhere to the cause of the proletariat is never great. But those who thus devote themselves are among the best of the bourgeoisie; they may, in a sense, be regarded as supermen, raised above the average of their class, it may be by love of their neighbors, it may be by compassion, it may be by moral indignation against social injustice or by a profound theoretical understanding of the forces at work in society, or, finally, by a greater energy and logical coherence in the translation of their principles into practice. In any case, they are exceptional individualities, these bourgeois who, deserting the class in which they were born, give a deliberate direction to the instincts still slumbering in the proletariat, and thus hasten the emancipation of the proletarian class as a whole.

The proletarian mass is at first aware by instinct alone of the oppression by which it is burdened, for it entirely lacks the instruction which might give a clue to the understanding of that historical process which is in appearance so confused and labyrinthine. It would seem to be a psychologico-historical law that any class which has been enervated and led to despair in itself through prolonged lack of education and through deprivation of political rights, cannot attain to the possibility of energetic action until it has received instruction concerning its ethical rights and politico-economical powers, not alone from members of its own class, but also from those who belong to what in vulgar parlance are termed a "higher" class. Great class-movements have hitherto been initiated in history solely by the simple reflection: it is not we alone, belonging to the masses without education and without legal rights, who believe ourselves to be oppressed, but that belief as to our condition is shared by those who have a better knowledge of the social mechanism and who are therefore better able to judge; since the cultured people of the upper classes have also conceived the ideal of our emancipation, that ideal is not a mere chimera.

The socialist theory has arisen out of the reflections of philosophers, economists, sociologists, and historians. In the socialist programs of the different countries, every word represents a synthesis of the work of numerous learned men. The fathers of modern socialism were with few exceptions men of science primarily, and in the second place only were they politicians in the strict sense of the term. It is true that before the days of such men there were spontaneous proletarian movements initiated by an instinctive aspiration towards a higher intellectual and economic standard of life. But these movements manifest themselves rather as the mechanical outcome of an unreflecting though legitimate discontent, than as the consequence of a genuine sentiment of revolt inspired by a clear consciousness of oppression. It was only when science placed itself at the service of the working class that the *proletarian* movement became transformed into a *socialist* movement, and that instinctive, unconscious, and aimless rebellion was replaced by conscious aspiration, comparatively clear, and strictly directed towards a well-defined end.

Similar phenomena are apparent in all earlier class struggles. Every great class movement in history has arisen upon the instigation, with the cooperation, and under the leadership of men sprung from the very class against which the movement was directed. Spartacus, who urged the slaves to revolt on behalf of their freedom, was, it is true, of servile origin, but he was a freed-man, a Thracian property owner. Thomas Münzer, to whose agitation the Thuringian Peasants' War was largely due, was not a peasant but a man of learning. Florian Geier was a knight. The most distinguished leaders of the movement for the emancipation of the *tiers état* at the outset of the French Revolution, Lafayette, Mirabeau, Roland, and Sieyès, belonged to the privileged classes, and Philippe-Egalité, the regicide, was even a member of the royal house. The history of the modern labor movement furnishes no exception to this rule. When the German historian, Theodor Lindner, affirms[3] that the contemporary socialist movement is always "called to life" by nonworkers, we must indeed criticize the statement, which recalls to our mind the working of the necromancer's magic wand: "Let there be a labor movement! And there was a labor movement." Lindner's statement is likewise inexact and incomplete, because it fails to recognize that this "calling to life" cannot produce something out of nothing, and that it cannot be the work of one of those famous "great men" whom a certain school of historians make the cornerstone of their theory of historical causation—for the coming into existence of the labor movement necessarily presupposes a given degree of social and economic development, without which no movement can be initiated. But Lindner's view, though badly formulated, is to this extent true, that the heralds of the modern labor movement are chiefly derived from the "cultured

[3] Theodor Lindner, *Geschichtphilosophie*, Cotta, Stuttgart, 1904, 2nd ed., p. 132.

classes." The great precursors of political socialism and leading representatives of philosophical socialism, St. Simon, Fourier, and Owen; the founders of political socialism, Louis Blanc, Blanqui, and Lassalle; the fathers of economic and scientific socialism, Marx, Engels, and Rodbertus, were all bourgeois intellectuals. Of comparatively trifling importance in the international field, alike in respect of theory and of practice, were Wilhelm Weitling, the tailor's apprentice, and Pierre Leroux, the self-taught philosopher. It is only Proudhon, the working printer, a solitary figure, who attains to a position of superb grandeur in this field. Even among the great orators who during recent years have been devoted to the cause of labor, ex-bourgeois constitute the great majority, while men of working-class origin are altogether exceptional. Pages could be filled with the names of leading socialist politicians sprung from the bourgeoisie, whereas in a single breath we could complete the list of political leaders of truly working-class origin whose names will be immortalized in the history of their class. We have Bénoît Malon, August Bebel, and Éduard Anseele; but not one of these, although they are great practical leaders of the working class and potent organizers, is numbered among the creative theorists of socialism.

The presence of bourgeois elements in the proletarian movement organized to form a political party is a historical fact, and one which may be noted wherever the political movement of the international working class is attentively observed. This phenomenon reproduces itself wherever the socialist tree throws out new branches, as may be seen, for example, in Japan and Brazil.

Moreover, this phenomenon must be considered as a logical consequence of historical evolution. Nay more, it has been shown that not merely the presence of ex-bourgeois in the party of the fighting proletariat, but further the leading rôle which these play in the movement for proletarian enfranchisement, is the outcome of historical necessity.

The question might arise, and it has in fact been mooted, whether the presence of a large number of bourgeois refugees among the proletarian militants does not give the lie to the theory of the class struggle. In other words, we have to ask whether the desired future social order in which all class distinctions are to be abolished (for this is the common aim, more or less distinctly formulated, of all socialists and other advanced reformers, ethical culturists, anarchists, neo-Christians, etc.) may not come to be realized by a gradual psychical transformation of the bourgeoisie, which will become increasingly aware of the injustice of its peculiar economic and social privileges. This consideration naturally leads us to ask whether the sharp line of cleavage which exists on the political field between class-parties representing class-interests is really necessary, or whether it is not a sort of cruel sport, and therefore useless and injurious. Rudolph Penzig, editor of "Ethische Kultur," in a controversy with the present writer, went so far as to claim that the deserters from the bourgeoisie to the socialist ranks were "precursors."[4] Now this expression logically involves the belief that these bourgeois pioneers will be followed by the whole mass of the bourgeoisie, who will thus come over to the camp of those who economically and socially are their mortal enemies. We might be inclined to speak of this as a theory of hara-kiri, did we not know that hara-kiri is not usually practiced as a deliberate voluntary act, but is affected in obedience to orders from above, to coercion from without. Let us briefly examine the soundness of the theory in question.

The socialist poet Edmondo de Amicis enumerates the factors which he regards as working most effectively for the ultimate victory of socialism. There is the general sense of weariness which, in his opinion, follows a great industrial crisis, and the utter disgust felt by the possessing classes with the unending struggle; there is the anxiety felt by these same classes to avoid at all costs a revolution in which they are destined to perish miserably, overcome by fire and sword; there is, finally, the indefinite need, with which the bourgeoisie is also affected, for rejuvenation and idealism, and for avoiding "the horror of living amid the ruins of an expiring world.[5] A similar train of thought was expressed fifty years earlier by Heinrich Heine, who lacked to make him a fighter for socialism merely the courage to give open expression to his political ideas. In his letters from Paris upon politics, art, and national life he writes, under date June 15, 1843: "I wish here to draw especial attention to the point that for communism it is an incalculable advantage that the enemy against which the communists contend has, despite all his power, no firm moral standing. Modern society defends itself simply because it must do so, without any belief in its own rights, and even without any self-respect,

[4] Rudolph Penzig, *Die Unvernunft des Klassenkampfes*, written in answer to R. Michels, *Endziel, Intransigenz, Ethik*, "Ethische Kultur," December 26, 1903. xii. No. 52.

[5] Edmondo de Amicis, *Lotte civili*, Nerbini, Florence, 1899, p. 294.

just like that ancient society which crumbled to ruin at the coming of the carpenter's son."[6]

In many respects, the views of these two poets may be accepted. And yet it seems more than questionable whether a dying bourgeois society would not defend itself to the last, and endeavor to maintain by force of arms, if need be, its property and its prerogatives, however greatly these might be undermined and threatened, in the hope that the final victory of the proletariat might at least be postponed. Unquestionably, too, Heine's opinion in 1843 that in the bourgeoisie of his day there was a widespread lack of confidence, is open to criticism, seeing that, as we all know, the bourgeois resistance is to this day animated by a vigorous belief in his own rectitude. But the fundamental thought of de Amicis and Heine is so far sound, in that a society which lacks a lively faith in its own rights is already in its political death-agony. A capacity for the tough and persevering defense of privilege presupposes in the privileged class the existence of certain qualities, and in especial of a relentless energy, which might thrive, indeed, in association with cruelty and unconscientiousness, but which is enormously more prosperous if based upon a vigorous faith in its own rectitude. As Pareto has pointed out,[7] the permeation of a dominant class by humanitarian ideas, which lead that class to doubt its own moral right to existence, demoralizes its members and makes them inapt for defense.

The same law operates likewise where men are absolutely convinced of their sacred right to existence. It is equally valid of national aggregates. Where a nation lacks the sense of such a right, decadence and ruin inevitably ensue. We may regard it as an established historical law that races, legal systems, institutions, and social classes, are inevitably doomed to destruction from the moment they or those who represent them have lost faith in their own future. The Poles, widely dispersed, and dismembered among three separate powers, have preserved their nationality and their faith in themselves and in their rights. No power in the world, not to mention the Prusso-Russian microcosm, can annihilate the Polish people whilst their brains still cherish the consciousness of their right to national existence. The Wends, on the other hand, a Slav people like the Poles, owing to the nature of the historical epoch in which they were subdued and to the peculiar circumstances under

[6] Heinrich Heine, *Lutetia in Sämtliche Werke*, Hoffmann u. Kampe, Hamburg, 1890, x, p. 93.

[7] Vilfredo Pareto, *Les Systèmes socialiste*, ed. cit., vol. i, pp. 37 and 57.

which this historical occurrence took place, did not succeed in retaining intact the consciousness of their national existence —if they ever possessed one. Even where, as in the Spreewald, they have retained their language, they have been thoroughly absorbed into the German system, and are in our day, as Wends, completely expunged from the history of civilization. Although they inhabit quite a large area of Germany, they have in many cases so utterly lost all sense of their Slav origin as to have become the most ardent Pan-Germanists, although they are in reality Germans only in virtue of the legal fiction of the state and of the customs and speech which have been imposed upon them by their ancient conquerors.

No social struggle in history has ever been permanently won unless the vanquished has as a preliminary measure been morally weakened. The French Revolution was rendered possible only because the ardent pre-revolutionary writers, Voltaire, D'Alembert, Rousseau, Holbach, Diderot, etc., who made so plainly manifest the "immorality" of the economic privileges possessed by the ruling classes of the old regime, had already demoralized (in the psychological sense of the word) a conspicuous portion of the nobility and the clergy. Louis Blanc remarked, apropos of the French Revolution: "The thrilling result of the *Encyclopédie*, that great laboratory of eighteenth-century ideas, in 1789 it had only to take material possession of a domain already conquered morally."[8] The unification of Italy, previously broken up into seven states, was effected with a minimal shedding of blood (if we except the deaths that resulted in the struggle against foreigners), and after the foundation of the kingdom there was hardly a single inhabitant of the peninsula who shed any tears over the fate of the fallen dynasties, this attitude of mind forming a strong contrast to what happened in Germany in the corresponding historical period. The reason for the difference was that in Italy the unification of minds had long preceded the unification of administration. In the war of secession in the United States of America, it was not merely the armed strength of the northern states which decided the issue, but also the consciousness of moral error which towards the end of the war began to spread among a large number of the slave owners of the southern states.[9] Examples of this nature could be multiplied at will.

[8] Trans. from Louis Blanc, *Organisation du Travail*, Camille, Paris, 1845, 4th ed., p. xiii.

[9] Woodrow Wilson, *A History of the American People*, Harper, New York and London, 1903, vol. iv, p. 311.

The aim of agitation is to shake the opponent's selfconfidence, to convince adversaries of the higher validity of our own arguments. Socialism can least of all afford to underrate the enormous force of rhetoric, the compelling power of persuasion, for it is to these means that socialism owes its great successes. But the force of persuasion has a natural limit imposed by social relationships. Where it is used to influence the convictions of the popular masses or of social classes to induce them to take part in a movement which is directed towards their own liberation, it is easy, under normal conditions, to attain to positive results. But attempts at persuasion fail miserably, as we learn again and again from the history of social struggles, when they are addressed to privileged classes, in order to induce these to abandon, to their own disadvantage, as a class and as individuals, the leading positions they occupy in society.

The individual human being is not an economic automaton. His life consists of a perennial conflict between his financial needs and the interests which bind him to a given class or caste, on the one hand, and, on the other, those tendencies which are outside class considerations, outside the orbit of social struggles, and which may arouse in his mind passions capable of diverting him from a purely economic path, attracting him within the sphere of influence of some ideal sun, leading him to act in ways more consonant with his own individual character. But all this applies only to the individual human being. The mass, if we leave out of consideration certain pathological influences to which it is exposed, and which may lead its members into activities conflicting with purely material advantage, is unquestionably an economic automaton. The common manifestations of its members are stamped with the seal of the economic interests of the mass, just as the individual sheep of a flock bear the mark of their owner. Consequently the seal need not necessarily be useful to the individual who bears it, nor correspondent with his ends; any more than is the imprint upon the back of the sheep, which often consigns the animal to slaughter. But in the human herd the economic imprint extends its influence into the physical life. The kind of work and of interests imposed by economic conditions makes spirit and body alike dependent on occupation.

It is doubtless true that the socialist doctrine has won over many children of bourgeois families, penetrating their minds so profoundly as to lead them to abandon everything else—to leave father and mother, friends and relatives, social position and respect. Without regret and without hesitation they have consecrated their lives to the emancipation of humanity as conceived by socialism. But we have here to do with isolated instances only, and not with compact groups representing an entire economic class. The class to which the deserters belong is no wise weakened by the desertion. A class considered as a whole never spontaneously surrenders its position of advantage. It never recognizes any moral reason sufficiently powerful to compel it to abdicate in favor of its "poorer brethren." Such action is prevented, if by nothing else, by class egoism, a natural attribute of the proletarian as of other social classes, with the difference that, in the case of the proletariat, class egoism comes in ultimate analysis to coincide—*in abstracto,* at least—with the ideal of a humanity knowing nothing of classes. It will not be denied that in the various strata of the dominant and possessing classes there are considerable differences in the extent to which this class egoism is developed. There are certain representatives of landed property, and above all the Prussian junkers, who bluntly declare even today that we should treat as criminals or lunatics all who claim political, economic, or social rights by which their own class privileges are endangered. There are other classes in modern society less hostile to reforms and less crassly egoistic than the numerically small class of the Prussian junkers; but these too are not accessible to considerations of social justice, except in so far as no sensible injury is offered to their instinctive class interests. The proletariat is therefore perfectly logical in constituting itself into a class party, and in considering that the struggle against the bourgeoisie in all its gradations, viewed as a single class, is the only possible means of realizing a social order in which knowledge, health, and property shall not be, as they are today, the monopolies of a minority.

There is no contradiction whatever between the necessity which leads the proletariat to fight the bourgeoisie on the lines of the class struggle and the necessity which leads it to lay so much stress upon the general principle of human rights. Unquestionably, in pursuit of the conquest of power, persuasion is an excellent means to employ, for, as has already been pointed out, a class which has been convinced even against its will that its adversary's ideal is based upon better reasons than its own and is inspired by loftier moral aims, will certainly lack force to continue the struggle; it will have lost that faith in its own rights which alone confers upon resistance a moral justification. Persuasion, however, does not suffice, for a class, even if partially paralyzed by its recognition of the fact that the right of the hostile class is superior to its own, would none the less, hypnotized by its own class egoism, continue the struggle, and would in the end yield to the force, not of words, but of facts. The writer believes that all these considerations suffice to establish as an axiom that the entrance of bourgeois elements into the ranks of the workers organized as a class party is determined mainly by psychological motives, and that it represents a process of spontaneous selection. It must be regarded as a logical consequence of the historical phase of development through which we are now passing, but in view of the special conditions which induce it there is no reason to interpret it as a preliminary symptom of a spontaneous and general dissolution of the bourgeoisie. To sum up, the issue of the struggle which is proceeding between the two great classes representing conflicting economic interests cannot possibly be decided by the passage of individual or isolated molecules from one side to the other.

Chapter 2

Analysis of the Bourgeois Elements in the Socialist Leadership

SOCIALIST LEADERS, considered in respect of their social origin, may be divided into two classes, those who belong primarily to the proletariat, and those derived from the bourgeoisie, or rather from the intellectual stratum of the bourgeoisie. The lower middle class, that of the petty bourgeois, the minor agriculturists, independent artisans, and shopkeepers, have furnished no more than an insignificant contingent of socialist leaders. In the most favorable conditions, the representatives of this lower middle class follow the labor movement as sympathetic onlookers, and at times actually join its ranks. Hardly ever do they become numbered among its leaders.

Of these two classes of leaders, the ex-bourgeois, although at the outset they were naturally opposed to socialism, prove themselves on the average to be animated by a more fervent idealism than the leaders of proletarian origin. The difference is readily explained on psychological grounds. In most cases the proletarian does not need to attain to socialism by a gradual evolutionary process; he is, so to speak, born a socialist, born a member of the party—at least, this happens often enough, although it does not apply to all strata of the proletariat and to all places. In the countries where capitalist development is of long standing, there exists in certain working-class milieux and even in entire categories of workers a genuine socialist tradition. The son inherits the class spirit of the father, and he doubtless from the grandfather. With them, socialism is "in the blood." To this it must be added that actual economic relationships (with the class struggle inseparable from these, in which every individual, however refractory he may be to socialist theory, is forced to participate) compel the proletarian to join the labor party. Socialism, far from being in opposition to his class sentiment, constitutes its plainest and most conspicuous expression. The proletarian, the wage-earner, the enrolled member of the party, is a socialist on the ground of direct personal interest. Adhesion to socialism may cause him grave material damage, such as the loss of his employment, and may even make it impossible for him to gain his bread. Yet his socialist views are the spontaneous outcome of his class egoism, and he endures the hardships to which they may lead all the more cheerfully because he is suffering for the common cause. He is comforted by the more or less explicit recognition or gratitude of his comrades. The action of the socialist proletarian is a class action, and in many cases it may notably favor the immediate interests of the individual.

Very different is the case of socialists of bourgeois origin. Hardly any of these are born in a socialist milieu. On the contrary, in their families the tradition is definitely hostile to the workers, or at least full of disdain for the aspirations of modern socialism. Among the bourgeois, just as much as among the proletarians, the son inherits the spirit of the father, but in this case it is the class spirit of the bourgeoisie. The young bourgeois has "in the blood" not socialism, but the capitalist mentality in one of its numerous varieties, and he inherits in addition an intellectualism which makes him proud of his supposed superiority. We have further, on the one hand, to take into account the economic conditions in which the bourgeois child is born and grows to maturity, and on the other the education which he receives at school, all of which predisposes him to feel nothing but aversion for the struggles of a working class pursuing socialist aspirations. In his economic environment he learns to tremble for his wealth, to tremble when he thinks of the shock his class will one day have to sustain when attacked by the organized masses of the *quatrième état*. Thus his class egoism becomes more acute, and is even transformed into an implacable hatred. His education, based upon official science, contributes to confirm and to strengthen his sentiments as a member of the master class. The influence which the school and the domestic environment exercise upon the youthful scion of the bourgeoisie is of such potency that even when his parents are themselves socialist sympathizers, and on moral and intellectual grounds devoted to the cause of the workers, it most commonly happens that his bourgeois instincts gain the upper hand over the socialist traditions of his family. We learn from actual experience that it is very rare for the children of socialists, when they have received the education of intellectuals, to follow in their parents' footsteps. The cases of the children of Marx, Longuet, Liebknecht, and Molkenbuhr, remain altogether exceptional. It cannot be doubted that the rarity of such instances is due to the methods of education which usually prevail in a socialist family, methods which have nothing in common with socialism. Even when it is otherwise, when the immediate family environment is not opposed to the development of the socialist consciousness, the young man of bourgeois origin is strongly influenced by the milieu in which he is brought up. Even after he has joined the Socialist Party, he will retain a certain solidarity with the class from which he has sprung; for example, in his relations with the servants in his household he will remain always an employer, an "exploiter," in the sociological if not in the coarser sense of the latter term. For the bourgeois, adhesion to socialism signifies an estrangement from his own class, in most cases extensive social and ideal injury, and often actual material loss. In the case of the petty bourgeois, the evolution towards socialism may occur peacefully, for by his intellectual and social conditions the petty bourgeois is closely approximated to the proletarian, and above all to the better paid manual worker, from whom he is in many cases separated by purely imaginary barriers composed of all kinds of class prejudices. But the wealthier the family to which the bourgeois belongs, the more strongly it is attached to its family traditions, the higher the social position that it occupies, the more difficult is it for him, and the more painful, to break with his surroundings, and to adhere to the labor movement.

For the son of a wealthy capitalist, of an official in the higher ranks, or for a member of the old-established landed aristocracy, to join the socialists is to provoke a catastrophe. He is free to give himself up to vague and harmless humanitarian dreams, and even in private conversation to speak of himself as a "socialist." But as soon as he displays the intention of becoming an active member of the Socialist Party, of undertaking public work on its behalf, of enrolling himself as an actual member of the "rebel" army, the deserter from the bourgeoisie is regarded by his own class as either a knave or a fool. His social prestige falls below zero, and so great is the hostility displayed towards him that he is obliged to break off all relations with his family. The most intimate ties are abruptly severed. His relatives turn their backs upon him. He has burned his boats and broken with the past.

What are the motives which may lead the intellectual to desert the bourgeoisie and to adhere to the party of the workers? Among those who do this we may distinguish two fundamental types.

There is first of all the man of science. The ends which he pursues are of an objective character, but to the vulgar these seem at first sight devoid of practical utility, and even fantastical and extravagant. The stimulus which drives him is idealistic in this sense, that he is capable of sacrificing all other goods to science and its gains. In thus acting, he obeys the powerful impulse of his egoism, though it is an egoism ennobled. Scientific coherency is an inborn need of his nature. Psychology teaches us that in human beings every free exercise of faculty produces a sentiment of pleasure. Consequently the sacrifices which the socialist man of science makes for the party serve to increase the sum of his personal satisfaction. Notwithstanding all the material injuries he will suffer as a bourgeois in joining the Socialist Party, he will have gained a greater inward content and will have a more tranquil conscience. In some cases, too, his sentiments will take the form of an ambition to render signal services to the cause. In his case, of course, this ambition is very different from the grosser ambition of those who look merely for an increase in personal well-being—for a career, wealth, and the like.

The second category consists of those who are inspired with an intense sentimental attachment to socialism, who burn, so to speak, with the sacred fire. Such a man usually becomes a socialist when he is quite young, before material considerations and precautions have erected a barrier in the way of obedience to the impulses of his sanguine and enthusiastic temperament. He is inspired with the ardor of the neophyte and the need for devoting himself to the service of his kind. The principal motives which animate him are a noble disdain for injustice and a love for the weak and the poor, a delight in self-sacrifice for the realization of great ideas, for these are motives which often give courage and love of battle to the most timid and inert characters. With all this, there is usually found in the socialist enthusiast of bourgeois origin a considerable dose of optimism, a tendency to overestimate the significance of the moral forces of the movement, and sometimes an excessive faith in his own self-abnegation, with a false mode of conceiving the rhythm of evolution, the nearness of the final victory, and the ease with which it will be attained. The socialist faith is also in many cases nourished by æsthetic sensibilities. Those endowed with poetical aptitudes and with a fervent imagination can more readily and intuitively grasp the extent and the depth of human suffering; moreover, the greater their own social distance from the imagined objects, the more are they able to give their fancies free rein. It is for this reason that among the ranks of those who are fighting for the emancipation of labor we find so many poets and imaginative writers, and so many persons of fiery, impassioned and impulsive dispositions.[1]

The question arises, which category is the more numerous, that of those who become socialists from reasoned conviction, or that of those who are guided by sentimental considerations. It is probable that among those who become socialists in youth the sentimentalists predominate, whereas among those who go over to socialism when they have attained maturity, the change is usually dictated by scientific conviction. But in most cases mixed motives are at work. Very numerous, in fact, are the bourgeois who have always given a moral approval to socialism, who have held that it is the only solution of the social problem which conforms to the demands of justice, but who do not make their effective adhesion to the doctrine until they acquire the conviction (which at times seizes them quite unexpectedly) that the aspirations of their heart are not merely just and beautiful, but also realizable in practice. Thus the socialist views of these persons are a synthesis of sentiment and science. In 1894, an inquiry was made as to the attitude towards socialism of the most distinguished Italian artists and men of learning. They were asked whether their sympathy with socialist aims, their indifference to socialism, or their hostility to the doctrine, was the outcome of a concrete investigation of socialist problems, or whether their feelings were of a purely sentimental character. The majority of those who replied declared that their attitude towards socialism was the outcome of a physical predisposition, reinforced by objective convictions. A similar answer might doubtless be given by the Marxists, notwithstanding their superb disdain for all ideology and sentimental compassion, and notwithstanding the materialism with which they love to dress their windows. In so far as they are not completely absorbed in party life, or rather so long as they have not been completely overpowered by the

[1] A few only of the most notable of such persons, who are or who have been active workers on behalf of socialism, may be mentioned here: William Morris, Bernard Shaw, H. G. Wells, Jack London, George D. Herron, Upton Sinclair; J. B. Clément, Clovis Hugues, Anatole France, Jules Destrée; Cornelie Huygens, Herman Gorter, Henriette Roland-Holst; George Herwegh, Wilhelm Holzamer, Karl Henkell, Emil Rosenow; Edmondo de Amicis, Mario Rapisardi, Diego Garoglio, Angelo Cabrini, G. Romualdi, Virgilio Brocchi, Tomaso Monicelli; Maxim Gorki; Gustav af Geijerstam.

ties of party life, they display a strictness of principle which is essentially idealist.[2]

Not all those, indeed, who sympathize with socialism or have a rational conviction of the truth of socialist principles become effective members of the Socialist Party. Many feel a strange repugnance at the idea of intimate association with the unknown crowd, or they experience an æsthetic disgust at the thought of close contact with persons who are not always clean or sweet-smelling. Still more numerous are those held back by laziness or by an exaggerated fondness for a quiet life or, again, by the more or less justified fear that open adhesion to the party will react unfavorably upon their economic position. Sometimes the impulse to join the party is given by some external circumstance, insignificant in itself, but sufficient to give the last impetus to resolution: it may be a striking instance of social injustice which stirs a collective emotion; it may be some personal wrong inflicted upon the would-be socialist himself of upon one of those dear to him, when a sudden explosion of egoism finishes the slow work of altruistic tendencies. In other cases it is a necessity of fate, or the outcome of the ill-will and stupidity of human beings, which forces the man who has been a secret socialist to cross the Rubicon, almost by inadvertence. For example, something may happen which discredits him in the eyes of the members of his own class, displaying to all the socialist ideas which he has hitherto jealously concealed. Many a person does not join the party of the workers until, after some imprudent manifestation of his own, an enemy has denounced him in the bourgeois press, thus placing him in a dilemma: he must either make a shameful retreat, at the cost of a humiliating retraction, or else must make public acknowledgment of the ideas which he has hitherto held secret. Such persons become members of the Socialist Party as young women sometimes become mothers, without having desired it. The Russian nihilist Netchajeff made the idea of unmasking these timid revolutionary-minded persons the basis of a scheme of revolutionary agitation. He contended that it was the revolutionist's duty to compromise all those who, while they shared most of his ideas, did not as

[2] "They remained faithful to the proposed outcome, faithful without taking heed of the difficulties which lay ahead. 'Forward! Come what may!' say the materialists, their eyes always fixed on their supreme ideal. This is not an idealism of words only, enervating and sterile, but one of action. This is daily life, broadened, enlarged, lighted by a high concept." (Trans. from Charles Rappoport, *La Philosophie de l'Histoire comme Science de l'Evolution*, Jacques, Paris, 1903, p. v).

yet share them all; in this way he would force them to break definitely with the enemy, and would gain them over completely to the "sacred cause."[3]

It has often been asserted that the receptivity to socialist ideas varies in the different liberal professions. It is said that the speculative sciences (in the strictest sense of the term), such as philosophy, history, political economy, theology, and jurisprudence, are so profoundly imbued with the spirit of the past that those engaged in their study are refractory *a priori* to the reception of all subversive ideas. In the legal profession, in particular, it is contended there is inculcated a love of order, an attachment to the thing which is, a sacred respect for form, a slowness of procedure, and, if you will, a certain narrowness of view, which are all supposed to constitute natural correctives to the errors inherent in democracy. In a general sense, we are told, the deductive and abstract sciences are authoritative and aristocratic in spirit, and those who pursue these paths of study incline to reactionary and doctrinaire views. Those, on the other hand, engaged in the study of the experimental and inductive sciences are led to employ their faculties of observation, which conduct them gradually to wider and wider generalizations, and they must thus be easy to win over to the cause of progress. The doctor, above all, whose profession is a continual struggle against human misery, must carry in his mind the germs of the socialist conception.

An analysis of the professions of the intellectuals belonging to the various socialist parties does not confirm this theory. It is in Italy and France alone that we find a considerable number of medical men in the socialist ranks, and even here they are less numerous than the devotees of pure science, and conspicuously less numerous than the lawyers. In Germany, the relations between the socialist workers and those medical men who are least well-to-do (the doctors of the insurance-bureaux) are far from cordial. To sum up, it may be said in general terms that the doctor's attitude towards socialism is colder and more hostile than that of the abstract philosopher or the barrister. One reason for his may perhaps be that among doctors, more than among other intellectuals, there prevails, and has prevailed for the past forty years, a materialistically conceived and rigidly held Darwinism and Häckelism. A supplementary cause may be found in the cynicism, often pushed to an ego-centric extreme, by which many doctors are affected, as a natural

[3] James Guillaume, *L'Internationale, etc.*, ed. cit., vol. ii, p. 62.

reaction against the smell of the mortuary which attends their life-work and as an outcome of their experience of the wickedness, the stupidity, and, the frailty of the human material with which their practice brings them in contact.

In certain Protestant countries, in Holland, Switzerland, Great Britain, and America, we find a considerable number of the clergy among the socialists (but this is not the case in Germany, where the state is vigilant and powerful whilst the Lutheran Church is strict and intolerant). These ministers, we are told, make their adhesion to socialism on account of an elevated sense of duty towards their neighbor, but perhaps in addition there is operative the need which is no less strong in the preacher than in the popular orator, to be listened to, followed, and, admired by the crowd—it is of little importance whether by believers or unbelievers.

Here some reference may be made to the abundance of Jews among the leaders of the socialist and revolutionary parties. Specific racial qualities make the Jew a born leader of the masses, a born organizer and propagandist. First among these qualities comes that sectarian fanaticism which, like an infection, can be communicated to the masses with astonishing frequency; next we have an invincible self-confidence (which in Jewish racial history is most characteristically displayed in the lives of the prophets); there are remarkable oratorical and dialectical aptitudes, a still more remarkable ambition, an irresistible need to figure in the limelight, and last but not least an almost unlimited power of adaptation. There has not during the last seventy-five years been any new current agitating the popular political life in which Jews have failed to play an eminent part. Not a few such movements must be distinctively considered as their work. Jews organize the revolution; and Jews organize the resistance of the state and of society against the subversive forces. Socialism and conservatisim have been forged by Jewish hands and are impregnated with the Jewish spirit. In Germany, for example, we see on the one side Marx and Lassalle fanning the flames of revolution, and on the other, after 1848, Julius Stahl working as the brilliant theorist of the feudal reaction. In England, the Jew Disraeli reorganized the forces of the Conservative Party. We find Jews at the head of movements which marshal against one another the nationalities animated by a reciprocal hate. At Venice, it was Daniel Manin who raised the standard of liberty against the Austrians. During the Franco-German war, the work of national defense was organized by Gambetta. In England, Disraeli was the inventor of the watchword "the integrity of the British Empire," while in Germany, the Jews Eduard Simson, Bamberger, and Larker, were the leading champions of the nationalist liberalism which played so important a part in the foundation of the empire. In Austria, Jews constitute the advance-guard of almost all the strongly nationalist parties. Among the German Bohemians, the Italian irredentists, the Polish nationalists, and in especial among the Magyars, the most fanatical are persons of Jewish race. The Jews, in fact, are capable of organizing every kind of movement; even among the leaders of antisemitism there are not wanting persons of Jewish descent.

The adaptability and the intellectual vivacity of the Jews do not, however, suffice to explain the quantitative and qualitative predominance of persons of Hebrew race in the party of the workers. In Germany, above all, the influence of Jews has been conspicuous in the labor movement. The two first great leaders, Ferdinand Lassalle and Karl Marx, were Jews, and so was their contemporary Moses Hess. The first distinguished politician of the old school to join the socialists, Johann Jacoby, was a Jew. Such also was Karl Höchberg, the idealist, son of a rich merchant in Frankfort-on-the-Main, founder of the first socialist review published in the German language. Paul Singer, who was almost invariably chairman of the German Socialist Congresses, was a Jew. Among the eighty-one socialist deputies sent to the Reichstag in the penultimate general election, there were nine Jews, and this figure is an extremely high one when compared with the percentage of Jews among the population of Germany, and also with the total number of Jewish workers and with the number of Jewish members of the socialist party. Four of the nine were still orthodox Jews (Stadthagen, Singer, Wurm, and Haase). In various capacities, Jews have rendered inestimable services to the party: Eduard Bernstein, Heinrich Braun, Jakob Stern, Simon Katzenstein, and Bruno Schönlank, as theorists; Gradnauer, Eisner, and Josef Bloch, the editor of the "Socialistische Monatshefte," as journalists; Hugo Heimann, in the field of municipal politics; Leo Arons, as a specialist in electoral affairs; Ludwig Frank, as organizer of the socialist youth. In Austria, the predominance of Jews in the socialist movement is conspicuous; it suffices to mention the names of Victor Adler, Ellenbogen, Fritz Austerlitz, Max Adler, F. Hertz, Therese Schlesinger-Eckstein, Dr. Diamand, Adolf Braun, etc. In America we have Morris Hillquitt, A. M. Simons, M. Untermann. In Holland, we have Henri Polak, the leader of the diamond workers, D. J. Wijnkoop, the independent Marxist, and M. Mendels. In Italy, Elia Musatti, Claudio Treves, G. E. Modigliani, Riccardo and Adolfo Momigliano, R. L. Foà, and the man of science Cesare Lombroso. Even in France, although here the rôle of the Jews is less conspicuous, we may mention the names of Paul Louis, Edgard Milhaud, and the shareholders of "l'Humanité" in 1904. The first congress of the Parti Ouvrier in 1879 was rendered possible by the liberal financial support of Isaac Adolphe Crémieux, who had been governor of Algeria under Gambetta.

In many countries, in Russia and Roumania for instance, but above all in Hungary and in Poland, the leadership of the working-class parties (the Russian Revolutionary Party excepted) is almost exclusively in the hands of Jews,[4] as is plainly apparent from an examination of the personality of the delegates to the international congresses. Besides, there is a great spontaneous export from Russia of Jewish proletarian leaders to foreign socialist parties: Rosa Luxemburg and Dr. Israel Helphant (Parvus) have gone to Germany; Charles Rappoport to France; Anna Kulishoff and Angelica Balabanoff to Italy; the brothers Reichesberg to Switzerland; M. Beer and Theodor Rothstein to England. Finally, to bring this long enumeration to a close, it may be mentioned that among the most distinguished leaders of the German anarchists there are many Jews, such as Gustav Landauer, Siegfried Nacht, Pierre Ramus, Senna Hoj (Johannes Holzmann).

The origin of this predominant position (which, be it noted, must in no sense be regarded as an indication of "Judaization," as a symptom of dependence of the party upon the money of Jewish capitalist comrades) is to be found, as far at least as concerns Germany and the countries of eastern Europe, in the peculiar position which the Jews have occupied and in many respects still occupy. The legal emancipation of the Jews has not there been followed by their social and moral emancipation. In large sections of the German people a hatred of the Jews and the spirit of the Jew-baiter still prevails, and contempt for the Jews is a permanent feeling. The Jew's chances in public life are injuriously affected; he is practically excluded from the judicial profession, from a military career, and from official employment. Yet everywhere in the Jewish race there continues to prevail an ancient and justified spirit of rebellion against the wrongs from which it suffers, and this

[4] Mermeix, *La France Socialiste*, ed. cit., p. 69.

sentiment, idealist in its origin, animating the members of an impassioned race, becomes in them more easily than in those of Germanic blood transformed into a disinterested abhorrence of injustice in general and elevated into a revolutionary impulse towards a grandly conceived world-amelioration.[5]

Even when they are rich, the Jews constitute, at least in eastern Europe, a category of persons who are excluded from the social advantages which the prevailing political, economic, and intellectual system ensures for the corresponding portion of the Gentile population. Society, in the narrower sense of the term, is distrustful of them, and public opinion is unfavorable to them. Besides the sentiment which is naturally aroused in their minds by this injustice, they are often affected by that cosmopolitan tendency which has been highly developed in the Jews by the historical experiences of the race, and these combine to push them into the arms of the working-class party. It is owing to these tendencies that the Jews, guided in part by reason and in part by sentimental considerations, so readily disregard the barriers which the bourgeoisie endeavors to erect against the rising flood of the revolution by the accusation that its advocates are *des sans patrie*.

For all these reasons, the Jewish intelligence is apt to find a shorter road to socialism than the Gentile, but this does not diminish the obligations of the Socialist Party to the Jewish intellectuals. Only to the intellectuals, indeed, for the Jews who belong to the wealthy trading and manufacturing classes and also the members of the Jewish petty bourgeoisie, while often voting socialist in the elections, steadily refuse to join the Socialist Party. Here the interests of class prevail over those of race. It is very different with the Jewish intellectuals, and a statistical enquiry would certainly show that not less than 2 to 3 per cent of these are members of the Socialist Party. If the Socialist Party has always manifested an unhesitating resistance to antisemite sentiment, this is due not merely to the theoretical socialist aversion for all "nationalism" and all

[5] Liebknecht declared in a speech: "Slavery does not merely demoralize; it illuminates the mind, elevates the strong, creates idealists and rebels. Thus we find that in the more powerful and nobler natures among the Jews a sense of freedom and justice has been inspired by their unworthy situation and a revolutionary spirit has been cultivated. The result is that there is proportionately a much larger amount of idealism among Jews than among non-Jews" (Wilhelm Liebknecht, *Ueber den Kölner Parteitag mit besonderer Berucksichtigung der Gewerkschaftsbewegung*, Buchdruckerei Volkswacht, Bielefeld, 1893, p. 33).—Regarding the revolutionary-idealist-fanatical tendencies of Judaism, see also the brilliant analysis by Guglielmo Ferrero in *L'Europa giovane*, Treves, Milan, 1897, pp. 358 et seq.

racial prejudices, but also to the consciousness of all that the party owes to the Jewish intellectuals.

"Antisemite socialism" made its first appearance about 1870. Eugen Dühring, at that time *Privatdozent* at the University of Berlin, inaugurated a crusade in favor of a "German" socialism as opposed to the "Jewish" socialism of Marx and his collaborators.[6] This movement was inspired by patriotic motives, for Dühring held that the victory of Marxian socialism could not fail to result in the complete subordination of the people to the state, to the advantage of the prominent Jews and their acolytes.[7] Towards 1875, Dühring became the center of a small group of Berlinese socialists of which Johann Most and the Jew Eduard Bernstein were members. The influence of this group, however, did not survive the great polemic which Dühring had to sustain with Friedrich Engels, the spiritual brother of "Marx the Jew."[8] Dühring's influence upon the socialist masses in fact declined in proportion as his antisemitism became accentuated, and towards 1878 it was extinct. In 1894 another attempt was made to give socialism an antisemite tendency. This was the work of Richard Calwer, another socialist of strongly nationalist views, at that time on the staff of the "Braunschweiger Volksfreund." "For every good Jewish writer," he declared, "there will be found at least half a dozen who are altogether worthless, but who possess an extraordinary power of self-assertion and an inexhaustible flow of words, but no real understanding of socialism."[9] Calwer's campaign had, however, no better success than that of Dühring. A year before, when petty bourgeois antisemitism was spreading through the country as an anti-capitalist movement which was forming itself into a poltical party and making victims everywhere, the Cologne congress (October 1893) took up a definite position towards this new political movement. Bebel's report (which in antisemite circles had been anticipated with satisfaction), although far from exhaustive, was inspired throughout by a sentiment friendly towards the Jews. Bebel said: "The Jewish student is as a rule industrious during the greater part of his university career, whereas the 'Germanic' student most commonly spends his time in the drinking-bars and restaurants, in

[6] Cf. Eugen Dühring, *Kritische Geschichte der Nationalækonomie u. der Sozialismus*, Th. Grieben, Berlin, 1871, pp. 589 et seq.

[7] Eugen Dühring, *Sache, Leben u. Feinde*, Carlsruhe, 1882, p. 207.

[8] Cf. Engels' work, *Herrn Eugen Dührings Umwälzung der Wissenschaft*, first published in 1877 in the Leipzig "Vorwärts."

[9] R. Calwar, *Das Kommunistische Manifest*, Günther, Brunswick, 1894, p. 41.

the fencing-schools, or in other places which I will not here more particularly specify (laughter).[10] Wilhelm Liebknecht, in his well-known speech at Bielefeld,[11] notably reinforced the impression hostile to antisemitism produced by the congress. Since that time (if we except certain observations made at the Lübeck congress in 1901 by the barrister Wolfgang Heine in a polemic against Parvus and Rosa Luxemburg[12]—remarks that were maladroit rather than expressions of principle, and at the worst foolish reminiscences of a youth passed as a leader in the *Verein deutscher Studenten*) the German socialists have remained immune to the virus of race hatred, and have shown themselves quite unconcerned when ignorant opponents have endeavored to arouse popular prejudice against them by speaking of them as a party of "Jews and their satellites."

We may now add certain observations upon the frequent adhesion to socialism of members of the plutocracy, an adhesion which at first sight seems so strange. Certain persons of a gentle and charitable disposition, abundantly furnished with everything that can satisfy their desires, are sometimes inspired by the need of undertaking propagandist activities. They wish, for example, to make their neighbors share in the well-being which they themselves enjoy. These are the rich philanthropists. In most cases their conduct is the outcome of hypersensitiveness or sentimentalism; they cannot endure the sufferings of others, not so much because they experience a genuine pity for the sufferers, but because the sight of pain arouses pain in themselves and shocks their æsthetic sense. They thus resemble the majority of human beings, who cannot bear to see pigeons slaughtered but whose sentiments in this respect do not impair their relish for a pigeon-pie.

In the sick brains of certain persons whose wealth is exceeded only by their love of paradox, there has originated the fantastic belief that in view of the imminence of the revolution they can preserve their fortunes from the confiscatory fury of the revolutionists only by making profession of the socialist faith, and by thus gaining the powerful and useful friendship of its leaders. It is this ingenuous belief which has thrown them into the arms of the socialists. Others, again, among the rich, hasten to enroll themselves as members of the Socialist Party, in the dread lest their lives should be threatened through the

10 *Protokoll*, p. 234.
11 Quoted above p. 248.
12 *Protokoll*, p. 195.

exasperation of the poor.[13] More frequently, however, as has been well shown by Bernard Shaw, the rich man is drawn towards socialism because he finds the greatest possible difficulty in procuring for himself any new pleasures. He begins to feel a disgust for the bourgeois world, and in the end this may stifle his class consciousness, or at least may suppress the instinct which has hitherto led him to light for self-preservation against the proletariat.[14]

It is a very striking phenomenon how large is the percentage of Jewish *rentiers* who become members of the Socialist Party. In part his may be due to the racial characteristics of the Jew to which reference has already been made. In part, however, it is the outcome of the psychological peculiarities of the wealthy man afflicted with satiety. In certain cases, again, the strongly developed love of acquisition characteristic of the Jews affords the explanation, where the possibility has been recognized of making a clever investment of capital even in working-class undertakings.

It may, however, be said without fear of error that the great majority of young bourgeois who come over to socialism do so, to quote an expression used by Felice Momigliano, in perfect sincerity and inspired by ardent goodwill. They seek neither popular approbation, nor wealth, nor distinctions, nor well-paid positions. They think merely that a man must set himself right with his own conscience and must affirm his faith in action.

These men, again, may be classed in two distinct categories. We have, on the one hand, the loving apostles of wide sympathies, who wish to embrace the whole of humanity in their ideal. On the other hand we have the zealots, fierce, rigid, austere, and uncompromising.

But among the socialists of bourgeois origin we find other and less agreeable elements. Above all there are those who make a profession of discontent, the neurasthenics and the *mauvais coucheurs*. Yet more numerous are the malcontents from personal motives, the charlatans, and the ambitious. Many hate the authority of the state because it is inaccessible to them. It is the old story of the fox and the grapes. They are animated by jealousy, by the unassuaged thirst for power; their

13 "O plutocrats, a solidarity of celestial origin chains you to their misery [the misery of the proletariat] through fear, and ties you by your very interest to their future deliverance." (Trans. from Louis Blanc, *Organisation du Travail*, ed. cit., p. 25).

14 Bernard Shaw, *Socialism for Millionaires*, Fabian Society, London, 1901.

feelings resemble those of the younger sons of great families who are inspired with hatred and envy towards their richer and more fortunate brothers. They are animated by a pride which makes them prefer the position of chief in proletarian Gaul to that of subordinate in aristocratic Rome. There are yet other types somewhat similar to those just enumerated. First of all, these are the eccentrics. It seems natural that those whose position is low should attempt to storm the heights. But there are some whose position is lofty and who yet experience an irresistible need to descend from the heights, where they feel that their movements are restricted, and who believe that by descending they will gain greater liberty. They seek "sincerity"; they endeavor to discover "the people" of whom they have an ideal in their minds; they are idealists to the verge of lunacy.

There may be added all those disillusioned and dissatisfied persons who have not succeeded in gaining the attention of the bourgeoisie to an extent proportionate to their own conception of their genius. Such persons throw themselves on the neck of the proletariat, in most cases with the vague and instinctive hope of attaining a speedier success in view of the deficient culture of the working classes, of gaining a place in the limelight and playing a leading part. They are visionaries, geniuses misunderstood, apostates of all kinds, literary bohemians, the unrecognized inventors of various social panaceas, *ratés*, *rapins*, *cabotins*, quack-salvers at the fair, clowns—all persons who are not thinking of educating the masses but of cultivating their own egos.

The numerical increase of the party, which is associated with an increasing prestige (in the popular esteem, at least, if not in the official word), exercises a great force of attraction. In such countries as Germany, above all, where the gregarious spirit is highly developed, small parties are condemned to a stinted and rickety existence. But numerous bourgeois believe that they will "find in the great Socialist Party what they have not been able to find in the bourgeois parties," a suitable platform for political activity upon a vast scale. For this reason, and above all when the party passes from opposition to governmental collaboration, there results a great increase in the number of those who regard the party as a mere means to their own ends, as a pedestal from whose elevation they can better satisfy their ambition and their vanity, those who regard success not as a goal to be attained for the good of the cause, or as the reward for arduous service in pursuit of ideal aims, but one coveted on its own account for the enlargement of their own personalities. As Arcoleo has well expressed it, we dread the triumph of such persons as if it were the unchaining of hungry wild beasts, but on closer examination we discover that after all they are no more than greedy molluscs, harmless on the whole. These considerations apply to petty affairs as well as to great ones. Whenever the party of the workers founds a cooperative society or a people's bank which offers to intellectuals an assured subsistence and an influential position, there flock to the scene numerous professional socialists who are equally devoid of true socialist knowledge and genuine socialist sentiment. In democracy as elsewhere success signifies the death of idealism.

Chapter 3

Social Changes Resulting from Organization

THE SOCIAL changes which organization produces among the proletarian elements, and the alterations which are effected in the proletarian movement through the influx of those new influences which the organization attracts within its orbit, may be summed up in the comprehensive customary term of the *embourgeoisement* of working-class parties. This embourgeoisement is the outcome of three very different orders of phenomena: (1) the adhesion of petty bourgeois to the proletarian parties; (2) labor organization as the creator of new petty bourgeois strata; (3) capitalist defense as the creator of new petty bourgeois strata.

1. The Adhesion of Petty Bourgeois to the Proletarian Parties

For motives predominantly electoral, the party of the workers seeks support from the petty bourgeois elements of society, and this gives rise to more or less extensive reactions upon the party itself. The Labor Party becomes the party of the "people." Its appeals are no longer addressed simply to the manual workers, but to "all producers," to the "entire working population," these phrases being applied to all the classes and all the strata of society except the idlers who live upon the income from investments. Both the friends and the enemies of the Socialist Party have frequently pointed out that the petty bourgeois members tend more and more to predominate over the manual workers. During the struggles which occurred during the early part of 1890 in the German Socialist Party against the so-called "youths," the assertion that during recent years a complete transposition of power had occurred within the party aroused a veritable tempest. On one side it was maintained that the proletarian elements were to an increasing extent being thrust into the background by the petty bourgeois. The other faction repudiated this accusation as a "calumny." One of the best established generalizations which we obtain from the study of history is this, that political parties, even when they are the advocates of moral and social ideas of profound import, find it very difficult to tolerate the utterance of inconvenient truths. We have seen that the most unprejudiced enquiries are apt to be regarded as the outcome of a vicious tendency to fault-finding. The truth is, however, that an objective and searching discussion of the question leads us to recognize the wrongheadedness at once of those who are content flatly to deny the embourgeoisement of the Socialist Party and also of those who are content to sing the praises of the great socialist petty bourgeois party. Neither view is sound. The processes at work are too complex for solution by easy phrasemaking.

It may sometimes happen (although statistical proof is lacking) that in South Germany in certain socialist branches, and still more in certain party congresses, the petty bourgeoisie, though not numerically predominant, can yet exercise a preponderant influence. It may even be admitted that under certain conditions the strength of the petty bourgeois elements and the respect which is paid to them may at times compromise the proletarian essence of the party. Even so rigid a Marxist as Karl Kautsky is of opinion that the attitude of socialists towards the minor distributive trade in general, so that, "on political grounds," socialists must oppose the foundation of cooperative societies wherever, as often happens, small traders offer a favorable recruiting-ground for socialism.[1]

Wherever it has been possible to analyse the composition of the socialist party, and to ascertain the classes and the professions of its adherents, it has generally been found that the bourgeois and petty bourgeois elements, although well represented, are far from being numerically preponderant. The official statistics of the Italian Socialist Party present the following figures:—Industrial workers, 42.27 per cent; agricultural laborers, 14.99 per cent; peasant proprietors, 6.1 per cent; independent artisans, 14.92 per cent; employees, 3.3 per cent; property owners, 4.89 per cent; students and members of the liberal professions, 3.8 per cent.[2] As regards the German Socialist Party, the writer has shown elsewhere[3] that in all the branches the proportion of proletarians is yet greater than in Italy, ranging from 77.4 per cent to 94.7 per cent. It may even be said, with Blank, that if there is a party in which the proletarian element predominates, it is the German Socialist Party

1 Karl Kautsky, *Der Parteitag von Hannover*, "Neue Zeit," anno xviii, No. 1.
2 Michels, *Proletariato e Borghesia, etc.*, ed. cit., p. 136.
3 Michels, *Die deutsche Sozialdemokratie. Parteimitgliedschaft u. sozials Zusammensetzung*, "Archiv f. Sozialwiss.," vol. xxiii, pp. 471–559.

—not indeed in respect of its voting strength,[4] but pre-eminently in respect of its inscribed membership. It is this social homogeneity which renders the Socialist Party so great an electoral force, giving to it a cohesion unknown to the other political parties, and especially to the other parties of the left German liberalism has always been (at any rate since the unification of the empire) a multicolored admixture of classes, united not so much by economic needs as by common ideal aims. Socialism, on the other hand, derives its human materials from the only class which presents those economic, social, and numerical conditions requisite to furnish the greatest possible vigor for the struggle to overthrow the old world and to install a new one in its place. Blind indeed must be he who fails to recognize that the spring which feeds the Socialist Party in Germany, a spring which shows no signs of running dry, is the proletariat, the class of wage-laborers.

We must therefore accept with all reserve the statements of those anarchizing socialists and bourgeois radicals who accuse the Socialist Party of "embourgeoisement" because it contains a certain number of small manufacturers and small traders. The embourgeoisement of the party is an unquestionable fact, but its causes will be found in a process very different from the entry into the organizations of the fighting proletariat of a few hundred members of the middle class. The chief of these causes is the metamorphosis which takes place in the leaders of working-class origin, with the resulting embourgeoisement of the whole atmosphere in which the political activities of the party are carried on.[5]

2. Labor Organization as the Creator of New Petty Bourgeois Strata

The class struggle, through the action of the organs whereby it is carried out, induces modifications and social metamorphoses in the party which has come into existence to organize and control the struggle. Certain groups of individuals, numer-

[4] R. Blank, *Die sociale Zusammensetzung der sozialdemokratischen Wählerschaft Deutschlands*, "Archiv f. Sozialwiss.," vol. xx, fasc. 3; but the author is wrong in drawing the conclusion (p. 535) "that the German social democracy is not a class party in respect of composition." He should have said, "In respect of the composition of the socialist electorate."

[5] Parvus writes: "There is a confusion between two distinct things: the petty bourgeois existences which are created by the party movement, and the entrance of petty bourgeois elements into the party. These should be separately considered" (Parvus, *Die Gewerkschaften und die Sozialdemokratie Kritischer Bericht über die Lager u. die Aufgaben der deutschen Arbeiterbewegung*, "Sächs. Arbeiterzeitung," Dresden, 1896, 2nd ed., p. 65).

ically insignificant but qualitatively of great importance, are withdrawn from the proletarian class and raised to bourgeois dignity.

Where, as in Italy, the party of the workers contains a considerable proportion of bourgeois, most of the posts which the party has at its disposal are in the hands of intellectuals. In England, on the other hand, and still more in Germany, it is otherwise, for here the demand on the part of the socialist movement for employees is met chiefly by a supply of persons from the rank and file. In these countries the party leadership is mainly in the hands of the workers, as is shown by the following table:—

SOCIALIST GROUP IN THE REICHSTAG, 1903–6

By Origin		By Profession	
I. Intellectuals and Bourgeois	13	I. Professional men	17
II. Petty Bourgeois	15	II. Independent means	2
		Manufacturers	1
		Publishers	2
		Bourgeois	5
III. Proletarians:			
Textile	3	III. Petty Bourgeois:	
Tobacco	8	Innkeepers	6
Printing	7	Independent artisans and working employers	6
Tailoring	3		
Glass-blowing	2		
Masonry	1	Small shopkeepers	3
Lithography	1	Small manufacturers	5
Basket-work	1	Owners of printing works	4
Glove-making	1		
Saddlery	1		
Stone-cutting	1	*Petty Bourgeois*	24
Turning	1		
Carpet-weaving	1		
Bootmaking	1		
Wood-working	10		
Bookbinding	1	IV. Employees in the labor movement	35
Mining	2		
Metallurgy	6		
Brush-making	1		
Pottery	1		
Manual workers	53		

By Origin	Per Cent	By Profession	Per Cent
13 intellectuals and bourgeois	= 16.05	17 professional men ..	= 20.99
15 petty bourgeois ...	= 18.52	5 bourgeois	= 6.17
54 proletarians *(skilled workers)*	= 65.43	24 petty bourgeois ...	= 29.63
		35 employees	= 43.21

Consequently an entry into the party hierachy becomes an aim of proletarian ambition.

An ex-member of the German Socialist Party who some years ago, having entered the service of one of the bourgeois parties, amused himself by caricaturing his former comrades, declared that the whole party organization with all its various degrees of propagandist activity was "cut upon the military model," and that the members were "promoted by seniority."[6] There is at least this much truth in Abel's assertion, that to every member of the party the possibility of gradual advance remains open, and that each may hope, should circumstances prove exceptionally favorable, to scale the olympian heights of a seat in the Reichstag.

Proletarian leaders of the socialist parties and of the trade unions are an indirect product of the great industry. At the dawn of the capitalist era certain workers, more intelligent and more ambitious than their fellows, succeeded, through indefatigable exertions and thanks to favorable circumstances, in raising themselves to the employing class. Today, however, in view of the concentration of enterprise and wealth and of the high cost of production, such a transformation can be observed only in certain parts of North and South America (which explains, it may be mentioned in passing, the insignificant development of socialism in the New World). As far as Europe is concerned, where there is no longer any virgin soil to exploit, the "self-made man" has become a prehistoric figure. Thus it is natural that enlightened workmen should seek some compensation for the lost paradise of their dreams. Numerous are today the workers whose energies and aptitudes are not fully utilized in the narrow circle of their professional occupations, often utterly uninteresting and demanding purely mechanical labor.[7] It is chiefly in the modern labor movement that such

[6] Abel, quoted by "Vorwärts," August 5, 1904.
[7] Heinrich, Herkner, *Die Arbeiterfrage,* ed. cit., p. 186; as regards Italy, Angelo Mosso, *Vita moderna degli Italiani,* Treves, Milan, 1906, pp. 249, 262–3.

men now seek and obtain the opportunity of improving their situation, an opportunity which industry no longer offers. The movement represents for them a new and loftier mode of life, and offers at the same time a new branch of employment, with a chance, which continually increases as the organization grows, that they will be able to secure a rise in the social scale. There can be no doubt that the Socialist Party, with its posts of honor, which are almost always salaried, exercises a potent stimulus upon active-minded youths of the working class from the very outset of their adhesion to its ranks. Those who are keen in political matters, and also those among the workers who possess talent as writers or speakers, cannot fail to experience the magnetic influence of a party which offers so rich a field for the use and development of their talents. Consequently we must accept as a logical truth what was pointed out by Guglielmo Ferrero, that while the adhesion of anyone of proletarian origin to the Socialist Party always presupposes a certain minimum of special aptitudes and favorable circumstances, yet such adhesion must be considered desirable and advantageous, not only upon ideal grounds and from motives of class egoism, but also for speculative reasons of personal egoism. For an intelligent German workman there is hardly any other way which offers him such rapid opportunities of "improving his condition" as service in the socialist army.[8] One of the first persons to recognize the bearing of these possibilities, and to utilize them, with considerable partisan exaggeration, for his own peculiar political ends, was Prince Bismarck. During the violent struggle between the government and the Socialist Party he declared: "The position of socialist agitator has today become a regular industry, just like any other. A man becomes an agitator or a popular orator as in former days he became a smith or a carpenter. One who adopts this new occupation is often much better off than if he had kept at his old work, gaining a more agreeable and freer life, one which in certain circles brings him more respect."[9] The allusion to the agreeable and free life of the socialist agitator recalls a phrase used by William II, who, apropos of the Krupp affair, spoke of the "safe ambush" from which socialist editors could shoot their carefully aimed arrows of calumny. The emperor's criticism is unjust, for the socialist editor who departs from the

[8] Guglielmo Ferrero, *L'Europa giovane*, ed. cit., pp. 72 et seq.

[9] Speech in the Reichstag, October 9, 1878. Cf. *Fürst Bismarck's Reden, mit verbind geschichtlicher Darstellung von Philipp Stein*, Reclame, Leipzig, vol. viii, p. 110.

truth is always exposed to the risk of prosecution and punishment. Bismarck hit the right nail on the head.

A gigantic and magnificently organized party like the German Socialist Party has need of a no less gigantic apparatus of editors, secretaries, bookkeepers, and numerous other employees, whose sole task is to serve this colossal machine. *Mutatis mutandis* the same is true of the other great branch of the working-class movement, the trade-union organizations. Now, for the reasons that have previously been discussed, there are available for the service of the German labor movement no more than a very small number of refugees from the bourgeoisie. It is for this reason that most of the posts are filled by men of working-class origin, who by zeal and by study have succeeded in gaining the confidence of their comrades. It may, then, be said that there exists a proletarian *élite* which arises spontaneously by a process of natural selection within the Socialist Party, and that its members come to perform functions altogether different from those which they originally exercised. To make use of a phrase which is convenient and comprehensible, despite its lack of scientific precision, we may say that such men have abandoned manual work to become brain-workers. For those who make such a change considerable advantages accrue, altogether independent of the advantages which attach *per se* to mental work when compared to manual. The manual worker who has become an official of the Socialist Party is no longer in a position of strictly personal and purely mercenary dependence upon his employer or upon the manager of the factory; he has become a free man, engaged in intellectual work on behalf of an impersonal enterprise. Moreover, he is bound to this enterprise, not solely by his strongest material interests, but also by the powerful ties of the ideal and of solidarity in the struggle. And notwithstanding certain exceptions which may confuse the minds of the profane, he is treated far more humanely than by an private employer. In relation to the party the employee is not a simple wage-earner, but rather a profit-sharing associate—not, of course, a profit-sharer in the industrial sense, since the party is not a commercial undertaking for the earning of dividends, but a profit-sharer in the ideal sense. It is not suggested that the party employee earns his bread in the most pleasant way in the world. On the contrary, as has been said in earlier chapters, the daily bread, which with rare exceptions is not unduly plentiful, must be earned by the fulfilment of an enormous amount of labor, prematurely exhausting health and energy. Nevertheless the ex-manual worker can live with dignity and comparative ease. Since he has a fixed salary, his position is more secure, and though outwardly more stormy, it is inwardly more tranquil, than that of the ordinary wage-earner. Should he be imprisoned, the party cares for him and his dependents, and the more often he is prosecuted the better become his chances of rapid advancement in his career of socialist official with all the advantages attaching to the position.

We may here consider the interesting question, What is the numerical ratio between the socialist bureaucracy and the organized masses; how many comrades are there for each party official? If we include in the term "official" all the mandataries of the party in the communes, etc., most of whom are unpaid, we sometimes attain to surprising results. For example, the socialist organization of the grand duchy of Baden, with a membership (1905) of 7,332, had more than 1,000 municipal councilors.[10] According to these figures, every seventh member of the Badenese party had the honor of being a party representative. This example, however, was quoted by the executive in its report to the congress of Jena precisely on account of its abnormality. Even though it may not be unique in southern Germany, it does not in truth bear upon the question we are now considering, which is the numerical relation between the enrolled membership and the party employees in the strict sense of the term, considered as a group of persons permanently and directly engaged in the service of the collectivity. The following figures give some idea of this ratio. According to a notice which in 1904 went the round of the German socialist press,[11] the party at that time employed, in addition to 1,476 persons engaged in the party printing establishment (about two-thirds of whom enjoyed the benefits of the eight-hour day, while many also had the right to regular holidays), 329 individuals working on the editorial staff and as delivery agents. The daily socialist press had in 1909 a circulation of one million, while the trade-union journals, weekly for the most part, had a far higher circulation.[12] Alike in the trade unions and in the Socialist Party the number of paid employees is rapidly increasing. The first regularly appointed and paid leaders in the European labor movement were the officials nominated in 1840 by the English Ironfounders' Society. Today in the trade-union organizations of

10 *Protokoll d. Verhandl. d. Parteitags zu Jena,* 1905, p. 16.
11 "Mitteldeutsche Sonntagszeitung," xi, No. 14.
12 Karl Kautsky, *Der Weg zur Macht, "Vorwärts,"* Berlin, 1909, p. 56.

the United Kingdom there are more than one thousand salaried employees.[13] In Germany, in the year 1898, the number of trade-union officials was 104; in 1904 it was 677, of whom 100 belonged to the metal-workers and 70 to the bricklayers and mason's union. This increase in the officialdom is accelerated, not merely by the steady increase in the membership, but also by the increasing complexity of the benefits offered by the organizations. Almost every meeting of the central executives discusses and determines upon the appointment of new officials, rendered essential by the further differentiation of the trade-union functions. There are always found advocates for the creation of fresh specialized posts in the labor movement, to fulfil various technical offices, to keep abreast of new discoveries and advances in methods of manufacture, to check the returns made by factory employers, to act as economists and compile trade statistics.

For some years past the same tendency has been manifest in the German Socialist Party. According to the report of the executive for the year 1909, very many district organizations now employ salaried secretaries. The number of district secretaries is 43, while in a single year the number of secretaries of constituencies increased from 41 to 62. There is a mutual aid society for officials of the Socialist Party and of the trade unions, and its membership continually increases. In 1902 it had 433 members; in 1905, 1,095; in 1907, 1,871; and in 1909, 2,474. But there must be officials who are not members of the society.

When he abandons manual work for intellectual, the worker undergoes another transformation which involves his whole existence. He gradually leaves the proletariat to become a member of the petty bourgeois class. At first, as we have seen, there is no more than a change in his professional and economic situation. The salaries paid by the party, although modest, are distinctly greater than the average wage which the worker gained before his entry into the socialist bureaucracy, and are calculated to enable the recipients to lead a petty bourgeois life. In one of the German Socialist Congresses, Wilhelm Liebknecht apostrophized the other leaders in the following terms: "You are for the most part aristocrats among the workers—aristocrats, I mean, in respect of income. The workers in the Erzgebirge or the weavers of Silesia would regard the salaries you earn as the income of a Crœsus.[14] It

[13] Fausto Pagliari, *Le Organ. e i loro Impiegati*, ed. cit., pp. 8–9.
[14] *Protokoll des Parteitags zu Berlin*, 1892, p. 122.

is true, at least in the majority of cases, that the career of the party or trade-union employee does not positively transform the ex-manual worker into a capitalist. Yet this career effects a notable elevation of the worker above the class to which he primarily belonged, and in Germany there is applied to the existence led by such persons the sociologically precise term of *gehobene Arbeiterexistenz* (a working-class life on a higher scale). Karl Marx himself did not hesitate to classify the working-class leaders under two heads, as *höherklassige* (workers of a superior class, intellectual workers) and *Arbeiter* (manual workers properly speaking).[15] As we shall show in fuller detail in a subsequent chapter, the manual worker of former days becomes a petty bourgeois or even a bourgeois. In addition to this metamorphosis, and despite his frequent contact with the mass of the workers, he undergoes a profound psychological transformation. The paid official, living at a higher social level, will not always possess the moral strength to resist the seductions of his new environment. His political and social education will seldom suffice to immunize him against the new influences. August Bebel repeatedly drew the attention of the party to the dangers by which the leaders were beset, the risks to their class purity and to their unity of thought. The proletarian party-officials, he said, are "persons whose life has become established upon a comparatively stable basis."[16]

A closer examination will show that the phenomenon here considered has a profound social significance, and that neither within nor without the party has it hitherto received the attention it deserves. For the German workers, the labor movement has an importance analogous to that of the Catholic Church for certain fractions of the petty bourgeoisie and of the rural population. In both cases we have an organization which furnishes opportunities to the most intelligent members of certain classes to secure a rise in the social scale. In the Church, the peasants' son will often succeed in achieving social advance, whose equivalent in all the other liberal professions has remained the monopoly of members of the aristocracy of birth or of wealth. No one of peasant birth becomes a general or a prefect, but not a few peasants become bishops. Pope Pius X was of peasant origin. Now that which the Church offers to peasants and to petty bourgeois, namely, a facility for ascent

[15] Karl Marx, *Briefe u Auszuge, etc.*, ed. cit., p. 159.
[16] August Bebel, speaking at the Dresden congress, 1903. *Protokoll über die Verhandlungen des Parteitags*, "Vorwärts," Berlin, 1903, p. 230.

in the social scale, is offered to intelligent manual workers by the Socialist Party.

As a source of social transformations the Socialist Party has many affinities with another institution, namely, the Prussian military organization. The son of a bourgeois family who adopts a permanent military career becomes a stranger to his own class. Should he attain to high rank, he will receive a title from the emperor. He loses his bourgeois characteristics and adopts the usages and opinions of his new feudal environment. It is true that these military officers are only manifesting the tendency to the attainment of "gentility" in which the whole bourgeoisie is involved,[17] but in their case this process is greatly accelerated, and is effected with a full consciousness of its consequences. Every year hundreds of young men from the upper and middle strata of the bourgeois class become officers in the army, simply from the desire to secure a higher position and more social consideration. In the Socialist Party a similar effect is often the result of necessity, the individual's social metamorphosis taking place independently of the will. But the general results are similar.

Thus the Socialist Party gives a lift to certain strata of the working class. The more extensive and the more complicated its bureaucratic mechanism, the more numerous are those raised by this machine above their original social position. It is the involuntary task of the Socialist Party to remove the proletariat, to deproletarianize, some of the most capable and best informed of its members. Now, according to the materialist conception of history, the social and economic metamorphosis gradually involves a metamorphosis in the realm of ideas. The consequence is that in many of the ex-workers this embourgeoisement is very rapidly effected. Naturally the change is less speedy in proportion as socialist theory is more deeply rooted in the mind of the individual. Numerous are those manual workers who, having attained a higher social and economic situation, none the less remain throughout their lives profoundly attached to the socialist cause. In this case, however, the ex-manual worker is, just like the ex-bourgeois socialist, an "ideologue," since his mentality does not correspond to his position in society. Sometimes, again, the psychological metamorphosis we are considering is, as it were,

17 Franz Mehring: "It is distressing that at a time when the army cannot exist without bourgeois money and bourgeois intelligence, the bourgeois youth should have no higher ambition than to force his way into the feudal caste" (*Der Krieg gegen die Troddeln*, "Leipziger Volkszeitung," xi, No. 4).

inhibited by a tenacious and vigorous hereditary socialist mentality: here we see the children and grandchildren following their parents as whole-hearted combatants on behalf of the labor party, notwithstanding the elevated position to which they have attained. Experience shows, however, that such cases are exceptional. Even when the deproletarianized socialist remains a sincere advocate of proletarian emancipation, and grows gray in his position of socialist editor or deputy, his children, sons as well as daughters, are thoroughgoing members of the higher social class into which they have been removed by the improvement in their father's social position, and this not merely in the material sense, but in respect of their ideas, so that it becomes impossible to distinguish them from their fellow-bourgeois. In most cases the only bond which remains to attach the father to the working class, his faith in the politico-social dogma of socialism, is slackened in the son to become an absolute indifference and sometimes an open hostility to socialism. To sum up, it may be said that these former working-class people, considered as families and not as individuals, are absorbed sooner or later into the new bourgeois environment. The children receive a bourgeois education; they attend better schools than those to which their father had access; their interests are bourgeois and they very rarely recall the revolutionary and anti-bourgeois derivation of their own entrance into the bourgeoisie. The working-class families which have been raised by the revolutionary workers to a higher social position, for the purpose of a more effective struggle against the bourgeoisie, thus come before long to be fused with the bourgeoisie.

Reference has previously been made to a similar phenomenon in the case of the families of working-class leaders who are refugees from the class of bourgeois intellectuals. The final result is the same, the only difference being that the children of the ex-manual workers forget their class of origin, while the children of the bourgeois intellectuals recall it. The result is that in the history of the labor movement we may observe a similar irony to that which may be seen in the history of the bourgeois resistance to the workers. The bourgeoisie has not been able to prevent a number of the best instructed, most capable, and most adroit among its elements from placing themselves at the head of the mortal enemies of the bourgeoisie; it is often these ex-bourgeois who stimulate the proletarians to resistance and organize them for the struggle. The proletariat suffers a similar fate. In the severe struggle it has undertaken for the expropriation of the expropriators, it elevates from the depths of its own class those who have the finest intelligences and the keenest vision, by serious collective sacrifices gives them the pen to use in place of ruder tools, and in doing so it throws into the arms of the enemy those who have been selected with the express purpose of fighting the privileged class. If the chosen combatants do not themselves go over to the enemy, their children at least will do so. This is indeed a tragical destiny: ex-bourgeois on the one side, and ex-manual workers on the other. The imposing political contest between the classes representing respectively capital and labor ends, however paradoxical this may appear, in a manner analogous with that which in the sphere of economic competition is determined through the operation of supply and demand, speculation, personal adroitness, etc.—in a social exchange among the classes. It is hardly necessary to repeat that this interchange of the ripples on the surface of the waves does not weaken, and far less annul, the profundity of social antagonisms. It is obvious that the process of social exchange can on either side effect no more than infinitesimal minorities. But it affects the most influential, and herein lies its sociological importance. It affects the self-made leaders.

3. Capitalist Defense as the Creator of New Petty Bourgeois Strata

The embourgeoisement of certain strata of the working-class party has other factors in addition to the influence of the bureaucratic apparatus of the Socialist Party, the trade unions, and the cooperative societies. This development, which is a necessary characteristic of every movement towards emancipation, is to a certain extent paralleled by the constitution of a petty bourgeoisie of strongly proletarian characteristics, itself also developed from below upwards, itself also an accessory phenomenon of the struggle of the organized workers for social emancipation, but which takes place outside the various forms of socialist organization. We allude to those proletarian elements which become particularly numerous in times of crisis, when the labor organizations are still weak and persecuted, as was the case in Germany during the days of the anti-socialist law. At such times numerous proletarians are victimized, it may be on account of their passive fidelity to party or trade union, it may be because their attitude is frankly socialist and "subversive." Forced by necessity, these victims of capitalist reprisals have no other resource than to adopt some form of independent enterprise. Abandoning their ancient handicraft, they open a small shop, fruit and vegetables, stationery, grocery, or tobacco; they become pedlars, keep a coffee-stall, or the like. In most cases their ancient associates support them with admirable solidarity, regarding it as a duty to assist these unfortunate comrades by giving them their custom. It sometimes happens that some of these new petty bourgeois find their way definitely into the middle class. Thus capitalist resistance has automatically created new strata of petty bourgeois.

In addition to these victims of the struggle for proletarian emancipation, there are not a few workers who leave their class, not from necessity, but influenced to a large extent by the love of speculation and the desire to improve their social position. Thus there has come into existence a whole army of ex-proletarians, petty bourgeois and small shopkeepers, who all claim, in virtue of a superior moral right, that the comrades must support them by dealing exclusively at their establishments. The mode of life of these small traders often reduces them, despite all their good wishes, to the level of social parasites; their command of capital being extremely small, the goods they offer to their customers, that is to say to the organized workers, are both bad and dear.

Still more important in German socialism is the rôle of those who are termed *Parteibudiger*, that is to say tavern-keepers who are members of the party. During the prevalence of the anti-socialist law their political mission was of incontestable importance. In many small towns the tavern-keepers belonging to the party still exercise multifarious and important functions. It is in their houses that the executive committee meets; often these are the only places where socialist and trade-union journals are found on the tables; and in many cases, since the owners of other halls are hostile or timid, it is here alone that public meetings can be held. In a word, they are necessary instruments in the local socialist struggle. In the more important centers, however, these places, with their unhygienic environment, become a veritable curse to the party. It may be added that the brutal struggle for existence leads the petty bourgeois tavern-keepers to exercise improper pressure upon the socialist organizations. They enjoy a considerable influence among the comrades, and this pressure is commonly exerted in a manner directly injurious to the interests of the proletariat. The attempts which have been made in Germany, especially since 1890, to induce the workers to abandon the unwholesome rooms of the old taverns and to frequent the great modern establishments with fine airy halls, have led, as was inevitable, to "a vigorous opposition" on the part of the socialist tavern-keepers.[18] For many years the members of the party whose living is made by the sale of drink have energetically resisted the foundation of "People's Houses"; notwithstanding the sympathy for such institutions they may theoretically possess, they dread this new form of competition, and act in accordance with their immediate personal interests. In most cases their opposition has proved ineffectual. Not always, however. Even today there exist German towns with from twenty thousand to thirty thousand inhabitants in which the existence of a *Parteikneipe* (which despite its name of "Party tavern" is the exclusive property of some individual member of the party) has proved an insuperable obstacle in the way of the local labor organizations when they have desired to build a place of their own, or even to obtain from other and nonsocialist inkeepers the use of a more commodious hall for their meetings.

For an additional reason, these socialist taverns are calamitous in their influence upon the party, in that they oppose a potent obstacle to the extension of the temperance movement which has been initiated during recent years. It is no secret in socialist circles that long before the congress of Essen (1907) the party would have declared openly against alcoholism, and that after this congress it would have applied its decisions with greater vigor, had not the party leaders been restrained by the fear that the measures recommended, and even a simple temperance propaganda, would react injuriously upon the interests of an influential category of the members of the party.

It is impossible to determine with any accuracy the number of individuals who have become independent petty bourgeois as the outcome of the struggles of the workers and the political reprisals of the employers. Tobacconists, grocers, etc., elude statistical investigation. The only definite information we possess relates to tavern-keepers. In the parliamentary group we find that in 1892, of 35 socialist deputies, 4 were publicans (11.4%); in 1903, of 58 socialist deputies, 5 were publicans (8.6%); and in 1906, of 81 socialist deputies, 6 were publicans (7.4%). In the local socialist sections, the proportion of tavern-keepers is considerable. At Leipzig, in 1887, there were 30 *Partiekneipen*. In 1900, among the socialist branches

18 R. Calwer, op. cit., p. 9.

of the Leipzig country districts with 4,855 members there were 84 restaurant-keepers and publicans (1.7%); in Leipzig city, where the socialists numbered 1,681, there were in 1900, 47 tavern-keepers, and in 1905, 63 (3.4%). Offenbach, in 1905, 1,668 members, 74 publicans and 2 retailers of bottled beer (4.6%). Munich, in 1906, 6,704 members; milk-retailers, tobacconists, sellers of cheese, etc., and publicans (wine merchants not included), 369 (5.5%). Frankfort-on-the-Main, in 1906, 2,620 members, 25 publicans (12 retailers of bottled beer and tobacconists excluded—approximately 1%). Marburg, in 1906, 114 members, 2 publicans (1.8%). Reinickendorf-Ost, near Berlin, in 1906, 303 members, 18 tavern- and restaurant-keepers (5.9%). These figures serve to show that in certain towns there is a socialist publican for every twenty members. Since the socialist publican depends mainly upon socialist customers, it follows that these twenty comrades must provide the chief financial resources of the enterprise.

The best proof of the numerical strength and the importance of this category of the members of the party is that they have founded at Berlin a powerful association, the Berlin League of Socialist Publicans and Innkeepers. It must not be forgotten that this association has largely come into existence from the consideration that the socialist publicans have other political tasks to fulfil from those which devolve upon their "bourgeois" colleagues, nor can it be denied that its members constitute a category of chosen socialists of tried fidelity, who have rendered important services to the party in its political campaigns and agitations, and whose socialist clientèle is actuated by a high spirit of solidarity in giving these comrades its custom. It is inevitable, however, that the existence of such an organization, which represents peculiar economic interests, should in certain cases involve inconveniences, not merely for its competitors, the bourgeois publicans, but also for the socialist comrades, and that it should tend to assume the aspect of a party within the party. In the summer of 1906, the increase in the cost of production of beer, which resulted from new taxation by which the breweries were especially hard hit, led the publicans to raise the price to the consumers. Thereupon the German workers in a great many towns protested most energetically, and declared what was known as the "beer war," boycotting certain breweries and the publicans who had raised the price—an agitation which led certain foreign socialists to observe sarcastically that you may take anything from the German worker except his beer. In this struggle, which was in many places conducted with great obstinacy, the organized workers encountered resistance from a notable proportion of socialist publicans. These, adopting a tactical outlook estranged from socialist principles, endeavored to alarm the comrades by insisting upon the dangers of their campaign, and by predicting that if the consumers should succeed in forcing the producers to bear the new taxes, the government, delighted to find that these taxes were not pressing upon the masses of the people but were borne only by a restricted class of brewers and factory owners, would hasten to introduce new and yet heavier taxation, which could not fail to affect the consumers.

To sum up, it may be said that the petty bourgeois of proletarian origin, although the conditions of their life are not as a rule notably better than those of the proletarian strata from which they derive, constitute in more than one respect, on account of the particular interests they represent, a serious obstacle to the forward march of the working class legions. Moreover, it has to be remembered that the influence of this new stratum impresses upon the party from the mental point of view (in consequence of the new place which these elements occupy in the general economic process) a markedly petty bourgeois stamp.

Chapter 4

The Need for the Differentiation of the Working Class

EVERY INDIVIDUAL member of the working class cherishes the hope of rising into a higher social sphere which will guarantee to him a better and less restricted existence. The workman's ideal is to become a petty bourgeois.[1] To noninitiates and to superficial observers the working-class members of the socialist parties seem always to be petty bourgeois. The proletariat has not been able to emancipate itself psychically from the social environment in which it lives. For example, the German worker, as his wages have increased, has acquired the disease which is in the blood of the German petty bourgeoisie, the club-mania. In every large town, and not a few small ones, there is a swarm of working-class societies: gymnastic clubs, choral societies, dramatic societies; even smokers' clubs, bowling clubs, rowing clubs, athletic clubs—all sorts of associations whose essentially petty bourgeois character is not destroyed by the fact that they sail under socialist colors. A bowling club remains a bowling club even if it assumes the pompous name of "Sons of Freedom Bowling Club."

Just as little as the bourgeoisie can the socialist workers be regarded as a great homogeneous gray mass, although this consideration does not modify the fact that since proletarians all live by the sale of their only commodity, labor, the organized socialist workers are, at least in theory, conscious of their own unity in their common opposition to the owners of the means of production and to the governmental representatives of these. Yet it cannot be denied that the actual system of manufacture which unites under the same roof all the different categories of workers employed in a modern establishment for the production of railway-carriages, for instance, does not serve to overthrow the barriers which separate the various sub-classes

[1] According to Tullio Rossi Doria (*Le Forze Democratiche ed il Programma socialista*, "Avanti," anno xiv, No. 30), every struggle for higher wages has the same end in view. But as a rule the struggle for higher wages is carried out by a trade union, and the aim of the trade unions is to secure a better position for the manual workers, not to make them petty bourgeois. The organized workers as a whole desire to live like the petty bourgeois, but not to fulfil the economic function of these. They wish to remain manual workers.

of workers.[2] Nor is it less true, looking at the matter from the other side, that there exists among the workers the sense of a need for differentiation which will readily escape those who do not come in personal contact with them. The kind of work, the rate of wages, differences of race and climate, produce numerous shades of difference alike in the mode of life and in the tastes of the workers. As early as 1860 it was said: "Among the workers there are many categories and an aristocratic stratification. Printers take the lead; ragpickers, scavengers, and sewermen close the line."[3] Between the compositor and the casual laborer in the same country there exist differences in respect of culture and of social and economic status more pronounced than those between the compositor in one country and the small manufacturer in another.[4] The discrepancy between the different categories of workers is plainly displayed even in the trade-union movement. We know, for example, that the policy of the compositors' unions in Germany, France, and Italy differs from that of the other unions, and also from that of the Socialist Party, exhibiting a tendency towards the right, being more opportunist and more accommodating. In Germany, the compositors' union has for its president a Rexhäuser, and in France a Keufer. We observe, too, in the conduct of the diamond-workers in Holland and in Belgium the same unsocialistic, unproletarian, and particularist tendencies. The aristocratic element of the working class, the best paid, those who approximate most closely to the bourgeoisie, pursue tactics of their own. In the active work of the labor movement, the division of the organized masses into different social strata is often plainly manifest. Working-class history abounds in examples showing how certain fractions or categories of the proletariat have, under the influence of interests peculiar to their sub-class, detached themselves from the great army of labor and made common cause with the bourgeoisie. Thus it happens, generally speaking, that the workers in armaments factories have little sympathy with anti-militarist views. At the London congress of the Independent Labor Party in 1910, the Woolwich delegate, largely representing the view of the employees at Woolwich arsenal, expressed strong

[2] Rudolf Broda and Julius Deutsch, *Das moderne Proletariat*, Reimer, Berlin. 1910, p. 73.

[3] Trans. from Edmond About, *Le Progrès, Hachette*, Paris. 1864, pp. 51–2.

[4] Cf. the interesting communication upon the increasing differentiation of the working classes made by Hermann Herkner to the congress of the Verein für Sozialpolitik held at Nuremberg in 1911 (*Protokoll*, pp. 122 et seq.).

dissent from the opinion of those delegates who had brought forward a resolution in favor of a restriction of armaments and of compulsory arbitration in international disputes.[5] Again, the check which was sustained at Venice by the general strike of protest against the Tripolitan campaign was due to the opposition of a section of the arsenal workers.[6] The very fact that the cessation of work on May 1st is but a partial demonstration renders it possible to divide the workers into two classes. One consists of those who thanks to better conditions of life and other favorable circumstances "can allow themselves the luxury" of celebrating the 1st of May; the other comprises those who by poverty or ill-fortune are compelled to remain at work.[7]

The need for differentiation is manifested still more clearly when we consider more extended groups of workers. The difference between skilled and unskilled workers is primarily and predominantly economic, and displays itself in a difference of working conditions. As time passes, this difference becomes transformed into a veritable class distinction. The skilled and better paid workers hold aloof from the unskilled and worse paid workers. The former are always organized, while the latter remain "free" laborers; and the fierce economic and social struggles which occur between the two groups constitute one of the most interesting phenomena of modern social history. This struggle, which by the physiologist Angelo Mosso is termed *ergomachia,* the struggle for the feeding-ground,[8] is waged with ever-increasing intensity. The organized workers demand from the unorganized the strictest solidarity, and insist that the latter should abandon work whenever they themselves are in conflict with the employers. When this demand is not immediately complied with, they insult the unorganized workers by the use of approbrious names which have found a place in scientific terminology. In France, in the days of Louis Philippe, they were called *bourmont* and *ragusa.* At the

5 "Volksstimme," 1910, No. 76, fourth supplement.

6 Exaggeration must be avoided here, and it is desirable to point out that in the election of March 1912 in the Venetian constituency in which the arsenal is situated, notwithstanding all kinds of adverse pressure, two thousand electors expressed their definite disapproval of the African campaign by voting for the intransigeant socialist Musatti ("Avanti," anno xvi, No. 85).

7 The phrase quoted in the text is used by a correspondent of the "Volksstimme," of Frankfort (*Die Maifeier am ersten Maisonntag,* Manifest-Nummer, 1910, seventh supplement). The same article shows from how distinctively capitalist an outlook the better-paid workers regard the May Day celebration.

8 Angelo Mosso, *Vita moderna degli Italiani,* ed. cit., p. 178.

present day they are in Germany termed *Streikbrecher;* in Italy, *krumiri;* in England, *blacklegs;* in America, *scabs;* in Hainault, *gambes de bos;* in France, *jaunes, renards,* or *bédouins;* in Holland, *onderkruipers;* and so on. It is incontestable that the grievances of the organized workers against the unorganized are largely justified. On the other hand, it cannot be denied that in the working class this ergomachia is not essentially the outcome of differences between the well-disposed workers and the ill-disposed, as masters and men naïvely believe, of course inverting the rôles. For the socialists, in fact, the strikers are always heroes and the strike-breakers are always villains; whilst for the employers the strike-breakers are honest and hardworking fellows, whilst the strikers are idle good-for-nothings. In reality, ergomachia does not consist of a struggle between two categories distinguished by ethical characteristics, but is for the most part a war between the better-paid workers and the poorer strata of the proletariat. The latter, from the economic aspect, consist of those who are still economically unripe for a struggle with the employers to secure higher wages. We often hear the most poverty-stricken workers, conscious of their inferiority, content that their wages are high enough, whilst the better paid and organized workers declare that the unorganized are working at starvation rates. One of the most indefatigable of French socialist women has well said: "One is almost tempted to excuse the betrayals of these 'scabs' when one has seen with one's own eyes all the tragedy of the unemployed in England. In the large ports of the south and west, one sees, ranged along the wall of a dock, thousands and thousands of famished people, pale, trembling figures, who hope to be hired as dockers. A few dozen are needed. When the doors open, there is a terrible scramble, a veritable battle. Recently, one of these men, pressed on all sides, died of suffocation in the melee."[9] The organized workers, on their side, do not consider themselves obliged to exhibit solidarity towards the unorganized, even when they are all sharing a common poverty during crises of unemployment. The German trades councils often demand that the subsidies which (in accordance with the so-called Strasburg system) are provided in certain large towns from the public funds to render assistance in cases of unemployment,

[9] Trans. from Madame Sorgue, *Retour d'Angleterre,* "La Société Nouvelle," xvi, No. 8, p. 197.

should be reserved for the organized workers, declaring that the unorganized have no claim to assistance.[10]

The more fortunate workers do not only follow their natural inclination to fight by all available means against their less well-to-do comrades, who, by accepting lower wages, threaten the higher standard of life of the organized workers—using in the struggle, as always happens when economic interests conflict, methods which disregard every ethical principle. They also endeavor to hold themselves completely aloof. The union button is often, as it were, a patent of nobility which distinguishes its wearer from the plebs. This happens even when the unorganized workers would like nothing better than to make common cause with the organized. In almost all the larger British and American trade unions there is manifest a tendency to corporatism, to the formation of sharply distinguished working-class aristocracies.[11] The trade unions, having become rich and powerful, no longer seek to enlarge their membership, but endeavor rather to restrict it by imposing a high entrance fee, by demanding a certificate of prolonged apprenticeship, and by other similar means, all deliberately introduced in order to retain certain privileges in their own hands at the expense of other workers following the same occupation. The anti-alien movement is the outcome of the same professional egoism, and is especially conspicuous among the Americans and Australians, who insist upon legislation to forbid the immigration of foreign workers. The trade unions in such cases adopt a frankly "nationalist" policy. In order to keep out the "undesirables" they do not hesitate to appeal for aid to the "class-state," and they exercise upon the government a pressure which may lead their country to the verge of war with the labor-exporting land.[12] In Europe, too, we may observe, although here to a less degree, the formation within the labor movement of closed groups and coteries (and it is in this that the tendency to oligarchy consist), which arise in direct conflict with the theoretical principles of socialism. The workers

[10] The reader will find a more copious and more detailed study of this matter in an essay compiled by the present writer in collaboration with his wife. Michels, *Das Problem der Arbeitslosigkeit und ihre Bekämpfung durch die deutschen freien Gewerkschaften*, "Archiv f. Sozialw.," xxxi, September 2, 1910, pp. 479–81.

[11] Cf., inter alia, Daniel De Leon, *The Burning Question of Trades-Unionism*, Labour News Co., New York, 1906, p. 13.

[12] The American labor organizations have played a notable part in producing tension between the United States and Japan, a tension which, a few years ago, nearly culminated in war.

employed at the Naples arsenal, who recently demanded of the government that "a third of the new places to be filled should be allotted to the sons of existing employees who are following their fathers' trade,"[13] are in sentiment by no means so remote from the world of our day as might at first be imagined. As has been well said, "The goal of the class struggle is to raise the lower classes to the level of the upper class. This is why revolutions frequently succeed, not in democratizing the classes, but in making the democrats class-conscious."[14]

The policy of social reform, which finds its most definite expression in labor legislation, does not entail the same advantages for all sections of the working class. For example, the law which raises the minimum age of the factory worker will have varying effects according as may vary the power of the labor organizations, the rate of wages, the conditions of the labor market, etc., in the different branches of industry or agriculture. Thus in certain categories of workers the effect of the law will be a transient depression of the standard of life, whilst in other cases it will lead to a permanent elevation in that standard. There results an even greater accentuation of the differentiation which the proletarian groupings already present as the outcome of national, local, and technical differences.

To sum up, it may be affirmed that in the contemporary working class there is already manifest a horizontal stratification. Within the *quatrième état* we see already the movements of the embryonic *cinquième état*. One of the greatest dangers to the socialist movement, and one which must not be lightly disregarded as impossible, is that gradually there may come into existence a number of different strata of workers, as the outcome of the influence of a general increase of social wealth, in conjunction with the efforts made by the workers themselves to elevate their standard of life; this may in many cases enable them to secure a position in which, though they may not completely lose the common human feeling of never being able to get enough, from which even millionaires are not altogether exempt, they will become so far personally satisfied as to be gradually estranged from the ardent revolutionary aspirations of the masses towards a social system utterly different from our own—aspirations born of privation. Thus the working class will become severed into two unequal parts, subject to perpetual fluctuations in their respective size.

13 Angelo Mosso, *Vita moderna degli Italiani*, ed. cit., p. 191.

14 Trans. from Cf. Raoul de La Grasserie, *Les Luttes sociales*, "Annales de l'Institut intern. de Sociologie," vol. xi, p. 185.

Chapter 5

Labor Leaders of Proletarian Origin

ATTEMPTS HAVE not been lacking to solve the insoluble problem, how to obviate the leaders' dominion over the led. Among such attempts, there is one which is made with especial frequency, and which is advocated with considerable heat, to exclude all intellectuals from leadership in the working-class movement. This proposal reflects the dislike for the intellectuals which, in varying degrees, has been manifested in all countries and at all times. It culminates in the artificial creation of authenticated working-class leaders, and is based upon certain general socialist dogmas, mutilated or imperfectly understood, or interpreted with undue strictness—on an appeal, for instance, to the principle enunciated at the constitutive congress of the first International held at Geneva in 1866, that the emancipation of the workers can be effected only by the workers themselves.

Above all, however, such proposals are based upon an alleged greater kinship between the leaders of proletarian origin and the proletarians they lead. The leaders who have themselves been manual workers are, we are told, more closely allied to the masses in their mode of thought, understand the workers better, experience the same needs as these, and are animated by the same desires. There is a certain amount of truth in this, inasmuch as the ex-worker cannot only speak with more authority than the intellectual upon technical questions relating to his former occupation, but has a knowledge of the psychology and of the material details of working-class life derived from personal experience. It is unquestionably true that in the leaders of proletarian origin, as compared with the intellectuals, we see conspicuously exhibited the advantages of leadership as well as the disadvantages, since the proletarian commonly possesses a more precise understanding of the psychology of the masses, knows better how to deal with the workers. From this circumstance the deduction is sometimes made that the ex-worker, when he has become immersed in the duties of political leadership, will continue to preserve a steady and secure contact with the rank and file, that he will choose the most practicable routes, and that his own proletarian experiences will afford a certain safeguard against his conducting the masses into regions and bypaths from which they are by nature totally estranged.

The central feature of the syndicalist theory is found in the demand for direct action on the part of the trade union, enfranchised from the tutelage of socialist leaders predominantly bourgeois in origin, the union being self-sufficient and responsible to itself alone. Direct action means that the proletariat is to pursue its aims without the intermediation of parliamentary representation. Syndicalism is described as the apotheosis of proletarian autonomy. Everything is to be effected by the energy, initiative, and courage of individual workers. The organized proletariat is to consist of an army of *franctireurs,* disembarrassed of the impotent general staff of effete socialist bureaucrats, unhampered, autonomous, and sovereign.[1] Passing, however, from fiction to fact, we find that the most substantial difference between syndicalism and political socialism, apart from questions of tactics, is to be found in a difference of social origin in the leaders of the respective tendencies. The trade union is governed by persons who have themselves been workers, and from this the advocates of syndicalism infer, by a bold logical leap, that the policy of the leaders of working-class origin must necessarily coincide with the policy of the proletariat.[2]

The syndicalist leaders are to be, both in the intellectual and moral sense, chosen manual workers.[3] The leader of working-class origin is regarded as the Messiah who will cure all the ills of proletarian organization; he is, in any case, the best of all possible leaders.

It is hardly necessary to point out that it is an illusion to imagine that by entrusting its affairs to proletarian leaders the proletariat will control these affairs more directly than if the leaders are lawyers or doctors. In both cases, all action is effected through intermediaries. In the modern labor movement it is impossible for the leader to remain in actual fact a manual worker. Directly a trade union selects one of the comrades in the factory to minister regularly to the collective interests in return for a definite salary, this comrade is, consciously or not, lifted out of the working class into a new class, that of the salaried employees. The proletarian leader has ceased to be a

1 Edouard Berth, *Les nouveaux Aspects du Socialisme,* Rivière, Paris, 1908, p. 30.
2 Emile Pouget, *Le Parti du Travail,* Bibl. Syndicaliste, Paris, No. 3, p. 12.
3 Fernand Pelloutier. *Histoire des Bourses du Travail,* ed. cit., p. 86.

manual worker, not solely in the material sense, but psychologically and economically as well. It is not merely that he has ceased to quarry stones or to sole shoes, but that he has become an intermediary just as much as his colleagues in leadership, the lawyer and the doctor. In other words, as delegate and representative, the leader of proletarian origin is subject to exactly the same oligarchical tendencies as is the bourgeois refugee who has become a labor leader. The manual worker of former days is henceforward a *déclassé*.

Among all the leaders of the working class, it is the trade-union leaders who have been most sympathetically treated in the literature of the social sciences. This is very natural. Books are written by men of science and men of letters. Such persons are, as a rule, more favorably disposed towards the leaders of the trade-union movement than towards the leaders of the political labor movement, for the former do not, as do so often the latter, encroach upon the writer's field of activity, nor disturb his circle of ideas with new and intrusive theories. It is for this reason that often in the same learned volume we find praise of the trade-union leader side by side with blame of the socialist leader.

It has been claimed that service as buffers between employers and employed has led in the leaders to the development of admirable and precious qualities; adroitness and scrupulousness, patience and energy, firmness of character and personal honesty. It has even been asserted that they are persons of an exceptionally chaste life, and this characteristic has been attributed to the comparative absence of sexual desires which, in accordance with the law of psychological compensation discovered by Guglielmo Ferrero, is supposed to characterize all persons exceptionally devoted to duty.[4] Two qualities in which

[4] Arturo Salucci, *La Teoria dello Sciopero,* Libr. Moderna, Genoa, 1902, p. 151. Salucci goes so far as to affirm that while the trade-union leaders marry quite young, marriage is for them not so much a union for sexual purposes as a matter of "comfort to them in their lives of continual agitation." The analyses produced by many authors of the psychology of trade-union leaders remind us at times of the reports of travelers in foreign lands, who tell us of human beings altogether different from those with whom we are acquainted, and even of actions which appear utterly opposed to nature. Herein we have a criterion which leads us to doubt the trustworthiness of such reports, even when they are not adorned with stories of matters demonstrably false, as of dragons, centaurs, and other mythical monsters. (Cf. David Hume, *Enquiries concerning the Human Understanding,* Ed. Clar. Press, edited by Selby-Bigge, Oxford, 1902, p. 84.) The exaggeration which is so often manifested in the enumeration and description of the good qualities of the trade-union leaders can be explained on political grounds. It arises from the satisfaction felt in bourgeois circles with the practical tendencies of these leaders, and from the hope that is placed in them by the opponents of revolutionary socialism.

most of the trade-union leaders unquestionably excel are objective gravity and individual good sense (often united with a lack of interest in and understanding of wider problems), derived from the exceptionally keen sense they have of direct personal responsibility, and in part perhaps from the dry and predominantly technical and administrative quality of their occupations. The trade-union leaders have been deliberately contrasted with the verbal revolutionists who guide the political labor movement, men of the type of the loquacious Rabagas in Sardou's play, and, not without exaggeration, there has been ascribed to the former a sound political sense which is supposed to be lacking in the latter—an insight into the extraordinary complexity of social and economic life and a keen understanding of the politically practicable. The nucleus of truth which such observations contain is that the trade-union leaders (leaving out of consideration for the present those of syndicalist tendency) differ in many respects from the leaders of political socialism.

Among the trade-union leaders themselves, however, there are great differences, corresponding to the different phases of the trade-union movement. The qualities requisite for the leadership of an organization whose finances are still weak, and which devotes itself chiefly to propaganda and strikes, must necessarily differ from those requisite for the leadership of a trade union supplying an abundance of solid benefits and aiming above all at peaceful practical results. In the former case the chief requisites are enthusiasm and the talents of the preacher. The work of the organizer is closely analogous to that of the rebel or the apostle. According to certain critics, these qualities may well be associated, above all in the early days of the proletarian movement, with the crassest ignorance. During this period, propaganda is chiefly romantic and sentimental, and its objective is moral rather than material. Very different is it when the movement is more advanced. The great complexity of the duties which the trade union has now to fulfil and the increasing importance assumed in the life of the union by financial, technical, and administrative questions, render it necessary that the agitator should give place to the employee equipped with technical knowledge. The commercial traveler in the class struggle is replaced by the strict and prosaic bureaucrat, the fervent idealist by the cold materialist, the democrat whose convictions are (at least in theory) absolutely firm by the conscious autocrat. Oratorical activity passes into the background, for administrative aptitudes are now of the first importance. Consequently, in this new period, while the leadership of the movement is less noisy, less brilliant, and less glorious, it is of a far more solid character, established upon a much sounder practical competence. The leaders are now differentiated from the mass of their followers, not only by their personal qualities as specialists endowed with insight and mastery of routine, but in addition by the barrier of the rules and regulations which guide their own actions and with the aid of which they control the rank and file. The rules of the German federation of metal-workers occupy forty-seven printed pages and are divided into thirty-nine paragraphs, each consisting of from ten to twelve sections. Where is the workman who would not lose himself in such a labyrinth? The modern trade-union official, above all if he directs a federation, must have precise knowledge of a given branch of industry, and must know how at any moment to form a sound estimate of the comparative forces of his own organization and the adversaries'. He must be equally well acquainted with the technical and with the economic side of the industry. He must know the cost of manufacture of the commodities concerned, the source and cost of the raw materials, the state of the markets, the wages and conditions of the workers in different regions. He must possess the talents at once of a general and those of a diplomatist.

These excellent qualities of the trade-union leader are not always compatible with the democratic regime, and indeed they often conflict unmistakably with the conditions of this regime.

It is especially in the ex-manual worker that the love of power manifests itself with the greatest intensity. Having just succeeded in throwing off the chains he wore as a wage-laborer and a vassal of capital, he is least of all disposed to induce new chains which will bind him as a slave of the masses. Like all freedmen, he has a certain tendency to abuse his newly acquired freedom—a tendency to libertinage. In all countries we learn from experience that the working-class leader of proletarian origin is apt to be capricious and despotic. He is extremely loath to tolerate contradiction. This trait is doubtless partly dependent upon his character as parvenu, for it is in the nature of the parvenu to maintain his authority with extreme jealousy, to regard all criticism as an attempt to humiliate him and to diminish his importance, as a deliberate and ill-natured allusion to his past. Just as the converted Jew dislikes references to his Hebrew birth, so also the labor leader of proletarian origin dislikes any references to his state of dependence and his position as an employee.

Nor must it be forgotten that, like all self-made men, the trade-union leader is intensely vain. Although he commonly possesses extensive knowledge of material details, he lacks general culture and a wide philosophical view, and is devoid of the secure self-confidence of the born leader; for these reasons he is apt to show himself less resistant than he should be towards the interested and amiable advances of bourgeois notables. In a letter to Sorge, Engels wrote of England:[5] "The most repulsive thing in this country is the bourgeois 'respectability' which has invaded the very blood and bone of the workers. The organization of society into firmly established hierarchical gradations, in which each one has his proper pride, but also an inborn respect for his 'betters' and 'superiors,' is taken so much as a matter of course, is so ancient and traditional, that it is comparatively easy for the bourgeois to play the part of seducers. For example, I am by no means sure that John Burns is not prouder in the depths of his soul of his popularity with Cardinal Manning, the Lord Mayor, and the bourgeoisie in general, than of his popularity among his own class. Even Tom Mann, whom I regard as the best of these leaders of working-class origin, is glad to talk of how he went to lunch with the Lord Mayor." In Germany, one of the few "class-conscious" German workers who have come into personal contact with William II did not venture in the royal presence to give expression to his convictions or to manifest his fidelity to the principles of his party.[6] There already exists in the proletariat an extensive stratum consisting of the directors of cooperative societies, the secretaries of trade unions, the trusted leaders of various organizations, whose psychology is entirely modeled upon that of the bourgeois classes with whom they associate.

The new environment exercises a potent influence upon the ex-manual worker. His manners become gentler and more refined. In his daily association with persons of the highest

[5] *Briefe und Auszüge, etc.*, Ed. cit., pp. 324–5.

[6] "Arbeiterzeitung" of Dortmund, September 16, 1903: "In the year 1900, the representatives of the Imperial Insurance Institute were commanded to an audience at the court, on the occasion of the inauguration of the new administrative building in Berlin. The stucco-worker Buchholz, well known in trade-union circles, was present with his colleagues. Buchholz, who was wearing the iron cross, attracted the personal attention of William II. The king was apparently aware of Buchholz's position as a socialist, and said: 'I believe the socialists are all opponents of the monarchy?' Buchholz promptly answered: 'No, Your Majesty, not all!' "

birth he learns the usages of good society and endeavors to assimilate them. Not infrequently the working-class deputies endeavor to mask the change which has occurred. The socialist leaders, and the same is true of the Democratic-Christians and the trade-union leaders, if of working-class origin, when speaking to the masses like to describe themselves as working men. By laying stress upon their origin, upon the characteristics they share with the rank and file, they ensure a good reception and inspire affection and confidence. During the elections of 1848 in France it was the mode for candidates to speak of themselves as *ouvriers.* This was not simply a title of honor, but also a title which helped to success. No less than twenty-one of these *ouvriers* thus secured election. The real signification of this title may be learned from a study of the list of candidates presented by the modern Socialist Party in France, Italy, and, elsewhere; here we find that a master-tinsmith (a man who keeps a shop and is therefore a petty bourgeois) describes himself as a "tinker," and so on. It even happens that the same candidate will describe himself as a workman in an electoral address intended for working-class readers, and as an employer in an appeal to the bourgeoisie. When they have entered Parliament, some of the ex-manual workers continue, more or less ostentatiously, to differentiate themselves by their dress from their bourgeois colleagues. But it is not by such external signs of a proletarian origin that they can hope to prevent the internal change, which was described by Jaurès (before his own adhesion to socialism) in the following terms: "The deputies of the working-class who arrive in Parliament quickly become bourgeois in the bad sense of the word; they lose their original vigor and energy and are left with only a sort of tribunal sentimentality."[7]

Inspired with a foolish self-satisfaction, the ex-worker is apt to take pleasure in his new environment, and he tends to become indifferent and even hostile to all progressive aspirations in the democratic sense. He accommodates himself to the existing order, and ultimately, weary of the struggle, becomes even reconciled to that order.[8] What interest for them

[7] Trans. from Jean Jaurès, "Dépêche de Toulouse," November 12, 1887.

[8] Max Weber, a few years ago, advised the German princes, if they wished to appease their terrors of socialism, to spend a day on the platform at a socialist congress, so that they might convince themselves that in the whole crowd of assembled revolutionists "the dominant type of expression was that of the petty bourgeois, of the self-satisfied innkeeper," and that there was no trace of genuine revolutionary enthusiasm (Max Weber's speech at the Magdeburg congress of the Verein für Sozialpolitik, stenographic report of the sitting, October 2, 1907).

has now the dogma of the social revolution? Their own social revolution has already been effected. At bottom, all the thoughts of these leaders are concentrated upon the single hope that there shall long continue to exist a proletariat to choose them as its delegates and to provide them with a livelihood. Consequently they contend that what is above all necessary is to organize, to organize unceasingly, and that the cause of the workers will not gain the victory until the last worker has been enrolled in the organization. Like all the *beati possidentes,* they are poor fighters. They incline, as in England, to a theory in accordance with which the workers and the capitalists are to be united in a kind of league, and to share, although still unequally, in the profits of a common enterprise. Thus the wages of the laborers become dependent upon the returns of the business. This doctrine, based upon the principle of what is known as the sliding-scale, throws a veil over all existing class-antagonisms and impresses upon labor organizations a purely mercantile and technical stamp. If a struggle becomes inevitable, the leader undertakes prolonged negotiations with the enemy; the more protracted these negotiations, the more often is his name repeated in the newspapers and by the public. If he continues to express "reasonable opinions," he may be sure of securing at once the praise of his opponents and (in most cases) the admiring gratitude of the crowd.

Personal egoism, pusillanimity, and baseness are often associated with a fund of good sense and wide knowledge, and so intimately associated that a distinction of the good qualities from the bad becomes a difficult matter. The hotheads, who are not lacking among the labor leaders of proletarian origin, become cool. They have acquired a conscientious conviction that it would be a mistake to pursue an aggressive policy, which would in their view not merely fail to bring any profit, but would endanger the results hitherto attained. Thus in most cases two orders of motives are in operation, the egoistic and the objective, working hand in hand. The resultant of these influences is that state of comparative calm proper to the labor leader, regarding which an employee of one of the trade unions has expressed himself with great frankness: "It is no matter for reproach, but is perfectly comprehensible, that when we were all still working at the bench and had to get along as best we could with our small wages, we had a keener personal interest in a speedy change of the existing social order than we have in our present conditions."[9] Such a state of mind will be yet further reinforced if the former manual worker should be, as he often is, engaged in journalistic work. Although in most cases he will with admirable diligence have amassed a considerable amount of knowledge, he has not had the necessary preliminary training to enable him to assemble, re-elaborate, and assimilate the elements of his knowledge to constitute a scientific doctrine, or even to create for himself a system of directive ideas. Consequently his personal inclinations towards quietism cannot be neutralized, as unquestionably happens in the case of many Marxists, by the preponderate energy of a comprehensive theory. Marx long ago recognized this defect in proletarian leaders, saying: "When the workers abandon manual labor to become professional writers, they almost always make a mess of the theoretical side."[10]

We see, then, that the substitution of leaders of proletarian origin for those of bourgeois origin offers the working-class movement no guarantee, either in theory or in practice, against the political or moral infidelity of the leaders. In 1848, when the elections ordered by the provisional government took place in France, eleven of the deputies who entered the Chamber were members of the working class. No less than ten of these promptly abandoned the labor program on the strength of which they had been elected.[11] A yet more characteristic example is furnished by the history of the leaders of the Italian branch of the International (1868-79). Here the leaders, who were for the most part derived from the bourgeoisie and the nobility, nearly all showed themselves to be persons of distinguished worth. The only two exceptions were men of working-class origin. Stefano Caporusso, who spoke of himself as "the model working-man," embezzled the funds of the socialist group of Naples, of which he was the president; while Carlo Terzaghi, president of the section of Turin, turned out to be a police spy and was expelled from the party.[12]

Speaking generally, we learn from the history of the labor movement that a socialist party is exposed to the influence of

[9] Kloth, leader of the bookbinders' union, speaking at the conference of the trade-union executives in Berlin, 1906 (*Protokoll*, p. 10). In the *Protokoll* it is here noted that there were vigorous cries of objection, and also the remark, "What you say applies still more to the employees of the socialist party." (Cf. *supra*, pp. 155–6.)

[10] Letter to Sorge, October 19, 1877, *Briefe u. Auszüge, etc.*, ed. cit., p. 159.

[11] Arthur Arnould, *Historie populaire et parlementaire de la Commune de Paris*, Kistemaekers, Brussels, 1878, vol. ii, p. 43.

[12] Cf. Michels, *Proletariato et Borghesia, etc.*, Bocca, Turin, 1908, pp. 72 et seq.

the political environment in proportion to the degree in which it is genuinely proletarian in character. The first deputy of the Italian Socialist Party (which at that time consisted exclusively of manual workers), Antonio Maffi, a type-founder, elected to parliament in 1882, speedily joined one of the bourgeois sections of the left, declaring that his election as a working man did not make it necessary for him to set himself in opposition to the other classes of society.[13] In France, the two men who under the Second Empire had been the leaders of the Proudhonists, Henri Louis Tolain, the engraver, and Fribourg, the compositor and who at the first international congress in Geneva (1866) had urgently advocated an addition to the rules to effect the exclusion of all intellectuals and bourgeois from the organization, when the Commune was declared in 1871 ranged themselves on the side of Thiers, and were therefore expelled from the International as traitors. It may be added that Tolain ended his career as a senator under the conservative republic. Odger, the English labor leader, a member of the general council of the International, abandoned this body after the insurrection in Paris. It is true that he was in part influenced in this direction by his objection to the dictatorial methods of Marx. But Marx could rejoin, not without reason, that Odger had wished merely to make use of the International to acquire the confidence of the masses, and that he was ready to turn his back upon socialism as soon as it seemed to him an obstacle to his political career. A similar case was that of Lucraft, also on the general council of the International, who secured an appointment as school inspector under the British government.[14] In a word, it may be said that when the forces of the workers are led against the bourgeoisie by men of working-class origin, the attack is always less vigorous and conducted in a way less accordant with the alleged aims of the movement than when the leaders of the workers spring from some other class. A French critic, referring to the political conduct of the working-class leaders of the proletariat, declares that alike intellectually and morally they are inferior to the leaders of bourgeois origin, lacking the education and the culture which these possess. The same writer declares that the behavior of many of the leaders of working-class origin cannot fail to contribute to the intensive culture of anti-parliamentarist tendencies. "After the rule of feudalism, we had the rule of the bourgeoisie. After the bourgeois, shall we have

[13] Alfredo Angiolini, *Cinquent'anni di Socialismo in Italia*, ed. cit., pp. 180–6.
[14] G. Jaeckh, *Die Internationale* ed. cit., p. 152.

the foreman? But our most formidable master is the one from our own ranks who through lies and cunning raised himself to power."[15]

It was hoped that the energetic entry of the proletariat upon the world-stage would have an ethically regenerative influence, that the new elements would exercise a continuous and unwearied control over the public authorities, and that (endowed with a keen sense of responsibility) they would strictly control the working of their own organizations. These anticipations have been disappointed by the oligarchical tendencies of the workers themselves. As Cesare Lombroso pointed out without contradiction in an article published in the central organ of the Italian Socialist Party, the more the proletariat approximates to the possession of the power and the wealth of the bourgeoisie, the more does it adopt all the vices of its opponent and the more does it become an instrument of corruption. "Then there arise all those subdivisions of our so-called popular parties, which have all the vices of the bourgeois parties, which claim and often possess a prestige among the people, and which easily become the tools of governmental corruption sailing under liberal colors in their name."[16] We have sufficient examples in European history, even in that of very recent date, of the manner in which the artificial attempt to retain the party leadership in proletarian hands has led to a political misoneism against which the organized workers of all countries have every reason to be on their guard. The complaint so frequently voiced by the rank and file of the socialists that almost all the defects of the movement arise from the flooding of the proletarian party with bourgeois elements are merely the outcome of ignorance of the historical characteristics of the period through which we are now passing.

The leaders of the democratic parties do not present everywhere the same type, for the complex of tendencies by which they are influenced necessarily varies in accordance with environment, national character, climate, historical tradition, etc.

The United States of America is the land of the almighty dollar. In no other country in the world does public life seem to be dominated to the same extent by the thirst for gold. The unrestricted power of capital necessarily involves corruption. In America, however, this corruption is not merely exhibited upon a gigantic scale, but, if we are to believe American

[15] Trans. from Flax (Victor Méric), *Coutant* (d'Ivry), "Hommes du Jour," Paris, 1908, No. 32.
[16] Cesare Lombroso, *I Frutti di un Voto*, "Avanti," No. 2987 (April 27, 1905).

critics, has become a recognized institution. While in Europe such corruption gives rise to censure and anger, in America it is treated with indifference or arouses no more than an indulgent smile. Lecky declares that if we were to judge the Americans solely by the manner in which they conduct themselves in public life, our judgments would be extremely unfavorable—and unjust.[17]

We cannot wonder, then, that North America should be pre-eminently the country in which the aristocratic tendencies of the labor leaders, fostered by an environment often permeated, as has just been explained, by a gross and unrefined materialism, should have developed freely and upon a gigantic scale. The leaders of the American proletariat have merely followed the lead of the capitalism by which the life of their country is dominated. The consequence is that their party life has also become essentially plutocratic. When they have secured an improved rate of wages and similar advantages, the officials of the trade unions, wearing evening dress, meet the employers in sumptuous banquets. At congresses it is the custom to offer foreign delegates, and even their wives, valuable gifts, jewelry, etc. The special services of the leaders are rewarded by increases of salary, which sometimes attain considerable figures. We learn from indisputable authority that many of the labor leaders, and especially of the trade-union leaders, regard their positions simply as a means for personal advancement. According to the testimony of the well-informed, the American working class has hitherto produced few leaders of whom it has any reason to be proud. Many of them shamelessly and unscrupulously exploit for personal ends the posts which they have secured through the confidence of their fellow-workmen. Taken as a whole, the American labor leaders have been described as "stupid and cupid."[18] We owe to Gaylord Wilshire, himself also an American and a socialist, the following unflattering picture of the socialist leader: "He is a man who often expresses a social dissatisfaction based upon personal failure. He is very apt to be loud rather than profound. He is, as a rule, not an educated man, and his demands and urgings are based too often on ignorance."[19] Intelligent and honest workmen are consequently repelled from the labor organizations or induced to follow false paths.

[17] W. E. Lecky, *Democracy and Liberty*, Longmans, London, 1899, vol. i, pp. 113–14.

[18] Austin Lewis, *The Rise of the American Proletariat*, ed. cit., p. 200.

[19] Gaylord Wilshire, *Wilshire Editorials*, Wilshire Book Co., New York, 1906, p. 140.

We have even been told that not a few labor leaders are altogether in the hands of the capitalists. Being uneducated parvenus, they are extremely sensible to flattery,[20] but this seems to be among the least of their defects. In many cases they are no more than paid servants of capital. The "Union Officer" then becomes a "boss" in the hands of the enemy, a "scab" or, to use a still more significant American expression, "a labor lieutenant of the capitalist class."[21] It is from the socialists themselves that we learn almost incredible details regarding certain categories of American workers who have achieved a privileged position, but who are utterly devoid of moral sense. Among the best organized unions there are some which enter into regular treaties with the capitalists in their respective branches of industry in order to exploit the consumer and to effect with the capitalist a friendly division of the spoil.[22] In other cases, the leaders of a federation of trade unions, bribed by one group of employers, will organize strikes among the employees of another group. On the other hand, many strikes which are progressing favorably for the workers come abruptly to an end because the employers have made it worth the leaders' while to call the strike off. The absence of socialist tendencies among the American workers, their lack of class consciousness, have been noted with admiration by distinguished writers and leading members of the employing class, who praise these workers for their exceptional intelligence, and hold them up as examples to the degenerate and lazy European working men.[23] Yet these same intelligent American workers are led by the nose by such men as we have been describing, and appear to be the only ones who fail to notice the misdeeds of the labor leaders. Indeed, they favor these misdeeds by refusing to work at the same bench with those of their comrades who, more perspicacious than themselves, have attracted the enmity of the leaders by discovering and unmasking the frauds of the latter.[24]

The history of the organized working class in North America certainly rivals, in respect of the frequent occurrence of corruption, the history of a part of the capitalist class in the same

20 Austin Lewis, op. cit., p. 202.

21 Daniel De Leon, *The Burning Question of Trades-Unionism*, ed. cit., pp. 10–12, 41–43.

22 George D. Herron, *The Day of Judgment*, Kerr, Chicago, 1904, p. 17.—See also Werner Sombart, *Warum gibt es in den Vereinigten Staaten keinen Sozialismus?*, ed. cit., p. 33.

23 Cf., for example, E. Cauderlier, *L'Evolution économique du XIX siècle*, Brussels, 1903, p. 209.

24 De Leon, ed. cit., p. 12.

country. A historian of the American labor movement exclaims: "It is in both cases a sordid and dreary tale and, in the case of organized labor, is unrelieved to a disappointing degree by the heroism and sentiment which have played such a conspicuous part in the labor movements of other countries. The cynicism of a civilization based on cash seems to have found its way into the bones of both capitalist and proletarian."[25] The American labor movement is the purest in respect of its proletarian composition and is at the same time the richest in examples of social perversion. Side by side with the vulgar and interested corruption to which we have referred, there exists, indeed, a corruption which arises from idealism, and the latter must not be confused with the former. It sometimes happens that the leader allows himself to be induced by pecuniary considerations to attack a given party, the money being furnished by other parties or by the government. That he should do this presupposes, indeed, that his point of view regarding money is *non olet*; but he acts as he does exclusively in the interest of his party, and not a penny of the money he receives goes into his own pocket. An American political economist has justly pointed out that such corruption sometimes involves a heroic capacity for self-sacrifice on the part of the leader who, to secure advantages for the party with the foreign money, faces the fiercest attacks and the worst suspicions, and even, if need be, accepts his own political annihilation. He offers up his honor to the party, the greatest sacrifice that a man of honor can make.[26] Of this kind, for example, is the corruption of which the leaders of the poltical labor movement have frequently been accused by the liberals, namely, when they have accepted money from the conservatives or from the government in order to fight liberals or radicals. There are not a few instances of this kind in the history of the international labor movement. Thus, in England, during the general election of 1885, the leaders of the Social Democratic Federation, in order to run two candidates in metropolitan constituencies, accepted money from the Tory Party, whose aim it was to split the votes of its opponents, and thus to secure the defeat of the liberal candidates; the sum payable in this case was determined by the number of votes given to the socialist candidate, £8 for every vote.[27] Similarly, Constantino Laz-

25 Austin Lewis, op. cit., p. 196.
26 Robert Clarkson Brooks, Dodd, Mead & Co., New York, 1910, pp. 65 et seq.
27 Bernard Shaw, *The Fabian Society: What it has done: How it has done it*, Fabian Society, Lond., 1892, p. 6.

zari, leader of the Milanese Labor Party, accepted from the government the sum of 500 lire to carry on an electoral struggle against the bourgeois radicals.[28] In Germany, the conduct of Schweitzer during the last years in which he was president of the Allgemeine Deutsche Arbeiterverein, conduct which led to accusations of corruption in which Bebel joined, appears to have been dictated by similar considerations. Such at least is the impression produced by a perusal of the various references to the matter made by Gustav Mayer.[29] In none of these cases is it fair to accuse the party leaders of personal corruption, since the money was not accepted for personal ends but for the supposed advantage of the party. Whether such procedures are politically wise, whether they make for the general advance of political morality, are different questions. Indubitably their influence on the mentality of the masses is not educational in a good sense. They are, moreover, especially dangerous to the leaders' own morale. Corruption for honorable motives is likely to be succeeded by corruption for dishonorable. If the method were to be accepted as a regular and legitimate element of party politics, it would be easy for able but unscrupulous leaders to put a portion of the price of corruption into their own pockets, and yet to remain more "useful" to the party than their disinterested and conscientious colleagues. This would be the beginning of the end, and would open the door to plutocracy in the party.

It cannot be said that the English labor leaders are in these respects greatly superior to the American, although in England, perhaps, corruption assumes a more subtle and less obvious form. At the Amsterdam congress (1906) Bebel related in a private conversation what Marx and Engels had said to him once in London: "English socialism would certainly be far more advanced than it is today had not the capitalists been clever enough to check the movement by corrupting its leaders."[30] Hyndman, the leader of the English Marxists, a man of bourgeois origin who sacrificed a diplomatic career for the sake of socialism, relates in his memoirs that many of the working-class leaders, and among these the most energetic and the most gifted, after having acquired a genuine political culture with the aid of socialist of bourgeois origin, have not

28 Alfredo Angiolini, *Cinquant'anni di Socialismo in Italia*, Nerbini, Florence, 1900, 1st ed., p. 135.

29 Gustav Mayer, *J. B. Schweitzer*, Fischer, Jena, 1909, pp. 129, 161, 181, 195, 321, 379.

30 Daniel De Leon, *Flashlights of the Amsterdam Congress*, Labor News Co., New York, 1906, p. 41.

hesitated to sell this new acquirement to the bourgeoisie. Nor do the workers themselves complain of this, for, full of admiration for what they call the cleverness of their leaders, they have by their votes rendered possible the gradual rise of these in public life.[31] Another writer well acquainted with the English labor movement declares: "A prominent labor leader remarked recently that the labor movement was a charnel-house of broken reputations. That puts it too strongly, but, in essence, how true!"[32]

Thus in the United States, and also, though to a less degree, in England, there exists a peculiar category of working-class leaders of proletarian origin. Among these there are unquestionably to be found many men of strong character, and many who are uninfluenced by selfish considerations, although but few who take lofty views, who are endowed with a fine theoretical insight, or capacity for coherent political work and the avoidance of opportunities for error. Most of them are excellent organizers and technicians. But apart from these somewhat exceptional categories, there can be no doubt that many of the labor leaders are half-educated and arrogant egoists. We might almost imagine that Diderot had a premonition of such individuals when he made his ambitious Parisian beggar, Lumpazius, say: "I shall be like all the beggars who have new clothes. I shall be the most insolent rogue you have ever seen."[33]

31 H. M. Hyndman, *The Record of an Adventurous Life*, Macmillan, London, 1911, p. 433.
32 S. G. Hobson, *Boodle and Cant*, loc. cit., p. 588.
33 Trans. from Diderot, *Le Neveu de Rameau*, Delarue, Paris, 1877, p. 44.

Chapter 6

Intellectuals, and the Need for Them in the Working-Class Parties

IN THE early days of the labor movement the bourgeois intellectuals who adhered to the cause of the workers were regarded by these with profound esteem; but as the movement matured the attitude of the proletariat became transformed into one of undue crticism. This antipathy on the part of the rank and file of the socialists is based upon false presuppositions, and proceeds from two antithetical points of view. Some, like the group of the "Neue Zeit" and the "Leipzige Volkszeitung" in Germany, with the support of the revolutionary-minded workers of Berlin, of the two Saxonies, and of Rhenish Westphalia, persisting in the maintenance of intransigent revolutionary conceptions, think themselves justified in accusing the intellectuals of a tendency to "take the edge off" the labor movement, to "water it down," to give it "bourgeois" characteristics, to rob it of proletarian virility, and to inspire it with an opportunist spirit of compromise. The others, the reformists, the revisionists, who find inconvenient the continued reminder *principiis obsta!* with which they are assailed by the revolutionists, in their turn attack the intellectuals, regarding them as meddlesome intruders, fossilized professors, and so on, as persons who are utterly devoid of any sound ideas of the labor movement and of its necessities, disturbing its normal course with their ideas of the study. Thus while the first group of critics regard the intellectuals as being for the most part reformists, bourgeois-minded socialists of the extreme right, the other group of critics classes the intellectuals as ultra-revolutionary, as anarchizing socialists of the extreme left. In Italy, towards 1902, the intellectuals found themselves placed between two fires. On one side the reformists claimed to represent the healthy proletarian energy of the economic organizations of the peasants as against the *circoletti ambiziosetti* ("the self-seeking petty circles"—i.e. socialist groups in the towns), which were composed for the most part, so they affirmed, of bourgeois and petty bourgeois. On the other side, the revolutionists of the "Avanguardia Socialista" group entered the lists against the employees and the bourgeois leaders, in the name of the class-conscious proletariat of industrial workers. Thus by both factions alike the intellectuals were treated as scapegoats and made responsible for all the mistakes and sins of the party. But both sides are wrong. Above all it is hardly possible to imagine the reasons which would induce refugees from the bourgeoisie to adhere to the extreme right wing of the working-class party. It is rather the adverse thesis which might be sustained by psychological and historical arguments which are good but not decisive.

1. Let us first consider the psychological arguments, Kautsky, referring to a period when "even by educated persons socialism was stigmatized as criminal or insane" (a period which Kautsky wrongly imagines to have passed away), makes the judicious observation that the bourgeois who adheres to the socialist cause needs more firmness of character, stronger revolutionary passion, and greater force of conviction, than the proletarian who takes a similar step.[1] The violent internal and external struggles, the days full of bitterness and the nights without sleep during which his socialist faith has ripened, have combined to produce in the socialist of bourgeois origin, especially if he derived from the higher circles of the bourgeoisie, an ardor and a tenacity which are rarely encountered among proletarian socialists. He has broken completely with the bourgeois world, and henceforward confronts it as a mortal enemy, as one irreconcilable *a priori.* The consequence is that, in the struggle with the bourgeoisie, the socialist intellectual will incline towards the most revolutionary tendencies.

There is, however, another reason which leads the ex-bourgeois to make common cause with the intransigent socialists, and this is his knowledge of history and his intimate acquaintance with the nature of the bourgeoisie. To the proletarian socialist it is often difficult to form any precise idea of the power of his adversaries and to learn the nature of the means at their disposal for the struggle. Often, too, he is inspired with an ingenuous admiration for the benevolent attempts at social reform patronized by certain strata of the bourgeoisie. Faced by the more or less serious or more or less deceitful offer of panaceas, he is often in the position of the peasant at the fair who listens open-mouthed while the quack vaunts the miraculous virtue of his remedies. Conversely the socialist of

[1] Karl Kautsky, *Die Soziale Revolution.* 1. *Sozialreform u. Soziale Revolution,* "Vorwärts," Berlin, 1902, p. 27; also *Republik u. Sozialdemocratie in Frankreich,* "Neue Zeit," xxiii, No. 11, p. 333.

bourgeois origin will interpret more precisely the efforts made by the bourgeoisie to put the labor movement to sleep. His experience as a bourgeois will enable him to penetrate more easily the real motives of the different proceedings of the enemy. That which to his proletarian comrade seems a chivalrous act and proof of a conciliatory spirit, he will recognize as an act of base flattery, performed for the purposes of corruption. That which a proletarian socialist considers a great step forward towards the end, will appear to the bourgeois socialist as an infinitesimal advance along the infinitely extended road of the class struggle.

The difference of intellectual level between those who advocate the same idea, dependent upon their respective derivation from a proletarian or a bourgeois environment, must necessarily reflect itself in the manner in which they represent this idea in the face of non-socialists, and in the tactics they employ towards adversaries and sympathizers. The psychological process which goes on in the socialists of these two categories rests upon a logical foundation. The proletarian adherent of the party who remains a simple member of the rank and file attentively follows the progress made in all fields by the idea on behalf of which he is an enthusiastic fighter; he notes the growth of the party, and experiences in his own person the increase in wages secured in the struggle with the employers; besides being a member of the party, he belongs to his trade union, and often to a cooperative society as well. His experience in these various organizations induces a feeling of comparative content. He regards social evolution in a rosy light, and easily comes to take an optimistic view of the distance which his class has to traverse in order to attain to the fulfilment of its historic mission. Ultimately social progress is regarded by him as a continuous rectilinear movement. It appears incredible, even impossible, that the proletariat should suffer reverses and disasters; when they actually occur, they seem to him merely transient phenomena. This state of mind renders him generous and considerate even towards his adversaries, and he is far from disinclined to accept the idea of peace with the enemy and of class collaboration. It need hardly be said that this disposition is yet more accentuated among those proletarians who attain to positions of eminence in the party.

2. These considerations do not lack historical corroboration. Their truth is confirmed by a study of the activities of those socialists who were born as members of the aristocracy,

or in the upper strata of the bourgeoisie, such as Bakunin and Kropotkin, both Russian nobles and both anarchists, Frederick Engels, Karl Marx. As a rule, in all the great questions with which the party has to deal the ex-bourgeois socialist is in actual fact one who gives the preference to the most radical and intransigent solutions, to those which accord most strictly with socialist principles. It is of course true, on the other hand, that the history of the working-class movement shows that many "reformist" currents have been strongly permeated by intellectual elements. It is indisputable that even if German reformism was not actually created by the little phalanx grouped round "Der Sozialistiche Student" of Berlin, the reformist tendency was, from the days of its first inception, vigorously and ostentatiously patronized by the members of this group. A closer examination, however, shows very clearly that the strongest impulse to the reformist tendency in Germany was given by the trade-union leaders, by persons therefore of proletarian origin. Moreover, it is the most exclusivist working-class movements which have everywhere and always been most definitely characterized by the reformist spirit. In illustration may be mentioned: the French group of the International Working-men's Association which assembled round Fribourg and Tolain; the English trade unionists; the "integralists" in France, whose origin was the "Revue Socialiste," edited by the gentle ex-manual worker, Benoît Malon (the note of alarm against this form of socialism was sounded first by the medical student Paul Brousse, next by the intransigent Marxists under the leadership of Paul Lafargue, who had just secured his medical diploma in England, and finally by the man of letters Jules Guesde); the Independent Labor Party with the Labor Representation Committee; the socialists of Genoa, led by the varnisher Pietro Chiesa; the peasants of Reggio Emilia. This tendency has been manifest from the very outset of the modern labor movement. Bernstein says with good reason that, notwithstanding all assertions to the contrary, in the English Chartist movement the intellectuals were distinguished by their marked revolutionary inclinations. "In the disputes among the Chartists, the radical or revolutionary tendency was by no means charactertistic of the proletarian elements, or the moderate tendency of the bourgeois elements. The most notable representatives of the revolutionary spirit were members of the bourgeoisie, men of letters, etc., whereas it was leaders of working-class origin who advocated moderate methods."[2] To sum up, and putting aside the question whether the reformist movement has been a good or an evil for the working-class, it may be affirmed that generally speaking, the working-class leaders of proletarian origin have a special tendency to adopt the reformist attitude. In proof of this assertion it suffices to mention the names of Anseele in Belgium, Legien in Germany, and Rigola in Italy. The term *possibilisme ouvrier* is far from being a malicious invention.

It is not easy to furnish statistical proof of the statement that the socialists of bourgeois origin are more often revolutionaries than reformists. On the other hand, the history of Italian socialism during recent years offers an interesting demonstration of the adverse thesis (the causes of this peculiarity will be subsequently discussed). The official socialist organization of Milan, the Federazione Milanese, suffering from a chronic impecuniosity due to the slackness with which the majority of the members paid their subscriptions, proposed in the year 1903 an expedient which is frequently adopted by the Italian socialists. Henceforward the monthly subscriptions were no longer to be equal for all the comrades, but those who were better off were invited to pay more in proportion to their means. This reform, which was inspired by a thoroughly socialist sentiment, led the Milanese reformists (who in consequence of their differences with the revolutionists had for a long time been on the lookout for an honorable excuse to leave the federation, in which the revolutionary current was predominant) to resign their membership, declaring that they regarded the new system of payment as altogether unjust. On this occasion it appeared that it was the well-to-do members who resigned, so that these, the bourgeois, manifested the reformist tendency.[3] It is also to be noted that during recent years (since 1901) the great majority of Italian socialist intellectuals have definitely declared themselves to be reformists by a more or less unconditional adhesion to the opportunism of Turati. The cases just quoted seem to conflict with the rule previously enunciated that the refugees from the bourgeoisie are adverse to opportunism. But the inconsistency is no more than apparent. It has several times been pointed out that the intransigence of the ex-bourgeois socialist depends

[2] Edward Bernstein, *Zur Theorie u. Geschichte des Sozialismus*, Ferd. Dümmler, Berlin, 1904, 4th ed., part ii, p. 18.

[3] *I Casi di Milane*, a memorial presented by the Milanese federation to the party executive and to the Italian comrades (Stamp. editr. Lombarda di Mondaini, Milan, 1903, p. 18).

upon the circumstance that on his way to join the class-conscious proletariat he has had to make his way through a thorny thicket, struggling violently and suffering many injuries, and his courageous progress proves him to be endowed with an exceptional capacity of sacrifice for the ideal and with the energy of the born fighter. As the years have passed, however, this primal source of revolutionary energy has to a large extent dried up, because the path of the bourgeois adherent to socialism has become so much easier. It is a general law that when we change the soil we change the quality of the fruit. This is what happened in Italy.

The recent history of socialism shows that the intellectuals are distributed in nearly equal proportions among the various tendencies. Confining ourselves to German examples, we find that it is a doctor of medicine, Raphael Friedeberg, who has inaugurated anarchizing socialism; a similar tendency is exhibited by the Tolstoian-Kantian Otto Buck, doctor of philosophy, and Ernest Thesing, doctor of medicine and at one time a cavalry lieutenant. If among the reformists we find the barrister Wolfgang Heine, the former theological student Richard Calwer, the former student of political science Max Schippel, the pastor of Göhre, the sometime gymnasium teacher Eduard David, the doctor of philosophy Heinrich Braun, and many other intellectuals—we find in the opposite camp, that of the revolutionaries, the doctor of philosophy Franz Mehring, the doctor of medicine Paul Lensch, Rosa Luxemburg, Israel Helphant (Parvus), the former student Max Grunwald, the ex-barrister Arthur Stadthagen, the barrister Karl Liebknecht, and Karl Kautsky, who escaped only by chance the disgrace of the doctor's title. We see, then, that in Germany the intellectuals cannot be classed exclusively as revolutionists or as reformists.

* * * * *

The struggle against the intellectuals within the socialist party is due to various causes. It originated as a struggle for leadership among the intellectuals themselves. Then there came a struggle between the representatives of different tendencies: strict logical adhesion to theory versus criticism, opportunism versus impossibilism, trade unionism after the English manner versus doctrinal Marxism as a philosophy of history, reformism versus syndicalism. From time to time these struggles assume the form of attacks made by the bulk of the party upon some small heterogeneous element which has invaded the labor movement. It is not always the genuine manual workers, or those who have been such, that are the first to raise the cry of alarm against the intellectuals. But it is true that the working class has ever been suspicious of those elements in the party who were derived from other social camps. Clara Zetkin writes very justly: "The bourgeois refugee is apt to find himself lonely and misunderstood among his comrades in the struggle. He is at once a stranger and a citizen in the valley of the possessing classes, with which he is associated by education and habits of life; at once, also, a stranger and a citizen upon the heights of the proletariat, to whom he is bound in a firm community by his convictions."[4] The power of tradition presses with peculiar force upon persons of culture.

The coldness of his reception in the new environment seems to him doubly hard. The intellectuals, who have entered the party under the spur of idealism, soon feel humiliated and disillusioned. The masses, moreover, are little capable of appreciating the gravity of the sacrifices which the intellectual often accepts when he adheres to the party. When Paul Göhre related to the Dresden congress how for love of the cause he had renounced his profession and his income, his social position, and even his family, a number of socialist journals answered that all this was, to put it politely, maudlin sentimentality, and that the socialist intellectuals, when they made such "sacrifices," were not thinking of the cause of the workers but of themselves. In a word, the comrades showed themselves utterly insensible of the greatness of the sacrifice which Göhre had made for love of them. The truth is that upon this point, as upon so many others, the intellectuals and the proletarians lack the capacity of mutual understanding.

In Germany, as in Italy, France, and in some of the Balkan states, the gravest accusations have been launched against the intellectuals. There have been times in the history of German socialism in which the educated members of the party have been exposed to universal contempt. It suffices to recall the Dresden congress (1903), during which the whole complicated question of tactics seemed to be reduced to "the problem of the intellectuals." Even today they are often treated as suspects. There are still intellectuals who think it necessary to demonstrate to the masses that, notwithstanding the aggravating circumstance of their social origin and their superior educa-

[4] Clara Zetkin, *Geistiges Proletariat, Frauenfrage, u. Sozialismus*, a lecture, Verlag "Vorwärts," Berlin, 1902, p. 32.

tion, they are nevertheless good socialists. It is surely far from heroic, this persistence with which the intellectuals are apt to deny their true social character and to pretend that their own hands are horny. But we need not be deceived. Merlino hits the bull's-eye when he ironically warns us that this state of affairs lasts only until the moment when the intellectuals succeed in getting control of the working-class movement.[5] They now feel themselves secure, and no longer need wear the mask, at least in their relations with the masses. If they continue, none the less, to assume the posture of the humble demagogue, this is done from a vague fear of being accused as tyrants by the bourgeois parties, but still more in order to ward off the criticism of their working-class competitors.

It is proper to recognize that mistrust of the intellectuals, although in large part an artificial product, has its good side. For this mistrust leads no small number of cranky and eccentric intellectuals, who incline to play a picturesque part in joining the socialists, to turn towards other pastures. Nothing would be more disastrous for the workers than to tolerate the exclusive rule of the intellectuals. University study is not possible to those choice individuals alone who are endowed with exceptional natural gifts; it is merely a class privilege of persons whose position is economically advantageous. Consequently the student has no right to be proud of his ability and his knowledge. He need not glory in being able to write Dr. before his name or M.A. after it. Every proletarian of average intelligence, given the necessary means, could acquire a university degree with the same facility as does the average bourgeois. Besides, and above all, it cannot be denied, that for the healthy progress of the proletarian movement it would be incomparably better that the mistrust of the workers towards the bourgeois refugees should be a hundred times greater than necessary, rather than that the proletariat should be deceived even once by overconfidence in its leaders. But unfortunately, as we learn from the history of the modern labor movement, even the total exclusion of intellectuals would not save the working class from numerous deceptions.

From the ethical point of view the contempt felt by the non-intellectuals for the intellectuals is utterly without justification. It is a positive fact that even today, in many countries,

[5] F. S. Merlino, *Collettivismo, Lotta di Casse e . . . Ministerol,* rejoinder to E. Tuarati, Nerbini, Florence, 1904, p. 34.

the bourgeois refugee who makes his adhesion to the party of the revolutionary workers, the party of "social subversion," or, as William II expresses it, "the unpatriotic rout of those who are unworthy to bear the name of Germans," suffers serious economic and social damage. On the other hand, the proletarian commonly derives advantage in these respects from joining the party of his own class, and is thus impelled to take this step from motives of class-egoism. Unquestionably the working class, struggling on the political field, needs recruits from its own ranks who can rise to the position of officers in the proletarian army. It is natural, too, that these leaders should be furnished with adequate means, and that they should be firmly secured in their positions. But it ill becomes the working men who have thus risen in the social scale to look down upon their ex-bourgeois associates, who have descended in the social scale, and have thereby become voluntary *déclasses* for love of the party.

It results from all that has been said that the campaign against intellectuals in the Socialist Party, however justified it may be in individual cases, is as a whole utterly unjust, and often inopportune and absurd. Even the German labor movement, despite the high degree of technical organization to which it has attained, could not dispense with intellectuals. Although, as we have seen, its general character is decisively proletarian, and although it has as authoritative leaders such men of proletarian origin as August Bebel, Ignaz Auer, Johannes Timm, Martin Segitz, Adolph von Elm, Otto Hué, etc., it may be affirmed that German socialism would lose much of its prestige if it were to eliminate the intellectuals.

According to Mehring, the use of the intellectuals to the proletariat is not so much to serve as fellow-combatants in the struggle, as to play the part of theorists who illuminate the road. He writes: "If they wish to be practical fighters and not theorists, they become altogether insignificant as adherents to the labor movement; for what could be the import of the adhesion of a few hundred intellectuals to the working-class millions, seeing that the latter are already much better equipped than the former for the rough and tumble of practical life?" On the other hand, he says, the intellectuals are of great value to the proletariat in the elaboration of the theory of class-struggle; they display the historical nexus between the labor movement and the world-process as a whole; they take care that the workers shall not lose sight of the purposive relationship of individual branches of their movement with the process of world-transformation which it must be their aim to effect with all possible speed. Thus the task of the intellectuals consists in "maintaining the freshness and vigor of the workers in their movement towards their great goal, and in elucidating for them the social relationships which make the approaching victory of the proletariat a certainty."[6]

It is not necessary here to undertake a defense of the intelligence of the proletariat against those who, seeing that intellectuals are historically necessary to the socialist party, wish on this account to impugn the political capacity of the manual workers. Any one who has attentively followed the history of the international working-class movement will know how much goodwill and capacity are to be found in that proletarian party which, permeated with class-consciousness, has conceived the design of fighting for its own emancipation; he knows how much intelligence, devotion to duty, calm and indefatigable energy, have been displayed in this cause by the workers of every country. As managers of cooperative societies, employees of trade unions, editors of socialist newspapers, the proletarians have from the technical point of view displayed themselves as models whom the bourgeois who undertake similar activities would do well to imitate. If, notwithstanding all this, we commonly find in the international working-class parties that the bourgeois refugees are usually assigned the task of dealing with theoretical problems and in many cases, the supreme guidance in matters of practical politics (although in the latter sphere the proletarians always retain great influence); this phenomenon, far from being a *testimonium paupertatis intellectualis* on the part of the fighting proletariat, finds a perfectly natural explanation in the economic organization of contemporary production. This organization (while it permits the wage-earner, when conditions are favorable, to cultivate his intelligence), since it monopolizes the supreme advantages of civilization *ad usum Delphinorum,* makes it impossible for the *intelligent* worker to become an *intellectual.* Unquestionably modern production needs intelligent workers, such as are found among the modern proletariat. But it has need also of intellectuals, that is to say of persons whose natural mental abilities have received suitable training. Now a sufficient supply of these intellectuals is

6 Franz Mehring, *Akademiker u. Proletarier,* II, "Leipziger Volkszeitung," xi, No. 95.

furnished by the master class, from among whose relatives they are recruited. Consequently it is not in the interest of private industry to open for the proletariat all the sluices of instruction. Moreover, as far as agriculture is concerned, many landowners cynically declare that the more ignorant the worker the better does he serve their turn. The consequence of all this is that the socialist of bourgeois origin has enjoyed that which the modern proletarian still necessarily lacks. The former has had time and means to complete his political education; he has had the physical freedom of moving from place to place, and the material independence without which political activity in the true sense of the word is inconceivable. It is therefore not astonishing that the proletariat should still be to some extent dependent upon bourgeois refugees.

In 1894, at the Frankfort congress of the German Socialist Party, a committee was appointed for the study of the agrarian question, and of the fifteen members of which it was composed no less than nine were intellectuals. This is a manifest disproportion, especially when we remember that among the leaders of the German Socialist Party there is an exceptional numerical preponderance of working-class elements. But the committee in question had to deal with scientific problems, and these could be solved by those alone who had received a scientific education. The same thing happens whenever legal, economic, or philosophical problems have to be treated with technical competence—in a word, whenever the questions under discussion are not fully comprehensible except by those who have made prolonged and profound preliminary studies. Cases in which the self-taught man is incompetent, present themselves daily. The increasing democratization of state institutions and the progressive socialization of the collective life, together with the securing of better conditions of labor for the workers, may perhaps gradually render the help of the intellectuals less essential. But this is a question for the remote future. Meanwhile, such a movement as that of the modern proletariat cannot afford to await that degree of maturity which would enable it to replace the ex-bourgeois among its leaders by men of proletarian origin.

The bourgeois elements in the socialist working-class party cannot be forcibly eradicated, nor excluded by any resolutions of party congresses; they are integral constituents of the movement for whose existence it is needless to offer any apologies.

A political labor movement without deserters from the bourgeoisie is historically as inconceivable as would be such a movement without a class-conscious proletariat. This consideration applies, above all, to the early days of the labor movement; but it is still applicable to the movement in the form in which we' know it today.

PART FIVE/ATTEMPTS TO RESTRICT THE INFLUENCE OF THE LEADERS

Chapter 1

The Referendum

IN THE domain of public law, democracy attains it culminating point in that complex of institutions which exists in Switzerland, where the people possess the right of the referendum and that of the initiative. The use of the referendum is compulsory in Switzerland upon a number of questions which are statutorily determined. The legislative measures drawn up by the representative body must then be submitted to a popular vote, for acceptance or rejection. In addition, the burghers exercise the power of direct legislation. When a certain number of voters demand the repeal of an existing law or the introduction of a new one, the matter must be submitted to popular vote. These important popular rights are supplemented by the direct popular election of the supreme executive authorities, as in the United States. Although these democratic ordinances have often in actual practice proved but little democratic in their results (the referendum, above all, having frequently shown that the democratic masses possess less democratic understanding than the representative government), and although leading socialists have therefore with good reason sharply criticized these manifestations of democracy, other socialists look to these institutions for the definitive solution of all questions of public law, and for the practical contradiction of the opinion that oligarchy arises by natural necessity, contending that by the referendum and by the initiative the decisive influence in legislative matters is transferred from the representative assembly to the totality of the citizens.

Now the democratic parties, as far as their internal organization is concerned, have either failed to adopt the principles of direct popular sovereignty, or else have accepted application of these only after prolonged hesitation and in exceptional cases. From the democratic point of view they are therefore inferior to many of the Swiss cantons. For example, German social democracy does not submit the deliberations of its congresses to ratification by the party as a whole. Moreover, and here the German arrangements differ from those which obtain among the socialists of Italy, France, and England (where the vote is based upon the number of the adherents in the local branches which the delegates respectively represent), in Germany the decisions at the congress are determined by the simple majority of the delegates. Thus we have parliamentarism in place of democracy. It is true that every member of the Socialist Party has the right of submitting any motion as he pleases to the annual congress. But the initiative thus secured is purely nominal. The motions sent in by individuals are hardly ever considered, and they are never passed, and the consequence is that none but a few cranks avail themselves of this right. When the congress is actually sitting, if a new resolution is to be submitted at least ten delegates must demand it. The only institution in the modern socialist parties which corresponds to the right of initiative is that in virtue of which the executive is compelled to summon an extraordinary congress upon the demand of a certain number of the members: in Germany, fifteen sections; in Italy, not less than one-tenth of all the members; in Belgium, two provincial federations or twenty sections.

In the Italian Socialist Party the referendum was practiced for a certain time, especially as regards questions upon which a preceding congress had not come to a decision, or where this decision had been insufficiently clear. From 1904 to 1906 the executive council had recourse to this means on four occasions. In one of these the question submitted was whether in the local branches the minority had the right of secession to form autonomous branches. Of the 1,458 sections consulted, 778 replied (166 for, 612 against). On another occasion it was necessary to consult the party upon the compatibility of freemasonry with socialism, and to ask whether members of the party could continue to be members of lodges. The participation of the members in this referendum was insignificant, but of the replies received, the majority were adverse to freemasonry. In the two other cases in which the referendum was employed, one related to a local Milanese question and the other to the choice of seat for a congress. Thus the use made in Italy of the referendum has been extremely restricted and the results have been mediocre. In England, many of the trade unions, after having for long made use of the referendum, have now discontinued the practice, on the ground that it led to a loss of tactical stability and was prejudicial to the finances and to the work of administration. In Germany, where, nothwithstanding the hesitation of the majority, the referendum was introduced in certain districts for the election of the delegates to the congress, it was soon perceived that those comrades alone had sufficient knowledge to participate in the election of delegates who had taken part in the meetings upon party questions and were familiar with the attitude assumed upon these by the various candidates. Consequently the application of the referendum to the election of delegates came to be regarded as a dangerous measure, tending to withdraw the electoral act from the sovereignty of the assembly. In Holland, where the referendum is obligatory for the election of the executive committee of the Socialist Party, in 1909 the participation of the rank and file in the election was so small that (notwithstanding the violent internal struggles then agitating the higher centers of the party) not more than one-half of the members exercised their right to vote.

The history of the referendum as a democratic expedient utilized by the socialist parties may be summed up by saying that its application has been rare, and that its results have been unfortunate. The results have been bad owing to the confused manner in which the questions have been formulated and owing to the inadequate participation of the masses. The rare application within the Socialist Party of this direct appeal to the members is in remarkable contrast with the frequent use made of the referendum by the bourgeois national organism of Switzerland, and it is in flagrant contradiction with the demand which all socialists make of the state for direct legislation by the people through the initiative and right of popular veto. Where party life is concerned, the socialists for the most part reject these practical applications of democracy, using against them conservative arguments such as we are otherwise accustomed to hear only from the opponents of socialism. In articles written by socialist leaders it is ironically asked whether it would be a good thing to hand over the leadership of the party to the ignorant masses simply for love of an abstract democratic principle. The conservative has views which harmonize perfectly with the thought here expressed, but he will speak of the "state" instead of the "party."

The referendum is open to criticism to the same extent and for the same reasons as is every other form of direct popular government. The two principal objections are the incompetence of the masses and the lack of time. Bernstein has said with good reason that even if none but the most important political and administrative questions are to be submitted to the popular vote, the happy citizen of the future will find every Sunday upon his desk such a number of interrogatories that he will soon lose all enthusiasm for the referendum. It is, however, especially in respect of questions demanding a prompt decision that the referendum proves impracticable; it conflicts with the militant character of the party, interfering with easy mobilization. Moreover, in all the more important cases, as when it is necessary to determine the attitude of the Socialist Party towards an imminent war, the use of a referendum would be rendered impossible by the forcible opposition of the state. It may be added that it is easy for the chiefs to lead the masses astray by clever phrasing of the questions, and by reserving to themselves the right of interpretation in the case of replies which are ambiguous precisely because the questions have been ambiguously posed. The referendum, through its absolute character and its withdrawal from all criticism, favors the dominion of adroit adventurers. George Sand describes the plebiscite, if not counterpoised by the intelligence of the masses, as an attack upon the liberty of the people.[1] The power of Bonapartism was, in fact, based on the referendum.[2]

	Votes	Favorable	Unfavor-able
Constitution of the year 1791, not submitted to popular vote			
Constitution of the year 1793	—	1,801,018	11.600
Constitution of the year III . . .	—	1,057,390	49,977
Election as Consul (year VIII)	3,012,569	3,011,007	1,562
Consul for life (1802)	3,577,259	3,568,888	8.371
Emperor (1804)	3,524,253	3,521,675	2,578

The institution of the referendum demands for its just working a perfectly conscientious bureaucracy, for the history of this electoral system shows with what ease its results are falsified.[3] Even if the operation should be effected strictly according to rule, the result of a referendum can never have a truly demonstrative value, for it always lacks the vivifying influence of

[1] G. Sand, *Journal d'un Voyageur, etc.*, ed. cit., p. 306.

[2] Result of the plebiscitary elections of Napoleon I (*Idées Napoléoniennes*, ed. cit., p. 19, by Louis Napoleon Bonaparte).

[3] Celebrated is the reproach hurled by Victor Hugo at Napoleon III on account of the plebiscite of the year 1851: "Who made the report? Baroche. Who investigated? Roucher. Who was in control? Pietri. Who made the count? Maupas. Who verified it? Troplong. Who announced it? You. This is to say that the villain reported, the hypocrite investigated, the rogue controlled, the false counted, the venal verified, the liar proclaimed." (Trans. from Victor Hugo, *Napoléon le Petit*, ed. cit., p. 313).

discussion. To conclude, it may be said that it can exercise no substantial influence upon the executive.

Plebiscites of Napoleon III

Election to the presidency (1848)	—	5,500,000	1,590,000 (for Cavaignac)
Re-elected president for 10 years (1851)	—	7,500,000	—
Emperor (1852)	—	7,800,000	—

Chapter 2

The Postulate of Renunciation

THE DISSOLUTION of the democratic consciousness of the leaders may doubtless be retarded, if not completely arrested, by the influence of intellectual or purely ideological factors. "So long as the guidance and representation of the party remains in the hands of persons who have grown gray in the great tradition of socialism,"[1] so long, that is to say, as the party is still dominated by vigorous socialistic idealism, it is possible that in certain conditions the leaders will retain their ancient democratic sentiments, and that they will continue to regard themselves as the servitors of the masses from whom their power is derived. We have already discussed the drastic measures that have been proposed to prevent the embourgeoisement of the leaders of proletarian origin. But it is not enough to prevent the proletarian elements among the leaders from adopting a bourgeois mode of life; it is also essential, on this line of thought, to insist upon the proletarianization of the leaders of bourgeois origin. In order to render it impossible for the socialist intellectuals to return to their former environment it has been proposed to insist that they should assimilate the tenor of their lives to that of the proletarian masses, and should thus descend to the level of their followers. It is supposed that their bourgeois instincts would undergo atrophy if their habits were to be in external respects harmonized as closely as possible with those of the proletariat.

This thesis is rooted in the records and experiences of popular history. A life in common awakens sympathy, attenuates the sentiments of class opposition, and may culminate in their entire disappearance. In the equalitarian state of Paraguay, which was founded and administered by the Jesuit order, those who were under tutelage felt themselves to be at one with the Jesuit fathers who were exploiting them, since there was no distinction between the leaders and the led in respect of clothing or general manner of life.[2] During the French Revolution, the peasantry took the castles of the nobles by storm; it was only in La Vendée that the two classes made common cause

[1] Heinrich Ströbel, *Gewerkschaften u. Sozialistische Geist*, "Neue Zeit," anno xxiii, vol. ii, No. 44.

[2] J. Guevara *Historia de la Conquista de Paraguay*, Buenos Ayres, 1885.

in the pitiless struggle with the centralized revolutionary government in Paris, because the patriarchal life in common, the common festivals and common hunting parties, had there effected a close psychological community between the peasants and their lords.[3] Similarly in Italian villages we do not usually find a well-marked hatred of the clergy, for the local curés, good-natured if uncultured individuals, are in no way elevated above the rest of the population, whose habits, and even whose poverty, they usually share.

Numerous measures, both material and ideal, have been proposed to prevent the formation of an oligarchy within the democratic parties. Speaking of the Italian students, Bakunin defines in the following terms the rôle which in his opinion the young refugees from the bourgeoisie ought to play in the ranks of the proletariat. "Neither guides nor prophets, neither instructors nor creators. The young intellectuals should consent to be obstetricians to the thought born of the people's life, to raise the aspirations of the proletariat—as unconscious as they are powerful—from a state of confusion to one of clarity."[4] Bakunin saw clearly that in certain countries, such as Italy and Russia, the working-class movement could not possibly dispense with the aid of bourgeois intellectuals, but he desired that those who by birth were the natural adversaries of socialism should be subjected to a very strict regime when they adhered to the socialist cause. In this respect he may be considered a precursor of Tolstoi. "Life dominates thought and determines will." It is by this aphorism, essentially based upon the materialist conception of history, that Bakunin defines his attitude to the question under consideration. He continues: "If a man, born and raised in a bourgeois milieu, wishes sincerely and without nonsense to become the friend and brother of the workers, he must renounce all the conditions of his past existence, all his bourgeois customs, break all his ties of sentiment, vanity, and intellect with the bourgeois world and, turning his back on this world, become its enemy, declare outright war against it, throw himself entirely, without restriction or reserve, into the worker's world. If he does not discover a passion for justice in himself sufficient to inspire this resolution and courage, let him not fool himself or the workers; he

[3] Adolphe Thiers, *Histoire de la Révolution Française*, Brockhaus u. Avenarius, Leipzig, 1846, vol. ii, pp. 395–6; Karl Kautsky, *Die Klassengegensätze von 1789*, Dietz, Stuttgart, 1889, p. 17.

[4] Trans. from Bakunin. *Lette inédite à Celso Cerreti*, 1872, "La Société Nouvelle," Brussels, February 1896, No. cxxiv, p. 179.

will never become their friend."[5] Thus it was above all for reasons of a psychological order that Bakunin demanded from the "bourgeois socialists," from the "intellectuals," a complete abandonment of their former mode of life. He believed that the outer world exercises a decisive influence upon the world of mental life. Self-renunciation, sacrifice, repudiation of all the forms of bourgeois existence—such were the conditions essential to the labor leader during the long history of the Russian revolution. In 1871 Netchajeff wrote his famous revolutionary catechism, enunciating the principle that the true revolutionary must be a man "consecrated to the cause." In the first paragraph we read: "He has neither personal interests nor affairs, neither feelings, attachments, nor propriety, not even a name. Everything in him is absorbed in a single exclusive interest, one thought, one passion: the Revolution."[6] Thus the aim was to attain to an absolute forgetfulness of the former bourgeois existence. Even more important than this elusory internal mortification was the external or environmental mortification which, among the Russian socialists, subsequently came to constitute the substratum of their activities, and which Bakunin described as "complete immersion in the life of the people."[7] The suppression of bourgeois instincts, this was the postulate which long dominated the history of Russian socialism. The apostles of the revolution, who were in many cases of the highest birth, must effect this suppression, in accordance with established custom, by living "among the people," by harmonizing their mode of life with that of the proletariat, by confounding themselves with the latter. Such was the theory of the "narodniki" or "populists," and its practical consequences were endured with the greatest heroism. Abandoning their social position, bidding farewell to all the intellectual comforts of the town, renouncing study and bourgeois career, men of science, schoolmasters, nobles, Jewish girl-students, and young women of family, withdrew to remote villages. Working as agricultural laborers, wheelwrights, locksmiths, blacksmiths, etc., they endeavored to acquire the most intimate knowledge of the common people, to gain their confidence, and whilst still keeping always in view the great revo-

[5] Trans. from Bakunin, *L'Empire knouto-germanique et la Révolution Sociale*, Œuvres de Michel Bakounine, P. V. Stock, Paris, 1897, vol. ii, p. 370.

[6] *Le Catechisme Révolutionnaire*, reprinted by Marx, *L'Alliance de la Démocratie Socialiste et l'Association internationale des Travailleurs*. A. Darson, successeur Foucault, London and Hamburg, 1873, p. 90.

[7] "Il bagno nella vita del populo" (Bakunin, *Il Sozialismo e Mazzini*, ed. cit., p. 24).

lutionary aim, they became the advisers of the people in the most varied conditions of their lives.[8]

After 1870 an analogous movement, thought a somewhat less extensive one, was manifest among the socialist intellectuals of other countries, and more especially among those of Italy, who for this reason were stigmatized by Marx, in a spasm of unjustified anger, as *déclassés*. This term, used in an insulting sense, presents the Italian socialists in a false light. Bakunin spoke of such *déclassement,* not as a historical fact, but as a psychological postulate of the effective socialist action of those who were not proletarians by birth. Thus in Bakunin's view the *déclassé* was not a social outcast, a bankrupt, an ineffectual genius, in a word, an involuntary outcast, but the very opposite, a voluntary outcast, one who has deliberately broken with the society in which he was born, in order to adapt himself to a strange environment and one hostile to that in which he was himself brought up. He is an intentional *déclassé,* and apart from the end which he pursues he must inspire us with respect for his spirit of self-sacrifice and for the invincible firmness of his convictions. It is a historical fact, though one of which the proof cannot be attempted here, that the bourgeois leaders of the early Italian labor movement were *déclassés,* but that they were such almost exclusively in the sense in which the word is used by Bakunin and not in the sense in which the word is used by Marx. Carlo Cafiero, the best-known leader of the Italian section of the International, derived from an aristocratic and wealthy family, placed the whole of his considerable fortune at the disposal of the party, whilst himself leading the life of a poor Bohemian. He may be considered the prototype of such idealists. Similar political tactics, of which perhaps idealists alone are capable (and these only in periods dominated by strong collective emotion), are based upon the psychological experience that the most ominously dictatorial tendencies of the leaders can be weakened, if not altogether suppressed, by one prophylactic means alone, namely, by the artificial creation of a social homogeneity among the various strata and fragments of which the revolutionary Socialist Party is composed. It thus becomes a moral postulate that all members of the party should live more or less in the same manner. This homogeneity of life is regarded as a

[8] Adolf Braun, *Russland u. d. Revolution,* p. 4.—Among numerous documents relating to this period of the Russian struggle for liberty, cf. also *Geheime Denkschrift über die Nihilistischen Umtriebe im Jahre 1875.* "Deutsche Rundschau."

safety-valve against the development of oligarchical forms within the working-class parties.

In our own day the principle that the leaders should practice economic renunciation and should identify themselves with the multitude is advocated only by a few isolated romanticists who belong to the anarchist wing of the socialist movement, and even by them only in timid periphrases. A similar principle, however, continues to prevail in the form of a political postulate, for the demand is made in certain working-class sections of the French and German socialist parties that the leaders should break off all social relationships with the bourgeois world, should devote themselves entirely to the party, and should have no other companions than "regularly inscribed members." In a Guesdist congress held in the north of France a resolution was passed that it was the duty of the socialist deputies to spend their lives among their comrades. In Germany we find traces of the same order of ideas in the absolute prohibition that members of the party shall write for the bourgeois press, or take any part whatever in bourgeois society. It is obvious that these attempts, which are inefficacious and impractical, can succeed at most in creating party fanaticism. They cannot establish identity of thought and action between the leaders and the proletarian masses.

Chapter 3

Syndicalism as Prophylactic

ACCORDING TO the syndicalist doctrine, it is essential to transfer the revolutionary center of gravity of the proletariat from the political party to the trade union. The union is conceived as a politically neutral organism, one which does not adhere to any party, but which is socialist in inspiration and aim.

It is the great merit of the syndicalists that they have understood how disastrous would be isolated syndicalist activity, devoid of any general theory, living simply from day to day; and to have advocated with much energy the indissoluble union of the working class, organized in its trade unions, with the socialist idea as *spiritus rector* and as ultimate aim. The syndicalists desire (and here, for once, they agree with the Marxist politicians) to diffuse among the organized workers the conviction that the trade union cannot attain its aim except by the elimination of capitalism, that is to say, by the abolition of the existing economic order. But the syndicalists also desire (and here they are in open conflict with all the other currents of contemporary socialism) that the trade union should not merely be an asylum for socialist ideas, but that it should also directly promote socialist activity, pursuing not simply a trade-unionist policy in the amplest sense of the term, but in addition and above all a socialist policy. Syndicalism is to put an end to the dualism of the labor movement by substituting for the party, whose sole functions are politico-electoral, and for the trade union, whose sole functions are economic, a completer organism which shall represent a synthesis of the political and of the economic function.[1]

Hence it is not the purpose of syndicalism to do away with organization as the basis of the labor movement. It expressly recognizes that this basis is indispensable. The syndicalists hold, and with good reason, that the dangers of organization cannot be eliminated simply by suppressing the organization, any more than we can prevent intoxication of the blood or diseases of the circulation by withdrawing the blood from the vessels. These would be quack cures, alike fatal in their result,

[1] Enrico Leone, *Che cosa è il Sindacalismo*, Tip. Industria e Lavoro, Rome, 1906, p. 28.

for the latter would kill the human organism and the former would kill the political and social organism. The problem rather is to discover an appropriate means for reducing to a minimum the chief defect which seems inherent in organization, namely, the rule exercised by the minority over the majority. Here we find a political school, whose adherents are numerous, able, well-educated, and generous-minded, persuaded that in syndicalism it has discovered the antidote to oligarchy. But we have to ask whether the antidote to the oligarchical tendencies of organization can possibly be found in a method which is itself also rooted in the principle of representation. Does it not rather seem that this very principle is in insoluble contradiction with the anti-democratic protestations of syndicalism? In other words, is not syndicalism itself affected by a manifest antinomy?

The great significance of sydicalism is found, above all, in the clear and penetrating manner in which it has recognized the dangers of bourgeois democracy. With a genuinely scientific scepticism it has stripped away the veils which conceal the power exercised by the democracy in the state, showing that this power is really no more than the hegemony of a minority, and demonstrating that it is in acute opposition with the needs of the working class. "Democracy intends to continue the exploitation of the producing masses by an oligarchy of professionals from the intelligentsia."[2] All the struggles which international syndicalism has undertaken against the German social-democracy, against the Italian and French intellectuals, and against the trade unions constituted upon a bureaucratic basis, may be reduced in ultimate analysis to a struggle against democratic demagogy.

Syndicalism is, however, mistaken in attributing to parliamentary democracy alone the inconveniences that arise from the principle of delegation in general. Mantica is right when he says that the syndicalists themselves have not succeeded in getting rid of the mental impedimenta with which all those are burdened who belong to any party, whether it participates in parliamentary elections or rejects such participation on principle.[3] *Nolens volens,* the syndicalist party is nothing more than a socialist party inefficiently revised and corrected. The syndicalists wish to stop where logically there is no stopping-place. All that the syndicalists have written upon political

[2] Georges Sorel, *Les Illusions du Progrès,* ed. cit., p. 263.

[3] Paolo Mantica, postscript to an article by Fiorino dal Padulo, *Elezionismo o Anti-Elezionismo?,* "Divenire Sociale," vi, fasc. 19 and 20, p. 272.

parties in general, and upon their big brother the Socialist Party in particular, applies to themselves as well, because it applies to all organizations as such without exception.

The more syndicalism endeavors to displace the axis of working-class policy towards syndicalist action, the greater is the danger it runs of itself degenerating into an oligarchy. Even in the revolutionary syndicalist groups the leaders have frequent opportunities of deceiving the rank and file. The treasurer of a strike, the secretary of a trade union, even the participator in a conspiracy or the leader upon a barricade, can betray those from whom they have received their instructions far more easily and with much more serious consequences than can a socialist member of parliament or municipal councilor. French syndicalists have frequently insisted with a certain violence upon what they speak of as "direct action" as the only means of bringing the working class into effective operation as an autonomous mass not represented by third persons, and of excluding *a priori* all representation "which could only be betrayal, deviation and bourgeois corruption."[4] But they arbitrarily restrict their one-sided theory to the political party alone, as if it were not inevitable that like causes should produce like effects when their action is displayed upon the field of the syndicalist movement. They reason as if they were immunized against the action of sociological laws of universal validity.

The organic structure of the trade unions is based upon the same foundation as that of the political party of the workers, namely, the representation of the interests of the rank and file by individuals specially elected for that purpose. In the decisive moments of the struggle for higher wages, the masses do not represent themselves but are represented by others. Trade unions without representatives, without some kind of executive, do not exist and are inconceivable.

The management of a trade union is sometimes a post of transition extremely favorable to a political career. In Germany 35 trade-union leaders sit in parliament, and in England 27. In France the two first permanent secretaries of the Metallurgical Federation have become deputies.[5] The strike, direct action by the proletariat, which the syndicalists regard as the

[4] Trans. from Cf., *inter al.*, Edouard Berth, *Bourgeoisie et Proletariat dans le Mouvement socialiste italien*, "Mouvement Socialiste," anno ix, series ii, p. 16; and reply by R. Michels, *Controverse socialiste*, in the same review, pp. 282 et seq.

[5] *Union Fédérale des Ouvriers Métallurgistes de France*, Bourse du Travail, Paris, p. 16.

panacea for all the ills affecting the labor movement, offers to men with a taste for political life, excellent opportunities for the display of their faculty for organization and their aptitude for command. The same may be said of the political strike, the general strike. For the professional leaders of the working-class, the economic strike is often precisely what war is for professional soldiers. Both present a good opportunity for rapid and splendid promotion. Many labor leaders have risen to extremely exalted and lucrative positions bcause they have directed a great strike, and have thus attracted the attention of the general public and of the government. The political position now [1912] occupied in England by John Burns is largely due to the celebrity he acquired as a strategist when he led the great dockers' strike in London during the year 1889. He then created a solid foundation for his subsequent popularity, and in particular he then gained the confidence of the most important categories of organized workers, and thus paved the way for his elevation from the bench of the working engineer to the rank of cabinet minister. This is one example among many which could be adduced in support of the assertion that very frequently the strike, instead of being a field of activity for the uniform and compact masses, tends rather to facilitate the process of differentiation and to favor the formation of an *élite* of leaders. Syndicalism is even more than socialism a fighting party. It loves the great battlefield. Can we be surprised that the syndicalists need leaders yet more than do the socialists?

The syndicalists reject the system of democractic representation and of bureaucracy. They desire to substitute for it "the more combative tactics of the revolutionary army of liberty, tactics founded upon the tried ability of the leaders." The modern labor leader, they tell us, must not be a bureaucrat. Already today, they add, the great strike-leaders arise suddenly from obscurity as did formerly the great leaders of revolution. In so far as it corresponds to historic truth, this conception does not at the best afford more than a general explanation of the institution of leadership. Its adequacy would be far greater were it possible to prove that these strike-leaders, whose necessity is admitted by the syndicalists themselves, when they have emerged from obscurity to fulfil a temporary need, were to prove sufficiently disinterested to undergo a spontaneous eclipse as soon as the strike was over. We know, however, that in general they seize the opportunity to secure a position of permanent influence. No form of strike, however much it may seem to be inspired by the autonomy of the masses, will be able to kill the dragon of demagogy, or even to prevent the formation of a class of independent leaders.

Under certain conditions, the mere theoretical propaganda of the idea of the strike and of direct action has sufficed to secure power and influence for the popular leader, to lift him upon the shoulders of the multitude to a position in which he could pluck at his ease the golden apples of life. Aristide Briand, born at Nantes of a family of small tavern-keepers, having joined the Socialist Party in Paris, speedily acquired fame and power among the workers by his defense of the doctrine of the general strike and the military strike. He soon gained so great a prestige as to require but a few years to climb to the position of premier of France. The starting-point of his triumphal march was the Nantes congress (1894), where he secured the acceptance of the idea of the general strike as part of the official program of the French trade unions.

Syndicalism is hostile to the "democratic" policy of the Socialist Party and the "authoritarian" syndicates, for the syndicalists hold that "democracy" affords a mere caricature of the fundamental principle of the labor movement, and they declare that from the democratic soil no fruit can spring but that of oligarchy. No other movement bases itself so energetically as does the syndicalist movement upon the right and ability of the masses for self-government. Where, as in France, the leadership of the labor movement is in their hands, they lay great stress upon the fact that their authority is restricted to carrying into effect the resolutions passed at the sovereign assemblies of the comrades. They assure us that the Confédération Générale du Travail, which sits in Paris, is not a directive organ, but a mere instrument for the coordination and the diffusion of the revolutionary activity of the working class. They describe this body as equally hostile to "centralization" and to "authoritarianism."[6] All impulse to action, we are assured, starts from the masses, and the syndicalist leaders are merely the exponents of this impulse. In strikes, the activity of the Comité Confédéral is not directive in the strict sense of the term; this body is a mere intermediary to ensure the solidarity of the workers to secure an element of *suractivité* and of *polarization*. Such is the theory. In practice, these same French syndicalists complain that in all decisive questions the masses wait until those above take the initiative, and that in

[6] Emile Pouget, *La Confédération Générale du Travail*, ed. cit., pp. 7, 23, 24.

default of such initiative the comrades remain with folded arms.

As in all groups characterized by an ostensibly democratic ideology, among the syndicalists the dominion of the leaders often assumes veiled forms. In France, the trade-union leaders are forbidden to seek election as deputies, for they must be preserved from all impure contacts. They must remain in constant communication with the masses, and their activities must be carried on in the full light of day. It is none the less true that the necessities of their position often oblige them, in the interest of the trade unions, to enter into relationships with the organs of state, in such a way that their anti-parliamentary attitude is apt to mean no more than that, instead of treating with the government in the open, from the summit of the parliamentary tribune, where their actions are, in part at least, visible to the rank and file, they negotiate mysteriously out of sight in antechambers and passages.

The theory of the masses professed by the syndicalists has a reverse side to which it is well to pay attention. The trade-union organizations, taken as a whole, do not include in their membership more than a minority of the workers susceptible of organization: in Italy, 11%; in England, 23%; in Sweden (where the proportion is highest of all), 42.21%. Among the organized workers, it is once more only a minority which plays an active part in trade-union life. The syndicalists at once lament this fact and rejoice at it, being inspired, in this respect, by sentiments which are by no means logically consistent. They rejoice to be rid of the dead weight of those who are still indifferent or immature. No doubt this attitude is inspired by the old Blanquist idea, that masses too vast and intellectually heterogeneous paralyze all activity by their lack of mobility, and that only alert minorities are enterprising and bellicose. If they were logical, the syndicalists would draw the conclusion that the general movement of the modern proletariat must necessarily be the work of a minority of enlightened proletarians. But the democratic tendencies of our time prevent the formulation of such a conclusion, or at least prevent its frank avowal, for this would bring the syndicalists into open conflict with the very basis of democracy, and would force them to proclaim themselves, without circumlocution, partisans of an oligarchical system. The syndicalist oligarchy, it is true, would not consist (like that of the socialist party) in the dominion of the leaders over the masses, but in the dominion of a small fraction of the masses over the whole. There are a few theorists of syndicalism who already speak unreservedly of socialism as an evolution based upon the action of working-class *élites*.[7]

The oligarchical character of the syndicalist movement is displayed most conspicuously in the demand (made for reasons which have nothing to do with democracy) for absolute obedience to the orders of the organized *élite*. "The indifferent, because they have neglected to express their will, can do more than acquiesce in decisions already made."[8] Following the example of the reformist trade unions of Germany and England, those French unions that are inspired by the doctrine of revolutionary syndicalism hold fast to the principle that the organized workers have the right to issue orders to the unorganized.

It may be admitted that the supreme directive organs of the French labor movement do not possess that plenitude of powers which the corresponding hierarchical grades of other countries have at their disposal—above all in Germany. There are various reasons for this difference, such as the national character of the French, the weakness of the organizations, etc. But even in France there is a great difference between theory and practice. In the first place the leaders exercise a powerful influence upon the organized comrades through the newspapers, which, as every one knows, are not edited by the masses. In addition there exists a whole hierarchy of sub-chiefs. The number of trade unionists enrolled in the Confédération Générale du Travail is about 350,000, whilst the number of subscribers to the "Voix du Peuple," the central organ of the Confédération, is no more than 7,000. These subscribers are described as "the most active militants, members of union shops and trade councils . . . Through their mediation the Confederation's ideas are diffused."[9] Here we have a frank confession that there exists a graduated intellectual subordination which conflicts with the syndicalist theory. Even the general strike was primarily conceived in France as a hierarchical procedure. A resolution voted at the Nantes congress (1894) specified that the general strike must be accurately prepared in advance by a central committee of eleven and by a large number of local sub-committees. These were to give the signal

[7] Cf. the essays of Angelo Oliviero Olivetti and Alfredo Polledro in "Pagine Libere," 1909–10; especially Polledro's article *Dal Congresso di Bologna alla Palingenesi Sindacalista* (anno iv, 1909, fasc. 14).

[8] Trans. from Emile Pouget, *La Confédération Générale du Travail*, ed. cit., p. 7.

[9] Trans. from Ibid., ed. cit., pp. 30 and 33.

and to direct the movement. Today the syndicalists reject this conception on account of its jacobin character; but in practice they are compelled to conform to the idea, notwithstanding the theoretical contradiction in which they are thus involved. In the works of some of the French syndicalist writers who have a strong tendency towards æstheticism, such as Edouard Berth, we find that the jacobin germs of the theory in question have undergone a full development.

The more syndicalism gathers power, the more conspicuous among the syndicalists become the effects which are everywhere characteristic of the representative system. From the ranks of the French syndicalists, leaders have already sprung whose sensitiveness towards the criticisms of their followers can be equalled only by that of an English trade-union leader. Youthful syndicalism, although born out of opposition to the authoritarianism of the leaders, is thus quite unable to escape the oligarchical tendencies which arise in every organization. For the syndicalist leaders, as for others, the preservation of their own power becomes the supreme law. So far has the process already gone in France, that they have abandoned the old tactics of taking advantage of the prosecutions instituted against them by the government to make propagandist speeches in court and to employ the language of heroes and prophets. Instead, on these occasions, they act with extreme prudence and display diplomatic reserve. Sorel himself speaks of the "progressive degeneration of trade-unionism," and he has declared: "The General Confederation of Workers takes on more and more the aspect of a government employee."

Chapter 4

Anarchism as Prophylactic

ANARCHISTS WERE the first to insist upon the hierarchical and oligarchical consequences of party organization. Their view of the defects of organization is much clearer than that of socialists and even than that of syndicalists. They resist authority as the source of servility and slavery, if not the source of all the ills of the world. For them constraint is "synonymous with prison and police."[1] They know how readily the individualism of the leaders checks and paralyses the socialism of the led. In order to elude this danger, anarchists, notwithstanding the practical inconveniences entailed, have refrained from constituting a party, at least in the strict sense of the term. Their adherents are not organized under any stable form. They are not united by any discipline. They know nothing of obligations or duties, such as elections, pecuniary contributions, participation in regular meetings, and so on.

It is a necessary consequence of these peculiarities that the typical anarchist leader differs considerably from the typical socialist leader, the characteristic product of the last twenty-five years. Anarchism has no party organization which can offer lucrative positions, nor does the anarchist pathway lead to parliamentary honors. Consequently there are fewer opportunities for contagion, fewer temptations, and much less field for personal ambition. Thus it may be expected, as a logical consequence of the theory that environment makes character, that in the average anarchist leader idealism should be more conspicuous than in the average socialist leader. The anarchist lives remote from the practice of politics, with all its passions, all its appetites, and all its allurements; consequently he is more objective in his judgment of persons and of things, more contemplative, more self-enclosed—but also more of a dreamer, more remote from reality. Among anarchist leaders we find many learned, cultivated, and modest men who have not lost the sentiment of true friendship, and to whom it is a

[1] Ferdinand Domela Nieuwenhuis, *Der staatssozialistische Charakter der Sozialdemokratie*, "Archiv für Sozialw.," xxviii, fasc. i, p. 144.

pleasure to cultivate and nourish that sentiment: sincere and high-minded men, such as Peter Kropotkin, Elisée Reclus, Christian Cornelissen, Enrico Malatesta, and many others less famous.[2] But though the anarchist leaders are as a rule morally superior to the leaders of the organized parties working in the political field, we find in them some of the qualities and pretensions characteristic of all leadership. This is proved by a psychological analysis of the characteristics of the individual anarchist leader. The theoretical struggle against all authority, against all coercion, to which many of the most eminent anarchists have sacrificed a large portion of their lives, has not stifled in them the natural love of power. All that we can say is that the means of dominion employed by the anarchist leader belong to an epoch which political parties have already outlived. These are the means utilized by the apostle and the orator: the flaming power of thought, greatness of self-sacrifice, profundity of conviction. Their dominion is exercised, not over the organization, but over minds; it is the outcome, not of technical indispensability, but of intellectual ascendancy and moral superiority.

Whilst anarchists repudiate the formation of political parties, they adhere none the less to the principle of organization in the economic field. Some of them, even, explicitly recognize the need for the technical guidance of the masses; whilst others declare their conviction that it would suffice to restrict the functions of the leaders to purely administrative work, to eliminate, once for all, the differences, so dangerous to the organization, which arise between the leaders and the led. As if the technical and administrative superiority of the leaders were not alone sufficient to establish their supremacy over the masses in all other respects! Not even Bakunin proposed to exclude the principiles of organization and discipline, but he desired that they should be voluntary instead of automatic.[3] He conceived the anarchist regime as a federation of perpetual barricades, and proposed to institute a council of the revolutionary commune, consisting of delegates, one or two in number from each barricade, or from each street or quarter, these

[2] We find some admirably drawn character-sketches of anarchist leaders in the work of Peter Kropotkin, *Memoirs of a Revolutionist*, Smith, Elder, London, 1899, vol. ii, p. 196. See also the psychological portrait of an unnamed anarchist in De Amicis, *Lotte civili*, Nerbini, Florence, 1904, pp. 128 et seq.

[3] Bakunin, *Œuvres*, ed. cit., vol. ii, p. 297.

delegates having an imperative mandate. The communal council thus composed would nominate from among its own members special executive committees for all the branches of the revolutionary administration of the commune. The capital, having effected a successful insurrection and constituted itself as a commune, would then declare to the other municipalities of the country that it put forward no claim to exercise any supremacy over them. But it would invite them to provide themselves also with a revolutionary organization, and to send delegates to a meeting-place to be determined by agreement, in order to establish a federation of insurgent associations, communes, and provinces, and thus to create a revolutionary power sufficiently strong to oppose any possible reaction. As Marx justly pointed out, these executive committees, if they were to do anything at all, must be furnished with powers, and must be sustained by public force. The federal parliament would have no reason for existence unless it were to organize this public force. Besides, this parliament could, just like the communal council, delegate its executive power to one or more committees, and each of these would in fact be invested with an authoritative character which the needs of the struggle would not fail continually to accentuate. In a word, according to Marx, the whole Bakuninian scheme would be characterized by an ultra-authoritative stamp.[4]

Like the syndicalists, the anarchists have extolled "direct action," which, they consider, possesses the value of an ethical principle. Direct action, "in contradistinction to the tactics of negotiation, of mutual compromise, of hierarchical organization, and of the representative system, tends to secure a higher standard of life for the workers, and the emancipation of the proletariat from capitalism and political centralization—to secure these advantages by the immediate self-help of the workers."[5]

Notwithstanding this, anarchism, a movement on behalf of liberty, founded on the inalienable right of the human being over his own person, succumbs, no less than the Socialist Party, to the law of authoritarianism as soon as it abandons the re-

[4] Karl Marx, *L'Alliance de la Démocratie socialiste et l'Association internationale des Travailleurs*, ed. cit., p. 14.—Regarding the autocratic tendencies of Bakunin see pp. 3, 9, 10–11, 18, 24–5.

[5] Erich Mühsam, *Die direkte Aktion im Befreiungskampfe der Arbeiterschaft*, "Generalstreik," monthly supplement of "Der Freie Arbeiter," anno i. October 1905.

gion of pure thought and as soon as its adherents unite to form associations aiming at any sort of political activity. Nieuwenhuis, the veteran champion of anarchizing socialism with a frankly individualist tendency, showed on one occasion that he had a keen perception of the dangers which anarchism runs from all contact with practical life. At the Amsterdam congress of 1907, after the foundation of the new anarchist international, he raised a warning voice against the arguments of the Italian Enrico Malatesta, an anarchist attached to the school of Bakunin. Malatesta, having dilated upon the strength of bourgeois society, declared that nothing would suit this society better than to be faced by unorganized masses of workers, and that for this reason it was essential to counter the powerful organization of the rich by a still more powerful organization of the poor. "If that is your thought, dear friend," said Nieuwenhuis to Malatesta, "you can go peacefully over to the socialists. They won't tell you anything else." In the course of this first anarchist congress there were manifest, according to Nieuwenhuis, the symptoms of that diplomatic mentality which characterizes all the leaders of authoritarian parties.[6]

Ostrogorski has proposed to substitute for party organization, which invariably leads to the institution of anti-democratic forms, a system of temporary associations, which should come into existence only for the attainment of definite ends, and should be dissolved as soon as these ends have been secured (*league system*).[7] He considers that the adoption of this system would tend to restore to political struggles the sincerity, honesty, and clarity which they lack today. Now, the analysis of political parties which has been effected authorizes us to doubt the efficiency of the proposed method. Its adoption would not secure any real progress, even were it possible to suppress by a simple decree the organizations which have been brought into existence by the necessary determinants of historical evolution. Whilst anarchism, which presents to us the most abstract and most idealistic vision of the future, has promised to the world an order from which all concentration of power shall be excluded, it has not known how to establish,

[6] Ferdinand Domela Nieuwenhuis, *Die Nieuwe Internationale*, "De Vrije Socialist," Hilversum, September 1907, vol. x, No. 71.

[7] M. Ostrogorski, *La Démocratie et l'Organisation des Partis politiques*, ed. cit., vol. ii, pp. 618 et seq.

as a part of anarchist theory, the logical elements of such an order.[8]

[8] "Most once said that only the dictatorial and the servile could be sincere opponents of anarchism. Even if the use of the 'only' be left uncriticized, these words seem to me to display a fatal defect in the psychological foundations of anarchism. For, in view of the natural endowments of human beings, it seems probable that the majority will always continue to belong to one or other of the two types here characterized by Most" (Walter Borgius, *Die Ideenwelt des Anarchismus*, Dietrich, Leipzig, 1904, p. 58).

PART SIX/SYNTHESIS: THE OLIGARCHICAL TENDENCIES OF ORGANIZATION

Chapter 1

The Conservative Basis of Organization

AT THIS point in our inquiry two decisive questions present themselves. One of these is whether the oligarchical disease of the democratic parties is incurable. This will be considered in the next chapter. The other question may be formulated in the following terms. Is it impossible for a democratic party to practice a democratic policy, for a revolutionary party to pursue a revolutionary policy? Must we say that not *socialism* alone, but even a socialistic *policy*, is utopian? The present chapter will attempt a brief answer to this inquiry.

Within certain narrow limits, the Democratic Party, even when subjected to oligarchical control, can doubtless act upon the state in the democratic sense. The old political caste of society, and above all the "state" itself, are forced to undertake the revaluation of a considerable number of values—a revaluation both ideal and practical. The importance attributed to the masses increases, even when the leaders are demagogues. The legislature and the executive become accustomed to yield, not only to claims proceeding from above, but also to those proceeding from below. This may give rise, in practice, to great inconveniences, such as we recognize in the recent history of all the states under a parliamentary regime; in theory, however, this new order of things signifies an incalculable progress in respect of public rights, which thus come to conform better with the principles of social justice. This evolution will, however, be arrested from the moment when the governing classes succeed in attracting within the governmental orbit their enemies of the extreme left, in order to convert them into collaborators. Political organization leads to power. But power is always conservative. In any case, the influence exercised upon the governmental machine by an energetic opposition party is necessarily slow, is subject to frequent interruptions, and is always restricted by the nature of oligarchy.

The recognition of this consideration does not exhaust our problem, for we have further to examine whether the oligarchical nature of organization be not responsible for the creation of the external manifestations of oligarchical activity, whether it be not responsible for the production of an oligarchical policy. The analysis here made shows clearly that the internal policy of the party organizations is today absolutely conservative, or is on the way to become such. Yet it might happen that the external policy of these conservative organisms would be bold and revolutionary; that the anti-democratic centralization of power in the hands of a few leaders is no more than a tactical method adopted to effect the speedier overthrow of the adversary; that the oligarchs fulfil the purely provisional function of educating the masses for the revolution, and that organization is after all no more than a means employed in the service of an amplified Blanquist conception.

This development would conflict with the nature of party, with the endeavor to organize the masses upon the vastest scale imaginable. As the organization increases in size, the struggle for great principles becomes impossible. It may be noticed that in the democratic parties of today the great conflicts of view are fought out to an ever-diminishing extent in the field of ideas and with the weapons of pure theory, that they therefore degenerate more and more into personal struggles and invectives, to be settled finally upon considerations of a purely superficial character. The efforts made to cover internal dissensions with a pious veil are the inevitable outcome of organization based upon bureaucratic principles, for, since the chief aim of such an organization is to enroll the greatest possible number of members, every struggle on behalf of ideas within the limits of the organization is necessarily regarded as an obstacle to the realization of its ends, an obstacle, therefore, which must be avoided in every possible way. This tendency is reinforced by the parliamentary character of the political party. "Party organization" signifies the aspiration for the greatest number of members. "Parliamentarism" signifies the aspiration for the greatest number of votes. The principal fields of party activity are electoral agitation and direct agitation to secure new members. What, in fact, is the modern political party? It is the methodical organization of the electoral masses. The Socialist Party, as a political aggregate endeavoring simultaneously to recruit members and to recruit votes, finds here its vital interests, for every decline in membership and every loss in voting strength diminishes its political prestige. Consequently great respect must be paid, not only to new members, but also to possible adherents, to those who in Germany are termed *mitläufer*, in Italy *simpatizzanti*, in Holland *geestverwanten*, and in England *sympathizers*. To avoid alarming these individuals, who are still outside the ideal worlds of socialism or democracy, the pursuit of a policy based on strict principle is shunned, while the consideration is ignored whether the numerical increase of the organization thus effected is not likely to be gained at the expense of its quality.

The last link in the long chain of phenomena which confer a profoundly conservative character upon the intimate essence of the political party (even upon that party which boasts itself revolutionary) is found in the relationships between party and state. Generated to overthrow the centralized power of the state, starting from the idea that the working class need merely secure a suffiicently vast and solid organization in order to triumph over the organization of the state, the party of the workers has ended by acquiring a vigorous centralization of its own, based upon the same cardinal principles of authority and discipline which characterize the organization of the state. It thus becomes a governmental party, that is to say, a party which, organized itself like a government on the small scale, hopes some day to assume the reins of government upon the large scale. The revolutionary political party is a state within the state, pursuing the avowed aim of destroying the existing state in order to substitute for it a social order of a fundamentally different character. To attain this essentially political end, the party avails itself of the socialist organization, whose sole justification is found precisely in its patient but systematic preparation for the destruction of the organization of the state in its existing form. The subversive party organizes the *framework* of the social revolution. For this reason it continually endeavors to strengthen its positions, to extend its bureaucratic mechanism, to store up its energies and its funds.

Every new official, every new secretary, engaged by the party is in theory a new agent of the revolution; in the same way every new section is a new battalion; and every additional thousand francs furnished by the members' subscriptions, by the profits of the socialist press, or by the generous donations of sympathetic benefactors, constitute fresh additions to the war-chest for the struggle against the enemy. In the long run, however, the directors of this revolutionary body existing within the authoritarian state, sustained by the same means as that state and inspired by the like spirit of discipline, cannot fail to perceive that the party organization, whatever advances it may make in the future, will never succeed in becoming more than an ineffective and miniature copy of the state organization. For this reason, in all ordinary circumstances, and as far as prevision is humanly possible, every attempt of the party to measure its forces with those of its antagonists is foredoomed to disastrous failure. The logical consequence of these considerations is in direct conflict with the hopes entertained by the founders of the party. Instead of gaining revolutionary energy as the force and solidity of its structure has increased, the precise opposite has occurred; there has resulted, *pari passu* with its growth, a continued increase in the prudence, the timidity even, which inspires its policy. The party, continually threatened by the state upon which its existence depends, carefully avoids (once it has attained to maturity) everything which might irritate the state to excess. The party doctrines are, whenever requisite, attenuated and deformed in accordance with the external needs of the organization.[1] Organization becomes the vital essence of the party. During the first years of its existence, the party did not fail to make a parade of its revolutionary character, not only in respect of its ultimate ends, but also in respect of the means employed for their attainment—although not always in love with these means. But as soon as it attained to political maturity, the party did not hesitate to modify its original profession of faith and to affirm itself revolutionary only "in the best sense of the word," that is to say, no longer on lines which interest the police, but only in theory and on paper. This same party, which at one time

[1] A classical example of the extent to which the fear of injuring the socialist organization will lead even the finest intelligences of the party to play tricks with socialist theory is afforded by the history of that celebrated preface which in 1895 Frederick Engels wrote for a posthumous edition of Marx's book, *Die Klassenkämpfe in Frankreich, 1848–9*. This preface became the subject of great international discussions, and has been justly considered as the first vigorous manifestation of reformism in German socialism. For Engels here declares that socialist tactics will have more success through the use of legal than of illegal and revolutionary means, and thus expressly repudiates the Marxist conception of the socialist revolution. It was not till some years later that Kautsky published a letter from Engels in which the latter disavowed his preface, saying: "My text had to suffer from the timid legalism of our friends in Berlin, who dreaded a second edition of the anti-socialist laws—a dread to which I was forced to pay attention at the existing political juncture" (Karl Kautsky, *Der Weg zur Macht*, Buchandlung "Vorwärts," 1909, p. 42). From this it would appear that the theory (at that time brand-new) that socialism could attain to its ends by parliamentary methods—and this was the quintessence of Engels' preface—came into existence from a fear lest the socialist party organization (which should be a means, and not an end in itself) might suffer at the hands of the state. Thus Engels was fêted, on the one hand, as a man of sound judgment and one willing to look facts in the face (cf. W. Sombart, *Friedrich Engels, Ein Blatt zur Entwicklungsgeschichte des Sozialismus*, Separat-Abdruck der "Zukunft," Berlin, 1895, p. 32), and was attacked, on the other hand, as a pacifist utopist (cf. Arturo Labriola, *Riforme e Rivoluzione sociale*, ed. cit., pp. 181 and 224); whereas in reality Engels would seem to have been the victim of an opportunist sacrifice of principles to the needs of organization, a sacrifice made for love of the party and in opposition to his own theoretical convictions.

did not hesitate, when the triumphant guns of the bourgeois governors of Paris were still smoking, to proclaim with enthusiasm its solidarity with the communards,[2] now announces to the whole world that it repudiates anti-militarist propaganda in any form which may bring its adherents into conflict with the penal code, and that it will not assume any responsibility for the consequences that may result from such a conflict. A sense of responsibility is suddenly becoming active in the Socialist Party. Consequently it reacts with all the authority at its disposal against the revolutionary currents which exist within its own organization, and which it has hitherto regarded with an indulgent eye. In the name of the grave responsibilities attaching to its position it now disavows antimilitarism, repudiates the general strike, and denies all the logical audacities of its past.

The history of the international labor movement furnishes innumerable examples of the manner in which the party becomes increasingly inert as the strength of its organization grows; it loses its revolutionary impetus, becomes sluggish, not in respect of action alone, but also in the sphere of thought. More and more tenaciously does the party cling to what it calls the "ancient and glorious tactics," the tactics which have led to a continued increase in membership. More and more invincible becomes its aversion to all aggressive action.

The dread of the reaction by which the Socialist Party is haunted paralyses all its activities, renders impossible all manifestation of force, and deprives it of all energy for the daily struggle. It attempts to justify its misoneism by the false pretense that it must reserve its strength for the final struggle. Thus we find that the conservative tendencies inherent in all forms of possession manifest themselves also in the Socialist Party. For half a century the socialists have been working in the sweat of their brow to create a model organization. Now, when three million workers have been organized—a greater number than was supposed necessary to secure complete victory over the enemy—the party is endowed with a bureauc-

[2] As is well-known, in 1871 Bebel, in open Reichstag, declared himself opposed to the annexation of Alsace-Lorraine, an annexation which had already been completed, and, with the sole support of Liebknecht, pushed his theoretical opposition to war to the point of voting, in war-time, against the military credits. Bakunin cherished no affection either for the Marxists or for the Germans, but he was unable to refuse his admiration to the youthful Marxist party in Germany, which had had the sublime courage to proclaim "in Germany, in the country where freedom is least known, under the triumphant military regime of Bismarck, its ardent sympathies for the principles and heroes of the Commune" (M. Bakunin, *Il Socialismo e Mazzini*, ed. cit., p. 9).

racy which, in respect of its consciousness of its duties, its zeal, and its submission to the hierarchy, rivals that of the state itself; the treasuries are full,[3] a complex ramification of financial and moral interests extends all over the country. A bold and enterprising tactic would endanger all this: the work of many decades, the social existence of thousands of leaders and sub-leaders, the entire party, would be compromised. For these reasons the idea of such a tactic becomes more and more distasteful. It conflicts equally with an unjustified sentimentalism and a justified egoism. It is opposed by the artist's love of the work he has created with so much labor, and also by the personal interest of thousands of honest breadwinners whose economic life is so intimately associated with the life of the party and who tremble at the thought of losing their employment and the consequences they would have to endure if the government should proceed to dissolve the party, as might readily happen in case of war.

Thus, from a means, organization becomes an end. To the institutions and qualities which at the outset were destined simply to ensure the good working of the party machine (subordination, the harmonious cooperation of individual members, hierarchical relationships, discretion, propriety of conduct), a greater importance comes ultimately to be attached than to the productivity of the machine. Henceforward the sole preoccupation is to avoid anything which may clog the

[3] In the year 1906 the total funds of the German trade unions amounted to about 16,000,000 marks. The richest union, that of the compositors, had accumulated funds amounting to 4,374,013 marks. Next came the bricklayers' union, with 2,091,681 marks; the metal-workers' union, with 1,543,352 marks; and the woodworkers' union, with 1,452,215 marks (Karl Kautsky, *Der neue Tarif der Buchdrucker,* "Neue Zeit," anno xxv, vol. 1, No. 4, p. 129). Since then, notwithstanding the intervening years of crisis involving exceptionally high claims for out-of-work pay, the financial position of the unions has become yet stronger. In 1909 the compositors owned 7,929,257 marks; the bricklayers, 6,364,647 marks; the metalworkers, 6,248,251 marks; the woodworkers, 3,434,314 marks (*Statistisches Jahrbuch für das deutsche Reich,* 1910, anno xxxi, pp. 376–7). These ample funds are of great importance for defensive purposes, but their value for offensive purposes is extremely restricted. It would be utterly absurd for the union to pursue the policy of heaping up funds in the hope of thus overthrowing capitalism. In Germany there are hundreds of capitalists in whose private treasuries are available means exceeding those of all the unions put together. Moreover, on the present system of depositing savings with private banks, the earnings of this accumulated capital yield profit, not to the trade unionist, but to the enemies of the working class who are shareholders in these banks, so that the trade-union funds are "ultimately employed against the labour movement" (Bruno Buchwald, *Die Gewerkschaftsbank,* "Die neue Gesellschaft," anno iii, fasc. x). Hence the trade-union funds help to strengthen the opponents of the trade unions. For this reason a scheme has long been on foot among trade unionists to institute a bank of their own.

machinery. Should the party be attacked, it will abandon valuable positions previously conquered, and will renounce ancient rights rather than reply to the enemy's offensive by methods which might "compromise" its position. Naumann writes sarcastically: "The war-cry 'Proletarians of all countries unite!' has had its due effect. The forces of the organized proletariat have gained a strength which no one believed possible when that war-cry was first sounded. There is money in the treasuries. Is the signal for the final assault never to be given? . . . Is the work of preliminary organization to go on for ever?"[4] As the party's need for tranquility increases, its revolutionary talons atrophy. We have now a finely conservative party which (since the effect survives the cause) continues to employ revolutionary terminology, but which in actual practice fulfils no other function than that of a constitutional opposition.

All this has deviated far from the ideas of Karl Marx, who, were he still alive, ought to be the first to revolt against such a degeneration of Marxism. Yet it is quite possible that, carried away by the spectacle of an army of three million men acting in his name, swearing on solemn occasions *in verba magistri*, he also would find nothing to say in reprobation of so grave a betrayal of his own principles. There were incidents in Marx's life which render such a view possible. He certainly knew how to close his eyes, in public at any rate, to the serious faults committed by the German social democracy in 1876.[5]

In our own day, which may be termed the age of the epigones of Marx, the character of the party as an organization ever greedy for new members, ever seeking to obtain an absolute majority, cooperates with the condition of weakness in which it finds itself vis-á-vis the state, to effect a gradual replacement of the old aim, to demolish the existing state by the new aim, to permeate the state with the men and the ideas of the party. The struggle carried on by the socialists against the parties of the dominant classes is no longer one of principle, but simply one of competition. The revolutionary party has become a rival of the bourgeois parties for the conquest of power. It therefore opens its doors to all those persons who may assist in the attainment of this end, or who may simply swell its battalions for the struggle in which it is engaged. With the necessary modification, we may well apply to the

[4] Friedrich Naumann, *Das Schicksal des Marxismus*, "Hilfe," October 11, 1908, p. 657.

[5] Karl Kautsky, Preface to Karl Marx, *Randglossen zum Programm der deutschen Arbeiterpartei* (1875), "Neue Zeit," anno ix, vol. 1, pp. 568 et seq.

internationalist socialist party the words which de Maupassant puts into the mouth of the *Neveu de l'Oncle Sosthène* in order to describe the essence of French freemasonry: "Instead of destroying it, you organize competition; that lowers the prices, that's all. And then again, if you did not admit free-thinkers among you, I would understand. But you admit everyone. You have Catholics *en masse;* even leaders of the party. Pius IX was one of you before he became pope. If you call a society composed in this manner a citadel against clericalism, I find your citadel weak. . . . Ah yes, you are rogues! If you tell me that French Masonry is an election factory, I will agree with you; that it serves as a machine for the election of candidates of all sorts I will not deny; that it has no other function than to make fools of good people, that it regiments in order to send them to the ballot box like soldiers to the front, I will agree; that it is useful because it changes each of its members into an electoral agent, I will cry out 'It is as clear as day!' But if you maintain that it serves to lessen the monarchic spirit, I will laugh in your face."[6]

Thus the hatred of the party is directed, not in the first place against the opponents of its own view of the world order, but against the dreaded rivals in the political field, against those who are competing for the same end—power. It is above all in the electoral agitation carried on by the socialist parties when they have attained what is termed "political maturity" that this characteristic is most plainly manifest. The party no longer seeks to fight its opponents, but simply to outbid them. For this reason we observe a continual recurrence in socialist speeches of a claim which harmonizes ill with socialist principles, and which is often untrue in fact. Not the nationalists, they say, but we, are the best patriots; not the men of the government, but we are the best friends of the minor civil servants [in Italy] or of the peasants [in Germany]; and so on. Evidently among the trade unions of diverse political coloring, whose primary aim it is to gain the greatest possible number of new members, the note of competition will be emphasized yet more. This applies especially to the so-called "free unions" of Germany, neutrally tinted bodies which on principle hold in horror all definiteness in respect of political views or conceptions of the world order, and which are therefore distinguishable in name only (a few trifling terminological differences apart) from the Christian unions. If we study the speeches and

6 Trans. from Guy de Maupassant, *Mademoiselle Fifi*, Libr. Ollendorff, Paris, 1907, p. 69.

polemic writings directed by the leaders of the free unions against the leaders of the Christian unions, we find that these speeches and writings contain no declarations of principle and no theoretical expositions, but merely personal crticisms and accusations, and above all accusations of treachery to the cause of labor. Now it is obvious that these are no more than the means vulgarly employed by competitors who wish to steal one another's customers.

By such methods, not merely does the party sacrifice its political virginity, by entering into promiscuous relationships with the most heterogeneous political elements, relationships which in many cases have disastrous and enduring consequences, but it exposes itself in addition to the risk of losing its essential character as a party. The term "party" presupposes that among the individual components of the party there should exist a harmonious direction of wills towards identical objective and practical aims. Where this is lacking, the party becomes a mere "organization."

Chapter 2

Democracy and the Iron Law of Oligarchy

WHILE THE majority of the socialist schools believe that in a future more or less remote it will be possible to attain to a genuinely democratic order, and while the greater number of those who adhere to aristocratic political views consider that democracy, however dangerous to society, is at least realizable, we find in the scientific world a conservative tendency voiced by those who deny resolutely and once for all that there is any such possibility. As was shown in an earlier chapter,[1] this tendency is particularly strong in Italy, where it is led by a man of weight, Gaetano Mosca, who declares that no highly developed social order is possible without a "political class," that is to say, a politically dominant class, the class of a minority. Those who do not believe in the god of democracy are never weary of affirming that this god is the creation of a childlike mythopœic faculty, and they contend that all phrases representing the idea of the rule of the masses, such terms as state, civic rights, popular representation, nation, are descriptive merely of a legal principle, and do not correspond to any actually existing facts. They contend that the eternal struggles between aristocracy and democracy of which we read in history have never been anything more than struggles between an old minority, defending its actual predominance, and a new and ambitious minority, intent upon the conquest of power, desiring either to fuse with the former or to dethrone and replace it. On this theory, these class struggles consist merely of struggles between successively dominant minorities. The social classes which under our eyes engage in gigantic battles upon the scene of history, battles whose ultimate causes are to be found in economic antagonism, may thus be compared to two groups of dancers executing a *chassé croisé* in a quadrille.

The democracy has an inherent preference for the authoritarian solution of important questions. It thirsts simultaneously for splendor and for power. When the English burghers had conquered their liberties, they made it their highest ambi-

[1] Cf. *supra*, p. 76.

tion to possess an aristocracy. Gladstone declared that the love of the English people for their liberties was equalled only by their love for the nobility. Similarly it may be said that it is a matter of pride with the socialists to show themselves capable of maintaining a discipline which, although it is to a certain extent voluntary, none the less signifies the submission of the majority to the orders issued by the minority, or at least to the rules issued by the minority in obedience to the majority's instructions. Vilfredo Pareto has even recommended socialism as a means favorable for the creation of a new working-class *élite*, and he regards the courage with which the socialist leaders face attack and persecution as a sign of their vigor, and as the first condition requisite to the formation of a new "political class."[2] Pareto's *théorie de la circulation des élites* must, however, be accepted with considerable reserve, for in most cases there is not a simple replacement of one group of *élites* by another, but a continuous process of intermixture, the old elements incessantly attracting, absorbing, and assimilating the new.

This phenomenon was perhaps recognized at an earlier date, in so far as the *circulation des élites* was effected within the limits of a single great social class and took place on the political plane. In states where a purely representative government prevails, the constitutional opposition aims simply at such a circulation. In England, for instance, the opposition possesses the same simple and resistant structure as the party which holds the reins of government; its program is clearly formulated, directed to purely practical and proximate ends; it is thoroughly disciplined, and is led by one lacking theoretical profundity but endowed with strategic talent; all its energies are devoted to overthrowing the government, to taking the reins of power into its own hands, while in other respects leaving matters exactly as they were; it aims, in a word, at the substitution of one clique of the dominant classes for another. Sooner or later the competition between the various cliques of the dominant classes ends in a reconciliation which is effected with the instinctive aim of retaining dominion over the masses by sharing it among themselves. The opinion is very generally held that as a result of the French Revolution, or that in any case in the Third Republic, the old order had socially speaking been completely suppressed in France. This view is utterly erroneous. In the present year of grace we find

[2] V. Pareto, *Les Systèmes socialistes*, ed. cit., vol. i, pp. 62 et seq.

that the French nobility is represented in the cavalry regiments and in the republican diplomatic service to an extent altogether disproportionate to its numerical strength; and although in the French Chamber there does not exist, as in Germany, a declared conservative party of the nobility, we find that of 584 deputies no less than 61 belong to the old aristocracy (*noblesse d'épée and noblesse de robe*).

As we have said, the theory that a directive social group is absolutely essential is by no means a new one. Gaetano Mosca, the most distinguished living advocate of this sociological conception, and, with Vilfredo Pareto, its ablest and most authoritative exponent, while disputing priority with Pareto, recognizes as precursors Hippolyte Taine and Ludwig Gumplowicz.[3] It is a less familiar fact, but one no less interesting, that the leading intellectual progenitors of the theory of Mosca and Pareto are to be found among the members of the school against which these writers more especially direct their attacks, namely among socialist thinkers, and especially among the earlier French socialists. In their work we discover the germs of the doctrine which at a later date was elaborated by Mosca and Pareto into a sociological system.

The school of Saint-Simon, while holding that the concept of class would some day cease to be characterized by any economic attribute, did not look for a future without class distinctions. The Saint-Simonians dreamed of the creation of a new hierarchy which was to be founded, not upon the privileges of birth, but upon acquired privileges. This class was to consist of "the most vital, the most intelligent and the strongest, the living personification of the threefold progress of society," and "capable of directing it in the widest course."[4] At the head of their socialist state the Saint-Simonians desired to place those whom they termed "hommes généraux," who would be able to prescribe for each individual his quantum of social labor, the individual's special aptitudes being taken into account in this connection; here it is obvious that dependence must be placed upon the discretion of these supermen.[5] One of the most ardent followers of Saint-Simon, an enthusiastic advocate of the "nouvelle dynastie," when forced to defend himself against the accusation that his doctrine paved the way

[3] Gaetano Mosca, *Piccola Polemica,* "Riforma Sociale," anno xiv, vol. xvii, fasc. 4.

[4] Trans. from E. Barrault, *La Hierarchie, in Religion Saint-Simonienne,* Receuil et Prédications, Aux bureaux du "Globe," Paris, 1832, vol. i, p. 196.

[5] *Œuvres de Saint-Simon et Enfantin,* vol. xli, *Doctrines Saint-Simoniennes,* Exposition par Bozard, Leroux, Paris, 1877, p. 275.

for despotism, did not hesitate to declare that the majority of human beings ought to obey the orders of the most capable; they should do this, he contended, not only for the love of God, but also on grounds of personal egoism, and finally because man, even if he could live in isolation, would always need some external support. The necessity for issuing orders on one side and the necessity for complying with them on the other are furnished with metaphysical justification. Such authority would only be "a political transformation of love which unites all men in God. And can you prefer the pathetic independence which at present isolates feelings, opinions, efforts, and which, beneath a pompous name, is nothing but egoism accompanied by all the habits it engenders?"[6] The Saint-Simonian system is authoritarian and hierarchical through and through. The disciples of Saint-Simon were so little shocked by the Cæsarism of Napoleon III that most of them joyfully accepted it, imagining that they would find in it the principles of economic socialization.

The school of Fourier went further still. With a wealth of detail bordering on pedantry and exhibiting more than one grotesque feature, Fourier thought out a vast and complex system. Today we can hardly restrain a smile when we study the tables he drew up describing his "spherical hierarchy," consisting of a thousand grades and embracing all possible forms of dominion from "anarchie" to "omniarchie," each of them having its special "hautes dignité" and its appropriate "hautes fonctions."[7] Sorel has well shown that the socialism of the days prior to Louis Blanc was intimately connected with the Napoleonic era, so that the Saint-Simonian and Fourierist utopias could not live and prosper elsewhere than in the soil of the idea of authority to which the great Corsican had furnished a new splendor.[8] According to Berth, Fourier's whole system presupposes for its working the invisible but real and indispensable ubiquity of Fourier himself, for he alone, the Napoleon, as it were, of socialism, would be capable of activating and harmonizing the diverse passions of humanity.[9]

Socialists of the subsequent epoch, and above all revolu-

[6] Ibid.
[7] Ferdinand Guillon, *Accord des Principes, Travail des Ecoles sociétaires. Charles Fourier*, Libr. Phalanst., Paris, 1850, p. 97.
[8] Preface by George Sorel to the work of Fernand Pelloutier, *Historie des Bourses du Travail*, ed. cit., pp. 7 et seq.
[9] Edouard Berth, *Marchands, intellectuels et politiques*, "Mouvement Socialiste," anno ix, No. 192, p. 385.

tionary socialists, while not denying the possibility, in the remote future, of a democratic government by majority, absolutely denied that such a government could exist in the concrete present. Bakunin opposed any participation of the working class in elections. He was convinced that in a society where the people, the mass of the wage-earners, is under the economic dominion of a minority consisting of possessors, the freest of electoral systems could be nothing more than an illusion. "He who speaks of power, speaks of domination, and all dominations presumes the existence of a dominated mass."[10] Democracy is even regarded as the worst of all the bourgeois regimes. The republic, which is presented to us as the most elevated form of bourgeois democracy, was said by Proudhon to possess to an extreme degree that fanatical and petty authoritative spirit (*zèle gouvernemental*) which believes that it can dare everything with impunity, being always ready to justify its despotic acts under the convenient pretext that they are done for the good of the republic and in the general interest. Even the political revolution signifies merely "un déplacement de l'autorité."[11]

The only scientific doctrine which can boast of ability to make an effective reply to all the theories, old or new, affirming the immanent necesssity for the perennial existence of the "political class" is the Marxist doctrine. In this doctrine the state is identified with the ruling class—an identification from which Bakunin, Marx's pupil, drew the extreme consequences. The state is merely the executive committee of the ruling class, or, to quote the expression of a recent neo-Marxist, the state is merely a "trade-union formed to defend the interest of the powers-that-be."[12] It is obvious that this theory greatly resembles the conservative theory of Gaetano Mosca. Mosca, in fact, from a study of the same diagnostic signs, deduces a similar prognosis, but abstains from lamentations and recriminations on account of a phenomenon which, in the light of his general political views, he regards not merely as inevitable, but as actually advantageous to society. Aristide Briand, in the days when he was an active member of the Socialist Party, and before he had become prime minister of the "class-state," pushed the Marxist notion of the state to its

[10] Trans. from Bakunin, *L'Empire Knouto-Germanique et la Révolution sociale*, ed. cit., vol. ii, p. 126.
[11] Proudhon, *Les Confessions d'un Révolutionnaire*, ed. cit., p. 24.
[12] Angelo Oliviero Olivetti, *Problema del Socialismo Contemporaneo*, Canoni, Lugano, 1906, p. 41.

utmost limits by recommending the workers to abandon isolated and local economic struggles, to refrain from dissipating their energies in partial strikes, and to deliver a united assault upon the state in the form of the general strike, for, he said, you can reach the bourgeoisie with your weapons in no other way than by attacking the state.[13]

The Marxist theory of the state, when conjoined with a faith in the revolutionary energy of the working class and in the democratic effects of the socialization of the means of production, leads logically to the idea of a new social order which to the school of Mosca appears utopian. According to the Marxists the capitalist mode of production transforms the great majority of the population into proletarians, and thus digs its own grave. As soon as it has attained maturity, the proletariat will seize political power, and will immediately transform private property into state property. "In this way it will eliminate itself, for it will thus put an end to all social differences, and consequently to all class antagonisms. In other words, the proletariat will annul the state, *qua* state. Capitalist society, divided into classes, has need of the state as an organization of the ruling class, whose purpose it is to maintain the capitalist system of production in its own interest and in order to effect the continued exploitation of the proletariat. Thus to put an end to the state is synonymous with putting an end to the existence of the dominant class."[14] But the new collectivist society, the society without classes, which is to be established upon the ruins of the ancient state, will also need elective elements. It may be said that by the adoption of the preventive rules formulated by Rousseau in the *Contrat Sociale*, and subsequently reproduced by the French revolutionists in the *Déclaration des Droits de l'Homme*, above all by the strict application of the principle that all offices are to be held on a revocable tenure, the activity of these representatives may be confined within rigid limits.[15] It is none the less true that social wealth cannot be satisfactorily administered in any other manner than by the creation of an extensive bureaucracy. In

[13] Aristide Briand, *La Grève Générale et la Révolution*. Speech published in 1907. Girard, Paris, p. 7.

[14] Friedrich Engels, *Die Entwicklung des Sozialismus von der Utopie zur Wissenschaft*, Buchhandlung "Vorwärts," Berlin, 1891, 4th ed., p. 40.

[15] Many believe with Hobson (*Boodle and Cant*, ed. cit., pp. 587 and 590) that the socialist state will require a larger number of leaders, including political leaders, than any other state that has hitherto existed. Bernstein declares that the administrative body of socialist society will for a long time differ very little from that of the existing state (Eduard Bernstein, *Zur Geschichte, etc.*, ed. cit., p. 212).

this way we are led by an inevitable logic to the flat denial of the possibility of a state without classes. The administration of an immeasurably large capital, above all when this capital is collective property, confers upon the administrator influence at least equal to that possessed by the private owner of capital. Consequently the critics in advance of the Marxist social order ask whether the instinct which today leads the members of the possessing classes to transmit to their children the wealth which they (the parents) have amassed, will not exist also in the administrators of the public wealth of the socialist state, and whether these administrators will not utilize their immense influence in order to secure for their children the succession to the offices which they themselves hold.

The constitution of a new dominant minority would, in addition, be especially facilitated by the manner in which, according to the Marxist conception of the revolution, the social transformation is to be effected. Marx held that the period between the destruction of capitalist society and the establishment of communist society would be bridged by a period of revolutionary transition in the economic field, to which would correspond a period of political transition, "when the state could not be anything other than the revolutionary dictatorship of the proletariat."[16] To put the matter less euphemistically, there will then exist a dictatorship in the hands of those leaders who have been sufficiently astute and sufficiently powerful to grasp the scepter of dominion in the name of socialism, and to wrest it from the hand of the expiring bourgeois society.

A revolutionary dictatorship was also foreshadowed in the minimum program of Mazzini's republican party, and this led to a rupture between Young Italy and the socialist elements of the carbonari. Filippo Buonarroti, the Florentine, friend and biographer of Gracchus Babeuf, a man who at one time played a heroic part in the French Revolution,[17] and who had had opportunities for direct observation of the way in which the victorious revolutionists maintained inequality and endeavored to found a new aristocracy, resisted with all his might the plan of concentrating the power of the carbonari in the hands of a single individual. Among the theoretical reasons he alleged against this concentration, the principal was that

[16] Karl Marx, *Randglossen zum Programm der deutschen Arbeiterpartei*, "Waffenkammer des Sozialismus," 10th semi-annual vol. Frankfort-on-the-Main, 1908, p. 18.

[17] Filippo Buonarroti, *Conspiration pour l'Egalité, dites de Babeuf*, Brussels, 1828. Cf. especially p. 48.

individual dictatorship was merely a stage on the way to monarchy. To Mazzini and his friends, Buonarroti objected that all the political changes they had in view were purely formal in character, aiming simply at the gratification of personal needs, and above all at the acquirement and exercise of unrestricted authority. For this reason Buonarroti opposed the armed rising organized by Mazzini in 1833, issuing a secret decree in which he forbade his comrades of the carbonari to give any assistance to the insurgents, whose triumph, he said, could not fail to give rise to the creation of a new ambitious aristocracy. "The ideal republic of Mazzini," he wrote, "differs from monarchy in this respect alone, that it possesses a dignity the less and an elective post the more."[18]

There is little difference, as far as practical results are concerned, between individual dictatorship and the dictatorship of a group of oligarchs. Now it is manifest that the concept *dictatorship* is the direct antithesis of the concept *democracy*. The attempt to make dictatorship serve the ends of democracy is tantamount to the endeavor to utilize war as the most efficient means for the defense of peace, or to employ alcohol in the struggle against alcoholism.[19] It is extremely probable that a social group which had secured control of the instruments of collective power would do all that was possible to retain that control. Theophrastus noted long ago that the strongest desire of men who have attained to leadership in a popularly governed state is not so much the acquirement of personal wealth as the gradual establishment of their own sovereignty at the expense of popular sovereignty.[20] The danger is imminent lest the social revolution should replace the visible and tangible dominant classes which now exist and act openly, by a clandestine demagogic oligarchy, pursuing its ends under the cloak of equality.

The Marxist economic doctrine and the Marxist philosophy of history cannot fail to exercise a great attraction upon thinkers. But the defects of Marxism are patent directly we enter the practical domains of administration and public law, without speaking of errors in the psychological field and even in more elementary spheres. Wherever socialist theory has

18 Giuseppe Romano-Catania, *Filippo Buonarroti*, Sandron, Palermo, 1902, 2nd ed., pp. 211–12, 213, 218, and 228.

19 "There continually recurs the dream of Schiller's Marquis Posa (in *Don Carlos*), who endeavours to make absolutism the instrument of liberation; or the dream of the gentle Abbé Pierre (in Zola's *Rome*), who wishes to use the church as a lever to secure socialism" (Kropotkin, *Die historische Rolle des Staates*, Grunau, Berlin, 1898, p. 52).

20 Labruyère, *Caractères*, ed. cit., p. 28.

endeavored to furnish guarantees for personal liberty, it has in the end either lapsed into the cloudland of individualist anarchism, or else has made proposals which (doubtless in opposition to the excellent intentions of their authors) could not fail to enslave the individual to the mass. Here is an example: to ensure that the literature of socialist society shall be elevated and moral, and to exclude *a priori* all licentious books, August Bebel proposed the nomination of a committee of experts to decide what might and what might not be printed. To obviate all danger of injustice and to secure freedom of thought and expression, Bebel added that every author must have the right of appeal to the collectivity.[21] It is hardly necessary to point out the impracticability of this proposal, which is in effect that the books, however large, regarding which an appeal is made, must be printed by the million and distributed to the public in order that the public may decide whether they are or are not fit for publication!

The problem of socialism is not merely a problem in economics. In other words, socialism does not seek merely to determine to what extent it is possible to realize a distribution of wealth which shall be at once just and economically productive. Socialism is also an administrative problem, a problem of democracy, and this not in the technical and administrative sphere alone, but also in the sphere of psychology. In the individualist problem is found the most difficult of all that complex of questions which socialism seeks to answer. Rudolf Goldscheid, who aims at a renascence of the socialist movement by the strengthening of the more energetic elements in that movement, rightly draws attention to a danger which socialism incurs, however brilliantly it may handle the problems of economic organization. If socialism, he says, fails to study the problem of individual rights, individual knowledge, and individual will, it will suffer shipwreck from a defective understanding of the significance of the problem of freedom for the higher evolution of our species—will suffer shipwreck no less disastrous than that of earlier conceptions of world reform which, blinded by the general splendor of their vision, have ignored the individual light-sources which combine to produce that splendor.[22]

The youthful German labor party had hardly succeeded in

21 A. Bebel, *Die Frau und der Sozialismus*, J. H. W. Dietz Nachf., Stuttgart, 34th ed., 1903, p. 423.

22 Rudolf Goldscheid, *Grundlinien zu einer Kritik de Willenskraft*, W. Braumüller, Vienna and Leipzig, 1905, p. 143.

detaching itself, at the cost of severe struggles, from the bourgeois democracy, when one of its sincerest friends drew attention to certain urgent dangers. In an open letter to the Leipzig committee of the Allgemeine Deutsche Arbeiterverein, Rodbertus wrote: "You are separating yourselves from a political party because, as you rightly believe, this political party does not adequately represent your social interests. But you are doing this in order to found a new political party. Who will furnish you with guarantees against the danger that in this new party the adversaries of your class (*die anti-sozialen Elemente*) may some day gain the upper hand?"[23] In this observation Rodbertus touches the very essence of the political party. An analysis of the elements which enter into the composition of a party will show the perfect justice of his criticism. A party is neither a social unity nor an economic unity. It is based upon its program. In theory this program may be the expression of the interests of a particular class. In practice, however, anyone may join a party, whether his interests coincide or not with the principles enunciated in the party program. The Socialist Party, for example, is the ideological representative of the proletariat. This, however, does not make it a class organism. From the social point of view it is a mixture of classes, being composed of elements fulfiling diverse function in the economic process. But since the program has a class origin, an ostensible social unity is thereby conferred upon the party. All socialists as such, whatever their economic position in private life, admit in theory the absolute pre-eminence of one great class, the proletariat. Those non-proletarians affiliated to the party, and those who are but partial proletarians, "adopt the outlook of the working class, and recognize this class as predominant."[24] It is tacitly presupposed that those members of a party who do not belong to the class which that party represents will renounce their personal interests whenever these conflict with the interests of the proletarian class. On principle, the heterogeneous elements will subordinate themselves to the "idea" of a class to which they themselves do not belong. So much for theory. In practice, the acceptance of the program does not suffice to abolish the conflict of interests between capital and labor. Among the members belonging to higher social strata

[23] Rodbertus, *Offener Brief, etc.*, in F. Lassalle's *Politische Reden u. Schriften*, ed. cit., vol. ii, p. 15.

[24] Eduard Bernstein, *Wird die Sozialdemokratie Volkspartei?*, "Sozial. Monatshefte," August 1905, p. 670.

who have made their adhesion to the political organization of the working class, there will be some who will, when the occasion demands it, know how to sacrifice themselves, who will be able to unclass themselves. The majority of such persons, however, notwithstanding their outward community of ideas with the proletariat, will continue to pursue economic interests opposed to those of the proletariat. There is, in fact, a conflict of interests, and the decision in this conflict will be determined by the relationship which the respective interests bear towards the principal necessities of life. Consequently it is by no means impossible that an economic conflict may arise between the bourgeois members and the proletarian members of the party, and that as this conflict extends it will culminate in political dissensions. Economic antagonisms stifles the ideological superstructure. The program then becomes a dead letter, and beneath the banner of "socialism" and within the bosom of the party, a veritable class struggle goes on. We learn from actual experience that in their conduct towards persons in their employ the bourgeois socialists do not always subordinate personal interests to those of their adoptive class. When the party includes among its members the owners of factories and workshops, it may be noticed that these, notwithstanding personal goodwill and notwithstanding the pressure which is exercised on them by the party, have the same economic conflict with their employees as have those employers whose convictions harmonize with their economic status, and who think not as socialists but as bourgeois.

But there exists yet another danger. The leadership of the Socialist Party may fall into the hands of persons whose practical tendencies are in opposition with the program of the working class, so that the labor movement will be utilized for the service of interests diametrically opposed to those of the proletariat. This danger is especially great in countries where the working-class party cannot disperse with the aid and guidance of capitalists who are not economically dependent upon the party; it is least conspicuous where the party has no need of such elements, or can at any rate avoid admitting them to leadership.

When the leaders, whether derived from the bourgeoisie or from the working class, are attached to the party organism as employees, their economic interest coincides as a rule with the interest of the party. This, however, serves to eliminate only one aspect of the danger. Another aspect, graver because more general, depends upon the opposition which inevitably arises between the leaders and the rank and file as the party grows in strength.

The party, regarded as an entity, as a piece of mechanism, is not necessarily identifiable with the totality of its members, and still less so with the class to which these belong. The party is created as a means to secure an end. Having, however, become an end in itself, endowed with aims and interests of its own, it undergoes detachment, from the teleological point of view, from the class which it represents. In a party, it is far from obvious that the interests of the masses which have combined to form the party will coincide with the interests of the bureaucracy in which the party becomes personified. The interests of the body of employees are always conservative, and in a given political situation these interests may dictate a defensive and even a reactionary policy when the interests of the working class demand a bold and aggressive policy; in other cases, although these are very rare, the rôles may be reversed. By a universally applicable social law, every organ of the collectivity, brought into existence through the need for the division of labor, creates for itself, as soon as it becomes consolidated, interests peculiar to itself. The existence of these special interests involves a necessary conflict with the interests of the collectivity. Nay, more, social strata fulfiling peculiar functions tend to become isolated, to produce organs fitted for the defense of their own peculiar interests. In the long run they tend to undergo transformation into distinct classes.

The sociological phenomena whose general characteristics have been discussed in this chapter and in preceding ones offer numerous vulnerable points to the scientific opponents of democracy. These phenomena would seem to prove beyond dispute that society cannot exist without a "dominant" or "political" class, and that the ruling class, while its elements are subject to a frequent partial renewal, nevertheless constitutes the only factor of sufficiently durable efficacy in the history of human development. According to this view, the government, or, if the phrase be preferred, the state, cannot be anything other than the organization of a minority. It is the aim of this minority to impose upon the rest of society a "legal order," which is the outcome of the exigencies of dominion and of the exploitation of the mass of helots effected by the ruling minority, and can never be truly representative of the majority. The majority is thus permanently incapable of self-government. Even when the discontent of the masses culminates in a successful attempt to deprive the bourgeoisie of power, this is after all, so Mosca contends, effected only in appearance; always and necessarily there springs from the masses a new organized minority which raises itself to the rank of a governing class.[25] Thus the majority of human beings, in a condition of eternal tutelage, are predestined by tragic necessity to submit to the dominion of a small minority, and must be content to constitute the pedestal of an oligarchy.

The principle that one dominant class inevitably succeeds to another, and the law deduced from that principle that oligarchy is, as it were, a preordained form of the common life of great social aggregates, far from conflicting with or replacing the materialist conception of history, completes that conception and reinforces it. There is no essential contradiction between the doctrine that history is the record of a continued series of class struggles and the doctrine that class struggles invariably culminate in the creation of new oligarchies which undergo fusion with the old. The existence of a political class does not conflict with the essential content of Marxism, considered not as an economic dogma but as a philosophy of history; for in each particular instance the dominance of a political class arises as the resultant of the relationships between the different social forces competing for supremacy, these forces being of course considered dynamically and not quantitatively.

The Russian socialist Alexandre Herzen, whose chief permanent claim to significance is found in the psychological interest of his writings, declared that from the day in which man became accessory to property and his life a continued struggle for money, the political groups of the bourgeois world underwent division into two camps: the owners, tenaciously keeping hold of their millions; and the dispossessed, who would gladly expropriate the owners, but lack the power to do so. Thus historical evolution merely represents an uninterrupted series of oppositions (in the parliamentary sense of this term), "attaining one after another to power, and passing from the sphere of envy to the sphere of avarice."[26]

Thus the social revolution would not effect any real mod-

[25] Gaetano Mosca, *Elemente de Scienza politica*, ed. cit., p. 62.—Among the socialists there are a few rare spirits who do not deny the truth of this axiom. One of these is the professor of philosophy, and socialist deputy of the Swedish Upper House, Gustaf F. Steffen, who declares: "Even after the victory, there will always remain in political life the leaders and the led" (Steffen, *Die Demokratie in England*, Diederichs, Jena, 1911, p. 59).

[26] Alexandre Herzen, *Erinnerungen*, German translation by Otto Buek, Wiegandt u. Grieben, Berlin, 1907, vol. ii, p. 150.

ification of the internal structure of the mass. The socialists might conquer, but not socialism, which would perish in the moment of its adherents' triumph. We are tempted to speak of this process as a tragicomedy in which the masses are content to devote all their energies to effecting a change of masters. All that is left for the workers is the honor "of participating in government recruiting."[27] The result seems a poor one, especially if we take into account the psychological fact that even the purest of idealists who attains to power for a few years is unable to escape the corruption which the exercise of power carries in its train. In France, in working-class circles, the phrase is current, *homme élu, homme foutu*. The social revolution, like the political revolution, is equivalent to an operation by which, as the Italian proverb expresses it: "Si cambia il maestro di cappella, ma la musica è sempre quella."[28]

Fourier defined modern society as a mechanism in which the extremest individual license prevailed, without affording any guarantee to the individual against the usurpations of the mass, or the mass against the usurpations of the individual.[29] History seems to teach us that no popular movement, however energetic and vigorous, is capable of producing profound and permanent changes in the social organism of the civilized world. The preponderant elements of the movement, the men who lead and nourish it, end by undergoing a gradual detachment from the masses, and are attracted within the orbit of the "political class." They perhaps contribute to this class a certain number of "new ideas," but they also endow it with more creative energy and enhanced practical intelligence, thus providing for the ruling class an ever-renewed youth. The "political class" (continuing to employ Mosca's convenient phrase) has unquestionably an extremely fine sense of its possibilities and its means of defense. It displays a remarkable force of attraction and a vigorous capacity for absorption which rarely fail to exercise an influence even upon the most embittered and uncompromising of its adversaries. From the historical point of view, the anti-romanticists are perfectly right when they sum up their scepticism in such caustic phraseology as this: "What is a revolution? People fire guns in a street; that breaks many windows; scarcely anyone profits but the

[27] Félicien Challaye, *Syndicalisme révolutionnaire et Syndicalisme réformiste*, Alcan, Paris, 1909, p. 16.

[28] There is a new conductor, but the music is just the same.

[29] Charles Fourier, *De l'Anarchie industrielle et scientifique*, Libr. Phalanst., Paris, 1847, p. 40.

glaziers. The wind carries away the smoke. Those who stay on top push the others under. . . . It is worth the suffering to turn up so many good paving stones which otherwise could not be moved!"[30] Or we may say, as the song runs in *Madame Angot*: "It's not worth the bother to change the government!" In France, the classic land of social theories and experiments, such pessimism has struck the deepest roots.[31]

[30] Trans. from Théophile Gautier, *Les Jeunes-France*, Charpentier, Paris, 1878, p. xv.

[31] The disillusionment of the French regarding democracy goes back to the Revolution. Guizot declared that this terrible experiment sufficed "to disgust the liberty-seeking world forever, and to dry up the noblest hopes of the human race at their source." (Trans. from F. Guizot, *Du Gouvernement de la France*, ed. cit., p. 165.)

Chapter 3

Party-Life in War-Time

NEVER IS the power of the state greater, and never are the forces of political parties of opposition less effective, than at the outbreak of war. This deplorable war, come like a storm in the night, when everyone, wearied with the labors of the day, was plunged in well-deserved slumber, rages all over the world with unprecedented violence, and with such a lack of respect for human life and of regard for the eternal creations of art as to endanger the very cornerstones of a civilization dating from more than a thousand years. One of the cornerstones of historical materialism is that the working classes all over the world are united as if by links of iron through the perfect community of economico-social interests which they possess in face of the bourgeoisie, this community of interests effecting a horizontal stratifiacation of classes which runs athwart and supersedes the vertical stratification of nations and of races. The greatest difference, in fact, in the views taken of economico-social classes and of linguistico-ethical nationalities, as between the respective adherents of nationalistic theories and of the theories of historical materialism, consists in this, that the former propound the hypothesis that the concept "nation" is morally and positively predominant over the concept "class," while the latter consider the concept and reality "nation" altogether subordinate to the concept "class." The Marxists, in fact, believed that the consciousness of class had become impressed upon the entire mentality of the proletariat imbued with socialist theories.

The war has shattered this theory at one terrible blow. The German Socialist Party, the strongest, wealthiest, and, best organized section of the working-class international, for thirty years past the leading spirit in that international, suddenly and emphatically declared its entire solidarity with the German Emperor. Throughout the proletarian mass there has not been reported a single instance of moral rebellion against the struggle which enlists socialists to fight on behalf of German imperialism and to contend with the comrades of other lands. Unquestionably, the tactics of the German socialists were largely due to the oligarchical tendencies which manifest themselves in modern political parties, because these parties, even if they pursue a revolutionary aim, and indeed precisely because they do so, that is to say because they make war against the existing state-system and desire to replace it by another, have need of a vast organization whose central strength is found in a trusted and stable bureaucracy, the members of which are well paid, and which has at its disposal the powers of a journalistic system and of a well-filled treasury.[1] This organization constitutes a state within the state. Now the forces of party, however well-developed, are altogether inferior and subordinate to the forces of the government, and this is especially true in such a country as Germany. Consequently one of the cardinal rules governing the policy of the Socialist Party is never to push its attacks upon the government beyond the limits imposed by the inequality between the respetcive forces of the combatants. In other words, the life of the party, whose preservation has gradually become the supreme objective of the parties of political action, must not be endangered. The result is that the external form of the party, its bureaucratic organization, definitively gains the upper hand over its soul, its doctrinal and theoretic content, and the latter is sacrificed whenever it tends to involve an inopportune conflict with the enemy. The outcome of this regressive evolution is that the party is no longer regarded as a means for the attainment of an end, but gradually becomes an end-in-itself, and is therefore incapable of resisting the arbitrary exercise of power by the state when this power is inspired by a vigorous will.

Inevitably such a party is unable to sustain so terrible a test as that of upholding its faith in principles when the state, determined upon war, and resolved to crush anyone who gets in the way, threatens the party in case of disobedience with the dissolution of its branches, the sequestration of its funds, and the slaughter of its best men. The party gives way, hastily sells its internationalist soul, and, impelled by the instinct of self-preservation, undergoes transformation into a patriotic party. The world-war of 1914 has afforded the most effective confirmation of what the author wrote in the first edition of this book concerning the future of socialist parties.

1 At the end of 1913 the central treasury of the German socialist trade unions owned property amounting to 88,069,295 marks (£4,400,000), whilst the local and independent unions owned 3,152,636 marks (£150,000). Now a rebellion against the government and its foreign policy would have endangered all these funds.

This natural tendency of the modern political party is reinforced, in the particular case under consideration, by the decision of the German socialists to support their government in all respects, owing to their fear and hatred of Czarism. This invincible aversion, upon which is dependent the general agreement with which the entire Germanic democracy has accepted the war, arises not solely from the foolish prejudice that the Slavs belong to an inferior race, but is also the outcome of a special historical theory held by Marx. Marx, in fact, regarded Russia as responsible for "the reaction" wherever this became manifest. More particularly, he considered that the militarist regime of the Prussian nobles, which he ardently abhorred, was merely the vanguard of the Russian autocracy. He added that the most infallible means for destroying the predominance of the German junkers would be to crush Russia, without whose aid the rule of the Prussian reaction would be impossible. This Marxist conviction had become a party dogma, deep-rooted in the mind of every individual member and diffused in a hundred writings. The German socialists who enthusiastically obeyed the mobilization order issued by the emperor believed themselves to be fulfiling a sacred duty, not only from the patriotic point of view, but also from the democratic, considering that they were thus hastening the day of their own final deliverance. It was by such a state of mind that were inspired the principal speeches delivered and the most authoritative articles written by the German socialists when William II declared war against the czar.

Moreover, an attitude which harmonized ill with the theoretical principle of historical materialism was defended by the socialists themselves as absolutely essential for the German proletariat. Substantially what the German socialists said was that, in the event of a defeat of the state to which they belonged, the proletarians would necessarily suffer greatly from unemployment and poverty; consequently it was their supreme interest, and must be the supreme aim of their representatives, to avoid this eventuality; hence it was their first and greatest duty to aid the German army by all the means at their disposal in its arduous taks of defeating the enemy. Now, there is no lack of positive clearness about the view which underlies this reasoning. Since the proletariat is an integral part of the state, it cannot but suffer when the state falls upon evil days. Above all, the lot of the workers is dependent upon the degree to which manufacture and commerce flourish. No doubt the most prosperous condition of manufacturing industry does not afford the workers an absolute guarantee that they will receive good wages and be able to enjoy a high standard of life, since there is no proof that the curve of wages will always follow that of industrial profits; indeed, it is notorious that while after 1870 the development of German manufacture was rapid and extensive, the condition of the German workers remained stationary for nearly two decades. But if the lot of the workers and that of the manufacturers are not always on the same footing in the matter of good fortune, it cannot be doubted that when bad times come they have to share the same distresses; if manufacturing industry is stagnant, any rise of wages is excluded *a priori*. While, however, this view of a community of interests in the national sphere between the bourgeoisie and the proletariat has a basis of reality, there can be no doubt that not only is it absolutely antagonistic to the *idealism* of class, that is to say, to the fraternal affection which denies national solidarity in order to affirm with enthusiasm the international solidarity of the proletariat, tending and aiming at speedy class-emancipation; but further that it undermines the very *concept* of class. In fact, the theoretical position assumed by the German socialists, and imitated more or less faithfully by their comrades in other lands, is dictated by a criterion altogether different from that which forms the basis of historical materialism. This latter doctrine presupposes the existence of a working class by nature one and indivisible, whereas in the nationalist view there exists only a national proletariat, included within a given state, living within definite geographical boundaries, and subject to all the influences of force or of destiny. Indeed, the social democratic concept of class (as manifested under stress of war by the majority of the German socialists) constitutes the negation of the Marxist concept, in so far as the former degrades the latter, and, instead of becoming the instrument of world liberation as it was conceived by the internationalist theorists, is made the instrument of patriotic, social, and military cooperation. Historical materialism aimed at securing the solidarity of the human race under the guidance of the revolutionary proletariat and through the overthrow of the bourgeoisie and of national governments. The social democratic concept of class aims at the aggrandizement of the fatherland and at the prosperity of the proletariat and of the bourgeoisie therein, through the ruin of the proletariat and of the bourgeoisie of other lands. Between these two conceptions there is, in fact, so great a gulf fixed, that the most learned attempts to bridge it over will inevitably prove futile. If the war has not demonstrated the fallacy of the theory that the working classes of various countries, considered as a whole, possess common interests in opposition to the interests of the various national bourgeoisies also considered as a whole, it has at least demonstrated the non-existence of the reaction which this supposed phenomenon ought to have exercised upon the mentality and consequently upon the activity of the proletariat which prolonged socialist propaganda had endeavored to indoctrinate with Marxist principles.

But while the German Socialists appealed to their right to be guided by strictly economic interests and to make common cause with those who had hitherto been their worst enemies, they had the bad taste to deny this right to their foreign comrades. Paul Lensch, socialist member of the Reichstag, editor of the ultra-Marxist "Leipziger Volkszeitung," has, with a seriousness worthy of a better cause, sustained the following remarkable assertions: that the victory of Germany is necessary for the destruction of militarism, which will become superfluous as soon as the enemies of Germany have been definitely defeated, while the defeat of Germany will necessarily provide militarism with new aliment (since Germany will have to take her revenge); for the German proletariat, the defeat of Germany would be equivalent to an ecnomic catastrophe, to the loss of the most essential means of subsistence, and to the ruin of the fruits of many years of labor; whereas for the English proletariat, the consequences of the defeat of England would unquestionably be extremely beneficial, by leading to the rapid diffusion of socialist ideas, to the distribution of monopolies, and to "the disappearance of the stupid pride which characterizes the English race."[2] According to this profound thinker, the same causes would produce different effects in England and France, on the one hand, and in Germany on the other. For Germany a defeat must be avoided at all costs, for its results would be disastrous, while in the case of England and France they could not fail to be salutary!

Speaking generally, it may be said that the war has further accentuated the oligarchical character of party leadership. In no country (Italy, of course, excepted, for Italy has had ten months for mature deliberation) were the rank and file of the party active factors in the adoption of a policy for which

[2] Paul Lensch, *Die deutsche Sozialdemokratie u. der Weltkrieg*, Buchhandlung "Vorwärts," Berlin, 1915, pp. 26, 42, 58.

every single member was accountable; in no country, except Italy, was the great question of the attitude of parties in relation to the problem of peace or war laid before the ordinary members; everywhere the supreme decision was in the hands of the leaders, and the masses had merely to accept an accomplished fact. In most cases the majority of the leaders established their absolute supremacy over the minority by means of the so-called party discipline which obliges the minority to accept the will of the majority. This explains the almost incredible unanimity with which, in the Reichstag, in the memorable August sitting, the German socialist parliamentary group voted the war credits. In the secret session of the group on the eve of the official session the opponents of the war were in the minority, and were therefore compelled on the following day, by the obligations of party discipline, to confound themselves publicly with the majority, and to give a vote which ran counter to their most sincere convictions. This amounts to saying that party life involves strange moral and intellectual sacrifices.

Moreover, by not a few party leaders the war was looked upon as a useful means of propaganda for the attraction of new recruits. This applies above all to the Socialist Party, eager to overthrow the barriers which separate from the party many sympathizers among the manual, operative, and shopkeeping classes, who are loth to join a party professing internationalist views. In a great public meeting held at Stuttgart on February 22, 1915, Heymann, a deputy to the diet of Würtemberg and one of the best-known leaders of the Socialist Party in the state, triumphantly declared: "Many have ardently desired to join our party. But there was an obstacle. Well, that obstacle no longer exists!"[3] Unquestionably principles are often a stumbling-block to a party whose main desire is to increase its membership; and to disregard inconvenient principles may bring electoral advantage, if at the cost of honor. The leaders are the first to favor such a tendency, for the more widely extended the foundations of their party, the greater grows their own individual power. In fact, the individual power of the leaders undergoes an immeasurable increase at a time when the majority of the members of all parties are under arms, and for this reason may be considered as politically non-existent because they are unable to exercise any influence upon the executive of the party to which they belong. On the Continent,

[3] *Zwei Reden*, by Hildebrand and W. Heine, Dietz, Stuttgart, 1915, p. 44.

even those members who have not been summoned to the colors no longer possess any power of controlling their leaders, owing to the suppression of the freedom of the press and of the rights of public meeting and of combination. Wherever martial laws prevails, the leader is omnipotent.

Chapter 4

Final Considerations

> *"A prendre le terme dans la rigueur de l'acception il n'a jamais existé de veritable democratie, et il n'en existera jamais. Il est contre l'ordre naturel que le grand nombre gouverne, et que le petit soit gouverné."*—J. J. ROUSSEAU, Contrat Social.

LEADERSHIP IS a necessary phenomenon in every form of social life. Consequently it is not the task of science to inquire whether this phenomenon is good or evil, or predominantly one or the other. But there is great scientific value in the demonstration that every system of leadership is incompatible with the most essential postulates of democracy. We are now aware that the law of the historic necessity of oligarchy is primarily based upon a series of facts of experience. Like all other scientific laws, sociological laws are derived from empirical observation. In order, however, to deprive our axiom of its purely descriptive character, and to confer upon it that status of analytical explanation which can alone transform a formula into a law, it does not suffice to contemplate from a unitary outlook those phenomena which may be empirically established; we must also study the determining causes of these phenomena. Such has been our task.

Now, if we leave out of consideration the tendency of the leaders to organize themselves and to consolidate their interests, and if we leave also out of consideration the gratitude of the led towards the leaders, and the general immobility and passivity of the masses, we are led to conclude that the principal cause of oligarchy in the democratic parties is to be found in the technical indispensability of leadership.

The process which has begun in consequence of the differentiation of functions in the party is completed by a complex of qualities which the leaders acquire through their detachment from the mass. At the outset, leaders arise SPONTANEOUSLY; their functions are ACCESSORY and GRATUITOUS. Soon, however, they become PROFESSIONAL leaders, and in this second stage of development they are STABLE and IRREMOVABLE.

It follows that the explanation of the oligarchical phenomenon which thus results is partly PSYCHOLOGICAL; oligarchy derives, that is to say, from the psychical transformations which the leading personalities in the parties undergo in the course of their lives. But also, and still more, oligarchy depends upon what we may term the PSYCHOLOGY OF ORGANIZATION ITSELF, that is to say, upon the tactical and technical necessities which result from the consolidation of every disciplined political aggregate. Reduced to its most concise expression, the fundamental sociological law of political parties (the term "political" being here used in its most comprehensive significance) may be formulated in the following terms: "It is organization which gives birth to the dominion of the elected over the electors, of the mandataries over the mandators, of the delegates over the delegators. Who says organization, says oligarchy."

Every party organization represents an oligarchical power grounded upon a democratic basis. We find everywhere electors and elected. Also we find everywhere that the power of the elected leaders over the electing masses is almost unlimited. The oligarchical structure of the building suffocates the basic democratic principle. That which IS oppresses THAT WHICH OUGHT TO BE. For the masses, this essential difference between the reality and the ideal remains a mystery. Socialists often cherish a sincere belief that a new *élite* of politicians will keep faith better than did the old. The notion of the representation of popular interests, a notion to which the great majority of democrats, and in especial the working-class masses of the German-speaking lands, cleave with so much tenacity and confidence, is an illusion engendered by a false illumination, is an effect of mirage. In one of the most delightful pages of his analysis of modern Don Quixotism, Alphonse Daudet shows us how the "brav' commandant" Bravida, who has never quitted Tarascon, gradually comes to persuade himself, influenced by the burning southern sun, that he has been to Shanghai and has had all kinds of heroic adventures.[1] Similarly the modern proletariat, enduringly influenced by glib-tongued persons intellectually superior to the mass, ends by believing that by flocking to the poll and entrusting its social and economic cause to a delegate, its direct participation in power will be assured.

The formation of oligarchies within the various forms of

1 Alphonse Daudet, *Tartarin de Tarascon*, Marpon et Flammarion, Paris, 1887, p. 40.

democracy is the outcome of organic necessity, and consequently affects every organization, be it socialist or even anarchist. Haller long ago noted that in every form of social life relationships of dominion and of dependence are created by Nature herself.[2] The supremacy of the leaders in the democratic and revolutionary parties has to be taken into account in every historic situation present and to come, even though only a few and exceptional minds will be fully conscious of its existence. The mass will never rule except *in abstracto*. Consequently the question we have to discuss is not whether ideal democracy is realizable, but rather to what point and in what degree democracy is desirable, possible, and realizable at a given moment. In the problem as thus stated we recognize the fundamental problem of politics as a science. Whoever fails to perceive this must, as Sombart says, either be so blind and fanatical as not to see that the democratic current daily makes undeniable advance, or else must be so inexperienced and devoid of critical faculty as to be unable to understand that all order and all civilization must exhibit aristocratic features.[3] The great error of socialists, an error committed in consequence of their lack of adequate psychological knowledge, is to be found in their combination of pessimism regarding the present, with rosy optimism and immeasurable confidence regarding the future. A realistic view of the mental condition of the masses shows beyond question that even if we admit the possibility of moral improvement in mankind, the human materials with whose use politicians and philosophers cannot dispense in their plans of social reconstruction are not of a character to justify excessive optimism. Within the limits of time for which human provision is possible, optimism will remain the exclusive privilege of utopian thinkers.

The socialist parties, like the trade unions, are living forms of social life. As such they react with the utmost energy against any attempt to analyze their structure or their nature, as if it were a method of vivisection. When science attains to results which conflict with their apriorist ideology, they revolt with all their power. Yet their defense is extremely feeble. Those among the representatives of such organizations whose scientific earnestness and personal good faith make it impos-

[2] Ludwig von Haller, *Restauration der Staatswissenschaften*, Winterthur, 1816, vol. i, pp. 304 et seq.

[3] Werner Sombart, *Dennoch!*, ed. cit., p. 90. Cf. also F. S. Merlino, *Pro e contro il Socialismo*, ed. cit., pp. 262 et seq.

sible for them to deny outright the existence of oligarchical tendencies in every form of democracy, endeavor to explain these tendencies as the outcome of a kind of atavism in the mentality of the masses, characteristic of the youth of the movement. The masses, they assure us, are still infected by the oligarchic virus simply because they have been oppressed during long centuries of slavery, and have never yet enjoyed an autonomous existence. The socialist regime, however, will soon restore them to health, and will furnish them with all the capacity necessary for self-government. Nothing could be more antiscientific than the supposition that as soon as socialists have gained possession of governmental power it will suffice for the masses to exercise a little control over their leaders to secure that the interests of these leaders shall coincide perfectly with the interests of the led. This idea may be compared with the view of Jules Guesde, no less antiscientific than anti-Marxist (though Guesde proclaims himself a Marxist), that whereas Christianity has made God into a man, socialism will make man into a god.[4]

The objective immaturity of the mass is not a mere transitory phenomenon which will disappear with the progress of democratization *au lendemain du socialisme*. On the contrary, it derives from the very nature of the mass as mass, for this, even when organized, suffers from an incurable incompetence for the solution of the diverse problems which present themselves for solution—because the mass *per se* is amorphous, and therefore needs division of labor, specialization, and guidance. "The human species wants to be governed; it will be. I am ashamed of my kind," wrote Proudhon from his prison in 1850.[5] Man as individual is by nature predestined to be guided, and to be guided all the more in proportion as the functions of life undergo division and subdivision. To an enormously greater degree is guidance necessary for the social group.

From this chain of reasoning and from these scientific convictions it would be erroneous to conclude that we should renounce all endeavors to ascertain the limits which may be imposed upon the powers exercised over the individual by oligarchies (state, dominant class, party, etc.). It would be an error to abandon the desperate enterprise of endeavoring to

[4] Jules Guesde, *La Problème et la Solution*, Libr. du Parti Socialiste, Paris, p. 17.

[5] Charles Gide et Charles Rist, *Histoire des Doctrines économiques depuis les Physiocrates jusquà nos jours*, Larose et Tenin, Paris, 1909, p. 709.

discover a social order which will render possible the complete realization of the idea of popular sovereignty. In the present work, as the writer said at the outset, it has not been his aim to indicate new paths. But it seemed necessary to lay considerable stress upon the pessimist aspect of democracy which is forced on us by historical study. We had to inquire whether, and within what limits, democracy must remain purely ideal, possessing no other value than that of a moral criterion which renders it possible to appreciate the varying degrees of that oligarchy which is immanent in every social regime. In other words, we have had to inquire if, and in what degree, democracy is an ideal which we can never hope to realize in practice. A further aim of this work was the demolition of some of the facile and superficial democratic illusions which trouble science and lead the masses astray. Finally, the author desired to throw light upon certain sociological tendencies which oppose the reign of democracy, and to a still greater extent oppose the reign of socialism.

The writer does not wish to deny that every revolutionary working-class movement, and every movement sincerely inspired by the democratic spirit, may have a certain value as contributing to the enfeeblement of oligarchic tendencies. The peasant in the fable, when on his death-bed, tells his sons that a treasure is buried in the field. After the old man's death the sons dig everywhere in order to discover the treasure. They do not find it. But their indefatigable labor improves the soil and secures for them a comparative well-being. The treasure in the fable may well symbolize democracy. Democracy is a treasure which no one will ever discover by deliberate search. But in continuing our search, in laboring indefatigably to discover the undiscoverable, we shall perform a work which will have fertile results in the democratic sense. We have seen, indeed, that within the bosom of the democratic working-class party are born the very tendencies to counteract which that party came into existence. Thanks to the diversity and to the unequal worth of the elements of the party, these tendencies often give rise to manifestations which border on tyranny. We have seen that the replacement of the traditional legitimism of the powers-that-be by the brutal plebiscitary rule of Bonapartist parvenus does not furnish these tendencies with any moral or aesthetic superiority. Historical evolution mocks all the prophylactic measures that have been adopted for the prevention of oligarchy. If laws are passed to control the dominion of the leaders, it is the laws which gradually weaken, and not the leaders. Sometimes, however, the democratic principle carries with it, if not a cure, at least a palliative, for the disease of oligarchy. When Victor Considérant formulated his "democratico-pacificist" socialism, he declared that socialism signified, not the rule of society by the lower classes of the population, but the government and organization of society in the interest of all, through the intermediation of a group of citizens; and he added that the numerical importance of this group must increase *pari passu* with social development.[6] This last observation draws attention to a point of capital importance. It is, in fact, a general characteristic of democracy, and hence also of the labor movement, to stimulate and to strengthen in the individual the intellectual aptitudes for criticism and control. We have seen how the progressive bureaucratization of the democratic organism tends to neutralize the beneficial effects of such criticism and such control. None the less it is true that the labor movement, in virtue of the theoretical postulates it proclaims, is apt to bring into existence (in opposition to the will of the leaders) a certain number of free spirits who, moved by principle, by instinct, or by both, desire to revise the base upon which authority is established. Urged on by conviction or by temperament, they are never weary of asking an eternal "Why?" about every human institution. Now this predisposition towards free inquiry, in which we cannot fail to recognize one of the most precious factors of civilization, will gradually increase in proportion as the economic status of the masses undergoes improvement and becomes more stable, and in proportion as they are admitted more effectively to the advantages of civilization. A wider education involves an increasing capacity for exercising control. Can we not observe every day that among the well-to-do the authority of the leaders over the led, extensive though it be, is never so unrestricted as in the case of the leaders of the poor? Taken in the mass, the poor are powerless and disarmed vis-à-vis their leaders. Their intellectual and cultural inferiority makes it impossible for them to see whither the leader is going, or to estimate in advance the significance of his actions. It is, consequently, the great task of social education to raise the intellectual level of the masses, so that they may be enabled, within the limits of what is possible, to counteract the oligarchical tendencies of the working-class movement.

[6] Victor Considérant, *Principes du Socialisme. Manifeste de la Démocratie au xix Siècle*, Librairie Phalanstérienne, Paris, 1847, p. 53.

In view of the perennial incompetence of the masses, we have to recognize the existence of two regulative principles:—

1. The *ideological* tendency of democracy towards criticism and control;

2. The *effective* counter-tendency of democracy towards the creation of parties ever more complex and ever more differentiated—parties, that is to say, which are increasingly based upon the competence of the few.

To the idealist, the analysis of the forms of contemporary democracy cannot fail to be a source of bitter deceptions and profound discouragement. Those alone, perhaps, are in a position to pass a fair judgment upon democracy who, without lapsing into dilettantist sentimentalism, recognize that all scientific and human ideals have relative values. If we wish to estimate the value of democracy, we must do so in comparison with its converse, pure aristocracy. The defects inherent in democracy are obvious. It is none the less true that as a form of social life we must choose democracy as the least of evils. The ideal government would doubtless be that of an aristocracy of persons at once morally good and technically efficient. But where shall we discover such an aristocracy? We may find it sometimes, though very rarely, as the outcome of deliberate selection; but we shall never find it where the hereditary principle remains in operation. Thus monarchy in its pristine purity must be considered as imperfection incarnate, as the most incurable of ills; from the moral point of view it is inferior even to the most revolting of demagogic dictatorships, for the corrupt organism of the latter at least contains a healthy principle upon whose working we may continue to base hopes of social resanation. It may be said, therefore, that the more humanity comes to recognize the advantages which democracy, however imperfect, presents over aristocracy, even at its best, the less likely is it that a recognition of the defects of democracy will provoke a return to aristocracy. Apart from certain formal differences and from the qualities which can be acquired only by good education and inheritance (qualities in which aristocracy will always have the advantage over democracy—qualities which democracy either neglects altogether, or, attempting to imitate them, falsifies them to the point of caricature), the defects of democracy will be found to inhere in its inability to get rid of its aristocratic scoriæ. On the other hand, nothing but a serene and frank examination of the oligarchical dangers of democracy will enable us to minimize these dangers, even though they can never be entirely avoided.

The democratic currents of history resemble successive waves. They break ever on the same shoal. They are ever renewed. This enduring spectacle is simultaneously encouraging and depressing. When democracies have gained a certain stage of development, they undergo a gradual transformation, adopting the aristocratic spirit, and in many cases also the aristocratic forms, against which at the outset they struggled so fiercely. Now new accusers arise to denounce the traitors; after an era of glorious combats and of inglorious power, they end by fusing with the old dominant class; whereupon once more they are in their turn attacked by fresh opponents who appeal to the name of democracy. It is probable that this cruel game will continue without end.

Index of Names

CPSIA information can be obtained
at www.ICGtesting.com
Printed in the USA
LVHW091221061122
732481LV00003B/462

9 780029 212509